The Henri Meschonnic Reader

The Henri Meschonnic Reader
A Poetics of Society

Edited by Marko Pajević

Introduction to Henri Meschonnic by John E. Joseph
Introduction to Meschonnic's theory, concepts and poetics of society by Marko Pajević

Translated from the French by Pier-Pascale Boulanger, Andrew Eastman, John E. Joseph, David Nowell Smith, Marko Pajević and Chantal Wright

EDINBURGH
University Press

Edinburgh University Press is one of the leading university presses in the UK. We publish academic books and journals in our selected subject areas across the humanities and social sciences, combining cutting-edge scholarship with high editorial and production values to produce academic works of lasting importance. For more information visit our website: edinburghuniversitypress.com

© editorial matter and organisation Marko Pajević, 2019, 2021
© Régine Blaig for *Un Coup de Bible*; *Critique du rythme* © Éditions Verdier, 1982; *Modernité modernité* © Éditions Verdier, 1988; *La Rime et la Vie* © Éditions Verdier, 1989; *Langage, Histoire, une même théorie* © Éditions Verdier, 2012; *Poétique du traduire* © Éditions Verdier, 1999; *Célébration de la poésie* © Éditions Verdier, 2001.

Edinburgh University Press Ltd
The Tun – Holyrood Road
12(2f) Jackson's Entry
Edinburgh EH8 8PJ

First published in hardback by Edinburgh University Press 2019

Typeset in 11/13pt Adobe Garamond Pro by
Servis Filmsetting Ltd, Stockport, Cheshire

A CIP record for this book is available from the British Library

ISBN 978 1 4744 4596 2 (hardback)
ISBN 978 1 4744 4597 9 (paperback)
ISBN 978 1 4744 4598 6 (webready PDF)
ISBN 978 1 4744 4599 3 (epub)

The right of Marko Pajević to be identified as the editor of this work has been asserted in accordance with the Copyright, Designs and Patents Act 1988, and the Copyright and Related Rights Regulations 2003 (SI No. 2498).

This publication was supported by the University of Tartu ASTRA Project PER ASPERA and financed by the European Regional Development Fund.

A research symposium on Henri Meschonnic's 'thinking language' and two workshops for the translator team were funded by a British Academy/Leverhulme Small Research Grant.

Contents

List of Translators   vii

Introduction, by John E. Joseph   1
Meschonnic's Theory of Rhythm, his Key Concepts and their Relation, by Marko Pajević   15
Meschonnic's Poetics of Society, by Marko Pajević   32
Preliminary Remarks to this Reader: *Some Comments on the Experience of Translating Meschonnic*, by Marko Pajević   46

Part 1. Critique of Rhythm   53

1. Poetics: *Theoretical Activity, Poetic Activity*   57
2. Rhythm: *What is at Stake in a Theory of Rhythm*   66
3. Metrics: *Pure Metrics or Discourse Metrics*   115
4. Sign: *Not the Sign, but Rhythm*   155

Part 2. Poetry and Poem   165

5. *The Rhythm Party Manifesto*   167

Part 3. Rhyme and Life   177

6. *Rhyme and Life*   179
7. *Orality, Poetics of the Voice*   198
8. *The Subject of Writing*   220

Part 4. Translating   225

9. Translating and Society: *Translating, and the Bible, in the Theory of Language and of Society*   229

10	Translating and the Biblical: *A Bible Blow to Philosophy*	244
11	Case Study of Poetic Translating: *The Name of Ophelia*	269

Part 5. Modernity — 279

12 *Modernity is a Battle* — 281

Part 6. Historicity and Society — 291

13 *For a Poetics of Historicity* — 293
14 *Rhythm, Theory of Language, Poetics of Society* — 297
15 *Realism, Nominalism: The Theory of Language is a Theory of Society* — 312

Glossary — 321
Chronological Bibliography of Meschonnic's Books — 326
Index — 329

List of Translators

Pier-Pascale Boulanger is a Professor at Concordia University (Montreal, Canada), where she teaches and researches literary as well as financial translation. She has translated novels and Henri Meschonnic's essay *Éthique et politique du traduire* into English (*Ethics and Politics of Translating*, John Benjamins, 2011). Her current research focuses on the financial discourse in the Canadian press during the Roaring 2000s using a corpus of 9 million words.

Andrew Eastman is *Maître de Conférences* in English at the University of Strasbourg. He has published numerous articles on rhythm and subjectivity in American modernist poetry, and has recently translated into French, with Chloé Laplantine, the Introduction to the *Handbook of American Indian Languages* by Franz Boas (Lambert-Lucas, 2018).

John E. Joseph is Professor of Applied Linguistics at the University of Edinburgh. His translation of Émile Benveniste's *Last Lectures: Collège de France, 1968 and 1969* has recently appeared with Edinburgh University Press. Other books of his include *From Whitney to Chomsky* (John Benjamins, 2002), *Language and Identity* (Palgrave Macmillan, 2004), *Language and Politics* (Edinburgh University Press, 2006), *Saussure* (Oxford University Press, 2012) and *Language, Mind and Body* (Cambridge University Press, 2018).

David Nowell Smith is Senior Lecturer in Poetry/Poetics at the University of East Anglia. He is author of *Sounding/Silence: Martin Heidegger at the Limits of Poetics* (Fordham University Press, 2013) and *On Voice in Poetry: The Work of Animation* (Palgrave Macmillan, 2015). He was editor of the poetics journal *Thinking Verse* from 2011 to 2016, and co-editor, with Abigail Lang, of *Modernist Legacies: Trends and Faultlines in British Poetry Today*, and, with Marko Pajević, of Special Issues on Wilhelm von Humboldt (*Forum for Modern Language Studies*, 2017) and Henri Meschonnic (*Comparative Critical Studies*, 2018).

Marko Pajević is Professor of German Studies at the University of Tartu. He taught at the Sorbonne, Paris IV and Paris I, at Queen's University Belfast, Royal Holloway and Queen Mary University of London. In his research, he develops a poetical anthropology, see his website apt.ut.ee. He is the author of the monographs: *Zur Poetik Paul Celans. Gedicht und Mensch – die Arbeit am Sinn* (C. Winter 2000), *Kafka lesen. Acht Textanalysen* (Bonn 2009), and *Poetisches Denken und die Frage nach dem Menschen. Grundzüge einer poetologischen Anthropologie* (Freiburg i.Br. 2012), and (co-)edited volumes on the relationship between poetry and musicality (Harmattan 2007) and on post-1945 poetics (Camden House 2011), as well as special issues on the language theories of Wilhelm von Humboldt (FMLS 2017/1) and of Henri Meschonnic (CCS 2018/3).

Chantal Wright is a literary translator and Reader in Translation as a Literary Practice in the Department of English and Comparative Literary Studies at the University of Warwick. She is the author of *Literary Translation* (Routledge, 2016) and the translator of Antoine Berman's *The Age of Translation* (Routledge, 2018). She won the inaugural Cliff Becker Book Prize in Translation and has twice been shortlisted for the Marsh Award for Children's Literature in Translation.

Introduction

by John E. Joseph

Henri Meschonnic (1932–2009) occupies a unique position in modern thought. He strove throughout his career to reform the understanding of language and all that depends on it, which is to say: all understanding. This put him, as a professor of linguistics in the Parisian university system, in conflict with his peers whose careers were tied up with the success of a field which, in the hope of improving it, Meschonnic critiqued relentlessly. Although not a 'post-structuralist' as that term is applied to a Deleuze or a Derrida, he did battle against structural and generative linguistics, semiotics and stylistics. For him, the word 'structuralism' encapsulated everything he stood against. What he envisaged was not, however, so much a dismantling of structuralism as, arguably, a vast consolidation and expansion of it.

'Arguably' is a particularly apt word to use about Meschonnic. It is hard to say anything about him that will not sound polemical. To call him ahead of his time is as much as to accuse his contemporaries of backwardly blocking their ears to his discomfiting critique. To say that he defies easy categorisation is an implicit rebuke to all of us who want our intellectual figures well contained by pinning their name to a set of labels for a profession, a specialisation, a movement, a religion and ethnicity.

Linguistics has long measured its success by the growth in its sub-fields, whose specialists stick to their own tightly focused questions. Even in the 1960s, when, especially in Paris, linguistics and the semiotics deriving from it were enjoying the status of master science – the methodological model for ethnography, psychoanalysis, literary analysis and many other fields besides – this did not result in an expansion of linguists' interests. Rather, scholars in other fields emulated their fragmentation and specialisation.

Linguists took a particular satisfaction in seeing literary studies turn to them for a model. The establishing of linguistics as a separate field from literature, or more precisely, their joint separation from the age-old study of philology, was still on-going, not least in the conservative French university system. Literature was the much bigger, more prestigious and institutionally powerful of the two. Traditional literary criticism was never entirely taken over by linguistics or semiotics but, for a decade or more starting in the mid-1960s, a wide consensus looked to them as the way forward. Redefining literary studies as a sub-branch of linguistics was a stunning achievement, and even those linguists who preferred not to think about literature at all saw their intellectual standing rise – and so they resented the dissenting voice insisting loudly that linguistics was on the wrong track.

It did not help matters that Meschonnic's output was not only prolific but of a learning and eloquence on a par with the great thinkers of the day, whose work he knew thoroughly and did not spare from his withering critique. When he found one of them getting something right, his praise sounded all the more genuine and glowing for its rarity. Sometimes it can be hard to tell whether his judgement on a particular thinker is acerbic or complimentary: when Merleau-Ponty's absorption of the environment into the Subject is equated by Meschonnic with the poetry of Walt Whitman, it would seem like high praise; but in the context of his general repudiation of phenomenology, especially of the Heideggerian brand, he may in fact be cocking a snook at Whitman.[1]

As for the eloquence, none of his opponents won any significant prizes for their poetry. Meschonnic did, starting with the Prix Max Jacob for his *Dédicaces proverbes* (Proverbial Dedications) in 1972, and including the Prix Mallarmé for *Voyageurs de la voix* (Voyagers of the Voice) in 1986. Nor are many poets quite as fixated on voice and language.

> les morts sont couverts de mots
> mes mots sont pour ceux qui vivent
> ils ne ferment pas une vie
> je ne fais que commencer
> de les dire des bouts de mots
> qui sortent à peine de nos bouches
> tant ils sont mêlés à nous
> que la phrase à dire c'est nous[2]
> *the dead are covered with words*

---

1. Henri Meschonnic, *Le Signe et le poème* (Paris: Gallimard, 1975), p. 328.
2. Extract from Henri Meschonnic, *Combien de noms* (Paris: L'Improviste, 1999); my translation, as are those which follow.

my words are for those who live
they do not close a life
I merely begin
to speak them bits of words
which barely exit our mouths
so much are they mixed up with us
that the sentence to be said is us

Unlike Noam Chomsky, who denies any significant link between his theoretical and political writings, Meschonnic never thought that his poetry and his poetics could be separated. He believed in living in language, practising what he thought, thinking through what he was doing. He advocated a self-reflecting creativity, and did not accept the cordoning off of his writing into separate tracks. That would be to surrender to those enforcing alienating boundaries carving up the university into career paths. The poetics, moreover, could not be detached from the understanding of language generally.

Meschonnic was interested in rhythm, scansion, and prosody at all levels. None the less, for him, what was needed was not structural linguistics or semiotics as a master science, but a science of the human Subject, with poetics at its centre. 'What is at stake in the poem', he said, 'is the subject of enunciation, who is not a privileged subject, but every subject.'[3] Enunciation is a term and concept introduced by Émile Benveniste, the French linguist of the previous generation who most inspired Meschonnic, along with Roman Jakobson, Mikhail Bakhtin and, from the previous century, Wilhelm von Humboldt. Enunciation is centred on what a subject *does* with the language, rather than on its form and functioning as a system (*langue*) or the texts which subjects produce using it (*parole*).[4] Benveniste's intent was for linguistics to follow a double track of the 'semiotic' study of the language system and the 'semantic' study of enunciation. Meschonnic, however, saw the semiotic as the obstacle to be eliminated. He was convinced that the semiotic will not explain the semantic, but that the semantic, properly grasped, opens up every dimension of the human subject for us; and that it is best grasped where it is most salient: not in everyday speech but in poetry, which he called 'the language of language'.[5]

---

3. 'Questions à Henri Meschonnic', interview with Jean Verrier, *Le Français aujourd'hui*, 51 (September 1980), pp. 95–7, p. 95.
4. See Translator's Introduction to Émile Benveniste, *Last Lectures: Collège de France, 1968 and 1969*, ed. by Jean-Claude Coquet and Irène Fenoglio, trans. by John E. Joseph (Edinburgh: Edinburgh University Press, 2019).
5. Henri Meschonnic, 'Poésie, langage du langage, pour Michel Deguy', *Cahiers du chemin*, 18 (April 1973), pp. 75–89. See also Henri Meschonnic, 'Benveniste: Sémantique sans sémiotique', *Linx*, 9 (1997), pp. 307–26.

And it is a test of the social: tell me what you do with poetry, and I'll tell you what you do with the subject, the social, the individual and the State. At stake in the poem is discourse as social practice, and the theory of discourse as theory of language and political theory. The *I* of the poem transforms the linguistic *I* into a system of discourse.[6]

For Meschonnic, then, poetics is not a narrow field of metrics and literary criticism, but expansive, subsuming linguistics, traductology (the science of translation), philosophy, poetry itself and other forms of literary production, and even political theory. Poetics brings them all back to a fundamental element which has figured in none of these discourses, apart from metrics, and even there it was vastly misunderstood. That element is *rhythm*.

Certainly, rhythm is part of poetry, and of all spoken and signed language, and of at least some written language. But in what sense is rhythm political? Meschonnic is of his time in equating the political with Marx, whose conception of the Subject was a semiotic one.

> [T]he subject–individual is therefore the creature of the systems of signs, whose social relationships are only a category. In this, Marxism not only is compatible with the theory of the sign but constitutes a culmination, a perfection of the politics of the sign.[7]

Bringing rhythm to the centre displaces the semiotic and the language system, and installs in their place the semantic and discourse, shattering the very foundation on which the Subject has classically been conceived, and so setting subjects free to take control of their own discursive definition.

> In the theory of rhythm that Benveniste made possible, discourse is not the use of signs, but the activity of subjects in and against a history, a culture, a language – which is only ever discourse, where the definition of language appears essentially grammatical, a particular relation of the syntagmatic to the paradigmatic which takes up, *redistributes* old categories. Rhythm as the organisation of discourse, and therefore of meaning, brings back to the fore what is empirically obvious, that there is only meaning by and through subjects. That meaning is in discourse, not in language.[8]

Rhythm is everyone's property, because it is embodied. The most impressive achievements in the scientific understanding of language of the last

---

6. 'Questions à Henri Meschonnic', p. 95.
7. Henri Meschonnic, *Critique du rythme* (Lagrasse: Verdier, 1982), p. 71 (this anthology, p. 68).
8. Ibid. Benveniste, an exquisitely careful writer, would probably have said that it is in both, in different forms.

fifty years have not come from linguistic theory (listen closely and you will hear Meschonnic's ghost wailing 'I told you so') but from new technology, such as functional magnetic resonance imaging (fMRI) of brains, and high-resolution ultrasound imaging of foetuses reacting to sound *in utero*. Your mother's heart beating – rhythm in its most basic form – was your formative experience of sound, and of touch, because you felt it as well as hearing it. With the ability to watch foetuses gesturing in response to rhythms, music and voices, we can say without fear of exaggeration that the foundation of language is laid months before birth.

You do not remember these experiences, not in the way you remember things after you were born, when your senses of sight and smell and taste were opened. Even then, memory is limited until we have another medium in which to capture and express these experiences. A language. And languages have rhythms of their own, which are distinct from those natural rhythms of the womb. Or are they?

Much of science revolves around general conceptions of time and space. Your sense of time began with those rhythms in the womb, before any sense of space was available to you. Time was the great problem of language for the linguist whom Meschonnic admired above all others, Ferdinand de Saussure. He was not satisfied with abstracting a grammatical system outside time, but constantly insisted that its operation *in* time was ultimately what needs to be understood. Occurrences in time: that is rhythm. Yet those structuralist linguists who claimed to be developing Saussure's heritage betrayed him, Meschonnic believed, by focusing only on the system of *langue* (Louis Hjelmslev being his particular *bête noire*). They compounded their sins by relegating poetics to an adjunct of their field, when they did not disown it completely.

Linguistics reserves a tiny corner of prosodic analysis for rhythm: students learn, for example, that French is a syllable-timed language, whereas English is stress-timed. But since this is not considered to affect meaning, it is devoid of semiological significance and treated as marginal. It matters in poetics, where rhythm is a central aspect of language – as a result of which structuralists separated out 'poetic language' as something apart, only tangentially connected to the 'real' language that they dealt with. Indeed, they regarded this separation as part of the maturing of linguistics as a science, distinct from the philology out of which it had developed in the previous century.

Meschonnic could see how self-defeating this was. Linguistics was setting itself up to be overwhelmed by an 'informatics' which treats language as a conduit for transferring information; and whilst representation and communication have been the functions focused on by philosophers and grammarians since ancient times, they are continuous with other functions which are not trivial – which, indeed, are arguably less trivial than the two traditionally recognised ones. Language is the medium of all our social relations, including with ourselves. It is life. That cardinal equation, continuous with but more radical than Wittgenstein's *Lebensform* (form of life),[9] is expressed in one way or another in nearly everything Meschonnic wrote.

The error of linguistics, for Meschonnic, is to have treated language in ways that range it on the side of the dead, in part by basing itself on dichotomies between form and content, sound and sense, which amounts to fatal vivisection; and by accepting rather than challenging the notion of poetry as being something distinct from ordinary language – something more organised, less chaotic. Yet organisation, dispelling chaos, these are exactly what linguistics itself aims for in the understanding of language, even as it excludes the poetic from the ordinary language which it takes as its subject matter. A perverse exclusion, because 'Poetry makes everything life. It is that form of life which makes everything language. It comes to us only if language itself has become a form of life.'[10]

For Meschonnic, the tragedy of structuralism lay in what he called its 'triumphalism of a scientism of the discontinuous'.[11] The result of discontinuity, as Meschonnic saw it, was to leave the unifying core of language – rhythm – relegated to the periphery, when it should be at the very centre of an investigative enterprise in which everything connects to everything else. *Tout se tient*: the motto of structural linguistics. If we take that interconnectedness as its defining criterion, Meschonnic rejected structuralism for not being structuralist enough.

* * *

Meschonnic was born in Paris on 18 September 1932, the only child of Tanya (*née* Schwartzmann, 1903–87) and Izya Meschonjinich (1902–82), who emigrated to France in 1926 from Kishinev, now Chișinău, capital of the Republic of Moldova.[12] Between the wars Kishinev was the capital

---

9. 'Und eine Sprache vorstellen heißt, sich eine Lebensform vorstellen' ('And imagining a language means imagining a form of life'): Ludwig Wittgenstein, *Philosophische Untersuchungen* (Oxford: Blackwell, 1953), §19.
10. Henri Meschonnic, *La Rime et la vie* (Lagrasse: Verdier, 1990), p. 247 (this anthology, p. 179).
11. Henri Meschonnic, 'Traduire, et la Bible, dans la théorie du langage et de la société', *Nouvelle revue d'esthétique*, 3 (2009), pp. 19–26, p. 20 (this anthology, p. 232).
12. The biographical information is from 'Henri, cousin', a memoir by Claude and Jacques Treiner, the sons of Meschonnic's maternal aunt Ida, available at <https://www.researchgate.net/profile/Jacques_Treiner/publication/297836097_HENRI_COUSIN/links/58f311d6458515ff23af9b81/HENRI-COUSIN> (last accessed 25 March 2019),

of Bessarabia, a region disputed between the Kingdom of Romania and the USSR. Kishinev had been the site of a notorious massacre of Jews in 1903,[13] the year Tanya was born. As Jews, Tanya and Izya were fortunate to escape, even if it was to a shoddy two-room flat in the place Balard, where Henri was raised. Tanya and her sister Ida, who followed her to France in 1929, worked as seamstresses, and Izya ran a stall in the St-Ouen flea market, said to be the world's oldest and largest, which, by a law still in force today, he could do for only three days per week. He spent the rest of his time playing cards in cafés and bistrots, whilst Tanya took charge of Henri's extracurricular education, 'devoting a veritable cult to her son', in her nephew's words,[14] ensuring that he was well acquainted with the museums of Paris and encouraging him in the oil paintings he did as an adolescent.

In 1939, they again found themselves in a precarious position, first being liable to arrest at the start of the war as citizens of Romania, an Axis power, then exposed to a far worse danger with the German Occupation in May 1940. When the round-up, imprisonment and deportation of Jews began in the summer of 1942, the Meschonjinich family fled south to the 'unoccupied' zone, where, however, they were by no means safe. They moved from place to place until the Liberation in August 1944, after which they returned to Paris. In 1948, Izya, Tanya and Henri were naturalised as French citizens and tweaked their surname to Meschonnic, an appropriately iconic change, given that the new name is neither French nor as un-French as the old one, similar to the interzone in which the family were themselves culturally located.

After completing his *baccalauréat*, Henri was admitted to advanced study in *lettres classiques* at the Sorbonne, which covered Greek, Latin and French literature together with linguistics, mainly historical. He had a student deferment from active duty in the Algerian War, and in 1957, he published the first of a steady stream of articles on the subjects in the *lettres classiques* curriculum, particularly French literature. He married his first wife, Marietta, and their first son was born in 1958; the second arrived in 1960, the year in which he was finally called up to do eight months of military service in Algiers. His interest in the Hebrew language began whilst there, despite Algiers not being an obvious place for this to happen. He had not had a

and from Meschonnic's entry in *Who's Who in France*, the information for which he probably supplied himself, and where his father's first name is given in its Hebrew form, *Israël*.
13. See Stephen J. Zipperstein, *Pogrom: Kishinev and the Tilt of History* (New York: Liveright, 2018), and the review article by Anthony Julius, 'Before the Holocaust, Jewish Suffering Had One Name: Kishinev', *New York Times Book Review* (24 July 2018), available at <https://www.nytimes.com/2018/07/24/books/review/steven-zipperstein-pogrom.html> (last accessed 25 March 2019).
14. Jacques Treiner, 'Henri, cousin', p. 3.

religious upbringing, his parents being good communists – indeed, militant ones in their youth, when they, or at least his mother, Tanya, had been part of the struggle to free Bessarabia from the Romanian Crown and unite it with the USSR. Throughout their long lives, Tanya and her sister Ida remained atheists; 'however, in their last years, they went together to the synagogue in the rue de la Victoire, in the 9th arrondissement of Paris, for the Day of Atonement, Yom Kippur'.[15] Clearly, some glimmer of their family's religious and cultural tradition remained.

Henri completed his *agrégation*, which qualified him to teach, and later a *doctorat ès lettres*. In 1961, he took up a post in the Lycée François I in Fontainebleau; the following year, a third son was born and Henri's first set of poems was published.[16] In 1963, he obtained his first university post, as *assistant* in linguistics at Lille, promoted to *maître-assistant* in 1967. Articles on literary subjects and original poetry continued to appear during these years, when he was collaborating on the *Dictionnaire du français contemporain* (Dictionary of Contemporary French) under the direction of the linguist Jean Dubois, a project aimed at creating a French dictionary which would incorporate the findings of modern linguistics, as *Webster's Third International Dictionary* of 1962 had done for English. Meschonnic also opened up another new and enduring avenue in his intellectual life: translating the Old Testament from Hebrew into French, starting with the Book of Ruth,[17] and aimed at 'initiating a new way of translating the Hebrew verse of the Bible according to its cantillation accent'.[18] In parallel, he was publishing articles about the nature and practice of translation.[19]

The student revolution of 1968 brought about a large-scale restructuring of the university system, including the creation of an Experimental University Centre at Vincennes in the eastern suburbs of Paris, with Meschonnic amongst the initial faculty cohort when the centre opened in January 1969. It became the Université de Paris 8 in 1971, at which point Meschonnic, originally brought to Vincennes to teach French literature, was made *maître-assistant* in linguistics. He remained at the Université de Paris 8 for the rest of his career, through its move to St-Denis in 1980, having been promoted to professor in

---

15. Claude Treiner, 'Henri, cousin', p. 3.
16. Henri Meschonnic, 'Poèmes d'Algérie', *Europe*, 393 (January 1962), pp. 68–70.
17. 'Ruth, introduction et traduction', *Le Nouveau Commerce*, 7 (spring–summer 1966), pp. 127–52. In the same journal he would publish translations of Ecclesiastes (1968) and the Song of Songs (1969).
18. Henri Meschonnic, interview with Gabriella Bedetti, *Diacritics*, 18/3 (1988), pp. 93–111, p. 95. The article notes that the interview was conducted in English, in August 1986.
19. Henri Meschonnic, 'Les Problèmes de la traduction', *Europe*, 449 (September 1966), pp. 216–20.

1978 and retiring as emeritus professor in 1998. In 1976, he married Régine Blaig, who supported his work immensely, both intellectually and by typing and editing his texts, and they were together for nearly thirty-three years until his death from leukaemia on 8 April 2009.

It was in April 1970 that his first book appeared in print: *Pour la poétique* (For Poetics), issued by the prestigious publisher Gallimard, which simultaneously put out *Les Cinq Rouleaux*, Meschonnic's translation of five books of the Bible traditionally grouped together as the five *megillot* (scrolls). The theoretical book's title became *Pour la poétique I* when two further volumes were issued in 1973, with a fourth following in 1977 and a fifth in 1978. Now, if a person wants to become notorious in the field of language, the most efficient way is to tamper with sacred texts, in a book issued by the publisher of the most famous writers of the day. Meschonnic had served his sacred-text-tampering apprenticeship on Dubois's dictionary, dictionaries being a genre which commands an authority that is possibly greater than scripture's, since it is recognised in secular contexts as well as religious ones. Had *Pour la poétique* been published on its own, it might have garnered only modest scholarly attention, but the Bible translations were another matter.

From this point on, Meschonnic was invited to contribute to widely read periodicals such as *Le Nouvel Observateur* and *La Quinzaine littéraire*, as well as to Gallimard's *Nouvelle Revue française* and *Cahiers du chemin*, which merged in 1977, and for which Meschonnic was 'the in-house poetry theorist'[20] until 1981. During this period, he published the book which, for him, signalled the development of his poetics into 'the critique of the theory of language',[21] *Le Signe et le poème* (The Sign and the Poem).[22] Here the Professor of Linguistics at Paris 8 burned any remaining bridges with the field in its contemporary state, whilst also waging war against the big intellectual beasts of the day, culminating in a searing attempt to eviscerate Derrida.

In 1981 he completed what is generally regarded as his magnum opus, the 736-page *Critique du rythme* – the intricacies of translating the title will be discussed below – which he saw as the natural culmination of all his work up to that point, including the biblical translations. Gallimard might have been expected to publish it, but did not.

> I was asked to reduce the book to a 200-page essay. I refused. I still think I was right in keeping *Critique du rythme* to its inner necessity and development.

---

20. Andy Stafford, review of Serge Martin, *Les 'Cahiers du chemin' (1967–1977) de Georges Lambrichs: poétique d'une revue littéraire* (Paris: Honoré Champion, 2013), *French Studies*, 69/2 (2015), p. 263.
21. Meschonnic, interview with Gabriella Bedetti, p. 95.
22. *Le Signe et le poème* is dedicated to Georges Lambrichs, Meschonnic's editor at Gallimard.

One does not write to please. One does not write *for* anybody. But for what has to be written.[23]

No more of Meschonnic's work would appear with Gallimard until 1990.

Critique du rythme was published in 1982 by Verdier, founded in 1979 by a group of militant Maoists of the Gauche Prolétarienne (Proletarian Left), with offices not in Paris but far south in the village of Lagrasse, with a population of about 500 (more than double that of nearby Verdier, for which the press was named). What drew Meschonnic to this obscure enterprise may partly have been its ambition to be the anti-Gallimard, but also its series Les Dix Paroles (The Ten Words, great texts of the Jewish tradition), though he would never publish any of his translations with them.

* * *

The present anthology is intended to be representative of Meschonnic's work, so the fact that it begins with substantial excerpts from *Critique du rythme* is an indication of that book's centrality to his *œuvre*. It draws together the key points that Meschonnic had been developing in his poetics over the preceding fifteen years, whilst pointing the way to what lies ahead. 'The optical illusion makes people see a big book in it,' he told an interviewer. 'Yet I know it is just a sketch of what remains to be done.'[24] Its title is deceptively polysemous. It seems straightforward enough, Critique of Rhythm, until you start to think about it. How can you critique rhythm? You can critique a particular musician's or dancer's or poet's or prose writer's or orator's rhythm, but rhythm in general? It dawns on you that *du* can indicate not only the object of something but also its possessor, its subject: *la critique du professeur*, the criticism of the teacher, can be someone's criticism of the teacher, or the teacher's criticism of someone. And *Critique du rythme* is, above all, Meschonnic's exposition of how rhythm itself provides a massive critique of the analysis of literature and language – starting with its irrational handling of, or failure even to try to handle, rhythm itself.

Rhythm brings us back to poetry as 'that form of life that makes language out of everything'. As the song says, the rhythm of life is a powerful beat, puts a tingle in your fingers and a tingle in your feet. It is bodily, as well as mental, or rather it overrides the division between the two. In one of his last articles, Meschonnic wrote, 'Language–body continuity is then the linking of the rhythms of position, onset and coda, inclusion, conjunction,

---

23. Meschonnic, interview with Gabriella Bedetti, p. 104.
24. Ibid., p. 110.

rupture, lexical repetition, syntactic repetition, prosodic series. It is a serial semantics.'²⁵

These two sentences project a revolution in how to conceive of language. Not as something 'cognitive', to use the most vacuous of modern linguistic terms, but as continuous with the body; and understood first of all as a sequence, not of phonemes, but of rhythms, of which he gives the nine types in the preceding quotation. The types ignore the canonical discontinuities of phonology, morphology and syntax, treating them all as part of the rhythmic repertoire. In the most revolutionary move of all, he refuses the fundamental doctrine that rhythm is separate from meaning, instead making language–body continuity itself a 'serial semantics'. Everything in language, on whatever level, occurs in a rhythm, including the series of the serial semantic.

A linguistics that shunts rhythm to its margins will not grasp language, not even on the page – least of all the scriptural page. The rhythms of the Hebrew Old Testament are sacred (a difficult concept, to which I shall return); in fact, they are what make the text sacred, whether or not one believes that they are the word of God. And where, Meschonnic wondered, have those rhythms gone to in the Greek New Testament? Many passages of it are translations of Old Testament verses, but without the music. And what about later translations? Can language–body continuity be restored in contemporary translational practice?

To address such questions, we must abandon our conventional disciplinary boundaries and embrace a unified linguistics–semiology–poetics–traductology. The obstacles to doing this lie partly in the institutionalised separation of disciplines, and partly in the incommensurable ways of talking about these problems and issues which the disciplines have spawned. And we must not neglect to include the political dimension – an unsurprising inclusion today, except in those areas of linguistics (probably the majority) whose practitioners conceive of themselves as doing pure science, devoid of politics, as was more common throughout the humanities when Meschonnic was launching his programme.

As the simplest example of his reformed translation practice, he would cite *ani shalom* (Psalm 120: 7). Two words – *ani* 'I', *shalom* 'peace':

> The verb *to be* in the present tense being implicit: thus, 'I am peace', and these two words joined by a hyphen, a conjunctive accent that welds them together in a single affect group. I have translated, to render this strengthening: *moi je suis la paix* (literally, 'me, I am the peace').²⁶

---

25. Meschonnic, 'Traduire, et la Bible', p. 20 (this anthology, p. 234).
26. Ibid., p. 24 (this anthology, p. 241), commenting on Meschonnic's *Gloires* (translation of the Psalms, Paris: Desclée de Brouwer, 2001).

He is true to his call for continuity: it is not a matter of reproducing just the sonic rhythm of the Hebrew verse, which would only reinforce the fundamental problem, the idea that rhythm can be separated from semiotics, semantics, syntax and all the rest of language. 'This strong formula', he says, 'is what the erasing-translations have applied all their cleverness to watering down, have competed with one another to trivialise,' and he gives a catalogue of translations from 1545 to 1985, explaining where each goes astray, and characterising the whole practice as 'obscene'. This includes the King James Bible, with its 'I *am for* peace,' though Meschonnic gives no consideration to the italics which the translators introduced to indicate words with no exact equivalent in the Hebrew. They are for the eyes, not the ears, so one might think that Meschonnic ignores them because of his insistence that *orality* is what the poem is about; but he does not mean orality in the usual sense of an opposition with the written. For Meschonnic, the oral–aural mode is synonymous with rhythm[27] – and, paradoxically, writing is where orality can have its fullest manifestation.

Another key issue that arose with the Bible translations, and that haunted Meschonnic, is the nature of the sacred. This is something structuralists were by no means scared of; Claude Lévi-Strauss, René Girard and Jacques Lacan each put it squarely amongst their concerns. Benveniste, who both was and was not a structuralist,[28] treated the sacred like any other institution for the purposes of examining its Indo-European linguistic heritage. But none of them was translating sacred texts, and trying not only to identify in what textual characteristics their sacred character lies but to transfer them into another language. That aspect of the undertaking was what the press and broad reading public found fascinating – and it frequently left Meschonnic

---

27. Anthony Cordingley, in 'L'Oralité selon Henri Meschonnic', *Palimpsestes: Revue de traduction*, 27 (2014), pp. 47–60, p. 56, says that in Meschonnic's work orality becomes *almost* a synonym with rhythm, but follows this immediately with a quotation from *Critique du rythme* (p. 705) which has no 'almost' about it: 'Rhythm, a subjective–collective organisation of a discourse, is its orality' (this anthology, p. 155).
28. In 'Seul comme Benveniste, ou Comment la critique manque de style', *Langages*, 118 (June 1995), pp. 31–55, Meschonnic insists that 'Benveniste *is not a structuralist*' (p. 51), and that what others take to be structuralist elements in his work are, in fact, effects of style. Meschonnic repeats the statement, this time without the italics, in 'Benveniste: sémantique sans sémiotique' (p. 317), where he adds that 'His term "systems", here in relation to "author" and "work", and his rejection of "convention", tied to the chain of conventionalism, along with any correlation between philology and general linguistics, and his deductive attitude, situate Benveniste outside structuralism.' In 'The Resistant Embrace of Formalism in the Work of Émile Benveniste and Aurélien Sauvageot', in *Form and Formalism in Linguistics*, ed. by James McElvenny (Berlin: Language Science Press, in press), I argue for seeing Benveniste's relationship to structuralism in a more complex way.

in the position of having to explain himself. His Bible translations were not an act of faith in the sacredness of the texts, in a personal religious sense. Or, at least, so said the son of the militant atheist who attended synagogue with her like-minded sister every Yom Kippur.

The sacred is such an overarching theme in Meschonnic's 1975 book *Le Signe et le poème* that it is surprising not to find *le sacré* in its title. The misunderstandings to which the word gave rise may help to explain its absence. The book treats the sacred as a problem of semiotics.

> The schema of the sign is the very schema of the sacred: a relationship to the Absent, the Other. [. . .] The sign as sign of something else and the sign of the Wholly Other are an identical relationship. Their level differs.[29]

Differences of 'level' or of 'orders' are always easy to pull out of the scholar's bag of tricks, but rarely stand up to enquiry into what exactly they are meant to represent. The sacred would continue to be an important thread in Meschonnic's writing, as can be seen repeatedly in this Reader. His various ways of trying to explain it embody, but never quite admit, the mystery it posed for him. His academic style was not one which betrayed uncertainty, in writing or in face-to-face debate, which by all accounts made him a reassuring friend and ally, and an insufferable opponent.

* * *

I have dealt with a few of the grand original themes running through Meschonnic's work, ones I consider important if only for the impact they have had on my own thinking about language. My first exposure to his work was during stays with my wife's uncle, Jean Verrier, who taught with Meschonnic at Paris 8 and always had his colleague's latest book on a table near the guest room. For twenty years I read these books, without being wholly won over, but retaining from each something that was iconoclastic and insightful. It is always a challenge reading Meschonnic: he often takes it for granted that readers of his later books will already know the earlier ones, and do not need reminding that key terms such as 'orality', 'poem' and 'rhythm' mean far more when he uses them than when others do. Once that is grasped, the overall vision becomes clear. In my case, that was what it finally took to become *meschonnicien*.

He is the great Absent of the twenty-first-century study of language, poetics and translation. His writing, in all the genres which he insisted we should treat as continuous, achieved a certain undefinable sacredness. He is

---

29. Meschonnic, *Le Signe et le poème*, p. 48.

not, however, a *monstre sacré*. In life, he was divisive because he said what he believed rather than what he was supposed to say. Mention him to linguists in France and they will react as though you have named either someone *sacré* or, more often, a *monstre*. That is shifting with time, as old academic–political struggles become historical trivia, whilst the great books endure. For my part, as for my fellow translators of this Reader, Henri Meschonnic has expanded and continues to expand and enrich our understanding of language, and of life, in a way that very few people have ever managed to do.

Meschonnic's Theory of Rhythm, his Key Concepts and their Relation

by Marko Pajević

The Sign as an Obstacle

In order to give a systematic account of Meschonnic's key ideas on poetics, we have to start with his critique of the sign.[1] The dominant contemporary conception of language, and therefore of the world, is based on the sign. I shall use the term semiotics to designate all theories based on the sign. The sign implies the binarism of a signifier and a signified, where the signifier is naturally perceived as secondary. This conception is so well established in Western thought that it is difficult to conceive of an alternative way of considering the world; it appears to be simply the truth. However, it is a historical phenomenon; not all times and cultures shared or share this conception and we should not expect it to be the final word. Meschonnic argues that it also represents an obstacle to the awareness of certain elements of human life. Semiotics as we know it cannot give a full account of what language or art does.

It is interesting to note that the English language does not have a transitive use of the verb 'to think', as German or French, for instance, does. The expression 'penser le langage' in French or 'Sprache denken' in German has no perfect equivalent in English; we would have to say 'to think about

---

1. The following presentation of key aspects of Meschonnic is a slightly revised version of my article 'Beyond the Sign: Henri Meschonnic's Poetics of Rhythm and Continuum. Towards an Anthropological Theory of Language', in *Forum for Modern Language Studies*, 47/3 (2011), pp. 304–18. Earlier versions of some parts of this introduction have been used in the introduction to the Special Issue of Marko Pajević and David Nowell Smith's 'Thinking Language with Henri Meschonnic', *Comparative Critical Studies*, 15/3 (2018).

language' or 'to reflect upon language'. However, one cannot think about language without already being in language. The transitive use 'to think language' would stress that the thinking is done in language, that language is not only a tool and that one is aware of what language is doing; this formulation already steps outside of the representation of language as sign but English does not traditionally allow for it.[2] This is only an initial difficulty on the way to a fuller awareness of what language and art do.

Rhythm and Discourse

It is best to begin a discussion of Meschonnic with his pivotal concept of rhythm. Rhythm is normally considered a regular wave-like coming and going associated with metrics. In contrast to this, Meschonnic's use of this term refers to the pre-Platonic concept as it is found in Democritus and Heraclitus, where there is an opposition between *rhythmos*, the organisation of what is in movement, and *schema*, the organisation of immobile things.[3] It was Émile Benveniste who drew Meschonnic's attention to the fact that it was only with Plato that the original meaning of the term changed. Benveniste was a major French linguist to whom we will return. His discovery of the original meaning of rhythm in his article 'La Notion de "rythme" dans son expression linguistique'[4] in the year 1951 has hardly made any waves. Benveniste demonstrates that *rhythmos* is related to *rhein*, to flow, and that this verb is never used for the sea but only for a river (PLF1, pp. 327–8). *Rhythmos* therefore originally referred to a constant flowing movement and not to the alternating tidal ebb and flow. The meaning of *rhythmos* was consequently the activity of giving form but with the particularity of being form in movement, without organic consistency, and always subject to change:

> la forme dans l'instant qu'elle est assumée par ce qui est mouvant, mobile, fluide, la forme de ce qui n'a pas consistance organique [. . .]. C'est la forme improvisée, momentanée, modifiable. [. . .] On peut alors comprendre que *rythmos*, signifiant littéralement 'manière particulière de fluer', ait été le terme le plus propre à décrire des 'dispositions' ou des 'configurations' sans fixité ni nécessité naturelle et résultant d'un arrangement toujours sujet à changer. (PLG1, p. 333)

---

2. Recently, however, the structure 'thinking plus noun' has been widely used in academic language.
3. In *Dans le bois de la langue* (Paris: Laurence Teper, 2008), p. 56; subsequently referred to in the text as BL plus page number.
4. In *Problèmes de linguistique générale 1* (Paris: Gallimard, 1966), pp. 327–35; subsequently referred to in the text as PLG1 plus page number.

(the form in the instant that it is assumed by what is moving, mobile, and fluid, the form of that which does not have organic consistency [. . .]. It is the form as improvised, momentary, changeable. [. . .] We can then understand how *rhythmos*, meaning literally 'the particular manner of flowing', could have been the most proper term for describing 'dispositions' or 'configurations' without fixity or natural necessity and arising from an arrangement which is always subject to change.)[5]

Plato then changed the meaning of rhythm as form in movement by applying it first to the human body in dance and then in song, and to all procedures demanding a constant activity that is organised by a metre in alternating phases. He thus made of *rhythmos* a structuring principle in which, as Benveniste comments, '[L]a notion de rythme est fixée' (PLG1, pp. 334–5) (The notion of rhythm is fixed).

Following this, the standard etymology for *rhythmos*, established in France in the late seventeenth century, saw rhythm as a periodic, even 'metrical', flow modelled on the coming and going of waves on the shore. Meschonnic takes rhythm in its pre-Platonic sense, which Benveniste identified in lyric and tragic poetry, and in Atomistic philosophy, as the activity of giving form, but form in movement, *without organic consistency* and *always subject to change*, as Benveniste wrote (PLG1, p. 333). Meschonnic, however, takes this far further than Benveniste imagined: in particular, transforming the notion of rhythm from a question of linguistic 'form' into the process of meaning-making itself. He applies Benveniste's archaeological linguistics to a total theory of language and society. He formulates it thus: 'Le rythme dépasse la mesure.'[6] This is a good example of his often witty style. A translation into English cannot work in the same way; I suggest 'Rhythm outmeasures metre.' When we talk about rhythm, we are not talking about regularity or measure but about form without fixed consistency, form assumed in a single moment. As such, the concept of rhythm has to be combined with another concept drawn from Benveniste: discourse. This is a crucial term for understanding Meschonnic's position. At its root is the opposition of the signified and the signifier, to use Saussure's terminology, even though the problem is obviously much older.[7] Even though Saussure considers the two parts of the sign as two

---

5. Translated by Mary Elizabeth Meek, in *Problems in General Linguistics* (Coral Gables, FL: University of Miami Press, 1971).
6. In *Critique du rythme: anthropologie historique du langage* (Lagrasse: Verdier), p. 225; subsequently referred to in the text as CR plus page number.
7. Actually, as we can know only now, after the publication of Saussure's *Écrits de linguistique générale*, text drawn up and edited by Simon Bouquet and Rudolf Engler (Paris: Gallimard, 2002), text from 1891, the structuralist reception of Saussure is one-sided

sides of a piece of paper, this conception still implies a static and secondary nature of the signifier with respect to the signified. Meschonnic therefore prefers to refer to Saussure's notion of *valeur* (value), which, in his eyes, allows for poetics as a form of analysis of the functioning of literature (BL, p. 470). Value, for Saussure, differs from signification in so far as value always depends on the system. *Sheep* in English and *mouton* in French, for instance, can have the same meaning, but the value is different because the word can be used for different things and applied to different contexts.[8] The term value shows that there is more to language than signs. But Saussure only hinted at this linguistics of discourse; he did not fully apply it. Language certainly is discontinuous in the sense that there is no inner continuous between a signifier and a signified, and that it is made up of a series of signs, but this is not all: beyond a certain level of understanding, it is also continuous. This is not to efface the sign; it always remains, but an additional dimension comes into play. The desire to make this continuous intelligible lies at the heart of Meschonnic's theory. It is a necessary condition in order to understand what takes place in art and literature.

Benveniste states that language has a double signifying function (double signifiance),[9] semiotically (all linguistic signs considered as and in their unitary form, distinct from all other units) and semantically (the globally conceived meaning). The semantic meaning is not the result of a combination of semiotic signs; on the contrary, it is considered globally, even though its meaning may be divided into particular 'signs' and their combination (PLG2, p. 64). This semantic functioning of language is engendered by discourse which is not recognised, as the sign in semiotics, but understood (PLG2, pp. 64–5). To illustrate this difference, we can think of Stanislavski, who famously made an actor pronounce the words *sevodnja večerom* (tonight) in forty different ways to express forty different meanings. Recognising the words is simply not enough to understand what is expressed by them.

There is consequently a shift in focus in this alternative way of considering language. The sign splits language up into discontinuous units; discourse considers language in its continuous. It is, of course, more practicable to analyse language in such small portions; none the less, the sign, claims Benveniste, is paradoxically in the way if one wants to understand how language functions,

since he has also thought about language as discourse in Benveniste's sense of the term.
8. Ferdinand de Saussure, *Cours de linguistique générale*, critical edition prepared by Tullio de Mauro (Paris: Payot, 1972), pp. 155–62.
9. Émile Benveniste, 'Semiologie de la langue', in *Problèmes de linguistique générale 2* (Paris: Gallimard, 1974), pp. 43–66, p. 63; subsequently referred to in the text as PLG2 plus page number.

if one wants to 'think language', since it is perceived as the unique principle on which the working of language entirely depends. He calls for a semantics that admits another dimension of significance – which is discourse, the semantics of enunciation (PLG2, p. 66).

To understand what is meant by a semantics of enunciation, it is important to see how Benveniste conceives of discourse and subjectivity. Discourse is, according to Benveniste, 'la langue en tant qu'assumée par l'homme qui parle, et dans la condition d'*intersubjectivité*' (language as it is appropriated by the person speaking, and in the condition of *intersubjectivity*).[10] He states that the basis of subjectivity lies in the exercise of language (PLG1, p. 262), inasmuch as each use of 'I' refers to an individual moment of speech (PLG1, p. 261). The 'I' cannot exist without reference to a 'you'; therefore language is necessarily dialogical and, as a result, the precondition of society. Language manifests itself exclusively as discourse. And in the moment of discourse the speaker manifests him- or herself as a subject. The enunciation of 'I' brings subjectivity into being; it is a new subject each and every time and therefore cannot be fixed or foreseen. Language is, for Benveniste, the possibility of subjectivity, and discourse is its realisation.

For Benveniste, the abstract system of language (*langue* as opposed to *langage*) does not make any sense. The single word may have a meaning, but without the context in the sentence it is meaningless. The meaning of a word always depends on the context. Benveniste actually defined the sentence as the smallest unit of meaning in language. This implies that the sign cannot render meaning; meaning is always in discourse – that is, in speech, in the concrete continuous speech in its historical situation.

Semioticians obviously know that there is more to language than mere signs: they are aware of grammar, of word play, of speech acts and so on. When Meschonnic, by drawing his conclusions from Benveniste's linguistics, dismisses other theories and thinkers, he is sometimes very categorical in his rejection. Instead of stressing common interests and questions, he confronts his peers head on. Derrida, for example, also criticised the binarism of the sign from his point of view, and Heidegger's ontology is in some crucial ways closer to that of Meschonnic than the latter admits. None the less, differing terminology implies a difference in focus that generates different attitudes and approaches to the world, and it is useful to point out crucial differences from other thinkers and their shortcomings from the perspective of the theory of language, as Meschonnic does. These differences are decisive for the role of art and literature.

10. Émile Benveniste, 'De la subjectivité dans le langage', in *Problèmes de linguistique générale 1* (Paris: Gallimard, 1966), pp. 258–66, p. 266.

Benveniste defined artistic expression in 1969 as 'semantics [. . .] without semiotics' (PLG2, p. 65) and, according to Meschonnic, this sums up in three words that it is art which demonstrates the fallacy of the mainstream theory of language. Semiotics refers to the functioning of the sign, semantics refers to discourse (PLG2, p. 64). Language is semantics and semiotics; it is the only system that has a double signifiance, as Benveniste calls it. Semantics can be more than, or something other than, semiotics, and in literature this is always the case. In literature – that is, language as an art form – language is primarily semantics without semiotics: that is, more than the sum of its parts. This does not mean that the signs are gone, but what makes art art is not the signs it is made of. Meschonnic writes:

> Ce que la sémiotique ne comprend pas [. . .] c'est que, dans l'œuvre d'art, l'unité n'est pas un signe; que l'œuvre ne devient une œuvre qu'à partir du moment où il y a en elle du sémantique sans sémiotique, même si, jusqu'à un certain niveau de lecture, elle est faite des unités à double articulation, comme toutes les autres pratiques du langage. (BL, p. 348)
>
> (What semiotics does not understand [. . .] is that in the work of art the unit is not a sign; that the work does not become a work unless it comports semantics without semiotics, even if, up to a certain level of reading, it is made of units of double articulation, like any other praxis of language.)

This does not deny the existence of the sign, but it does deny the sign an exclusive role. An artwork does not cease to be semiotic; it can still be analysed as being composed of signs. The difference from this perspective is that its specificity as a work of art is not taken into account when considered semiotically and not semantically. According to Meschonnic, only semantics considers it in its continuous. The perspective of semiotics is discontinuous and cannot see the entire work, only parts of it. This is the old problem of reasoning: the analysis seems to destroy its object, at least certain kinds of object. For some problems or phenomena reasoning is quite adequate, but there are other phenomena or problems for which reasoning is not the correct tool, and which do not 'give themselves up' to it. Art works are certainly amongst these phenomena. It is poetics that constantly interrogates our system of thought. As long as we cannot integrate artistic expression into it, there is something missing in the state of our mind and we have a blinkered vision of the world and of human life. The continuous, to which art draws our attention, requires concepts that make us capable of thinking it – this is the task of poetics. Of course, when using this term, I am not referring to the traditional notion of the poetic arts, understood as rules for how to write a poem. I am talking about poetics in a particular sense of the term: poetics defined as the theory of the specificity of literature, as the search for concepts that allow us to fathom the functioning of literature, and therefore also the functioning of the subject, and consequently, of ethics, politics and society as a whole. It is here that Meschonnic's theory is very helpful.

Since all our concepts have to be in language, we can certainly feel and perceive outside of language, but we cannot conceptualise and grasp anything intellectually without language. In order to configure the world mentally, we need language. We can give meaning to our life only by using language. If we can entertain this contention, then the theory of language is crucial for all the humanities; they are all dealing with meaning, whether they know it or not.[11] Émile Benveniste goes so far as to say that only language allows for society to exist: 'seule la langue permet la société' (PLG2, p. 62).

In describing the tendency of reason and analysis to divide the unity of presence, we arrive at Meschonnic's central theory, the intelligibility of presence.[12] Poetics is concerned with this question.[13] According to Meschonnic, what makes it so difficult to understand presence is the fact that our age, perhaps more than any other before it, has developed an epistemology that is based completely on semiotics. The sign, however, does not allow us to comprehend the specificity of art. We have built up an immensely vast knowledge, admirable in many respects, but like all knowledge it produces its own particular form of ignorance, making it almost impossible even to become aware of blind spots, since the whole system of knowledge makes it easy to brush aside as irrational everything that falls outside the binary logic of the sign. The sign can foster thinking only in terms of the discontinuous (not discontinuity in the meaning of chronological interruption, but discontinuous as a splitting apart of unity).

Heidegger's ontology was the most influential attempt to deal with this question of presence but it was not based on historicity, as Meschonnic's theory is. Instead, it had to rely on linguistic mysticism. Jacques Derrida has shown with his concept of *différance* that a direct access to presence is impossible, that there is always an imperceptible difference between being and our awareness of it. This position, while implying a criticism of the sign, is nevertheless based on the sign to some degree: Derrida's *différance* presents a negative hermeneutics, but it is still a hermeneutics preoccupied with the

---

11. That is what Meschonnic says in BL, p. 101: 'qu'elles le sachent ou non, toutes les sciences humaines sont des disciplines du sens'.
12. For instance, BL, p. 192, or *Pour sortir du postmoderne* (Paris: Klinksieck, Hourvari series, 2009), p. 8; subsequently referred to in the text as SP.
13. In *Politique du rythme, politique du sujet* (Lagrasse: Verdier, 1995), p. 93; subsequently referred to in the text as PRPS plus page number.

meaning of signs rather than with the mode of signifying. And obviously, Derrida only points to the problem; he does nothing to solve it. But we have to deal with this question of presence in some way since it is life itself that is at stake, life considered in the moment it passes, always ephemeral.

Meschonnic might be criticised for categorising as binary things that are more complex than that, but it remains true that in order to understand presence we must develop a theory of language that considers language as discourse (Benveniste) and not as signs strung together. And our terminology falls short in this respect.[14] Meschonnic's concepts of the continuous and rhythm, which will be employed in the following discussion, overcome these shortcomings to some degree.

Meschonnic defines rhythm as that which makes discourse discourse. Each enunciation is unique; the repetition of an enunciation is another enunciation. Rhythm is consequently what reigns over speech. Meschonnic formulates this as follows:

> À partir de Benveniste, le rythme peut ne plus être une souscatégorie de la forme. C'est une organisation (disposition, configuration) d'un ensemble. Si le rythme est dans le langage, dans un discours, il est une organisation (disposition, configuration) du discours. Et comme le discours n'est pas séparable de son sens, le rythme est inséparable du sens de ce discours. (CR, p. 70)
>
> (From Benveniste on, rhythm cannot be a sub-category of form any more. It is an organisation (disposition, configuration) of an ensemble. If rhythm is in language, in discourse, it is an organisation (disposition, configuration) of discourse. And since the discourse cannot be separated from its meaning, the rhythm is inseparable from the meaning of this discourse.)

Rhythm, for Meschonnic, is consequently no formal metrical principle, but a semantic principle; the way each concrete instance of speech makes sense, creates meaning. This also implies that there is no structure to be drawn from it; it is different each time, unique and unforeseeable, and an apparent repetition of an enunciation is different from a previous instance, too, because the context is necessarily different, even if only by virtue of the one instance having preceded the other. An example is repetition in music – a repeated phrase is never the same phrase as any of the previous instances precisely because they have already been heard, and the listener, by having already heard them, is different.

14. It is interesting that in recent years terms like *Stimmung* (mood) and 'atmosphere' have become more and more important in Germany and that many researchers are trying to find applications for them in academic discourse.

Meschonnic's most important forerunner for this conception of language is certainly Wilhelm von Humboldt. Humboldt stated very clearly that grammar and dictionaries are nothing but a 'dead skeleton': 'Die Sprache liegt nur in der verbundenen Rede, Grammatik und Wörterbuch sind kaum ihrem todten Gerippe vergleichbar' (Language exists only in connected speech; grammar and dictionary are barely the equivalent of its dead skeleton).[15] Just as Benveniste did much later, Humboldt stressed that it is not the words that give meaning in speech, but that it is, on the contrary, speech that grants the words their meaning: 'In der Wirklichkeit wird die Rede nicht aus ihr vorangegangenen Wörtern zusammengesetzt sondern die Wörter gehen umgekehrt aus dem Ganzen der Rede hervor' (VII: p. 72) (In reality, speech is not the connection of words that exist prior to it, but on the contrary the words emanate out of the ensemble of speech). Humboldt insists that language is not a product but an activity ('kein Werk [Ergon], sondern eine Thätigkeit [Energeia]', VII: p. 46), and characterises speech as living ('lebendig') and grounded in each particular instance ('jedesmalig'). This is thinking language as speech, not as an abstraction. His central terms for 'thinking language' are continuous ('Zusammenhang') and interdependency ('Wechselwirkung'). Meschonnic comments on Humboldt: 'C'est toute la pensée du discours' (BL, p. 181) (The whole thinking of discourse is there).

Rhythm for Meschonnic is not the rigid metrical arrangement of language; it is language in movement, the flow of language in its continuous. He often points out that Saussure also used the metaphor 'le fleuve du langage' ('the stream of language'). Consequently, rhythm always refers to the whole. Meschonnic describes this continuous of language as 'le vivant dans son histoire' (PRPS, p. 129). This leads him to use the term of historicity very often, to refer to the unique moment of speech with its context and its situation. The continuous is what connects the words, which are otherwise meaningless. Rhythm is the organisation of this continuous. It obviously does not and cannot create a totalising unity of meaning. Rhythm always remains open; it finds its unity only momentarily and inscribes a subject and its situation in discourse (CR, p. 73). The movement of language is organised by discourse; rhythm testifies to the uniqueness of this speech and thus of its radical historicity.

However, Meschonnic insists that it is less Benveniste's text about rhythm than his own experience with translating the Bible that lies at the source of his theory. What informed his thinking about language was the discovery that in the Bible there is neither verse nor prose but a complex system of eighteen

---

15. Wilhelm von Humboldt, *Über die Verschiedenheiten des menschlichen Sprachbaues*, 1827–9, in *Gesammelte Schriften*, ed. by Albert Leitzmann (Berlin: Behr, 1907), VI: p. 147.

disjunctive and conjunctive accents with melodic, pausal and semantic value, which establishes a serial signification and in which this pan-rhythm creates meaning.[16] The signifier as presented in the Bible shows the insufficiency of our representation of language and therefore of meaning: 'le signifiant n'a pas de garant. Puisqu'il est radicalement historique. Il n'a que le sujet, et le sujet se fait de se défaire. Il n'a que le risque, l'inconnu qui recommence' (JSE, p. 133) (the signifier has no guarantor. Since it is radically historical. It has only the subject, and the subject comes into being by vanishing. It has only the risk, the unknown that starts all over again).

Consequently, the thinking of rhythm is opposed to the thinking of the sign with its binary structure of signifier and signified. This sign model can function only on the level of the word; it does not have the concepts to think discourse and the flow of language. Even if the word can always also be perceived as sign, this is shown to be insufficient by poetry. For Meschonnic, rhythm has more, or perhaps another meaning, than the words: 'Le rythme dans un discours peut avoir plus de sens que le sens des mots, ou un autre sens' (CR, p. 70) (Rhythm in discourse can have more sense than the meaning of the words, or another sense).

Poetics and Poem

Rhythm focuses the attention on the historical moment of speech and thereby opens up the mind towards infinity, since it is aware that meaning is always created anew in each moment of speech. This is more than repetition or iterability as we find it in Chomsky, Derrida and others. It is more, precisely because it is not the signs in their variability that are considered, but the utterance as a whole.

With this in mind, the term poetics here can no longer refer to the art of writing poems or literature in general in the traditional way. The poem is defined by Meschonnic in a much broader manner: it is not the product or work of art any more (*ergon*), but an activity (*energeia*), as Humboldt put it. The emphasis in this process lies on transformation. Poetry should not be seen as a literary genre, as opposed to prose or to ordinary language. Poetry is, from Meschonnic's point of view, an ordinary speech activity (BL, p. 11); there is no way of distinguishing between poetic and ordinary language. Meschonnic actually carried on a lifelong battle against the celebration of poetry, which he considered poetry's worst enemy, since it pretends to know what poetry is and thus simply uses it or regards it as a form or convention

---

16. He explains this in most detail in *Jona et le signifiant errant* (Paris: Gallimard, 1981), subsequently referred to in the text as JSE, and more recently, for example, in *Éthique et politique du traduire* (Lagrasse: Verdier, 2007), pp. 46–7.

(this is the opposite of poetry as transformation and presence). He opposes to this his notion of *poésie-transformation*, which is actually to act on the poet and on the reader by changing their relationship with the world.[17]

There is consequently an interaction between poetry and life which leads to Meschonnic's following definition of the poem: 'je définis le poème comme l'invention d'une forme de vie par une forme de langage et l'invention d'une forme de langage par une forme de vie' (BL, p. 17) (I define the poem as the invention of a form of life by a form of language and the invention of a form of language by a form of life). A poem is invention, a transformation of life and of language, resulting from the interaction of language and life.

This fact that the poet and the reader are invented by the poem, as Meschonnic says (we must always keep in mind that he is talking about a way of thinking, not about a few written lines), shows that we are dealing with a real 'speech act', and this leads to an impact on ethics: a poem also transforms ethics and is thereby associated with anthropology (BL, p. 18), inasmuch as it is a transformation of the subject.

Such a process – I repeat, because a poem is not a literary form but a process of transformation – naturally cannot be defined formally. Meschonnic calls poetry a way of thinking ('une pensée'), the maximal relationship between life and language.[18] This is also the difference between the general fact of linguistic subjectivity created in language when the speaker says 'I', and a more charged idea of the subjectivity of art and literature. He coins the term poem of thought, 'poème de la pensée' (SP, p. 67), even used as the sub-title of his book on Spinoza,[19] to refer to the constant invention and reinvention of a subject in writing.

Subject and Poem

Some explanation is now needed to clarify how this conception of language and poetics has broad consequences for our ideas about the subject and therefore for all the humanities and for society.

Baudelaire's notion of modernity is a useful starting point to grasp these consequences. For Meschonnic, modernity is almost interchangeable with the notions of presence, subject and poem. By referring to Baudelaire, he contrasts the philosophical term 'modernity', meaning post-Enlightenment rationalism, with modernity in art and literature. Meschonnic also differentiates

17. For this aspect of his theory see the book with the ironic title *Célébration de la poésie* (Lagrasse: Verdier, 2001).
18. 'La poésie n'est pas une forme. Mais une pensée. D'une certaine manière, le maximum du rapport entre la vie et le langage' (BL, p. 18).
19. *Spinoza, poème de la pensée* (Paris: Maisonneuve & Larose, 2002).

at least thirteen subjects, one of them being the subject of philosophy (the conscious, unitary and voluntary subject) and another being the subject of art and literature.

In 1859/60, Baudelaire wrote in *Le Peintre de la vie moderne*, IV: 'La modernité, c'est le transitoire, le fugitif, le contingent, la moitié de l'art, dont l'autre moitié est l'éternel et l'immuable' (Modernity, that is the transitory, the fleeting, the contingent, the half of art, of which the other half is the eternal and the immovable). He concludes with the following sentences (XIII):

> Il [the artist who serves as a model for modernity] a cherché partout la beauté passagère, fugace, de la vie présente, le caractère de ce que le lecteur nous a permis d'appeler *la modernité*. Souvent bizarre, violent, excessif, mais toujours poétique, il a su concentrer dans ses dessins la saveur amère ou capiteuse du vin de la Vie.[20]

> (He [the artist who serves as a model for modernity] has looked everywhere for the passing beauty of present life, for the character that the reader has allowed us to call *modernity*. Often bizarre, violent, excessive, but always poetic, he has managed to concentrate in his drawings the bitter or sensuous taste of the wine of life.)

We are dealing here with a conception of modernity that is one and the same thing as Baudelaire's conception of presence and life – and not only his, obviously. It fits in perfectly with what has been said about the thinking of language as *discours* (Benveniste), or *Zusammenhang* (Humboldt), or *rythme* (Meschonnic). Baudelaire uses the words *transitory* and *fleeting* for it. Art then manages to render this eternal and unchanging – but without losing the transitory side of it. Modernity would consequently be exactly what *rhythmos* meant before Plato: form in movement. We can say together with Baudelaire, life; or with Meschonnic, presence.

Meschonnic identifies 'thinking modernity' with 'thinking the subject'.[21] He defines modernity as 'l'activité continue d'une forme-sujet, la découverte de sa propre historicité comme une présence au présent' (PRPS 377) (the

---

20. Charles Baudelaire, 'Le Peintre de la vie moderne', in *Œuvres*, ed. by Y.-G. Le Dantec (Paris: NRF, Bibliothèque de la Pléiade, Gallimard, 1954), pp. 892/920.
21. Meschonnic, *Pour sortir du postmoderne*, p. 21: 'penser le sujet et penser la modernité sont une seule et même pensée' (thinking the subject and thinking modernity means one and the same thinking). This is his last book on the issue. It concentrates on the cul-de-sac of post-modernism, as opposed to his concept of modernity, and picks up on his earlier *Modernité modernité* from 1988 (Lagrasse: Verdier), which gives his sources in more detail. In 2002, Meschonnic also co-edited with Shigehiko Hasumi the volume *La Modernité après le postmoderne* (Paris: Maisonneuve & Larose, 2002).

continuous activity of a subject-form(er), the discovery of its proper historicity as a presence to the present). He can therefore define modernity in art and literature as 'l'activité même du sujet du poème comme transformation continuée du présent des rapports à soi et aux autres' (SP, p. 141) (the activity of the subject of the poem as continuous transformation of the present, transforming the relationship to oneself and to others).

This transformation is the precondition for modernity to take place, and so much so that the two terms are almost interchangeable for Meschonnic. Through the transformative activity of art and literature, our relationship to the world is transformed; and this consequently transforms the world, for, as Meschonnic states, the world consists largely of our relationship with it.[22]

Unlike the philosophical subject understood by the modernity of reason, the Baudelairean modernity in art and literature does not separate subject and object; it unites them.[23] Meschonnic even claims provocatively that poetics is more competent for ethics and politics than the specialists in these latter fields, since poetics does not confuse these different subjects and modernities (BL, pp. 43–4). But this politics of rhythm is, of course, a utopia, a term which refers to the future for Meschonnic and is an absolute necessity for things to change; by no means does it imply resignation (BL, p. 104).

For Meschonnic, the subject of art and literature is possible only by first being ethical and political; this is its precondition. Its transformative activity is ethical and political; it changes the relationships among human beings. Without it, there would be no subject of art and literature. We should perhaps rule out the possible confusion of this subject with the author. The subject in question is not the author but rather, for Meschonnic, a process of subjectivation; it is the activity itself, not the person who acts. And the activity is the activity of the poem, which Meschonnic defined as the invention of a form of language by a form of life, and vice versa. It follows that the subject

---

22. 'La modernité n'advient que s'il y a transformation. Elle est cette transformation même. [. . .] La modernité est ce qui ne cesse de transformer par l'art et la littérature notre rapport au monde. Et le monde n'est pour sa plus grande part que notre rapport au monde' (Modernity emerges only when there is transformation. It is this transformation itself. [. . .] Modernity is what never stops transforming, by art and literature, our relationship with the world. And the world is for its major part our relationship with the world) (SP, pp. 165–6).
23. 'La modernité de la Raison suppose le sujet philosophique qui sépare sujet de connaissance et objet. La modernité en art et en littérature unit l'éthique et l'art, contre la Raison des Lumières; unit l'objet et le sujet' (BL, p. 43) (The modernity of Reason presupposes a philosophical subject which separates the subject of knowledge and the object. Modernity in art and literature unites ethics and arts, against the Reason of the Enlightenment; it unites object and subject).

is actually its own modernity. Poetry, as the activity of language, exposes the subject; and it exposes that what is at stake in language, in its historicity, is the subject (CR, p. 35). This subject of the poem, which includes its modernity and which represents the subjectivation of discourse, is, then, for Meschonnic the alternative to universalising thinking: an alternative which he calls a counter-coherence to the syncretic subject of universalisation (SP, p. 142). This is the case because it is radically historical. It is particular, each time anew; it exists only in the mode of presence, infinitely so, and cannot be applied to or forced on to anything. It cannot be considered in the past and it is unforeseeable for the future. This model proposes a real interaction between the activity of art, ethics and politics described above. Each one of them transforms the others.

Meschonnic claims that his thinking about the continuous engages with the theory of language, with the theory of literature and art, and with ethics and politics (SP, p. 15). The continuous for him is life in its historical moment ('Le continu, lui, c'est le vivant dans son histoire'; PRPS, p. 129), since thinking the continuous in language and art places human life in the infinity of history and of meaning, and therefore represents life. It also represents diversity and plurality, whereas thinking in terms of the sign is an abstraction, detached from the concrete historical situation. The latter way of thinking represents the death of the poem, the poem here equalling life (BL, p. 27). Meschonnic considers language asemiotically, starting from the subject: that is, from the subjectivation of language in speech. This implies historicity instead of structure. Language and subject are constantly starting anew in speech.

This does not happen only in poetry as an art form. But poetry is a test for the status of the subject. It demonstrates the failure of the sign with its dualism of form and content, or of sound and meaning. One can exchange one sign for another, but a poem cannot be expressed differently. It is this poem exactly in this form, as a whole; one cannot replace any of its words with another one. The sign fails when confronted with a poem; it cannot give an account of the plurality of the activities of language (BL, p. 207). It cannot even explain the existence of the continuous (BL, p. 401). Even if a poem is linguistically composed of signs, it is more than that. Considered semantically, it cannot be reduced to the sum of its elements. It actually creates a new meaning precisely in its continuous, and in this sense it goes beyond the meaning of its signs. Meschonnic says, 'Le poème passe à travers les signes' (CR, p. 72) (The poem slips through the signs): that is to say, even though the poem is made up of signs, this is not where its specificity resides. The poem slips through the signs, constituting its particular meaning in spite of them.

The discontinuous of the sign is qualified as madness by Meschonnic, 'une folie' (BL, p. 11). This, he says, is a madness that has been globalised by science and that renders the thinking of the continuous very difficult. Poetics tries to show up its limits and its flaws, and to propose another way of thinking.

Continuous and Consequences

It is clear that we are dealing here with a theory that lacks any obvious and direct application. It is, rather, a way of understanding the world and oneself, and as such it concerns all things. It allows for the critique of various discourses (the term being used here in Foucault's sense, as a way of thematising an issue in a given social situation). One might well feel that all this terminology somehow returns to the same issue, and indeed it does: the subject, the poem, poetics, modernity, transformation, historicity, discourse, continuous. All these are often interchangeable concepts; they are ways of approaching the most profound question that we cannot grasp – the intelligibility of presence. It is not possible to seize and master it – which is all for the good – but we have art and literature to be aware of it and to cultivate it. This poetics of the continuous is about developing concepts with which to approach art and literature, but it cannot be a question of seizing and mastering the intelligibility of presence, as that would return us to the mode of scientific knowledge (in which semiotics and the two-part sign reside) that involves a final analysis and final conclusions. The point about presence is its openness and its flux, its non-final and living character, precisely denied in the mode of knowledge and acquiring knowledge to which we are accustomed. Poetics constantly flees any system of thought and provides points of flight from any such system. This is why semiotics is so dismally unfit for the task of rendering presence intelligible, and why poetics is such a challenge. In some sense, then, poetics will never succeed, but that too is inherent in its task. If it succeeded – in our usual sense of full knowledge as scientific success – it would have failed: hence the paradox. And we would lose a truly essential dimension of human life if we gave up on this paradoxical task. The efforts to think it are of the highest importance.

If we look at language in this way and, consequently, at the subject, at ethics and politics, what does this change in society? The answer is that it offers another interpretation of the world, and as such it is an intervention. Another attitude can change everything, though it has to be shared to be effective. It is also a defence against all *langues de bois* (political cant, or prefigured, empty speech, which is usually ideologically motivated) and it makes us aware of any abuse of language (BL, p. 126).

This thinking of language cannot offer a generally valid, solid and always reliable ethics, but we should not regard this purely as a weakness. Any clear representation develops an institutionalisation, and the institution by its nature has to protect itself against anything that threatens its unity: it becomes dogmatic and rigid. Meschonnic's theory provides a form of what I call poetic thinking.[24] It cannot build a system; its strength consists in being a counterforce, possibly a corrective force, against all institutionalisation. Paradoxically, society needs both: the system, and a way of thinking that undermines it. Only in this way can humanity function and persist. A system without poetic thinking becomes inhuman; poetic thinking without the framework of the system is incapable of community. This is why society has to be as open to poetic thinking as possible; it has to represent a space pervaded by the poetic in which the systemic and the poetic exist together, complementing one another. Poetics in itself is, then, the effort to develop a rational discourse about poetic thinking. This explains the tension between semiotics and poetics: poetics, to a certain degree, has to function semiotically to demonstrate the limits of the sign, transcending it in a way that recalls Wittgenstein's famous ladder that has to be pushed away after use.

Meschonnic's formulation 'est sujet celui par qui un autre est sujet' (BL, p. 42) – a result of his conviction that in language one is a subject only by making somebody else a subject – is ethically important. It places every human being in a mutual interrelationship with the other. 'Le langage, c'est être des sujets les uns pour les autres' (BL, p. 515) (Language means being subjects one for the other), says Meschonnic.[25] Without this, the thinking of the sign leads to a world in which pure biologism rules. The thinking of the continuous, on the other hand, comprehends human life not biologically but historically (BL, p. 12), always considering each moment anew, with its context and situation. It cultivates the internal plurality of the subject (BL, p. 27), against all the efforts of totalitarian thought. Historicity demonstrates the infinity of meaning.

According to Meschonnic, the poem is a manifestation of the power of small things ('la puissance de l'infime') for human life (BL, p. 13), and he finds happiness in this presence, of which his ideas about language make us aware: 'Le bonheur, c'est de savoir à chaque instant que c'est ici et maintenant qu'on vit par le langage, qu'on vit une vie humaine' (BL, p. 515) (Happiness is to know at any moment that it is here and now that we live by language, that we live a human life). That is what he calls an anthropology of language.

---

24. Marko Pajević, *Poetisches Denken und die Frage nach dem Menschen: Grundzüge einer poetologischen Anthropologie* (Freiburg im Breisgau: Karl Alber, 2012).
25. This evokes the mostly Jewish tradition of dialogic thought, especially as it is developed by Martin Buber, but also by Emmanuel Levinas, with whom Meschonnic is thoroughly familiar.

Poetics, as Meschonnic understands it, affects all human sciences, since the latter work with meaning. It directly transforms the philosophy of the subject, which is the basis for our understanding of the world. Its lessons can be applied to a variety of questions. Meschonnic has shown very convincingly what its value is for the theory of translation,[26] and of course for translation itself, or for pedagogy, where he seeks not only to transfer knowledge but to develop the subject's potential and to give him or her the pleasure of inventing thought (BL, p. 19). He shows that poetry is far from being of interest only to a few old-fashioned romantics. Poetry, in the elaborated sense of the term, concerns everybody because it is in poetry that things take place in a privileged form that are decisive for the meaning of language and for the meaning of the subject. The fact that our society has not pursued this specific idea of language suggests to Meschonnic that our society is underdeveloped: 'C'est toute une culture, toute une société qui est jugée et qui se joue dans ce qui arrive à la poésie'[27] (CP, p. 10) (It is an entire culture, an entire society that is judged and that is at stake in what happens to poetry). Finally, to quote Benveniste once again: 'bien avant de servir à communiquer, le langage sert à vivre'[28] (much more than to communicate, language serves to live). There is no possibility of society and of humanity without it.

This poetics of rhythm and of the continuous cannot offer the same certainties as the thinking of the sign, which seems to provide clear, matter-of-fact statements regarding the things of the world. But, as Meschonnic writes, 'Nous n'avons pas affaire à un savoir, avec le rythme. Nous avons essentiellement affaire, à travers le rythme, avec notre ignorance. C'est ce que les notions reçues font beaucoup pour nous cacher' (With rhythm, we don't deal with knowledge. We deal essentially, via rhythm, with our ignorance. That is what the received notions try hard to hide from us).[29]

Meschonnic admits the uncertainty necessarily inherent in his theory, but he points out as well that in poetics there is more to search for than in the sign, and also more to find (BL, p. 418).

---

26. Most recently in *Éthique et politique du traduire* (Lagrasse: Verdier, 2007) or in *Poétique du traduire* (Lagrasse: Verdier, 1999).
27. In *Célébration de la poésie* (Lagrasse: Verdier, 2001), p. 10; subsequently referred to in the text as CP plus page number.
28. In 'La Forme et le sens dans le langage', in *Problèmes de linguistique générale 2*, pp. 215–40, p. 217.
29. Henri Meschonnic, *Les États de la poétique* (Paris: Presses Universitaires de France, 1995), p. 86.

Meschonnic's Poetics of Society

by Marko Pajević

We have established the central position of meaning-making in Meschonnic's theory of rhythm. This is closely connected to his criticism of the sign. In order to understand 'signifiance', we must work also outside of the remit of the sign; in order to overcome the practice of 'sign-thinking', the smallest unit of meaning cannot be the word but has to be the entire enunciation.

To grasp the act of enunciation, however, involves not just the speaker but his or her whole environment, for which a key element is the interlocutor. After all, one never speaks without an addressee (even if this addressee might be absent, fictional or oneself). Again following Benveniste, Meschonnic argued that discourse is language *spoken in the condition of intersubjectivity*.[1] If speaking constitutes the speaker as an I – that is, as a subject – and this I is inconceivable without reference to a you, then language becomes the precondition of subjectivity, but more than this, it becomes the precondition of society itself. In each moment of speaking, this social subjectivity is established anew. And if rhythm is the configuration of the subject in its discourse, then rhythm too produces and transforms the subject. Here we start to see why *Critique du rythme* was sub-titled 'historical anthropology of language', for Meschonnic's theory of rhythm entails a theory not just of discourse, but of the constitution of subjects in discourse, as they inhabit and transform their historical moment. What starts as a conceptual problem of linguistic rhythm expands outwards to comprise an alternative approach to grasping language, the subject and society.

---

1. Émile Benveniste, 'De la subjectivité dans le langage', in *Problèmes de linguistique générale 1* (Paris: Gallimard, 1966), pp. 258–66, p. 266.

What is at Stake in a Poetics of Society?[2]

Meschonnic's vast *œuvre* was continuously preoccupied with the question of a *poetics of society*; he constantly connected the theory of language to its practice in various fields and interrogated what that means for society. In 2012, three years after his death, a book on which he had worked since the late 1970s until almost the end of his life was finally published: *Langage, histoire, une même théorie* (Language, History, One and the Same Theory).[3] This very important publication of almost 750 pages clarifies the overarching rationale for his work and connects language theory to ethics and politics. This book assembles various text forms – essays, notes, prefaces and forewords – written over the past thirty years, but they all turn around that same issue which represents the core of Meschonnic's work: the interaction of life and language. And related to this is what he is always refining in his efforts to conceptualise that which flees the conceptual, and which he considered to be the philosophical issue par excellence: the intelligibility of presence.

Realism/Nominalism

On the basis of the fundamental ideas of Meschonnic's poetics, as presented above, the following will go more into the details at the example of a short text in the 2012 Meschonnic volume on the identity of the theory of language and of society. This text was first published in 2005 and its title is telling: 'Réalisme, nominalisme: la théorie du langage est une théorie de la société' (LH, pp. 717–26) ('Realism, Nominalism: The Theory of Language is a Theory of Society'). With this, he refers back to the debate on realism and nominalism, admitting that this might seem outdated, dusty and museum-like (LH, p. 721). This is a debate dating back to Antiquity, with its apogee in medieval scholastics. Meschonnic, however, claimed a vital importance for these terms when it comes to thinking the interaction of language, ethics and politics: that is, for a poetics of society. They are indeed omnipresent, he stated, albeit without people being aware of it. He himself had invoked realism and nominalism in connection to language theory as far back as 1970.[4] And in one of his last books, *Heidegger ou le national-essentialisme* (Heidegger or National-Essentialism), he used these terms again to denounce

---

2. The following is taken from my article 'A Poetics of Society: Thinking Language with Henri Meschonnic', in the Special Issue 'Thinking Language with Henri Meschonnic' of *Comparative Critical Studies*, 15/3 (2018), ed. by Marko Pajević and David Nowell Smith.
3. Henri Meschonnic, *Langage, histoire, une même théorie* (Lagrasse: Verdier, 2012); subsequently referred to in the text as LH plus page number. All translations are my own.
4. Henri Meschonnic, *Pour la poétique I* (Paris: Gallimard, 1970), p. 48.

the essentialism in Heidegger's philosophy and thereby to demonstrate the ethical dimension of language theory.[5]

What, then, is the import of these terms? The problem goes back to Plato's theory of ideas, most famously laid out in his allegory of the cave, concerning the existence of an essence of things. A table, for instance, can take various forms, be built of various materials and so on, but everybody has an idea of what a table is generally. Plato believed that something like an essential table exists on its own, as the truth of 'tableness', even though humans can see only individual forms of it. *Realism* is the position of believing in the real existence of such abstract entities, in the existence of universals *ante res* (anterior to things). *Nominalism* represents the opposing position, the belief that all general concepts are abstractions created by humans, arbitrarily but in community and consensually; for nominalists, there is consequently no essence of a table as such. 'Table' is a term to designate a group of objects. Only the individual objects are real.

The debate is, of course, much more sophisticated and differentiated, and in some ways still on-going; Meschonnic's focus, however, was not simply epistemological, but also political. If there exists the one true thing or idea, then the one with the power to define it has a claim to the truth. What matters for a poetics of society is that institutions and authorities have an interest in the existence of essential objects because they increase their authority (admittedly, today, many institutions see themselves as serving the public interest rather than their own interests – fortunately so). This is an approach to the world based outside of the human realm, a metaphysics. If, on the other hand, the starting position is individual objects, and people agreeing to group them under certain terms, then we are dealing with a historical approach to the world; concepts and terms are subject to change and everybody participates in these processes. It is not astonishing that the medieval Church, together with the medieval university with its ecclesiastical foundations, struggled to admit the nominalist position and that modern empirical science and democracy are based on nominalism. Nominalism led to a shift in paradigm: instead of the principle of *deduction* of the specific case from an accepted dogmatic position, it is now rather the *induction* from the specific, empirical fact that leads to a general insight.

Against the Sign

Meschonnic qualified realism as 'theological' and the sign, in mainstream linguistics, as a realist notion. As we have already seen, the sign is the enemy

---

5. Henri Meschonnic, *Heidegger ou le national-essentialisme* (Paris: Laurence Teper, 2007).

in Meschonnic's theory of language. He did not dispute the existence of the sign and its necessity, but argued that in mainstream linguistics the sign was taken to be all that the language consists of. Against this, he insisted that the sign is only one representation of language, one perspective in the history of language amongst others, and one which, in its hegemonic and omnipotent claim, keeps us from fully thinking language.

According to Meschonnic, Saussure's presentation of the sign as consisting of signifier and signified has generally been misinterpreted in favour of a binary notion where the signified is interpreted as the referent (the real thing in the world) and the signifier occupies a secondary position. In Saussure, however, the signifier cannot be separated from the signified. The split into signifier and signified — the latter lending itself to being considered to be the actual object, or the political real, whereas the signifier is considered to be merely the technical, material means of coming to grips with it — results in the opposition of content and form,[6] or of sense and sound, which, for Meschonnic, ignores crucial parts of *signifiance*: that is, of how meaning is constituted. If one has wrong ideas about how meaning comes into being, one has necessarily wrong ideas about political processes.

Evidently, hardly any literary scholar or linguist would nowadays explicitly defend a clear-cut distinction between content and form; none the less, elements of this prevail and Saussure's own formulation of 'le fleuve de la langue' ('the stream of language')[7] has hardly been taken into account by post-Saussurean linguistics. The sign, argued Meschonnic, grasps language as *discontinu* (discontinuous): it splits up the stream of language and reduces language to a means of expressing something else. The signified, however, does not equal the meaning of the sign, neither for Saussure nor for Meschonnic; there is more to meaning-making than the 'meaning' of words, or, rather, we have to enlarge our notion of meaning. This is why Meschonnic was at war with what he called *la pensée du signe* (sign-thinking) and hermeneutics. For him, the sign stands for the discontinuous of signifier and signified, and that represents an obstacle to thinking life and society, because life and society is of the order of the continuous, of subjects acting in language and in history. Poetry puts in evidence the failure of the sign: 'La poésie ne renvoie

---

6. This understanding of Saussure was largely due to Bally and Sechehaye's presentation in their edition of his *Cours*; cf. John E. Joseph, 'The *Arbre*-Tree Sign: Pictures and Words in Counterpoint in the *Cours de linguistique générale*', Semiotica, 217/1 (2017), pp. 147–71.
7. Meschonnic refers to this formulation time and again without ever giving the source or without providing any context in Saussure. The term suffices for him, even though it is used by Saussure in the context of diachrony, at the start of the third part on diachronic linguistics; Ferdinand de Saussure, *Cours de linguistique générale*, critical edition ed. by Tullio de Mauro (Paris: Payot, 1972), p. 193.

pas à une *expérience*. Elle la fait' (CR, p. 62) ('Poetry does not refer to an *experience*. It creates it'). It is not a sign, representing something else. Only a poetic approach as explained earlier allows for a full understanding of how a subject constitutes itself and its relation to society and the world. That is why Meschonnic wanted to develop a poetics of society, poetics being the only approach that allows us to think beyond the remit of the sign.

It is against this conception of the sign that he developed his theory of rhythm and of the continuous. Meschonnic considered language to be in movement; he considered language in its continuous flow. The logic of the sign breaks this continuous; rhythm, on the other hand, refers to the whole, to language in its continuous, which Meschonnic defined as 'le vivant dans son histoire' ('the living in its history').[8] Society, in Meschonnic's terms, is necessarily 'rhythmic'; a poetics of society would think society's rhythms.

The Biblical

Here I would like to take a detour via one aspect Meschonnic referred to also in connection with the issue of realism and nominalism, and which underpins his language theory, even if at first it seems quite remote from a 'poetics of society': the discourse of the Bible (LH, p. 722). For Meschonnic, it is the Bible – in Hebrew! – which allows us to free ourselves from realism in the sense of an essentialism, and of its damaging anti-democratic political effects. Paradoxically, then, it is the Bible that detheologises our language and our thinking. This is because Meschonnic did not consider 'le biblique' ('the biblical') as a sacred text, but as 'un fonctionnement' (LH, p. 722) ('a way of functioning').[9]

This functioning of the Bible is nominalist and at the extreme opposite of the essentialising logical realism:

> Le biblique, je le vois comme l'opposé majeur du signe et de sa théologisation du langage, dans son dualisme généralisé, son anthropologie de la totalité, qui oppose la forme au contenu, l'affect au concept, le langage à la vie (LH, p. 722).

> (I see the biblical as the major opponent to the sign and its theologisation of language, in its generalised dualism, its anthropology of totality, which opposes form to content, affect to concept, language to life.)

---

8. Henri Meschonnic, *Politique du rythme, politique du sujet* (Lagrasse: Verdier, 1995), p. 129.
9. For the distinction Meschonnic makes between the sacred, the religious, the divine and the theological, see John E. Joseph's article in the Special Issue of *Comparative Critical Studies*, 15/3 (2018).

Meschonnic detects a contradiction in that, on one hand, the West purports to be founded on the two pillars *Athens* and *Jerusalem*, on Greek philosophy and the Bible, but on the other hand, European philosophy constituted itself by effacing its biblical origin.

Meschonnic often said that he developed his language theory as a result of his experience of translating the Bible; he also called the Bible the 'levier théorique pour transformer toute la pensée du langage' ('theoretical lever to transform the entire thinking of language').[10] One could say with some justification that, throughout his life, he pursued the goal of reintroducing the biblical – specifically, the functioning of the Hebrew language in the Old Testament – into Western thinking. That leads to the question: what is this particularity of biblical functioning? Meschonnic presented biblical Hebrew as organised by a complex system of rhythmic accents, the *te'amim* (singular *ta'am*), constitutive of the verses, and which leads to a generalised rhythmisation of the language. Meschonnic called this the parable of his notion of *corps-langage*, body-in-language, because *ta'am* also literally means the taste of what is in the mouth, the flavour. And this flavour is an essential part of what is said, and why.

This demonstrates that the physicality of language was dear to Meschonnic. He aimed for a generalised *ta'amisation* of thinking language, and thus of thinking altogether. This system of accents creates connections within the text that are constitutive of meaning, thus manifesting a serial organisation of the movement of speech which the sign cannot account for. This meant, for Meschonnic, that the Bible 'impose de penser autrement, et d'entendre ce que le signe ne sait pas entendre. Parce qu'elle est toute entière organisée par les *te'amim* – pluriel de *ta'am*, "gout" et "raison"' ('requires that we think differently, and hear what the sign is unable to hear. Because it is completely organised by the *te'amim* – plural of *ta'am*, "taste" and "reason"').[11] Since it relies on a nominalist approach to language and understands meaning-making in a poetic way, the result of this *ta'amisation* would be a linguistic, poetic, and consequently also a political, detheologisation.

When it comes to political detheologisation, Meschonnic gives examples for the formation of certain abstract nouns in Hebrew, to demonstrate the

---

10. Henri Meschonnic, *Un Coup de Bible dans la philosophie*, revised, corrected and expanded edition (Chalifert: Les Cahiers de Peut-être, Association des Amis de l'Œuvre de Claude Vigée, 2016) (originally Paris: Bayard, 2004). Meschonnic often explained the importance of the biblical, starting with the introduction to his translation of the Song of Songs, *Les Cinq Rouleaux* (Paris: Gallimard, 1970). I also refer to 'Traduire, et la Bible, dans la théorie du langage et de la société', *Nouvelle Revue d'esthétique*, 3/1 (2009), pp. 19–25, particularly p. 23, originally published in *La Rime et la vie* (1989) (Reader pp. 229–43).
11. Meschonnic, *Un Coup de Bible*, p. 146.

nominalist functioning of thinking in Hebrew, which is 'particulièrement symbolique pour le présent de la pensée' (LH, p. 725) ('particularly symbolic for the presence of thinking'). One recurrent example is the formation of the word for *life*: *'hayim*, the masculine plural of *'hay*, which means *alive*. Meschonnic concluded that, in the biblical, life is first of all the living. This confirms the nominalist attitude for him: it is not an abstract, essentialised idea that takes precedence, but individuals come first and one can deduce larger ideas from them. Life is necessarily what is done by a living person. Another example would be the word for *youth*, *ne'ourim*, plural masculine of *ná'ar*, a *young man* – again, it is the individuals which form the first term and the general term derives from it.[12]

The Ethical and Political Consequences of the Nominalist Theory of Language: Humanity

This is a way of thinking which does indeed have an impact on the way we conceive of the world. This is why this conception of language is of importance for ethics and politics; it is what gives sense to the phrase *poetics of society*. When Meschonnic speaks of the political in this context, he does not refer to politics directly in the sense of the concrete measures taken by politicians, but sees the reciprocal interaction of the political with the ethical and with language, forming a whole of the functioning of interhuman relations. He thus opposes a splitting up of the different aspects of society (LH, p. 719). Thinking this interaction is crucial in order to think human life in a way that extends beyond the limits that Meschonnic reveals and decries, as a constant invention of subjectivity in dialogical speech. Meschonnic accorded great importance to literature and philosophy; it is exactly for this reason that he attacked writers who, in their writing, strengthen realist or essentialist language – in our main reference text he named Céline and Heidegger explicitly (LH, p. 719). He led a lifelong combat against Heideggerianism, so strong in France, and consecrated two book-length studies to this.[13]

Meschonnic offered another key example of the difference between

---

12. Émile Benveniste, in his linguistic archaeology of the European institutions, made a comparable point about the term *politics*, which derives from the Greek *pólis*. The Greek *pólitēs* 'citizen' is a derivation from *pólis*, with similar derivations in most modern European languages, where the linguistic relation between State and citizens implies priority of the State over the citizen: *city – citizen*, *Burg – Bürger*, *cité – citoyen*, *gorod – graždanin*. Only in Latin is this anti-individualistic linguistic logic reversed, and the root is the *civis*, the citizen, from which derives the city, *civitas*. See Benveniste, 'Deux modèles linguistiques de la cité', in *Problèmes de linguistique générale 2* (Paris: Gallimard, 1974), pp. 272–80.
13. Henri Meschonnic, *Le Langage Heidegger* (Paris: Presses Universitaires de France, 1990) and *Heidegger ou le national-essentialisme* (Paris: Laurence Teper, 2007).

the realist and the nominalist attitudes manifest in language: the notion of *humanity*, which was at the heart of the medieval debate. He summarised the opposing positions: 'Du point de vue réaliste, l'humanité existe, et les hommes sont des fragments de l'humanité. Du point de vue nominaliste, les individus existent, et l'humanité est l'ensemble des individus' (LH, p. 723) ('From the realist point of view, humanity exists, and humans are fragments of humanity. From the nominalist point of view, individuals exist, and humanity is the ensemble of individuals'). Meschonnic also pointed out that, from their own perspective, both sides are right. The logical, ethical and political consequences are, however, very different.

It is, then, a question of perspective – as always in language, as he added. Meschonnic expanded on this example in another text, 'L'humanité, c'est de penser libre' ('Humanity, that means free thinking') (LH, p. 62, n. 14).[14] There he commented that even if, in both perspectives, there are individuals, the status of the human is different in each. From the realist perspective, the person counts only as a number – and Meschonnic does not shy away from drawing a parallel with the tattooed numbers on the arms of the Jews in the concentration camps, qualifying Nazism as political and racist realism. From the nominalist perspective, however, any single individual embodies the entire form of the human condition in its potentiality.

The key term here is *point de vue* (point of view). The speaker's stance is revealed in his or her use of language. An awareness of the functioning of language consequently abolishes the idea of a truth that is merely communicated in language, independent of language, and even of the notion of truth as an external independent fact altogether, in favour of a conception of an individual truthfulness and commonly accepted, historically determined ideas, subject to change.

Meschonnic was cautious enough, however, to oppose the confusion between individual and individualism explicitly; the realist approach to humanity and society often represents the latter as the destruction of Western society (LH, p. 84). There is no contradiction between the individual and the social; on the contrary, the social builds on the individual. For Meschonnic, 'tous les totalitarismes sont réalistes' (LH, p. 84) ('all totalitarianisms are realist'), as is racism (LH, p. 93). This is why the nominalist representation of humanity implies for him 'un combat' ('a fight') against the realist abstraction which he identifies with death: 'Le réalisme produit du bloc, en donnant de la réalité à une abstraction. En ce sens, le réalisme du langage est un danger et un ennemi pour une vie humaine' (LH, p. 93) ('Realism produces blocks,

---

14. First published in *Qu'est-ce que l'humanité?* (Bibliothèque de Toulouse, 2005), pp. 5–14.

by endowing an abstraction with reality. In this way, linguistic realism is a danger and an enemy for a human life').

With this *vie humaine*, he refers to Spinoza, who, in his *Traité politique* (ch. V, §5), defined human life as determined not only by the circulation of the blood and other things shared with all animals, but mainly by 'reason, true virtue and the life of the mind' (LH, p. 78). He thus rejected the biological definition of humanity, which ignores the specificity of humanity and takes away its value (LH, p. 79). Meschonnic opposed this nominalist approach of 'les vivants d'abord' ('the living first') to the death of individuals in essentialism (LH, p. 726).

An important consequence of this theory is that it establishes another way of thinking the universal. According to this nominalist theory of language, it is individuals, the infinite diversity of specificities, which each time constitute the universal:

> Contre la pensée abstraite, et vide d'humanité, de l'universel, du théologico-linguistique qui ne donne en réalité que l'universalisation de son propre modèle abstrait, il est vital de poser que la seule pensée forte de l'universel est que seul le singulier chaque fois est l'universel. Autrement dit, l'universel est l'infinie diversité des spécificités, à réaliser chaque fois pour elle-même, par elle-même, à reconnaître comme telle par toutes les autres spécificités. (LH, p. 726)

> (Against the abstract thinking – devoid of humanity – of the universal of the theologico-linguistic that in reality does not give forth anything but the universalisation of its own abstract model, it is vital to argue for the only strong thinking of the universal: that only the singular, in each case, is the universal. In other words, the universal is the infinite diversity of specificities, to be realised each time for itself, by itself, to be recognised as such by all the other specificities.)

Meschonnic does not oppose abstract universalism to the singular; rather, he argues that we must always consider the singular as the universal.[15]

This is indeed an important redefinition. At a time when universalism has lost its credibility, in the aftermath of European colonialism, the question of how still to establish or defend universal values – human rights in the first instance – is pressing. Here we come to see the beginnings of a universalism which is not based on values imposed by one position but which indeed offers the possibility of a universalism where every individual, no matter

---

15. 'Il n'y a plus à opposer le singulier à l'universalisme abstrait, mais que chaque fois c'est le singulier qui est universel' (LH, p. 617) ('One cannot oppose the singular to the abstract universalism any more, but in each case it is the singular which is universal').

from which cultural background, has his or her say. This has tremendous ethical and political ramifications and it is based on this particular nominalist reconception of language.

Meschonnic therefore pleaded for a more developed awareness of this theory of language, of what is at stake in this conflict between realism and nominalism. This is of the utmost importance, since 'Le langage fait de nous des marionettes si on ne le pense pas dans tous ses effets de société' (LH, p. 93) ('Language makes puppets of us if we do not think it in all its effects on society'). Of course, propaganda and ideology – forms of realism for Meschonnic – have an interest in people not thinking about this (LH, p. 93). The only way of inoculating ourselves from linguistic manipulation is through becoming aware of how language operates as the activity of subjects, which, for Meschonnic, means we must transform the education system and how we teach the humanities so that humanity can be transformed. By this, he meant the training of an awareness of this theory of language and its ethical and political consequences (p. 94) – working on the awareness of what language is and does.

Two Objections: Linguistic Determinism and Beyond *Sprachkritik*?

We need to question this position, however. Does this not imply a linguistic determinism? Are we, then, who are not Hebrew native speakers or, more generally, who are conditioned by our language, condemned to think in an essentialist manner? This is clearly not the case for Meschonnic. Wilhelm von Humboldt, one of his most important reference points, stressed that there are always two forces in speech: on the one hand, there is the force of tradition in language, on which every speaker necessarily depends in order to make him- or herself understood; on the other hand, however, there is also the force of the individuality each speaker represents against these traditions when speaking.[16] That means that each real moment of speech is a renegotiation between tradition and transgression, and Meschonnic, with his notions of historicity and subjectivity as developed above, followed him in this.

Meschonnic's other main linguistic reference point, Émile Benveniste, gives a clear answer to this objection: it is not the language itself that favours or hinders the activity of the mind, but rather the capacities of the individual, and the general cultural conditions.[17] It is consequently true that our

---

16. Wilhelm von Humboldt, *Gesammelte Schriften*, 17 vols, ed. by Albert Leitzmann (Berlin: Behr, 1903–36), vol. VII, p. 64. Humboldt's position is at times too simply presented as linguistic determinism.
17. Émile Benveniste, 'Catégories de pensée et catégories de langue', in *Problèmes de linguistique générale 1* (Paris: Gallimard, 1966), pp. 52–74, p. 74.

thinking is inseparable from our language, but with *langage* not *langue*: that is, with language spoken by a subject in its historicity and not language as a convention. The linguistic form it takes depends on what we make of our language in each moment of speech, *parole*, and there we dispose of infinite options. The qualities attributed to a language are always in the subject that is speaking – even though a tradition of thought in a culture facilitates certain ideas and obstructs others. But the facilitation and obstruction are only ever partial; were it otherwise, speakers of the same language would never disagree, nor would languages change, which they do constantly. Language has to be considered historically and culturally, and even where its formal aspects are concerned, with a much broadened range of vision, whereas Meschonnic saw twentieth-century linguistics as equating progress with a narrowing of focus.

Another counterforce against determinism is plurilingualism: as each language constitutes a *Weltansicht*, a worldview, to use Humboldt's famous term, thinking in another language relativises any essentialist language notion and makes the nominalist position evident. The force of determinism due to language convention can thus be overcome both by the power of the subjective historicity of speaking and by an awareness of alternative worldviews due to plurilingualism.

Other examples given by Meschonnic imply that essentialism is not a question of language in the sense of a particular language (*langue*), but rather a question of the use of language (*langage*). He mentioned the use of 'the black', 'the Jew' and 'the woman', where the ethical and political implications are obvious, noting that 'blacks', 'Jews' and 'women' can be used in the same way – the singular and the plural can both demonstrate the essentialist perspective.

He summed up the realist attitude as follows: 'L'essentialisation est une massification. C'est etymologiquement le fascisme de la pensée' (LH, p. 723) ('Essentialism is massifying. It is etymologically the fascism of thought'). This is why only nominalism allows for an ethics of the subject: 'Le nominalisme est seul à permettre une éthique des sujets, donc une politique des sujets' (LH, p. 724) ('Nominalism alone can permit an ethics of subjects, and therefore a politics of subjects'). And this is vital for the defence against the fascism of thought (LH, p. 730) by constantly working on an awareness of our meaning-making processes in language.

Another possible objection would be that this seems well known and amounts to nothing more than the traditional critique of language. As a German, I am attentive to this and deeply immersed in *Sprachkritik*, as prominently brought forward directly after the end of the National Socialist regime by critics such as Victor Klemperer and Dolf Sternberger. Indeed, on several occasions, Meschonnic referred explicitly to Klemperer as an example of the 'rapport fort qu'il y a entre langage et histoire' (LH, p. 55) ('strong relation that exists between language and history').

Klemperer, a Jewish philologist who survived the Nazi period in his home in Germany, took notes on the Nazi use of language and published them after the war under the title *LTI*, a reference to the typical Nazi habit of acronyms, meaning here *Lingua Tertii Imperii*, the language of the Third Reich.[18] He demonstrated how, through the constant repetition of certain ways of using language, the language of the Third Reich penetrated the minds of Germans and their unconsciousness. He stated clearly that the power of language is such that only awareness of the mechanisms at stake can protect against being manipulated: 'Sprache dichtet und denkt nicht nur für mich, sie lenkt auch mein Gefühl, sie steuert mein ganzes seelisches Wesen, je selbstverständlicher, je unbewußter ich mich ihr überlasse' (LTI, p. 21) ('Language does not only create and think for me, it also directs my feeling; it directs my entire soul-being, the more naturally, the more unconsciously I abandon myself to it').[19] Essentialisation is only one of the forms of language transformation used by the Nazis.[20]

To my knowledge, all studies of Nazi German are in agreement that its specificity is not an issue of German linguistic structures, but of a particular *use* of them, of their application to certain situations, thus conveying certain ideas. The other main study of Nazi German directly after World War II makes this very clear: *Aus dem Wörterbuch eines Unmenschen* (Dictionary of a Fiend) by Dolf Sternberger.[21] It is not the words as such that are the

---

18. Victor Klemperer, *LTI: Notizbuch eines Philologen* (Leipzig: Reclam, 1980 [1946]). I have dealt in more detail with the German criticism of language at that time in my article 'German Language and National Socialism Today: Still a German "Sonderweg"?', *Edinburgh German Yearbook 8* (2014), pp. 7–24.
19. Jürgen Trabant has recently drawn attention to the fact that Klemperer was part of a determinist tradition existing since Bacon, understanding that words can have a negative impact on decency, and working for a politically correct use of language. Trabant is highly critical of this language cleansing in the name of a political agenda and considers this to be totalitarian, but concedes that Klemperer did not intend a political language reform but made a concrete historical analysis. He pleads for a linguistic liberalism, since language is no prison of the mind but functions on different levels. Cf. Jürgen Trabant, 'Die Erfindung der Sprachwaschmaschine', *Idee: Zeitschrift für Ideengeschichte*, XI/1 (2017), pp. 123–6.
20. James W. Underhill gives an insightful commentary on Klemperer's analysis, in a chapter of his book *Creating Wordviews: Metaphor, Ideology and Language* (Edinburgh: Edinburgh University Press, 2011), pp. 128–71.
21. Dolf Sternberger, Gerhard Storz and Wilhelm E. Süskind, *Aus dem Wörterbuch eines Unmenschen: Neue erweiterte Ausgabe mit Zeugnissen des Streites über die Sprachkritik*, third edition (Hamburg: Claassen, 1968 [1957, as individual articles starting in 1945]).

problem – the terms in this 'dictionary' are often perfectly normal words such as *Problem* or *intellektuell* – but their *use*. In his preface Sternberger stated:

> Soviel und welche Sprache einer spricht, soviel und solche Sache, Welt oder Natur ist ihm erschlossen. Und jedes Wort, das er redet, wandelt die Welt, worin er sich bewegt, wandelt ihn selbst und seinen Ort in dieser Welt. Darum ist nichts gleichgültig an der Sprache, und nichts so wesentlich wie die façon de parler. Der Verderb der Sprache ist der Verderb des Menschen. (p. 7)

> (However much and which language one speaks, that much and such things, world or nature, is unlocked for him. And each word he speaks transforms the world he moves in, transforms him himself and his place in this world. Therefore nothing is indifferent in language, and nothing is more of the essence than the *façon de parler*. The corruption of a language is the corruption of people.)

This means nothing else but that our world is determined by our use of language and this obviously also evokes Ludwig Wittgenstein's famous statement: 'Die Grenzen meiner Sprache bedeuten die Grenzen meiner Welt' ('The limits of my language mean the limits of my world').[22]

How does Meschonnic's poetics of society go beyond Klemperer and Sternberger's criticism of language? Most obviously because their scope is strictly lexical – limited to the sign – whereas Meschonnic is committed to digging much deeper, down to rhythm in particular. Still, in his conviction about the importance of language and a critical attitude towards its use, as well as in its social, ethical and political motivation, Meschonnic can indeed be compared to these thinkers. This attitude is also evident in his critical approach: meticulously reading other thinkers, and showing in detail their problematic use of language and notions, are consistent with his theory. Gérard Dessons, in his foreword to *Langage, histoire, une même théorie* (cf. footnote 1), commented on this method: 'Sa prise sur le monde est néces-

---

22. Ludwig Wittgenstein, *Logisch-philosophische Abhandlung, Tractatus logico-philosophicus*, critical edition (Frankfurt am Main: Suhrkamp, 1998), Statement 5.6. Another important German reference for Meschonnic is the Critical Theory of the Frankfurt School, particularly Max Horkheimer and Theodor W. Adorno, and their conviction that everything is interconnected and that in every detail concerning the social, the entire social sphere is represented and at stake. Meschonnic also performs a criticism of the myths of reason. But the Frankfurt School, according to Meschonnic, did not have a theory of language, and that is what he wanted to remedy (for example, *Langage, Histoire, une même théorie* (2012), p. 70/p. 110). For his analysis of the Frankfurt School, see, for instance, Meschonnic (2012), pp. 420–527, here particularly on Horkheimer, Adorno and Habermas.

sairement une prise sur les discours qui donnent sens au monde' (p. 9) ('His take on the world is necessarily a take on the discourses that give meaning to the world').

Continuing this *Sprachkritik* is, in any case, a ceaselessly crucial task and obligation if we are not to be swept away by an essentialising use of language. Sternberger stated quite dramatically – but no less correctly – that the destiny of humankind depends on it. However, in Meschonnic, this poetics of society is intricately linked to, and actually part of, his theory of language, which is incomparably more developed than Klemperer's or Sternberger's in so far as it goes beyond the lexical and looks at how rhythm and the continuous in discourse shape our subjectivity in its historicity, including its dialogical condition, thus transforming our outlook on life generally. In Meschonnic, this impetus leads precisely to a real poetics of society and of life.

Conclusion: A Poetics of Society!

What have we gained by establishing this intricate connection between the theory of language and the theory of society? What can we do with it? Is there any pragmatic utility?

Most academics probably accept the usefulness of discourse analysis and socio-linguistics. Nazi Germany represents an extreme case of how language use and abuse have very concrete political effects. It has become very evident that, since we live in language, in order to live a good life we need an ethics of language.

Promoting a poetics of society takes this to a different level, demonstrating the relevance of our attitude towards language for life and society by establishing it as our access to the other and to the world. It helps to create an awareness that language shapes our life, constantly, and how that takes place. This chapter aims to contribute to the elaboration of this approach and thus to a shift in the episteme, changing the way we think and interact. The knock-on effects would go well beyond linguistics, literary and translation studies, and would touch at our conceptions of the subject, ethics, politics, the universal, truth – to name just a few aspects which came up earlier – with concrete consequences for education and social policies. Working on our awareness of what language is and does is an endless process.

Poetics has been defined here as the interaction of the form of life and the form of language. *Poetic thinking* means to create and live our lives according to this idea. If we take politics in its wider sense, understood as the way humans organise their life in society and grant meaning to things, then poetics is the political, and vice versa.

Preliminary Remarks to this Reader
Some Comments on the Experience of Translating Meschonnic

by Marko Pajević

When I managed to secure funding from the British Academy/Leverhulme Fund for a project on Henri Meschonnic in 2017, I was extremely pleased to be able to win the support of a fantastic team of very competent and experienced researchers and translators for the tremendously difficult task of making Meschonnic's thinking, which goes so wholly counter to mainstream traditions, palatable for an Anglophone readership.

The project comprised two elements: the first of these was a symposium on Meschonnic's thinking language, held at Queen Mary University of London in September 2017, resulting in a Special Issue of *Comparative Critical Studies* (15/3, 2018), with contributions by myself, John E. Joseph, Serge Martin, David Nowell Smith, Clive Scott and Pier-Pascale Boulanger. The second element consisted of two translation workshops to prepare this Meschonnic Reader, with six translators contributing: myself, Pier-Pascale Boulanger, Andrew Eastman, John E. Joseph, David Nowell Smith and Chantal Wright. Pier-Pascale Boulanger had already translated a book by Meschonnic, *Ethics and Politics of Translating*, while David Nowell Smith had translated *The Rhythm Party Manifesto*, and Pier-Pascale initially exposed her own experience of the difficulties of translating Meschonnic.

For the first workshop, we also had the support of Serge Martin and his PhD students, Rafael Costa Mendes and Shungo Morita. Each member of the translator team had translated beforehand the same short text of about ten pages so as to familiarise him- or herself with the issues at stake, and to think in advance about possible problems concerning translation strategy and terminology. We took a full day to discuss the best solutions, all of us having the six versions in front of us and comparing them. I had the illusion that we would manage to get through this text, or almost, but in a very intense, full-day working session, we actually only managed to agree on the first two and a half pages. However, we all did agree that this was not only a very enjoyable experience but also an extremely valuable and useful one. Discussing in depth all the various difficulties involved, with high-profile scholars from different disciplines (German, English, French, Comparative Literature, Language Theory and Translation Studies) bringing in their experience and deep understanding of language and translation, as well as their knowledge of the traditions of language theory, made this a very enriching exchange and we all learned much about language, translation and Meschonnic. It is a rare privilege to combine the attention and knowledge of several specialists in translating. I would say today that in Humanities translation, it should be the norm.

Building on this day's discussions and results, the participants translated their share of the Reader. Before we met again for a second workshop five months later, we checked in rotation the translations of one of our peers, and then, during our session, presented the problematic parts, which we discussed together, based on the principles established during the first session. With these discussions and results in mind, everybody went over their translations once more, the translation partner checked it, and finally, I worked through all the translations one last time for consistency and any remaining errors. This Reader is thus the product of real teamwork and each translation received considerable input from all of us. It is none the less appropriate to indicate the translator of each text.

Translating Meschonnic confronts the translator with particular difficulties.[1] As mentioned earlier, Meschonnic's writing purposefully resists being easily readable, as he is opposed to ready-made ideas. He developed a series of stylistic peculiarities which are intended to break up an easy flow – he wanted to make ideas erupt so as to be more easily perceived, just as the Russian Formalist Viktor Šklovskij believed that a certain degree of disruption was necessary to reawaken meaning. Meschonnic was a poet and this also comes through in his theoretical writings. Though his French syntax is often trying and unconventional, when read aloud it actually works very well and sounds fluent and right. As one reads him, his concept of the 'poem of thought' becomes convincing.

None the less, his French contains many uncommon features. Translating them into English will probably make it even harder to digest them. A translation which does justice to Meschonnic's writing will certainly not correspond to the ordinary expectations of fluency and naturalness. His syntax

---

1. See also Pier-Pascale Boulanger's report on her experience in the above-mentioned Special Issue of *Comparative Critical Studies*, 15/3 (2018). I draw here on her observations.

is disruptive, using parataxis, parenthesis, repetitions and run-on sentences. Often he forms verbless sentences, sentences consisting of only a direct object complement, orphaned adjectival clauses, comma splices. This disruptive writing creates leeway for interpretation and at times makes it difficult to understand what he means, the references being ambiguous. It slows down reading and transforms thinking patterns since the reader is forced to read parts all over again. But, of course, as one becomes more familiar with his theory and his thinking, reading gets easier.

Our translation strategy was to maintain all these features since they are part of this particular thinking; they are thought in action. Depriving Meschonnic's theory of its language does not make any sense but would, on the contrary, completely alter its sense. Of course, this often takes place: it is well known that French theory is considerably changed when put into English. Reading Jacques Derrida or Jean-Luc Nancy in French or in English is often a very different experience.[2]

Thinking unconventionally demands an unconventional use of language – this is the first thing one should learn from Meschonnic. If he wanted to think against the categories of the sign, he had to find ways to grant importance to other ways of meaning-making. It is impossible to remain on the level of the signified; in his writing, significance also takes place in prosodic sound patterns. His style is in line with his language theory. With his own Bible translations, Meschonnic had the ambition of transforming Western thinking. He put this into practice by paying attention to the rhythm of biblical Hebrew, finding ways to render this particular accent system into French. A translation of Meschonnic's work has to make every possible effort to render the connections he created by such rhythmic means of syntactic and sound patterns. This is what Meschonnic called an ethics of translation: listening to what a text does with language and finding the same activity of language in the target language instead of idiomatising it. This is what makes Meschonnic an important thinker of foreignisation in translation. When translating Meschonnic, one cannot ignore this.

Taking style to be an accessory without signification would be the demonstration of an utter lack of understanding of everything Meschonnic says. Even if it taxes the good will of many Anglophone readers, then, this is Meschonnic and he is interesting because he differs. He is also interesting for the spoken quality of his writing, which might come across as a lack of discipline and academic rigour.

Another recurrent feature of Meschonnic's style is the nominalisation of

---

2. I have shown this deformation of thought in an English translation of Jean-Luc Nancy in 'Translation and Poetic Thinking', *German Life and Letters*, 67/1 (2014), pp. 6–21.

verbs, quite uncommon in English but done more often in French, as in *le vivre, le dire, le traduire*. This emphasises the action, thereby subscribing to Humboldt's idea of language as *energeia*. When Meschonnic entitles a book *Poétique du traduire*, it is important to keep the gerund and translate this title, as Pier-Pascale Boulanger rightfully did, as *Poetics of Translating*, not *Poetics of Translation*. It is about the process, not the product.

Alongside syntactic unconventionalities, Meschonnic also cultivated neologisms, as in such verbs as *to decurrentfrenchify* or *to embible*.

But such coinages are easy to understand, also in translation. Harder to translate are his witty wordplays: for example, the sub-title 'Casser la figure' (in *Politique du rythme, politique du sujet*), which means *to break the figure (of speech)*, but could also be *to beat someone up*, or *to be screwed or annoyed by something*. In such cases, often, translating is confronted with its limits.

Since the success of Barbara Cassin's great work on the *Untranslatables*,[3] people have become more aware that concepts do not always travel easily from one language into another. Even the most basic concepts are far from being universal. An obvious and recurrent case in translating Meschonnic would be the word *language*. In French, there are two words, *langage* and *langue*, corresponding to it, made even more complex by the existence of *parole* and *discours*, and all these terms are defined differently and not always consistently by different traditions. Now, translating these terms – and *langue*, in particular, creates problems – requires us to be aware of these traditions and to be cautious of what the text refers to and how the respective translations would be perceived in various systems of thought in the target language. It is not always possible to translate such a term consistently throughout but, depending on the context, one has to opt for one solution or another. It took much debate about the use of the article, 'the language' or simply 'language', and other options such as 'language system', until we finally settled for keeping the French *langue* when other options would be problematic – a word easy enough to understand by all potential readers of this book.

There are other terms lacking so far in English. In this Introduction, I have already on several occasions used the word *signifiance* – which is consistently changed to *significance* by the automatic spell-checker. We thought about explaining it as *ways of signifying* or something similar but finally, after we learned from John E. Joseph that *signifiance* is indeed an English word,

---

3. Barbara Cassin (ed.), *Vocabulaire européen des philosophies: Dictionnaire des intraduisibles* (Paris: Seuil/Le Robert, 2004), published in English as Barbara Cassin (ed.), *Dictionary of Untranslatables: A Philosophical Lexicon*, translation ed. by Emily Apter, Jacques Lezra and Michael Woods (Princeton: Princeton University Press, 2014).

albeit out of use, we decided here again simply to stick to it also in English – a solution also suggested by Meschonnic himself.[4] In Meschonnic's theoretical writing, often enough, significance plays a crucial role: that is, he uses sound patterns to associate words or parts of sentences to create semantic links.

All of these uncommon usages of language had to be kept in mind by six translators to form a consistent ensemble and to be true to Meschonnic's theories and his value system. I hope the result will prove worthy of all these efforts and establish a solid basis for further work.

I had established a selection of texts in view of a representative Reader and gratefully accepted one suggestion by the team to complement this. My choice aims at presenting key texts covering crucial aspects of Meschonnic's *œuvre* in sections: namely, on poetics, rhythm, metrics, the sign, the poem, rhyme and life, orality, the subject, translating, modernity, historicity and society. This was a tricky task because of Meschonnic's habit of reformulating his ideas in search of more precision or better presentation, and also in order to adapt them to different contexts. Another problem is that many passages are barely readable in translation; Meschonnic's critical approach involves making very detailed comments on other theoreticians, mainly French ones, often not well known outside of the French debates, and working on the French formulations, which means that they would be unpleasant to read and of little interest to an Anglophone readership. Choosing suitable extracts was consequently of the essence, but there cannot be a perfect solution to this task.

Meschonnic makes difficult reading. Theory for him is not about establishing a system of knowledge, nor is it programmatic; rather, he considers thinking an indefinite, open-ended activity. Meschonnic dedicated his *Critique du rythme* 'À l'inconnu' (To the unknown), and he told me that he is mostly interested in what he cannot know. His work is not so much about consumable knowledge, facts, but about the process of thinking. His constellation of concepts – rhythm, the continuous, the subject, modernity, historicity, the poem, orality – operates as an interdependent system: one cannot fully understand one concept without grasping them all in their ensemble. Each of his concepts opens up this particular universe of thought, and yet, the concept unfurls itself only from within this universe. Consequently, the reader needs to invest some time to understand the ensemble in order to appreciate the full significance of each single element. The end matter provides a succinct glossary of the most important terms that are specific to Meschonnic and might – without an explanation – lead to misunderstand-

---

4. Cf. Henri Meschonnic, interview with Gabriella Bedetti, *Diacritics*, 18/3 (1988), pp. 93–111, p. 106.

ings, alongside indexes of names and terminology, and a bibliography of Meschonnic's published books.

While finalising this Reader, I am preparing a key note on Meschonnic's notion of rhythm for a conference on *Rhythms* at University of Wisconsin – Madison, and am receiving invitations to participate in research and translation projects on Meschonnic's work from Germany and Russia. This confirms that, ten years after his death, the time has finally come for Meschonnic's ideas.

In preparing this book, I came to realise how difficult it is to put across this theory in English but I am confident that readers will agree that we have made a good start and that Meschonnic's theory of rhythm is worth every effort it requires.

It should inspire anyone working on what language is and does.

---- PART 1 ----

CRITIQUE OF RHYTHM

The first four texts are all taken from Meschonnic's magnum opus, *Critique du rythme: anthropologie historique du langage* (Lagrasse: Verdier, 1982) (Critique of Rhythm: A Historical Anthropology of Language), in which he presented for the first time his overarching theory in a more systematic manner. The monograph lays out the main elements of his universe of thought, always with a clear focus on the key term of rhythm, which functions as the operator of subjectivity and historicity. He does this in 1982, when structuralism, extremely strong in France, comes to an end. Meschonnic positions himself against structuralism and his work as a critique of his time.

The term critique, part of the title of the book, is also central to its first two chapters. The first chapter states the interchangeability of critique and theory. The task of critique is to demonstrate the historicity of any theory or discourse generally. This key term, historicity, means the situatedness and subjectivity of any discourse. This also implies that the critique itself is situated and part of the discourse. Thus, both art and critique are activities – they act on the debate. They cannot provide answers from an outside position; they raise questions, they are work in progress.

The first text in this Reader needs to be seen in this context. The first chapter, entitled *Theoretical Activity, Poetic Activity* (pp. 55–64 of CR), introduces Meschonnic's approach to theory, which is inseparable from poetics and poetry in his understanding of the terms. In his view, and in opposition to general opinion, there exists no contradiction between theory and poetry; together they are a double activity. Poetry, Meschonnic specifies, is neither signification nor expression, but an activity. The question of poetics is therefore always: what does it *do*?

In the second text, Chapter Two of the book, entitled *What is at Stake in a Theory of Rhythm* (pp. 65–115 of CR), Meschonnic discusses the relation of his theory of rhythm to key concepts such as sense, discourse, subject and semiotics. The text presents itself from the outset as a critique of sense, based on Émile Benveniste's linguistics. Benveniste demonstrated that, originally, rhythm did not mean a cadenced coming and going but a general flowing movement. If we accept, with Benveniste, the original meaning of rhythm as form in movement and, consequently, Meschonnic's definition of rhythm as the organisation of life in the moment of its movement, or as the organisation of sense in discourse, rhythm is inseparable from sense. The term Meschonnic uses here is *signifiance*, by which he means the ensemble of signifiers, the way of signifying. And rhythm is, for Meschonnic, a major signifier.

Since sense is the activity of a subject, Meschonnic claims a close connection between his theory of rhythm and the theory of the subject. They determine each other mutually. Rhythm therefore configures not only the utterance, but also the uttered, and, by extension, transforms the utterer. The theory of language taking rhythm into account goes beyond a theory of communication. It takes into consideration the creative, cognitive aspect of language. The theory of rhythm thinks language as an activity, not as a product, to refer to Wilhelm von Humboldt, who is one of Meschonnic's major references. Language is not only about passing on preconceived ideas, but also, and even more so, about conceiving ideas. Indeed, we also have here the anthropological dimension of this theory, *A Historical Anthropology of Language*, as the sub-title of the book states. This is because if humankind is not simply one with nature in an imitation of the metre of nature, if language is not simply an impression of the cosmic on humankind, but humans do create their own rhythms and organise sense, rhythm as flowing movement becomes anthropologically determining. That is what also makes the poetic element of this approach, poetics coming from *poein*, which means *to make/to create*. When Meschonnic talks about the poem, he is not actually referring to the literary form but to this transforming activity of language, which cannot be grasped by the category of the sign because it resides not in the sense of the signified but in the entirety of signifiance.

Meschonnic thus wants to oppose the dominance of semiotics, understood as a totalising claim of everything being reducible to signs, in the theory of language and beyond. Building on Benveniste, his critique of semiotics presents a counterforce to the sign, bringing to light aspects of language covered up by the sign.

Another aspect of Meschonnic's ideas about rhythm as inseparable from the subject is that language and life are interconnected. He will, later in his *œuvre*, define poetics as the interaction of the form of language and the form of life.

But this is life, 'the undefined empirical'. And that is why Meschonnic also defines rhythm as the sense of the unpredictable, which, only in retrospect, seems to be 'an interior necessity'. It represents the inscription of a subject in its history – that is never a unity, but always only a fragmented, open, undefined unity. And that is why rhythm, as anti-unity, is also anti-totality – which actually makes it a political necessity to think rhythm.

Meschonnic claims that what a society says and does about its literature is a sign of what it does to the subject, whereas the novel relates to the individual and the poem to the subject. Rhythm is a non-semiotic representative of the subject which is anterior to sense. After these initial two chapters of the book, Meschonnic goes on to demonstrate how his ideas on poetics show the problems and limitations of linguistics, literary theory and philosophy of language. The book now becomes a critique of the various traditions which, so far, have defined rhythm. That is first and foremost music and metrics, but also orality, the voice, the page as spatial representation of language, and a mathematical approach to language.

The third text of this Reader, *Pure Metrics or Discourse Metrics* (pp. 522–62 in CR), is one of these chapters. It elaborates a critique of metrics, demonstrating that metrics traditionally does not consider meaning and is a formalism, often an artificial one. While there are rules for metrics, there are none for rhythm. Rhythm is not measured, since it is in the unknown of a discourse. Discourse, in the sense of Benveniste, is the fundamental notion that all of Meschonnic's language theory builds upon. Meschonnic postulates and starts to elaborate a discourse metrics: that is, he is not introducing discourse into metrics but, inversely, transforms metrics to lead it toward discourse rhythmics to reconcile discourse and metrics.

Meschonnic finally develops a critique of the idea that rhythm is seen in its relation to the cosmos and installs an anthropology where body and language are considered as an ensemble. Both body and language share the same history, in an individual.

The final extract in this section, *Not the Sign, but Rhythm* (pp. 705–15 in CR), serves as a concluding chapter. It opens up the field of language studies and offers a view of the ambition of Meschonnic's critique of rhythm, which was to run throughout his *œuvre*: the theory of language and history it contains actually represents what he calls a poetics of society (see the Introduction to this Reader and Part 6). Hence, in the final paragraph of his book *Critique du rythme*, he writes, 'Speaking of rhythm, I am speaking of you.'

1

Poetics
Theoretical Activity, Poetic Activity

(in *Critique du rythme*, Lagrasse: Verdier, 1982, pp. 55–64)

Translated by Pier-Pascale Boulanger

The theory of rhythm stands with the theory and history of literary practices. Rhythm runs two dangers: either it can be disassembled like an object into form on one side and sense on the other, form supposedly repeating what sense said, redundant, expressive; or it can be understood in psychological terms that sidestep it to the point of seeing it as being beyond words, absorbed by sense, or emotion. Both are aspects, each one as customary as the other, of dualism and of the sign. The only defence is to situate the question of rhythm in the interaction of theory and practice as two activities that stand together historically.

Hence the theoretical intuitions of poets – similar to what painters say about painting –, being the discourses of a practice, the language of an activity (more than of experience), can be matrices more valuable than all the books written by critics and philosophers. Nowadays, everything fragments, consigns to the past the era of totalities. To illustrate this, I offer here a polemical sentence from Adorno: 'Hegel and Kant were the last who, to put it bluntly, were able to write major aesthetics without understanding anything about art.'[1] Baudelaire, who was above all a theorist, came up with the idea of the value of lexical frequency. He was practically the only one in his time to speak of a French prosody.

Technique is not the formal, because it is inseparable from practice. It was technique that defined Ezra Pound's criterion: 'I believe in technique as

---

1. Theodor W. Adorno, *Aesthetic Theory*, newly trans. from German by Robert Hullot-Kentor, ed. by Gretel Adorno and Rolf Tiedemann (London: Bloomsbury, 2013 [1997]), p. 441.

the test of a man's sincerity.'² Technique is all of art only if it is overwhelmed by the unknown that carries away the I entirely. Here lies the difference between a poetics that comes after the work, empirically, as with Victor Hugo, and a poetics that comes before, dogmatic, as with René Ghil: 'after my Poetics, my Poetry'.³ But in the interaction of poetry and poetics, the idea that thought is posterior, or anterior, to doing, is pure fiction.

Only the interaction of poetry and theory can avoid the common confusion between theory and literary critique. A confusion still made, for instance, by Ritsos, when he repeats the common belief that critique 'sometimes wears out the poem once and for all'.⁴ The poem has nothing to fear. Literary critique never wears out the poem. It wears itself out as well as the reader, but not the poem. Because it doesn't tell us anything about the poem. It speaks of it, or it speaks it: exterior or mimetic. The danger for the poem is the theory of the sign, its dualism that only recognises forms in the poem, or applies tastes and values directly to it. What diverts the poem is the sign, and its teaching. Where theory is definitely vital for the poem, against this pseudo-critique.

The critique of rhythm does not consist in a commentary on a verse, or a poem, whose effect or value it would wear out, or whose sense it would tell, if the verse or the poem has not done so itself. The critique of rhythm discovers how they signify, and the situation of this 'how'.

* * *

The truth about poetry, about rhythm, is not sought in poets the way scientific truth is sought in the consensus of scholars.⁵ Consensus probably just means belief. Even if it is universal, it remains a belief. And not proof. Accordingly, it is not a question of finding a concordance, nor even a correspondence. The best that truth could provide would be an irrespondence, more incomprehension than is usually needed for comprehension. Poets are not necessarily more intelligent or proficient in the theory of rhythm or of language. Their writings are saturated with literary ideologies, which are related to positions as well, and lead them to reject critique. Discussions among poets look more like the mad tea party in *Alice's Adventures in Wonderland* than a theoretical

2. Ezra Pound, 'A Retrospect', in *Literary Essays of Ezra Pound*, ed. by T. S. Eliot (London: Faber and Faber, 1918), p. 9.
3. René Ghil, *Traité du verbe: états successifs (1885–1886–1887–1888–1891–1904)*, ed. by Tiziana Goruppi (Paris: Nizet, 1978), p. 95.
4. Yannis Ritsos, *La Sonate au clair de lune et d'autres poèmes (1956–1963)* (Paris: Seghers, 1976), p. 90.
5. A first version of this chapter was published as a letter to Michel Deguy in *Po&sie*, 1 (1977).

reflection. There is no we. No super-poet who would be the epitome of a specific period or group. They are no more united by their disagreement than by a common doctrine. The reason is that the ways they relate to culture, and to the social sciences in particular, vary greatly. The quality of the relation, or any philosophical imprint, affects how they relate to theory, how they conceptualise and practise rhythm.

In searching for the historicity of my own discourse, in order to situate myself, the historicity of the discourses that precede and surround anyone who writes, or reflects on language, I start, in order to situate the theory of rhythm, by trying to show that there is no struggle between poetry and theory, between practice and theory, but that poetry struggles within a double activity, that is poetic and theoretical.

According to the current cliché they exclude one another. Whereas they stand together, as far as one can remember. From rhetoricians to surrealists, to cite only two examples. The separation that is presumed of these two activities is in itself indicative of an ahistorical notion of literature. Which immediately dehistoricises both of them. This cliché circulates as much among poets as in general. Critique, or theoretical intuition, should not be confused with ideas. There was a time when a painter had to be dim-witted to be good. That idea is no longer with painters. It remains with some poets.

Writing is empirical. It is a craft. It can seem to have nothing in common with theory. Nothing predisposes it in that regard. Apparently theoretical activity is opposed to action, which does things. It is suspect. Suspected of contemplation. Yet another trick played by etymology. Theory is frowned upon, as an abstraction. It is seen as difficult. Appears useless. At least for practical and immediate purposes. The term is commonly used pejoratively: 'an ounce of common sense is worth a pound of theory'. That is to say: theory is disconnected from reality. After the structuralist Reign of Terror, tired minds said: 'too much theory'. Theory was condemned. An addition to the dictionary of received ideas.

To situate writing historically as an activity makes it impossible to separate writing, something easy, from theory, something difficult. Or the other way around, by confusing theory with critique taken in the trivial sense, where critique is opposed to doing. In short, the notion Sainte-Beuve had of it, and found humiliating.

But then it was the opposite excess, just as ahistorical. The intolerable hierarchy was reversed – proof that *amour-propre* was always put in the same place. Now, the 'scriptor' also writes. Even the inkstand writes: its memoirs. All the inverted cliché has done is substitute the cliché. They are the two faces of the *same* cliché. Some therefore believed there was a continuous between writing and critique, refusing to see critique as secondary, or even second.

They extended to their critique the features they attributed to writing. At the same time, they denied they were using a metalanguage. That is, speaking of language. They recognised unknowingly that by overturning Sainte-Beuve they remained in Sainte-Beuve. The commentary on a poem was a poem, or rather was *imitating* that poem. Illusions, imposture: the term '*mise en abyme*' is well coined indeed. In the vertigo of the endless poem of the poem, no one noticed that this process *reconciles* writing and writing on writing: eliminates their tension. Such laxity has become widespread. The relation between the two activities has been cancelled out in their conflation.

But writing pursues a logic of indefinite contradiction, tension between practice and theory. To reconcile is to dedialecticise. Easy, difficult, these effects are due to culture. They may vary. Just as literature is the cultural integration of writing. Same thing for writing and translation. Either translation is writing, transforming, or it is literature – that which has already been transformed, whose role is to inform: to introduce a 'literature'. This is why translation matters for poetry, and for theory: it produces an experimental poetics.

The opposition between theory and poetry belongs to the myth of reason. This opposition falls within the known paradigm which makes the rational and the irrational, norm and deviation, into two inseparable poles – Husserl's normal adult against the madman–child–genius. Under which falls the prose–poetry couple which I will analyse further on. According to the theory of the sign, the transcendence of the signified and the delirium of the signifier belong *naturally* to this paradigm. In it as well, theology and poetry bolster one another by adding, on one side, the profane-day-to-day against the sacred-celebration. Everything is coherent. There is consensus between the cosmic and reason. This rationalism has never seen better days than under structuralism. Reason is optimistic. It developed a science of the object, in the dualism of the sign.

The mutual exclusion of poetry and theory has its historicity, but its timeline is not the same for everyone. The University had its part to play in it. Here Péguy is a benchmark: poets are not scholars, and vice versa. There is a conflict. Péguy has epitomised that conflict. With the lag that always exists between stereotypes and social transformations, the University, up until recent polemics, remained situated in a dual representation, produced by dualism and returning to dualism, within the air-tight coherence of consensus: the poet, outlaw; the scholar, tutor.

But the twentieth century has been, for this, especially during the second half, a period of sociological modification. Occasionally or through their profession, or their training, some poets, some writers are scholars, teachers. From Bonnefoy to Butor, from Deguy to Jude Stefan. A few. I am not talking about the United States. Over there, a new relation has developed between theoretical activity and writing. By definition I am neglecting the writing of professors of this or that or philosophy, who write their knowledge. Model pupils are everywhere. Their writing is an erudite variant of sub-literature. I argue that the interaction between writing and theory can no longer exclude teaching, unless it is reduced to problems of pedagogy – a poetic and political error.

The University can end its bad reputation as what writers outside the university perceive as the haven for academic writing. There are also, it is true, writers who are academics as didactic and dualistic as if they were not writers. However, teaching requires that one work on writing through literature. If this work is not historically situated, it is not long before the eclecticism of the day ends up teaching literature to the advantage of the sign. If the relation between poetry and philosophy, writing and theory of language is to be renewed, teaching is a prime and strategic site, one that is irreplaceable. Those who do not understand this defer to the order of the sign, to the 'Traditional Theory'.

Theoretical activity seeks a knowing that it does not have. It cannot enunciate a knowledge – which is what the didactic does. It stands on the edge of ignorance. It is the writing of ignorance. Contrary to its etymology, which would make it the action of seeing, observation–contemplation, it is the discourse of what it cannot see, which it yet manages to show.

The contradiction between the theoretical and the didactic, which imparts knowledge as truth, omitting contradictions and the history of errors, reinforces the ancient opposition between the writing activity and the didactic profession. Repetition and drills, selective admiration, lead to poetisation, which is an anti-poetry. Traditional resignation sends each activity back to itself. It *resolves* the contradiction.

But contradictions should be *upheld*, especially when intellectuals are made into professionals. That is, when their role is reduced. Any crisis contributes to their social isolation, presenting them as privileged. Misknown, they are soon hated. They even go along with this. For instance, through their lax notion of *text*. If everything is text, there is no point in teaching literature. A pseudo- and anti-democratisation creates 'civilisation' and 'expression skills'. Hence a deculturation towards a mass culture that is no longer popular culture. Where the notion of text, and the negation of metalanguage, produce a political as well as an epistemological effect. Gullible scholars macluhanise. They have contributed to the narrowing of minds under a new form, and for themselves. In fact, they chose, or thought they had chosen, the right side.

Theoretical activity is the questioning of a practice on its how, its why. Which makes it possible to distinguish knowledge that knows itself as such from that which does not, and which manœuvres. Both often coexist in ignorance of one another. It is possible to know and give a commentary on Saussure, all the while putting into practice a pre-Saussurean manipulation of the word, a mythology of etymology and a nature-motivated sign. That is the reason why critique must be a theory of sense, and of what, in sense, overwhelms sense, where rhythm operates.

A poetisation of poetry has taken poetry away from discourse. The myth of reason and the myth of poetry are one and the same. Poetry was too irrational to fit in narrative, demonstrative discourse. This rhetorical depreciation of discourse still lurks. It gets in the way of the linguistic notion of discourse, according to which poetry is a discourse, because any language activity is a discourse. Discourses are all that can be grasped from languages, and not only extinct ones. Discourse is the language activity of a subject in a society and a history. It is as important for a theory of discourses as it is for poetry to consider poetry as a discourse. As specific. The notion of discourse is a strategy.

Critique *does not speak of* poetry. *To speak of*, the dualism of the sign in a nutshell. A sense, which is paraphrased. To refrain right off the bat from looking for, and looking at, the specificity of the mode of signifying in the poem, thus the specificity of the relation between rhythm and sense, thus the specificity of understanding or of not understanding, which calls understanding into question. Critique is not a discourse-on, a gloss. That comes in several varieties. Simply, not to mix things up. Rhetoric, for instance, identifies figures, which it refers to *langue*: for works as well as for rhythm, it is an anti-poetics. But poetics does incorporate the instruments of rhetoric.

Critique is the very interaction of theoretical activity and poetic activity. To which it probably owes its share of non-conceptualised, of non-conceptualisable matter. It works *towards* the concept. There is a passion, a theoretical affectivity. Saussure's theoretical writing was his way of writing his life. Nothing is more opposed to it than, for instance, Hjelmslev's arrogance and lack of precision. There is a poetics, and an ethics, of theory. What the theoretical discourse and the activity of the poem have in common is that they are both specific modes of the subjective tending at once towards the referential and the intersubjective, the impersonal, which should be called the *transpersonal*.

Critique, poetics are thus, like the poem, personal and impersonal. Social sciences, language sciences create a knowledge that affects writing, and the problem is then: does one write *with* that knowledge? *Through* that knowledge? Or *in* and *despite* that knowledge? Matisse, in *Jazz*, spoke of the painter who knows everything, but forgets what he knows when he paints. And Apollinaire: *Where is the Christopher Columbus to whom we will owe the forgetting of a continent.*

Theoretical activity may sometimes not take place. So it seems. But the absence of an explicit theory is as worth analysing as a theory is. Theory may be only a fragment: the notes for a preface to *Fleurs du mal*. Or a literary genre, like the manifesto, in Breton. It may outgrow the poem disproportionately – as with Valéry.

But if there is a theoretical activity, there is a necessary, internal, relation to a poetic activity. The cliché that opposed them forgot about Dante, Du Bellay, Goethe, Hugo, Flaubert, Rimbaud, Mallarmé, Rilke, Brecht, Éluard, among others. When there is no theory, it may be that our current notion of theory is hiding relations between poetry and theory that are anterior, exterior to our grid. Relations which are included in poetry itself. When what has survived disasters can bear testimony.

To the idea that modern literature is experimental, it is more historical to counter that all writing has always been experimental. That it is by definition. Which is a theoretical proposition, a poetic universal. Synonymous with historicity. Against the illusion that established Mallarmé, Flaubert, Proust or Joyce, Khlebnikov or Cummings as points of departure of the experimental. A normative illusion.

Theory may subsume itself into practice. With an ostentatious rejection of theory, identified with a *speaking-of*. This rejection does not mean that theory is absent. A practice necessarily includes a poetics, even if it does not show it. Which is what happens with Jacques Réda, who theorises not to theorise.

Theory has shifted questions. It is no longer: what is literature, what is poetry? But: what does poetry *do*? Poetry is *not expression*. Everything is expression and everyone expresses themselves. We owe it at least to Roman Jakobson – to his six functions of language – to consider this reductive view of poetry as pure regression due to ignorance. Poetry *is not signification*. To say that a poem signifies, is to ask *what* that poem signifies, to presuppose that it partakes of the sign, thus to separate it into a sense and a form, which is the residue of sense. The usual way out of this trap is itself a trap: it turns poetry into the anti-arbitrariness of the sign. A triple status as nature, as celebration, as sacred. The cosmic and the religious betray the historicity of language and of poetry. It is why poetry is the critique of the sign, of the serial opposition of the body and the soul, of the letter and the spirit, of form and content, signifier, signified. Just when everything was going well for the sign, poetry introduced a question to which it obstructed the answer: what is to signify?

Poetry does not refer to the *world*, a notion belonging to phenomenology. Because it is an activity that rejects the division that phenomenology has made in language and in history, between play of the world and play in the world. Poetry does not refer to an *experience*. It *is* the experience. It transforms itself and transforms you us while transforming experience. A game whose rules change as it is being played. As soon as the rules are set, poetisation sets in, a variant of cultural programming. The point is not what poetry speaks of. It is as much a counter to poetry to say 'love poems' or poems on this or that than it is a counter to painting to judge a painting according to the object that is painted. Paraphrase is the weakness of the sign. Poetry does not respond. It is a revealer. But the sign applies perfectly to narrative: to the forms of the content, which are the universal language of universal literature, where there are no more problems of translation, only problems of putting things in their proper order.

Poetry stands with theory, and with knowing. These, in turn, stand with poetry. Which is illustrated by the place of parody in intertextuality, such as the Lautréamont effect. The logic of language in Husserl, the contemporary anthropology of Lévy-Bruhl, the dada-surrealist poetics all partake, despite their different positions or tensions, of the same anthropology of language. Either this anthropology accepts the 'normal', or it rejects it to *imitate* its opposite, in both cases it remains lexicalist, and fundamentally theological. In the same way the use of dictionaries, from Mallarmé to Ponge, displays a nomenclature that applies a pre-Saussurean conception of the word. The 'disordering of all the senses' has become a processing of words which takes *langue* directly for discourse. Any example that could be given inevitably leads the critique of poetry to a historical critique of language.

The proposition 'poetry is a language activity' is a situated one. It designates a functioning. Not a function, in Jakobson's sense, which calls for a structuralist descriptive formalisation. And Jakobson's functions cannot be separated from his opposition to Saussure's arbitrariness, his fascination with the *natural* expressivity of phonemes. *Activity* includes, compels the subject and history. Implies a linguistics of enunciation. *Activity* supposes an *actor*, who is also an *author*. Eustache Deschamps in *Art de dictier* [the Art of Dictation] used the word '*faiseur*' [doer], and Jean Molinet, '*acteur*' [actor], '*facteur*' [maker].[6] Not only the originator, the initiator – formalism recently evicted the term 'author' and skirted around ethics – but also the one who leads the poem, through whom the poem is active.

Activity supposes that language does something at the same time that it says something. It does not necessarily do what it says. If there is knowing through the poem, it comes from doing as much as from saying. The poem saps the opposition between speech and action which, in our culture, comes from the cosmic, and a metaphysics that condemns language.

6. In Ernest Langlois, *Recueils d'arts de seconde rhétorique* (Geneva: Slatkine, 1974 [1902]), pp. 223, 251.

The exclusion of poetry, since *The Republic*, is the embodiment of the condemnation of language – for being an obstacle, a lie, an artifice by nature. *Activity* and *actor* give the *I* a status that extends its linguistic attribute as a shifter, to an entire discourse.

Activity is not *act*. The poetic act is the making of a poem. A theory of *language* has no say in the matter. It would relapse into psychology, conscience, intention. As for the study of the *stages* of this act, through manuscripts, variants, it is skewed by a teleology inherent to its very process, from a text in limbo to a text in full fruition. The only escape is the rejection of the text as a definitive one, which destroys this required hierarchy simply through instating a plurality of versions, the last of which is but one variant among others. An eternalisation of the act that interiorises activity entirely. A philological form (by some editors of Hölderlin, for instance) of the primacy of the virtual and of genesis over what is actualised, which is just as questionable.[7] Is no longer the truth of the text. I am not debating questions of genesis, but strictly the question of functioning. It too is a value inherent to the term *activity*. Poetic activity is the practice of poetry, but also the mode of signifying of the poem. All questions on poetry derive from this mode of signifying. Only this mode of signifying is important for the theory of language, ensures rhythm its rightful place.

The *act–activity–actor* relation is the exercise of contradiction, between the individual subject and the social, writing and literature, indefinitely: not in the binary, but in the multiple. Shifting, maintaining the contradiction between living and writing, which reproduces the *duel* of the soul and the body, of signified, signifier. Which is what Aragon implied in *Traité du style*, when he wrote that dreams are not opposed to life, but to the absence of dreams, life to the absence of life. Poetic activity *embodies* language in that it shows, exemplarily, that language takes place and has always taken place within this contradiction. Against any substitutive poetics. Which suffices to link poetry and theory.

Against the schizophrenia of our culture, poetic activity and theoretical activity do the same work. Their work is conducive to situating the stakes of a theory of rhythm beyond what, traditionally, limits it to erudite quarrels on poetry.

---

7. See Friedrich Hölderlin, *Sämtliche Werke* (Collected Works), ed. by Dietrich Sattler (Frankfurt am Main: Roter Stern, 1975), and François Fédier, 'La Nouvelle Édition de Hölderlin', *Poésie*, 10 (1979), pp. 125, 126.

2

Rhythm
What is at Stake in a Theory of Rhythm

(in *Critique du rythme*, Lagrasse: Verdier, 1982, pp. 67–115)

*Translated by Chantal Wright (sections 1–3) and
David Nowell Smith (sections 4–8)*

The internal relationship between rhythm and sense ruins sense as unity, as totality. It shifts *langage* away from *langue* towards discourse, away from the language of pretend didactic–scientific neutrality towards the discovery of strategies, of stakes. Rhythm is the critique of sense. This has to be stipulated prior to any definition of rhythm. Beginning with a definition turns out to be not only an uncritical step, but an anti-critical one.

* * *

and it would, perhaps, be rather difficult to exclude the dimension of life from those who speak.

Jacques Lacan[1]

1. Rhythm, Sense, Subject

There is something at stake in the theory of rhythm, within language, and it is not the notion of rhythm, but that of sense, the status of sense, and thus the entire theory of language. From the beginning one can posit that a theory of rhythm, whatever it may be, is a critical situation for a theory of language. What is at stake with sense is either the question of its belonging to the theory of the sign, or the establishment of a theory of discourse. From one to the other, the definition of rhythm has changed. The relationship between sign, language, discourse has changed. I will outline a critique of the current

---

1. Jacques Lacan, *Séminaire XX* (Paris: Seuil, 1975), p. 32. (English version: Jacques Lacan, *The Seminar of Jacques Lacan, Book XX: On Feminine Sexuality, the Limits of Love and Knowledge, 1972–3 (Encore)*, trans. by Bruce Fink (New York: W. W. Norton, 1999), p. 30.)

notion of rhythm following an analysis of what is at stake, because that is the framework and the orientation of the conflict, and determines its terms. Their sense.

It suffices, in order to pose the question, to invoke the fact that the current notion of rhythm is compatible with the theory of the sign. Because it is included within it. It makes of rhythm a formal element. Relations with sense, where it sees them, are imitative relations. Juxtaposed, secondary. Rhythm is not a semantic notion. It is a structure. A level. The distinction between form and sense, rhythm and sense, is homologous with distinctions between the categories of grammar, lexis, syntax, morphology. Traditional and unproblematic. Allowing for philological study, the essence of structuralism.

Benveniste, in his critique[2] of the etymology that furnishes, and more or less constitutes, the current definition, has destabilised, turned upside down not only the notion of rhythm, but its insertion into the theory of the sign, and at the same time, destabilised the theory of the sign itself. In rewriting the history of the word, it is in fact not only the sense of the notion that has changed. It is that it no longer fits solely within a form, it is no longer an auxiliary of dualism. Characterised as an arrangement, 'the particular configurations of moving'[3] or as 'the characteristic arrangement of the parts in a whole',[4] *form of movement*,[5] rhythm has abandoned a static definition which kept it within the sign and within the primacy of language. It can enter into discourse.

The paradox is that Benveniste did not develop this work, even though he was the first and the only one to have made it possible. That is because he created a linguistics of discourse and, perhaps, a poetics of discourse was necessary – which analyses the poem as revelatory of the functioning of rhythm in discourse. And Benveniste makes this poetics possible, but doesn't himself establish it.

Following Benveniste, rhythm can no longer be a sub-category of form. It is the organisation (disposition, configuration) of an ensemble. If rhythm is in language, in discourse, it is the organisation (disposition, configuration) of that discourse. And since discourse is inseparable from its sense, rhythm is inseparable from the sense of this discourse. Rhythm is the organisation of

---

2. Émile Benveniste, 'La notion de "rythme" dans son expression linguistique', in *Problèmes de linguistique générale* (Paris: Gallimard, 1966), pp. 327–35. (English version: 'The Notion of Rhythm in its Linguistic Expression', in *Problems in General Linguistics*, trans. by Mary Elizabeth Meek (Coral Gables, FL: University of Miami Press, 1966), p. 281–8.)
3. Benveniste, *Problems in General Linguistics*, p. 286.
4. Ibid., p. 283.
5. Ibid., p. 287.

sense in discourse. If it is an organisation of sense, it is no longer a distinct, juxtaposed tier. Sense is created in and via all the elements of discourse. The hierarchy of the signified is now only one variable within it, depending on the discourse and situation. Rhythm in a discourse can have more sense than the sense of words, or a different sense. The 'suprasegmental' of intonation, in former times excluded from sense by linguists, can have all the sense, more than the words. It is not only the hierarchy of the signified that is disturbed, it is the 'traditional divisions', as Saussure put it: syntax, lexis. . . . Sense is no longer the signified. There is no longer a signified. There are only signifiers, present participles of the verb *signifier* [to signify].

In the theory of the sign, the language unit [*la langue*] is first and discourse second. It cannot be any other way. Within this theory, discourse is a use of signs, a choice, a series of choices within the pre-existing system of signs. In relation to language, the speaker can only have a grammatical definition: the one that is furnished by this choice. Which is where style and stylistics come from. Corresponding to this grammatical definition is Marxism's social definition, which makes the individual the creature of social relations.[6] Choice or the absence of choice, the subject–individual is therefore the creature of the systems of signs, whose social relationships are only a category. In this, Marxism not only is compatible with the theory of the sign but constitutes a culmination, a perfection of the politics of the sign.

In the theory of rhythm that Benveniste made possible, discourse is not the use of signs, but the activity of subjects in and against a history, a culture, a language – which is only ever discourse, where the definition of language appears essentially grammatical, a particular relation of the syntagmatic to the paradigmatic which takes up, *redistributes* old categories. Rhythm as the organisation of discourse, and therefore of sense, brings back to the fore what is empirically obvious, that there is sense only by and through subjects. That sense is in discourse, not in language. The notion (and the privilege) of the signified was not only the product of a description, its result and its stakes were also to exclude the subject. The extreme form of this linguistics was without a doubt Bloomfield's, the most coherent from this point of view, and which therefore also excluded sense.

If sense is an activity of the subject, if rhythm is an organisation of sense in discourse, rhythm is necessarily an organisation or configuration of

---

6. Karl Marx, 'Preface to the First Edition', in *Capital*, vol. 1, trans. by Ben Fowkes (London: Penguin, 1976), pp. 89–93, p. 92. 'My standpoint, from which the development of the economic formation of society is viewed as a process of natural history, can less than any other make the individual responsible for relations whose creature he remains, socially speaking, however much he may subjectively raise himself above them.'

the subject in their discourse. A theory of rhythm in discourse is therefore a theory of the subject in language [*langage*]. There cannot be a theory of rhythm without a theory of the subject, nor theory of the subject without theory of rhythm. Language is an element of the subject, the most subjective element, of which the most subjective in turn is rhythm.

The theory of language is therefore privileged terrain for the theory of the subject. Perhaps more so than psychoanalysis, which has been made to play the role of furnishing such a theory, for Marxism, or for anthropology in general. Like Sartre in *Questions de méthode* [*Search for a Method*] or *L'Idiot de la famille* [*The Family Idiot*]. The anthropological interest of literature, its effect as a social laboratory is, from this point of view, to reveal – at the price of vulnerability – the functioning of the subject, through which society itself is revealed. A theory of discourse, of the subject, is therefore above all a theory of literature. And the theory of literature is perhaps the last thing the discovery of which Freud makes possible.

The subject is comparable to the origins of language. Searched for as though it were indefinitely hidden. Nothing is hidden in language. But what is shown there slips through seeing. Like the origin, it is produced in all mouths and all ears constantly. It is the very functioning of language, the *I* of interchangeable utterance. Moving from the linguistic sphere to literature, it extends from the use of the agents of utterance to organisation into a system of an entire discourse. The subject of utterance is a relation. A dialectic of the unique and the social. A linguistic, literary, anthropological notion, not to be confused with that of the individual, which is cultural, historical, emerging from histories of individuation. The subject is an ahistorical linguistic universal: subject has always existed, everywhere language has existed. The individual is historical: it didn't always exist. Whence the history of relations between subject and individual. In discourse, the subject of discourse is historical, socially and individually.

Writing, exposing the political state of the subject in a society, shows and creates of the subject of writing a trans-subject. But there is a subject of writing only when there is a transformation of the subject of writing into a subject of re-utterance.

Just as there is sense only by and for subjects, there is rhythm only by and for subjects. The relation of rhythm to sense and to subject, in discourse, frees rhythm from the sphere of metrics. Studying rhythm no longer begins with verse (identified with poetry), as is normally the case, but with ordinary discourse, in all discourses. The theory of rhythm demonstrates that a poetics is worth what its theory of ordinary language is worth. And that it is certainly more difficult to develop a theory of prose than a theory of poetry. Caught in the paradigmatic and syntagmatic of discourse, sense- and subject-rhythm create a generalised semantics, a function of the ensemble of signifiers, which is *signifiance*.[7]

Rhythm in sense, in the subject, and the subject, sense, in rhythm, make rhythm a configuration of uttering just as much as of the utterance. This is why rhythm is the major signifier. It encompasses, with the uttered, the infra-notional, the infra-linguistic. *Rhythm is not a sign.* It shows that discourse is not only made up of signs. That the theory of language further exceeds the theory of communication. Because language includes communication, signs, but also actions, creations, relations between bodies, the shown–hidden of the unconscious, everything that the sign cannot manage and that means we move from one attempt to another. There can be no semiotics of rhythm. Rhythm entails an anti-semiotics. It shows that the poem is not made of signs, even if linguistically it is composed only of signs. The poem slips through signs. This is why the critique of rhythm is an anti-semiotics.

Rhythm, particularly in the poem, places the theory of the sign in difficulty. Not that it prevents it from functioning. The theory has functioned perfectly, from the Stoics to the present day. But it functions because it isn't merely a linguistic theory of the sign. It is also a pragmatics and a politics of the sign. Those of instrumentalism. Of the State. Of reason and of State reason. Which the centralising policies of language reinforce. The State can have no theory of language other than instrumentalism. In this, structuralism has been the good conscience of the theory of the sign. This theory can only exclude the poem, as a deviation, or as anti-arbitrary. This exclusion – which is also adoration, luxury, *celebration* – shows that in rhythm, the subject, the poem, the same thing is at stake, that of the historical anthropology of language, which also has a political sense, through the primacy of discourse, which is to say of the multiple in the empirical, of the indefinite dialectic of subjects and of the State. Historicity, plurality are indissociable.

Rhythm is therefore the primary anthropological element in language, more so than the sign: because it pressures the theory of the sign, and pushes towards a theory of discourse. Exceeding signs, rhythm comprehends language with all the might of the corporeal. It necessitates a shift from sense as totality–unity–truth to a sense that is no longer totality, nor unity, nor truth.

---

7. Which is why I give a value specific to poetics to the term *signifiance*, in contrast to that given to it by Benveniste as 'signifying property' in 'Sémiologie de la langue', *Problèmes de linguistique générale 2* (Paris: Gallimard, 1974), pp. 43–66, p. 51. (English translation of 'Sémiologie de la langue': 'The Semiology of Language', in Robert E. Innis (ed.), *Semiotics: An Introductory Anthology*, trans. by Genette Ashby and Adelaide Russo (Bloomington: Indiana University Press, 1985), pp. 228–46, p. 234.) [Translator's note: Ashby and Russo translate Benveniste's 'signifiance' as 'significance'. I have retained 'signifiance' here.]

There is no unity of rhythm. The only unity would be a discourse as the inscription of a subject. Or the subject itself. This unity can only be fragmented, open, undefined.

The question of rhythm maintains what is inseparable between a theory of language and a theory of literature. Because if a subject can be a unity of rhythm, if a discourse can be a unity of rhythm, this is possible only when a subject inscribes itself to the maximum degree possible into its discourse, inscribes its situation to the maximum degree possible into its discourse, and this becomes the system of it – maximal constraint. Whereas the majority of discourses are inscribed into a situation, and only make sense with it. Unity therefore is made up of them and their situation. When the situation shifts, they shift with it. But the unity of the text, which can fragment (the poem, the collection of poems, the novel, the entire work), is a unity of writing, subjective (in the sense of a transformation of the social), distinct from the rhetorical, narrative, metric unities that it contains and that it informs.

Rhythm brings to life the conflict between an epistemology that is specific to the problems of language and the ascendancy of science, or philosophy, with its idealising effects. Its paradox is the fact of being the most empirical activity, the most common to all discourse, like *I*. And theorised as belatedly, if not even later so.

2. Against Semiotics

Semiotics currently takes up the greater part of the theory of language. After structuralist triumphalism, semiotic triumphalism. It presents itself both as a science, and therefore universal, and omnipresent, therefore international.[8] Science, 'new scientific *savoir-faire*'.[9] It is not merely an epistemology, but also an ethics, and a politics, that are at stake in a theory of sense, because a theory of sense also influences theories of history and society. An epistemology is not merely a technical evaluation, it is also a strategy. Whence the importance of semiotics, and the urgency of a critique of semiotics.

If everything is sign and systems of signs, everything is semiotisable, and semiotics is the science of sciences – 'the method of methods' – to cite

---

8. This is what the edited volume *Le Champ sémiologique, perspectives internationales* displays. André Helbo (ed.), *Le Champ sémiologique* (Brussels: Éditions Complexe, 1979). The pagination system that I use from here on in is the one used by this book: letters followed by numbers. [Translator's note: All translations from this French-language encyclopaedia of semiotics are my own. Subsequent footnotes containing references to this work will include the name of the author of the entry cited and the page number reflecting the work's own idiosyncratic system of pagination (letter plus number), e.g. B3.]
9. Jean-Claude Coquet. Ibid., p. I1.

Sebeok.[10] This totalitarianism is part of the history of American semiotics,[11] from Peirce to Charles Morris. It is indissociable from the temptations of unity, of totality. Its ambition leads it to integrate everything, to the detriment of rigour, and at the price of taxonomic difficulties. The sign therefore includes, for Sebeok, the medical symptom, which makes Hippocrates the first semiotician. Along with Saussure and Peirce, therefore, following a metaphor that is just as rickety as the table that it suggests, a 'semiotic tripod'; the third leg 'unequal' but 'the most deeply rooted' – medicine. This would be unobjectionable were it not for the state in which semiotics places language, in offering itself as a common denominator for incommensurable units.

Poetics, rhetoric, stylistics, semiotics not only have a different history, so that they cannot be 'synchronically harmonised'.[12] Their strategies are different, their units, their relations with the theory of the sign. Like Hjelmslev's linguistics, semiotics has an ambiguous relationship to epistemology: as if it both constituted it and assumed it to be anterior, exterior: 'linguistics depends on an *episteme* which is not constitutive of it and over which it has no control. The epistemology that, in a given era, governs the majority of the humanities influences both the choice of method and the choice of object. This is why all epistemological slippage in the humanities inevitably has consequences for the linguistic field.'[13] Epistemology is not an outside, does not entrust itself to others. Each piece of work develops and critiques its very being. Hjelmslev's work is invalidated by its epistemological weakness, by the theorisation that masks its empiricism, its approximations, even its grammatical work on cases. Semiotics is positioned through its linguistics: Hjelmslev's – a few specifics notwithstanding – not Saussure's. Linguistics orients semiotics towards an ahistorical formalisation.

What is at stake for the humanities can only be the historicity of anthro-

---

10. Thomas A. Sebeok. Ibid., p. B28. [Translator's note: This entry by Sebeok in *Le Champ sémiologique* was originally published in English as 'The Semiotic Web: A Chronicle of Prejudices', *Bulletin of Literary Semiotics*, 2 (December 1975), pp. 1–63. It was translated into French for the Helbo volume by Jean-Jacques Thomas; a footnote on p. B6 of the volume explains the English-language provenance of this entry. The citation that Meschonnic attributes to Sebeok here is in fact referenced in Sebeok's article ('The Semiotic Web', p. 25) as a summary of Peirce's thought by Max H. Fisch and Jackson I. Cope, from 'Peirce at the Johns Hopkins University', in Philip P. Wiener and Frederic H. Young (eds), *Studies in the Philosophy of Charles Sanders Peirce* (Cambridge, MA: Harvard University Press, 1952), pp. 277–311, 355–60, p. 289.]
11. I refer the reader to *Le Signe et le poème*, pp. 140–56, 173–81, 232–47. Henri Meschonnic, *Le Signe et le poème* (Paris: Gallimard, 1975).
12. Michel Arrivé, in *Le Champ semiologique*, p. J7.
13. Jean-Jacques Thomas. Ibid., p. B5.

pology, or the variants of its status outside history. This is the situation and the sense of the conflict between the sign and the poem. Now, *the more semiotics acts like a science, the more it reinforces the metaphysics of the sign.* This is its constitutive contradiction. It both masks it and augments it by ever increasing totalisation, increasing scientificity. Its effects are: the reciprocal maintenance of post-structuralism and phenomenology; compartmentalisation into specialisms (a semiotics of painting, cinema etc.), which augments the blurriness of the notion of the sign, and the blurriness of borrowings from an ideology of pleasure that is derived from an 'articulation' with psychoanalysis. The strategy of a polemic of details, for internal use, like generative grammar, masks what is at stake through technical discussion, striving only to reinforce its academic standing. The manœuvres of conventional theory, to cite Horkheimer. Semiotics therefore contributes to the current confusionism. It lends its dehistoricisation to millenarian irrationalism. It leaves the field open to it, offering the prospect of an absence of critique that is the political effect of its epistemology.

Because there is a radical ahistoricity to semiotics. The sign is a universal which, as such, knows neither historicity nor historicisation. This is what Jean-Claude Coquet emphasises, perhaps without wanting to, when he speaks of the 'achronic structure' of Greimas's 'constitutional model'.[14] The 'Locke–Peirce–Morris pattern', as Sebeok says,[15] is Leibniz's lineage. The sign has lost what was linguistic about it in its trajectory from Saussure to contemporary semiotics, just as narrative function, in its trajectory from Propp to Greimas, has lost what was historical about it.

Going in a different direction from Peirce, whom Sebeok cites, for whom 'all this universe is perfused with signs, if it is not composed exclusively of signs',[16] an attentiveness to empirical discourse reduces the sign component in the strict sense (doubly articulated), and multiplies the pseudo-signs component. The semiotisable is lessened. It is unclear whether there is interest, among both the natural sciences and the linguistic sciences, in understanding the universe as a system of signs. The immediate effect of this is a generalised metaphor. Its effect on biology, genetics, is scarcely more than an effect of pan-semiotic discourse, via the usage of terms such as *code, message*. . . . Its effect on language is an insertion into the cosmic to the detriment of

---

14. Jean-Claude Coquet. Ibid., p. 17.
15. Sebeok, 'The Semiotic Web', p. 4.
16. Peirce, as cited by Sebeok in 'The Semiotic Web', p. 25. [Translator's note: Sebeok's reference for the Peirce citation is: Charles S. Peirce, *Collected Papers of Charles Sanders Peirce*, V (Cambridge, MA: Harvard University Press/The Belknap Press, 1965/6), note on p. 448.]

empirical signifiance. The classic privilege of the signified is thus reinforced, as is the blurriness between sign, signal, symptom, indication. . . . But this blurriness is of a fashionable sort.

The myth of the totality–unity that drives semiotics can also be found in theories of rhythm. To combat this myth, I will try to show that a *general theory of rhythm* – encompassing all rhythms, everything that is rhythm – inevitably finds itself to be a metaphysics of rhythm, as semiotics finds itself to be a metaphysics of the sign. Since only discourse is historical, not the sign, a theory of language must constitute itself in accordance with the specificity of its object. It can only lose its historicity by merging with semiotics. This is why a theory of rhythm in discourse would not necessarily have a relationship with a theory of rhythm anywhere other than in discourse. As if the sense of the notion of rhythm in language could only be the particular realisation of a universal, which presupposes a universal rhythm, or rather a universal notion of rhythm. Which, curiously, is the very one that Benveniste recognised and condemned. Even though he deprived the notion of rhythm of the historical foundations of its sense, in fact, nothing has changed.

Against semiotics and its effect on language, on literature, Benveniste did more than simply sketch a strategy, in *Sémiologie de la langue* [The Semiology of Language].[17] Against the attempt at 'one system alone' (ibid., p. 229), Benveniste noted the insurmountable difference between Saussure and Peirce, where Sebeok's already rickety 'tripod' – which placed these two 'feet' into a continuous series, made them *equal*, since the only 'unequal' was Hippocrates – starts to break down. There is a 'non-convertibility of systems with different bases' (ibid., p. 235); 'There is no sign [. . .] that is trans-systemic' (ibid.). Benveniste showed that there is no *unity*, in the plastic arts, for example, therefore no semiotics. Only 'the work of a particular artist' (ibid., pp. 237–8) would be an 'approximation' (ibid., p. 237) of such unity – in other words, an 'individual characteristic' (ibid., p. 238): unity ruins the notion of unity. It becomes one unicity: 'Art is nothing more than a specific work of art' (ibid., p. 239). The double 'relationship of *interpretance*' (ibid., p. 240) instituted by Benveniste allows us to distinguish systems that are purely semiotic from those that are purely semantic. If there is occasion to 'go beyond Saussure's concern for the sign as a unique principle' (ibid., p. 243). Benveniste's analysis is the only one to uphold the historicity and specificity of each practice. He outlined the programme, announcing on the one hand a linguistics of discourse, and on the other 'the translinguistic analysis of texts and other manifestations through the elaboration of a metasemantics

---

17. Benveniste, 'The Semiology of Language', pp. 228–46.

founded on the semantics of enunciation' (ibid.). This is where a poetics of rhythm takes off. It is inscribed in an investigation of semantics, the theory of the particular. But semiotics, with its dream of a universal science, has got its epistemology wrong.

In semiotics, binarism – with its phonological origins – indefinitely repeats the dualism of the sign. Just as the Saussure–Peirce–Hippocrates triad is unstable, so too the concept of *seme*, constantly employed by vulgate semiotics, is confused. An introductory textbook defines it as follows: 'an element of signification rigorously determined by these two relations of disjunction on the basis of conjunction'.[18] Disjunction, conjunction refer to phonology, and binarise difference, which is plural in Saussure. Retaining, despite an allusion to the critiques directed at it, the isomorphism of expression and content, in Hjelmslev, the notion of a minimal element of signification bases its combinatory principle on the logic of identity and the primacy of the signified, conjoined in the notion of *isotopy*. Greimas defined isotopy as a 'bundle of redundant semantic categories underlying considered discourse'.[19] Isotopy is the repetition of the same, the 'thing resulting from the repetition of elements of signification of the same category'.[20] One proceeds to its 'extraction'. In other words, to a series of conceptual reductions. A variant on the paraphrase concealed by scientism. Classification into categories rests on binarism (euphoria/dysphoria); mimics the generative: the 'manifest text' of the surface, 'abstract elements' in their depth (ibid., p. 103); divides polysemy into monosemies; has an almost non-existent power of discovery: the 'semiotic square' of oppositions into contraries and contradictories is only 'universally applicable' (ibid., p. 133) by finding abstract categories everywhere, by being vague, where *death* contrasts with *life*.

Confusionism and regression combine to give the semiotic definition of discourse. The same introductory textbook includes in its glossary: '*Discourse* (or parole) is the result of choices made by a given speaker, from the stock of language, in order to realise a particular message, inscribed in a concrete and specific situation' (ibid., p. 181). Parole given as equivalent to *discourse* muddies the entire history of linguistic concepts, from Saussure to Benveniste, renders Saussure unintelligible, and the term unusable for a linguistics of discourse. The notion of *choice* reveals the primacy of *langue*, towards a stylistics that cannot work either because it is an individualism without a theory of the subject, since *langue* reduces the subject to a structure. Finally, *stock*, which

---

18. Anne Hénault, *Les Enjeux de la sémiotique* (Paris: Presses Universitaires de France, 1979), p. 49.
19. Algirdas Julien Greimas, *Du sens* (Paris: Éditions du Seuil, 1970), p. 10.
20. Hénault, *Les Enjeux*, p. 81.

reshapes language as a nomenclature of words instead of a system, discovers both, like a slip of the tongue, the anti-Saussure and the pre-Saussure at work in semiotics.

This degeneracy of the sign is not a timely failing, which would scarcely merit a mention. It is the combined product of a linguistics borrowed from Hjelmslev, of a pseudo-scientific formalisation, of the very history of American semiotics, particularly after Charles Morris. Confusion and regression are precisely most visible where discourse is at stake. Cinema, painting tolerate this scienticism better. But there too, semiotics is less and less in touch with the reality of those practices.

Rhythm rejects semiotics. It rejects it on its own account, first of all. It can also signal a critique that semiotics itself does not appear ready to grasp, labouring under the illusion that it is partaking in a 'gold rush' (ibid., p. 175).[21]

Semiotics and poetics are only one aspect of a conflict revealed by poetics. This conflict is insurmountable. It reveals that it is impossible to think language without thinking in terms of conflict. In langage, it is always war. Whether it is a matter of discourse that is an endless *agon*, or the status of the subject, or the relationship between words and things. Semiotic science is caught up in its positivity. And in the poise of the semiotician.

3. Negativity of Rhythm

If rhythm, sense, subject are in a relationship of reciprocal inclusion where the critique of rhythm and discourse are concerned, linguistics, by contrast, says nothing about rhythm, for reasons which meant that Bloomfield left sense out of linguistics.

Neither a theory of rhythm, nor a theory of sense, nor a theory of the subject is constituted. But no theory is ever constituted. The initial mistake would be to wait for one before an other can be further determined. None of the three is a prerequisite for the rest. That would mean waiting indefinitely. If sense, subject, rhythm are linked, working on one means working on all of them.

A theory of rhythm is necessary for a theory of the subject and of the individual, since it finds fault with the metaphysics of the sign. This metaphysics operates through the effacement of the subject–observer, conflated with the truth of what is observed, the *object*, as if the conditions of observation were not inseparably subjective–objective. This is the solidarity of the sign and of the dualist anthropology of the logical and the pre-logical. And the solidarity

---

21. Ibid., p. 175.

of discourse with a decentred anthropology. Which also underlines the fact that a theory is only a 'mode of representation',[22] not an objective truth-universal of the object.

If theory recognises itself as relative, as a 'mode of representation', it is in a better state than the metaphysics of the sign to recognise that its object of knowledge is an empirical variable – sense, not truth. The literary work, grasped as a discourse among discourses, no longer allows for an aesthetics of mimicry, of the lie, nor an aesthetics of the truth. No more than is the case on the logical level of true or false. Adorno contrasted truth with *mimesis*: 'The spirit of works of art is neither their meaning nor the intention behind them but their truth content.'[23] He added: 'Jettisoning the idea of imitation from aesthetics would be just as wrong as accepting it uncritically' (ibid., p. 399 A-58). The subjectivity of sense, of reception, changes, prevents – at least in part – the moralisation that is truth. Adorno wrote: 'Great works of art are unable to lie', hence 'it is only the botched and misconceived ones that are untrue' (ibid., p.188). Which reduces art to psychology. But subjectivity stands in the way of mimetics by withdrawing its transcendence to make of it an adventure of subjects.

The historicity of discourse no longer makes of the work a beautiful lie or a truth. Because it doesn't trace it back to an intention, as Adorno continues to do, nor to a content (ibid., cf. pp. 187, 209). The link between sense and subject neutralises these oppositions. The organisation of sense as significance, value, means in turn that rhythm can no longer be envisaged as a form, which would be the 'logicality' (ibid., p. 197), the coherence of works of art. That are 'determined objectively' (ibid., p. 198).

Adorno wanted to eliminate the concept of 'aesthetic enjoyment': 'The concept of aesthetic enjoyment was a bad compromise between the social essence of art and the critical tendencies inherent within it' (ibid., p. 20), and further on: 'the very idea that enjoyment is of the essence of art deserves to be thrown overboard' (ibid., p. 22). The critique of rhythm is a critique of pleasure. But Adorno cannot eliminate this concept, which carries an entire aesthetics along with it, by remaining, as he does, with art-as-imitation. *Mimesis* remains, for Adorno, the 'ideal of art' (ibid., p. 164). Adorno adapts Kant's 'purposefulness without a purpose' (ibid., p. 201) to an instrumentalist idea of language. But rhythm as the sense of the subject is both subjective and social, sense and history. The theoretical division therefore eliminates this

---

22. Henri Bergson, 'Durée et simultanéité', in *Mélanges* (Paris: Presses Universitaires de France, 1972), p. 213.
23. Theodor W. Adorno, *Aesthetic Theory*, trans. by C. Lenhardt (London: Routledge and Kegan Paul, 1984), p. 398 A-56.

'aesthetic enjoyment as a constitutive concept'. It eliminates it as a product of dualism. Pleasure is the organisation of signifiance via the integration of the body and history in discourse. It is no more an aesthetic concept than one can differentiate between rhythm and metaphors in the 'thrill of the new' that Hugo perceived in Baudelaire.

At the same time, a maximalist rejection of the very notion of investigation into the subject suggests itself in a particular Marxist position. It has to be refuted but also analysed for its strategic importance, for the weakness of its arguments, and for what it indirectly anticipates: 'There can be no more a "theory of sense" or a "theory of the subject" than there can be "theories of God"; these objects are ideological categories, not objects of knowledge.'[24] Althusserian Marxism presupposes in this the identification between science and theory that is necessary for it to contrast itself radically with the ideological. The object of knowledge actually belongs to science. Or at least to this particular concept of science. But the rejection of sense in ideology does not recognise the effect of its own action on the theory of language.

It is the logical continuity from Marx to Marr that, taking up or rejecting together both sense and ideology, places ideology in *langue*, rejects the philosophy of *langage* along with the language of philosophers (in *The German Ideology*) and prepares the unthinkable of *langage* via superstructure. Hence the unthinkable of the subject. The *articulation* of Marxism and structuralism is by itself the negation of the subject: 'social formation is not composed of subjects: one can only define spaces to which conditions of production and the reproduction of significations are attached' (ibid., p. 77). A *subject* that is so negated that it is a confusion of the individual and the subject, the moral and the psychological: 'the subject–individual' is the 'specific subject–form' of 'bourgeois ideologies' (ibid., p. 159). A negation of the possibility of the *subject* that says more about its own strategy, its own ignorance, than about the subject. To this is added the 'articulation of historical materialism and of psychoanalysis' (ibid., p. 125), combined with the *articulation* of Marxism and of generative grammar (to articulate all of the avant-gardes at once), and which fails to perceive the theoretical and *political* incompatibility of the two.[25] Whence this proposition that doesn't know what it is saying, because it is ignorant of the opposing strategies of *langue* and *discourse*: 'syntax is

---

24. Paul Henry, *Le Mauvais outil: langue, sujet et discours*. With an afterword by Oswald Ducrot (Paris: Klinksieck, 1977), p. 20.
25. For a political analysis of generative grammar, I refer the reader to *Poésie sans réponse: pour la poétique*, V, pp. 317–95. Henri Meschonnic, *Poésie sans réponse: pour la poétique*, V (Paris: Gallimard, 1978).

situated in *langage* for the articulation of *langue* and discourse'.[26] The final obstacle to the subject, the unconscious, is strangely opposed to syntax: 'As for what the already said or heard articulates with all its *parole* or utterance, it is not properly syntax – that has its roots in the unconscious, not in the subject' (ibid., p. 144). The confusionism of an era, already out of date, which establishes a specious paradigm between the subject of the uttering and the unconscious, the subject of the uttered and the psychological subject (ibid., p.155).

This example characterises some of the current obstacles to a theory of the subject and of discourse. It shows that an epistemological obstacle is also a political obstacle. It confirms that a theory of discourse also maintains (contains, retains) a theory of syntax (which is not that of language). It displays the ambient naivety, of Sartre through to the Marxists, which entrusts to psychoanalysis the potential theory of the subject. Which, coincidentally, does not make it more of a science, but an ideology. Ducrot partially re-establishes the subject, as much as he draws it back to himself, via the presupposition: 'declaring X the subject of his uttering is to assume that he knows the sense of this uttering at the moment he brings it about' (ibid., p. 200).

It is here that the analysis of poetic activity can rejoin that of the presupposition. It is a matter of analysing modes of signifying. A poem is neither an intention nor a consciousness. There is a theoretical regression, following on from Valéry, that links the subject to this psychological and moral couple: in other words, unity.

The subject is no more a unity than a poem is made of signs. Which doesn't prevent it from being a relative unity. The text-unit(y) mistakes the notion of unity. Adorno wrote: 'Oneness is an illusion. Therefore works of art constitute illusion as they establish oneness.'[27] It breaks down into lesser unities, which are rhetorical, linguistic. The *word*, which is the smallest unit of sense, tends in the opposite direction, to designate larger units metaphorically. Mallarmé sees in *verse* the 'mot total'. Mandelstam goes further: 'Any unit of poetic speech, be it a line, a stanza or an entire lyrical composition, must be regarded as a single word.'[28]

Rhythm intervenes in poetry to the extent that poetry is the language that is least made up of signs. Which is what Diderot said, in his own way, in his *Letter on the Deaf and Dumb*, that discourse is:

26. Henry, *Le Mauvais outil*, p. 155.
27. Adorno, *Aesthetic Theory*, p. 425 A119.
28. Osip Mandelstam, 'Conversation about Dante', trans. by Jane Gary Harris and Constance Link, in Peter S. Hawkins and Rachel Jacoff (eds), *The Poets' Dante* (New York: Farrar, Straus, and Giroux, 2002), pp. 40–93, p. 52.

not merely [. . .] a chain of well-ordered terms which convey facts to our mind, but [. . .] a series of hieroglyphics which picture the thought to us vividly; in fact, I may say that all of poetry consists of emblems.

(But it is not every one who can understand these emblems. In order to feel their meaning we must almost have the power of creating them ourselves.)[29]

The emblem or the hieroglyph escapes unity. The poem, or rhythm, by this itself, escapes the subject, assumed to be unitary from the outset. But at the same time, only one subject of uttering has emitted a rhythm, a poem. Rhythm, conceived in continuity with sense and the subject, disunites sense, subject. The metaphor of the hieroglyph signals that one can think this activity only in the indirect, the provisional.

This is the same metaphor that Freud used for the dream: 'The dream-content [. . .] is expressed as it were in a pictographic script, the characters of which have to be transposed individually into the language of the dream-thoughts.'[30] He added: 'A dream is a picture-puzzle [rebus]' (ibid., p. 382). But rhythm is not a rebus. The rebus fragments unity into pieces of sense. Unity is merely inconvenienced along its path. Coded. It is reconstituted at the end, when the decoding has gone well. If rhythm is the configuration of a sense, nothing allows us, as we will see, to see in it the same sense, the same unity, differently arranged.

Just as separating rhythm and sense has appeared for the longest time 'an enterprise of doubtful value',[31] so too associating them through a vague identification would be of doubtful value. This would easily reveal the old homology of form and content, logico-grammatical parallelism. If the relationship of rhythm to sense is not conceived of technically as a relationship of discourse to the subject, it is, from the outset, a classic oscillation between living and *langage*.

A theory of rhythm is a theory of sense not because rhythm is sense, but because rhythm is in interaction with sense. The poem is the discourse where this interaction is most visible. Doubtlessly also where it is the most specific. Tynianov, in 1923, postulates this '*modification of the semantic value of the word that operates from the fact of its rhythmic value*'.[32] It is a semantics

---

29. Denis Diderot, *Œuvres complètes, II* (Paris: Le Club Français du Livre, 1969), p. 459. (English version: Denis Diderot, 'A Letter on the Deaf and the Dumb', trans. by Beatrix L. Tollemache, in *Diderot's Thoughts on Art and Style* (London: Rivingtons, 1904), pp. 146–69, p. 163.)
30. Sigmund Freud, *The Interpretation of Dreams*, trans. by James Strachey (London: Penguin, 1991), p. 381.
31. I. A. Richards, *Practical Criticism* (London: Routledge, 1966), p. 361.
32. Iouri Tynianov, *Le Vers lui-même: problème de la langue du vers*, trans. from Russian

of position, the 'semantic value of a word in verse through the function of its position' (ibid., p. 116). Because of the fact that rhythm was the 'constructive principle of verse' (ibid., p. 76), for Tynianov, creating a theory of verse meant creating, or rather announcing, as necessary, an 'analysis of changes *specific to the signification and sense of words* by function of the construction *of verse* itself' (ibid., p. 40). Tynianov's postulate has become, strangely, both a truism and an abandoned programme. I am certainly not aware that it has been realised. If it is to be taken up, extended, this can no longer be with its notion of the word, and of lexis: 'The very *structure* of the lexis of verse is radically different from that of the lexis of prose' (ibid., p. 126). Which is true, however, of certain poetries, certain cultures. The critique of rhythm owes to Tynianov the constructive function of rhythm. But Tynianov remains in a functionalism where there is neither utterance, nor subject, nor discourse. Nothing but sense, *langue*.

Rhythm is not sense, nor redundancy or substitute, but sense material, even the material of sense. If it is of the subject, it is an ensemble of subjective-social relations that drive discourse. The major importance that Gerard Manley Hopkins accorded rhythm confirms his pioneering significance, not only for poetic modernity, but for the theory of rhythm. He sought 'an immense advance in notation [. . .] in writing as the record of speech'[33] and referred to the accents of the Bible. A rhythm is a sense if it is a passage of the subject, the production of a form – arrangement, configuration, organisation – of the subject, which is the production of a subject-form(er) for any subject. Which is what, to use a well-known example, Nerval does in 'Je suis le Ténébreux, – le Veuf –, l'Inconsolé' [literal translation: I am the Shadowy One, – the Widowed –, the Unconsoled'] through the double internal break in the line, isolating 'le Veuf', the paradigm of solitude, which belongs as much to the work of the words as to that of the typography: the italics and the capital letters of 'Il appela le *Seul* – éveillé dans Solyme' [He summoned the *Lone One* – aroused in Solyme'], 'Et c'est toujours la Seule, – ou c'est le seul moment' [And it is always the Lone One, – or it is the lone moment'].

[*Problema Stixotvornovo Jazyka* (Leningrad, 1924)] by Jean Durin, Blanche Grinbaum, Hélène Henry and Danielle Konopnicki (Paris: Union générale d'éditions, 1977), p. 108. [Translator's note: The translations into English here are based on the French translation that Meschonnic cites.]

33. Gerard Manley Hopkins, in a letter to Robert Bridges dated 6 November 1887: 'it would be an immense advance in notation (so to call it) in writing as the record of speech, to distinguish the subject, verb, object, and in general to express the construction to the eye; as is done already partly in punctuation by everybody, partly in capitals by the Germans, more fully in accentuation by the Hebrews'. C. C. Abbott (ed.), *The Letters of G. M. Hopkins to R. Bridges* (Oxford: Oxford University Press, 1955), p. 265.

If the subject of writing is a subject through writing, it is rhythm that produces, transforms the subject, to the extent that the subject emits a rhythm. Closer to value than to signification, rhythm installs a receptivity, a mode of seizure that inserts itself despite our contemporary comprehension, that of the sign; the rationality of the identical identified with reason. It imposes a multiplicity of logics: 'When a verse is extremely beautiful one does not even dream of understanding. It is no longer a signal, it is a fact.'[34] It is perhaps this pre-, or one might say, peri-rational effect that certain metaphors of rhythm note, such as, in Hebrew, *michqal*, etymologically 'weight', for 'rhythm', or, to name the accents of cantillation in the Bible (rhythmic–semantic–melodic accents), *te'amim*, from *ta'am*, 'taste' (*ta'ām*, food, in Arabic). In Indian poetics, the term *rasa*, identified with the sense of 'taste' and 'lifeblood, essence', designates a theatrical mode.[35] The sensory metaphor designates absorption by the body. The metres in the *Brāhmaṇa* have a 'nutritional virtue' analysed by Mauss: 'the principle of this theory is that song is of the voice, which is of the breath, which is of food'.[36]

Anti-unity, rhythm is an anti-totality. It is the undefined empirical that prevents a Hegelian poetics from being realised. A Hegelian poetics wants to 'perceive the poem in its totality'.[37] Kibédi Varga looks for 'the superior unity of synthesis, such that it establishes itself in the reader during the actualisation of the poem' (ibid., p. 42). Some confusion follows: between a phenomenology of reading – 'a dialectic of the apprehension of the poem' (ibid., p. 35) – and an analysis of the mode of signifying; between the mode of signifying and individual realisation, the 'read poem'. This 'dialectical poetics of the actualised poem' (ibid., p. 149) continues to start out from the *word*, 'poetic or poeticised'. It therefore returns to the rhetoric of figures of words (ibid., p. 194). To grasp the 'constants of poetry' (ibid., p. 270), it

---

34. Paul Valéry, *Cahiers*, vol. II (Paris: Gallimard, 1916), p. 1076.
35. See Edwin Gerow, *Indian Poetics* (Wiesbaden: Otto Harrassowitz, 1977), pp. 245–9.
36. Marcel Mauss, *Anna-Virāj*, in *Œuvres*, 2 (Paris: Éditions de Minuit, 1969), p. 593. Kant perceived this metaphor: 'How could it have happened that modern languages in particular have designated the aesthetic faculty of judging with an expression (*gustus, sapor*) that merely refers to a certain sense organ (the inside of the mouth) and to its discrimination as well as choice of enjoyable things?' Immanuel Kant, *Anthropology from a Pragmatic Point of View*, trans. by Robert B. Louden (Cambridge: Cambridge University Press, 2006), p. 139 (§67). But he concluded by paraphrasing: 'the feeling of an organ through a particular sense has been able to furnish the name for an ideal feeling' (ibid., p. 141), and 'an unconditionally necessary end requires neither reflection nor experiment, but comes into the soul immediately by, so to speak, tasting what is wholesome' (ibid.). It appears to me that the relation cannot be explained by words, by relinking *sapor* to *sapientia*, and that it supposes a theory of the body in *langage*, therefore rhythm.
37. Kibédi Varga, *Les Constantes du poème* (Paris: Picard, 1977), p. 4.

misses the poem, because it places it in traditional categories, the image being a mode of representation: 'The constants of the poem are therefore movement and cessation, sonoric flow and rhyme, centre and distance of terms of the image, the relationship of each of these constants with the reader's effort of apprehension' (ibid.).

The rhythm of sense as the sense of the subject demands that we no longer accept this repartition, of the 'sonorous' and the 'image', which scarcely varies from that of form and content. The critique of rhythm is firstly the critique of criteria. There are criteria belonging to metrics. Are there any for rhythm? Rhythm is the sense of the unpredictable. The realisation of which, *in retrospect*, will be called 'an interior necessity': 'The artist does not create according to the criteria of beauty, but according to interior necessity'.[38] Rhythm is the inscription of a subject in its history. It is therefore both an irreversible and that to which it constantly returns. Not unitary, not totalisable, its only possible unity is no longer its own: discourse as system.

In writing, in art, a subject has become its work. Which is what the common designation indicates: the name of an author operates differently from the name of a person which is not the name of an author. It signifies, at the same time as it designates. It assembles semantics. Beyond the futurist provocation, this is one effect of Mayakovsky's title, *Vladimir Mayakovsky, Tragedy*.

4. System of the I

Writing, in particular that of the poem, is a specific practice of rhythm only when it is a specific practice of a subject, across all social codifications. Turns of phrase, rhythms, the entire language of a work is the activity of a system, its formation. It does not take place in a language [*la langue*]: the language takes place in it. Literature, from this point of view, is nothing but a specification of the fact that there is, concretely, no *langue*: there is only discourse. Literature, the parable of the subjective, found itself for this reason either sacralised or rejected, for the same imputation of subjectivity, coupled with that of individualism. This is however one of the universals of literature, the very banality, its foundational paradox, that a work, any work, has, in order to belong to all, something which only belongs to a unique individual. Ezra

---

38. Arnold Schoenberg, Introduction au *Traité d'harmonie*, trans. from German (from *Finale und Auftakt* (Salzburg: Otto Mueller, 1964) pp. 281–7) by Erika Dickenherr and Jean-Yves Bosseur. In: L. Brion-Guerry (ed.), *L'Année 1913: les formes esthétiques de l'œuvre d'art à la veille de la première guerre mondiale. 3. Manifestes et témoignages* (Paris: Klinksieck, 1973), pp. 216–24. [Translator's note: I have translated here from Dickenherr and Bosseur's French translation.]

Pound put in the entry for *Rhythm* in his *Credo*: 'A man's rhythm must be interpretative, it will be, therefore, in the end, his own, uncounterfeiting, uncounterfeitable.'[39] Rhythm, the *I*: both concern the same functioning, in order that literature should be, as Pound wrote in the *ABC of Reading* in 1934, 'news that stays news'.

The idea is traditional. It has for a long time even been associated with the idea of *style*, since style was a choice, and hence personal. Which is illustrated by Northrop Frye: 'The conception of style is based on the fact that every writer has his own rhythm, as distinctive as his handwriting, and his own imagery, ranging from a preference for certain vowels and consonants to a preoccupation with two or three archetypes.'[40] Every writer would have their style, their rhythm, as they have their voice, their fingerprints. This is indeed one conception of the I, and one which has the benefit of not placing any mystery into what is the most common thing in the world. But this is not a conception of the I as system. Moreover, it does not come out of poetics, nor a critique of rhythm, from out of that apperception which is strong despite being a truism.

Here, poets have multiplied theoretical intuitions. The subject of writing had been anticipated, before psychoanalysis and the theoreticians of the assumption that there was only subject when at the same time it was also non-subject. From Gérard de Nerval, 'I am the other,' to Rimbaud, subjectivity is not an egotism, not the private, not the ego. It is the interchangeable. Aragon wrote in 1925: 'I do not place myself on stage [*je ne me mets pas en scène*]. But the first person singular expresses for me all that is concrete in man. All metaphysics is in the first person singular. All poetry as well. / The second person, it is also the first.'[41] Which did nothing more than develop the fundamental, linguistic, functioning of discourse. It is in no way distinctive of poetry. Poetry is the discourse which exposes this functioning.

But it does not expose it through the use of personal pronouns. Like all discourse. It realises itself as figure of subjectivity only *if the discourse as a whole is carried to the state of subjectivity*. Which is to say, to the status of a value system. The subjectivity of a text results from the transformation of what is sense or values in *la langue* into values in a discourse, and only in that discourse. Whatever the linguistic levels. At every linguistic level. Maximal subjectivity is thus wholly differential, wholly systematics. Rhythm is system. It is not associationist. Literary, poetic specificity is thus the maximum of

---

39. Ezra Pound, 'A Retrospect', in *The Literary Essays of Ezra Pound*, ed. by T. S. Eliot (New York: New Directions, 1954), p. 9.
40. Northrop Frye, *Anatomy of Criticism* (Harmondsworth: Penguin, 1957), p. 268.
41. Louis Aragon, 'Avis', in *La Révolution surréaliste*, 5 (15 October 1925), p. 25.

constraints (varying according to dimension, 'genre') that a discourse can produce. Only a history – not a consciousness, not an intention – can make a discourse into a system. The system of the I is neither liberty, volition, choice, nor refusal. It is not wanting-to-say. It is unpredictable, as is everything that is history, and, like history, it gives rise in retrospect to facile teleologies. Thus I am not *explicating*, but situating writing as system among the other practices and activities of language.

If a writing produces a perhaps indefinite reprise of reading, its subjectivity is an *intersubjectivity*, a *trans-subjectivity*. Not an intra-subjectivity, which one pretends to conflate with subjectivism, individualism. This writing is an enunciation which ends not simply with an utterance, but with a chain of re-enunciations. It is an enunciation which is trans-historic, trans-ideological. A *hypersubjectivity*. A language which knows more about us than we do ourselves. Hypersubjectivity can be a self-prophetism. Apollinaire knew this to the point of superstition. Hugo wrote: 'Poets are scared of becoming prophets.' But that saying which implies the greatest amount of unsaid is quite distinct from ambiguity. It is the activity of language which draws back most powerfully the limits of the never-said, the greatest labour on the extra-linguistic and the infra-linguistic.

The poem, particularly, is a knowing [*savoir*] that we do not know [*connaît*], which we cannot consult. In the ignorance of the future, the partial knowing of the past, the poem is a knowing of the future to the extent that it inscribes the determinations of a subject. This is why no one writes what they want, even less what they wish. But whereas each of us has nothing but our past, the poem passes from I to I. It is that discourse which can recognise the past of others. It does not simply tear a part of life from oblivion. If it is different to memory, this is because rhythm is an actualisation of the subject, of its temporality.

Slippage of the I, rhythm is a present of the past, of the present, of the future. It both is and is not in the present. It is always a return. In which it is the poem, and not verse, which is *versus*. And one can understand why *verse*, and rhyme, and the other forms of return are, have been, associated with the poem to the point of being identified with it. Rhyme is, has been, nothing more than a privileged figure, in our culture, of this return. I speak of a *versus*, of a 'rhyme', which make the whole system of a work, and of the I. Not of the 'terrible concert for the ears of an ass', as Éluard said – before turning back on himself [*d'y revenir*]. Rhyme in the current sense has become a vulgar image, wholly external, wholly cultural, of this generalised return. This is what was able to render it insupportable as code, at least in a certain historicity, even if the reasons for and against have not always been understood. In order to be justified – to be a writing, and not simply literature, or poetisation – the *versus* must be system, value. Inner form, as Humboldt said of grammatical systems, and of the 'character' of languages, which still remains to be theorised. System, the return of temporality on itself, of sense on itself, of the I on itself, inseparably. Through which a mode of signifying overflows the practices and theory of the sign.

Impersonal writing is thus not the writing of a zero subject, nor, naively, the use of the 'third person'. Biographical truth or 'lie' (the fictive dates of Hugo's poems), it doesn't matter which, if the writing makes the particular into a generalisable concrete. The true bio-graphy, writing of life, is poetic activity. It is this activity, subsequently, which makes 'life' appear as non-poem; 'man' is nothing but a product of the 'work'. Both, products of what comes after the event and dualism combined.

Fiction pluralises, disseminates the subject. Generally, first through the plurality of characters, everything which sustains the plot. Rhythm, in fiction, is that of narrative unities as much as of signifiers. All the turnings back of a story do not change its character as a story. Even if the time of the story restarts a revolved past. The completed and the incompleted are not the same in fiction and in the poem. It is that every story turns them into something completed. The poem places them into the incomplete. Wherein there is a sadness in the novel. Which imitates that of life: of non-return. Which has its price. And a joy of the poem. The poem even continues the bygone [*revolu*]. This is what makes the epic.

Also, against Western modernity which for the last hundred and fifty years has so identified poetry with what used to be called lyricism (bringing together directly subjective poetry and the short piece), I would say, disaggregating the epic and the long, the lyric and the short, that the poem, *every poem, is fundamentally epic*. Long or short. A fragment can be epic. The very brief can be epic. This is what brings the poem so close to the tale, the legend. Its relation to the sacred.

The received idea is the filiation, taken for a continuity, of the epic to the novel. But we can no more confuse filiation with functioning than etymology with meaning. However incontestable the genesis of the novel, this genesis is far away. The ancient functionings had time to transform themselves. Nothing is further from the epic than the contemporary French novel. Not only because it no longer has its orality, its mode of collectivity, but because the lives and times it depicts are finite. It is not by chance that the sociological functioning of the novel today, in our society, includes a literature of forgetting. Airport novels. An *escape*. Crime novels, spy novels, the triumph of structure and the disappearance of the subject. There are no airport poems.

Even if the history of French poetry had not helped isolate poetry, the novel in our culture would have more readers than the poem. The poem in-completes the time of the subject. It is more difficult both as a result of itself, and for cultural reasons. Because it is a mode of temporality, a mode of subjectivity which imposes upon the subject a return. Which is why the traditional reduction of systems of versification to mnemotechnics is a misrecognition, an anthropological caricature. The poem memorises, and passes through techniques of memorisation, not in order that we remember things, or in order that we remember the poem, but because it is a memory of the subject. We learn our memory with it. A novel brings us back to ourselves through the forgetting of ourselves. It has this in common with the greatest novelty, the most famous, most recently redone, the most whatever. This function is the same in sub-literature, in commercial cinema. Their differences lie elsewhere.

But the poem makes us into this continuous only through an effort, a reminder to oneself, about oneself. The ethics of the poem and the ethics of the novel, their relation to the social, their relation to rhythm, constitute the two in opposition to one another. The poem gravitates towards making the individual into a subject. The novel multiplies the individual. Which does not have the effect of constituting the individual into a subject. On the contrary, since this is what best favours the subjective illusion of already being a subject, and a super-subject. If the author knows everything, in the narrative-novel of the nineteenth century, so does the reader. An effect that the *nouveau roman* did not cancel. As a result, the worst novel is assured a more *massive* success than any poem. The successful novel that we know here tends towards the mass, tends the individual towards the masses, because it is a merchant of illusions. There is an essential demagogy in the mode of subjectivity that it constructs.

I do not speak of the American or Latin American novel. I merely observe a situated sociological effect. I propose to see in this effect a subject-effect. Which seems to be confirmed by the success of the witness-history. Whence its non-critical role. Historicism, in place of historicity. In another society, the roles could be reversed: a poetry that sends us to sleep, where 'the poet reigned with the hangman', as Milan Kundera wrote in *Life is Elsewhere*, where the novel is critical.[42] This inversion invalidates nothing of the relation between the subject-effect and the effect of the mass. What a society says and does about its poetry and its novels is a sign of what it does to the subject.[43]

42. Milan Kundera, *La Vie est ailleurs* (Paris: Gallimard, 1973), p. 383. But this passage is about a derision of poetry, of a fake poet, which Kundera takes in a debatable manner as the representative of the 'true poet' (p. 239). He turns the 'frenetic desire for admiration' into something which 'belongs to the very nature of poetic talent' (p. 304). The 'force of lived sentiment' is not enough to make 'beautiful poetry' (p. 384). It is therefore no longer poetry, but the trap 'held out to poetry' which Kundera criticises. His critique, through the novel, rejoins poetry, which after all can appear only where there is a critique of poetry.
43. This passage was the object of a discussion at the poetics seminar at the Université de Paris

Poetry also has its demagogy, somewhat diverse, from Prévert to Neruda. I privilege neither one nor the other. I am trying to situate the relations between their functioning and their effects. Not only do the poem and the novel not have the same history, but they do not go towards the same history. The difference in their workings of language, in the relation of rhythm to sense, is consubstantial with what each makes of history, of the subject.

5. I-history, I-origin

The paradox of the I, a universal of language, is to make the historicity of discourse. Poetry carries the I to the systematicity of a discourse. It is thus not an origin, as in the poetics of Vico, but a figure of the historicity of all discourse. The primacy of the signified in the sign refers back to etymology, to the origin as the true discourse of sense. Rhythm as sense of the subject, putting poetry into the historical adventure of subjects, neutralises the opposition of subject and object through the creativity of the generalised I. It borrows neither from the structuralist rapture for the object with the 'forgetting' of the subject, nor from the phenomenological rapture for the subject, through a hermeneutics which no longer says anything about the mode of signifying. And which turns towards the origin to dissolve through effusion, empathy, *Einfühlung*, 'infusion', as Mikel Dufrenne says: 'even if art is not at the beginning, it is the return to beginnings, to the primordial confusion of subject and object, of the imaginary and the real, of desire and representation'.[44] Rhythm as history brings the origin into the functioning.

The cliché that Nietzsche denounced in *The Birth of Tragedy* has remained active. The cliché is of a 'release and redemption from the "I"'.[45] Nietzsche asked: 'how the "lyric poet" can possibly be an artist at all, since he is someone who, so the experience of the ages tells us, always says "I", and who stands before us singing the entire chromatic scale of his passions and desires?'. He maintained the separation between man and work, which renders both incomprehensible, good for the sign, when he opposed this *I* to man: 'this "I"-ness is not the same as that of the waking, empirically real human being, but rather the only "I"-ness which truly exists at all, eternal and resting in the ground of things, and through the images which are copies of that "I" the lyric genius can see down to that very ground of all things' (ibid., p. 31). The *copy* maintains Platonism, and a 'longing for what is original' (ibid., p. 41).

8.
44. Mikel Dufrenne, 'L'Esthétique en 1913', in Brion-Guerry (ed.), *L'Année 1913*, p. 37.
45. Friedrich Nietzsche, *The Birth of Tragedy*, in Raymond Geuss and Ronald Speirs (eds), *The Birth of Tragedy and Other Writings* (Cambridge: Cambridge University Press, 1999), p. 29.

The subject of enunciation, which is subject through its discourse, is in solidarity with the 'radically arbitrary' of Saussure. It is not the generative abstraction of the 'speaking subject'. Jean-Claude Milner distinguished between an 'ethics of science', which starts from the abstract subject, and an 'ethics of truth', which appeals to a 'subject of enunciation, capable of desire'.[46] The theory of rhythm in discourse demands that we recognise yet one more ethics, an ethics of sense, whose stakes are the historicity of the values and status of sense.

The arbitrary, far from being a technical, fixed notion, changes value according to the strategy it serves. Milner understands it as an 'absolute dualism' (ibid., p. 87) between signs and things, sound and sense, whose relation is thus returned to *Chance*, thus to a 'refusal of knowing', in Saussure, whereas a 'knowing is possible', in Mallarmé and Lacan (ibid., p. 96). We need only recall the *Mémoire* of 1878, to give greater nuance to this 'refusal of knowing': a refusal, effectively, of a metaphysics of origin and of nature, not a refusal of history. I have shown elsewhere that Chance brought back [the concept of] nature.[47] If the arbitrary is taken as Milner takes it – which is the traditional, structuralist understanding – it is effectively little more than a blockage of knowing, the sterility of science which Genette opposed, in *Mimologics*, to the profusion of dreams, on the side of nature. In other words, the arbitrary is a weak strategy, which remains firmly within in the dualist conception. Because it is taken on its own. If it is envisaged in and as an inseparable fourfold: *system–value–functioning–arbitrariness* in relation to the strategy of the sign and the cosmic, the strategy of *la langue* (word–sense–origin–nature), it constitutes a strong strategy, because it is that of the empirical, of discourse, which historicises motivation. But Milner, who represents Saussure's 'network of differences' as a 'nothing' (ibid., p. 110), overstates Saussurean negativity. In exaggerating it, he weakens it. He de-dialecticises it, since it is an ensemble of both negativity and positivity. Through this, he exposes his strategy.

Milner is quite aware that the arbitrary is not simply convention: 'the thesis of the arbitrary has for its function the elimination of any question of origins. It has hence only a superficial resemblance to conventionalism. It is in no way helpful to evoke apropos of the *Course* the opposition of the Greeks *thesei/phusei*, which is a statement about origins, and bears, not on *langue*, but on *langage*' (ibid., p. 96). But the distinction that Milner makes only obtains its value through his strategy. Returning the arbitrary to chance, and difference to an absolute negativity, he rules out Saussure's attempt by radicalising

---

46. Jean-Claude Milner, *For the Love of Language*, trans. by Ann Banfield (New York: St Martin's Press, 1990), pp. 78–9 (trans. modified).
47. 'Langage, histoire, une même théorie', *N.R.F.*, 296 (September 1977), pp. 94–5.

it. He reinforces *la langue*, and *nature*. So much so that this distinction amounts to neutralising the arbitrary, instead of unmasking the situation of conventionalism, which is involved in what it is opposed to.

The strategy of the arbitrary is that of the sign, for Milner: 'the arbitrariness of the sign, by which is only meant that the sign cannot have any master other than itself, and is master only of itself' (ibid., p. 51). The linguist here imperialises 'science' (ibid., p. 53). Equivocating, he also plays with irrationalism: '*lalangue* is what makes one language not comparable to any other, insofar as it has precisely no other, insofar also as what makes it incomparable could not be said' (ibid., p. 61).[48] Equivocation mimed by that which confuses 'systematically sound and sense', and which, against Saussure, brings back substance: 'it becomes substance as well, the possible material for phantasies' (ibid.). Continuity with nature returns in the opposition between the language which '*touches* upon no real' (ibid., p. 62) and 'the desire of the linguist' through which, 'like the truth itself, *lalangue* touches upon the real' (ibid., p. 66).

This strategy of psychoanalysis in linguistics proceeds through certain negative homologies which make a paradigm of sexual 'prohibition' and 'impossibles', and of the 'lack of words',[49] 'there is something for which words are always wanting, or, there is something impossible to say' (p. 98). It thus makes it clear that the conception of language which manœuvres it is metaphysical. This 'lack of words' presupposes that each thing that is to be said has a word for saying it. Which is not self-evident. It is the identification of concept and word, which weighed heavily on the anthropology of Lévy-Bruhl. This presupposes, beyond nomenclature (pre-Saussurean), naming, which brings with it its theology, and a logic of monosemy. Without counting the comparisons between morphologically poor and rich languages. The only truly linguistic position is that which situates things to say – like their impossibility, or their prohibition – not in words, but in discourse. *Lack of words* is the name that we give to something else. Which is precisely where literature intervenes, and rhythm – *which is signifiance without being composed of words*.

Unitarism leads Saussure on a unique quest, the 'key to Saussure', Milner writes (ibid., p. 126), which unifies the *Course* and the anagrams in one

---

48. [Translator's note: *Lalangue*, spelled as one word, is a term used by Lacan to point towards a side of language where language is not made up of signifiers, linked one to another. He proposes with this term that there was a signifier without such links, combining signifier and libido. See Jacques Lacan, *The Seminar of Jacques Lacan, Book XX: Encore, On Feminine Sexuality, The Limits of Love and Knowledge*, 1972–3, trans. by Bruce Fink (New York: W. W. Norton, 1998). See also footnote 72, where another translator translated it as *Llanguage*.]
49. [Translator's note: I changed the official translation, *loss*, to *lack*, since it is misleading and does not render *manque* well here.]

and the same madness, 'one and the same move which leads him to wish to maintain the One', 'the One that marks the languages comes to them from elsewhere' (ibid.). Saussure is brought back towards myth, towards the origin – whilst from 1878 onwards what he discovered was a *system*, building on but also in opposition to pointillist historical philology. Milner in turn identifies himself with the unitary desire of origin and mastery, where nature reappears, becoming the super-subject: 'it is no longer the linguist who knows, but *lalangue* which knows through the linguist' (ibid., p. 139). A conception of mastery which confuses authority and mastery, in the Greco-German lineage of the masters of truth: the will of the *Witz* of psychoanalysis.

At stake in the critique of rhythm is the theory and practice of the system, against the reduction to the word, to the name. The critique of rhythm thus proceeds through a critique of the metaphysics of language which psychoanalysis includes in its many forms, since to this very extent psychoanalysis is invested in the theory of language. What is at stake in the arbitrary and in rhythm are ultimately one and the same thing.

This is what is produced and regulated by a poem. An organisation which is something completely different from the group of stimulations perceived by a psychological subject, which led Paul Fraisse to write that 'every rhythmisation is *subjective*'.[50] Which means: wholly in the receiver. The reception of a poem is in the organisation of the poem before being in the interpreter. The specificity of writing makes the specificity of the subject which utters itself, and distinguishes it from the speaking subject.[51] This is what puts it in a critical relation with psychoanalysis. Adorno presented psychoanalysis as 'more productive psychologically than aesthetically'.[52] The critique remains to be taken back up. The unconscious functioning of language plays concurrently with the unconscious of subjects. Rhythm brings into the poem the linguistic unconscious in its value as a system, as figure, in its being stripped bare as *means*, in Reverdy's sense. Because it is the organisation of the sense of the subject, which neutralises the opposition between the conscious and the unconscious to the extent that it neutralises meaning [*le vouloir-dire*] with significance. Significance, not intention, carries the text.

Rhythm in a poem does not transgress the conventions of discourse. It

---

50. Paul Fraisse, *Les structures rythmiques: Étude psychologique* (Louvain: Publications universitaires de Louvain, 1956), p. 9.
51. As is indicated, after Benveniste, by Jean-Claude Coquet, in 'Prolégomènes à l'analyse modale, le sujet énonçant', in *Documents de recherche*, 3 (Paris: École des Hautes Études en Sciences Sociales, CNRS).
52. Theodor W. Adorno, *Aesthetic Theory*, trans. by Robert Hullot-Kentor (London: Continuum, 2002), p. 8.

transforms them. It is the subject to the extent that it can be neither form nor content, but its own realisation, its actualisation. It does not symbolise, does not interpret itself as a dream does. There is no proper meaning of rhythm, or figurative meaning. Being the power to signify without the sign, it cannot but challenge the pseudo-mathematical dualist formalisation, the increasingly numerous appeals Lacan makes to Hegel and Heidegger.[53] Subject, sense, are floating in rhythm. This is how they communicate – how they contain those 'to whom they address themselves' (*Écrits* 9). Nevertheless rhythm is not a reverse of discourse whose place would be sense. It has nothing in common with the veiled that must be unveiled, or remain veiled. It is not the unconscious of the subject in discourse, as Chinese characters were the unconscious of alphabetic Europe. If this unconscious manifests itself in it, it is as much in all the rhetoric and semantics of discourse. Rhythm, as the sense of the subject, is as evident, as invisible, as the sense of one's history is to oneself. Which also is not made of signs.

6. The Subject is Individuation

In 'The State and Rhythm', Mandelstam wrote in 1920: 'An amorphous man, without form, a disorganized individual is the greatest enemy of society.'[54] Without 'the organization of the individual', he anticipated the 'threat of remaining in a collectivism without collectivity' (ibid.). Which is to say, without individuals. This analysis is political because it comes from poetry. Poetry acts as a revealer of society, because an individual is at stake, and where an individual is at stake, the social is at stake. Which does not mean that every poet is a politician. One of the possibles of poetry is the sense of theory – which starts, in poets, by the sense of their own history. Cassandra 1920.

This is why one could declare that society is in play just as seriously, if not more so, in the relation of the poem to society as in the direct critique of society. Marxism, Critical Theory have demonstrated, through their regionalisation of problems (economism, sociologism, politism), their theoreticist–pragmatic oscillations (a function of their predictive incapacity) that, like all political ideologies, they continue to employ individuals as a representation of society, not society as a representation of individuals. To the myth of the masses corresponds the countermyth of the individual.

Adorno thus wants to establish that 'what speaks in art . . . is its veritable subject, not the individual who makes it or the one who receives

---

53. For example, for Hegel: Jacques Lacan, *Écrits* (Paris: Seuil, 1966), p. 292, and the annex on p. 897; *Le Séminaire*, book 1 (Paris: Seuil, 1975), p. 267.
54. Osip Mandelstam, *Collected Works, Sobranie sočinenij* (New York: Inter-Language Literary Associates, 1967–9) vol. 3, p. 123.

it'.⁵⁵ It is not simply a question of not conflating the subject with the biographical I. It is a question of reducing the individual-conflated-with-the-subject to the social. Because after all, the subject is social. And the individual is supposed to be the anti-social, the incompatible – whereas collectivity exists only if the individual exists. But a romanticism of the masses is substituted in its place. Power play. Since we speak in its name: 'The labor in the artwork becomes social by way of the individual, though the individual need not be conscious of society; perhaps this is all the more true the less the individual is conscious of society' (ibid., p. 167). The recourse to *consciousness*, like the individualist notion of the individual – ideological manœuvre more than historian's analysis – are two obstacles to a historical theory of language, and of the subject, in art. The individual is thus emptied of its intolerable unicity. Yet, art is the observatory, and the laboratory, which more than any other social practice makes it clear that *it is in the individual that both the subject and the social realise themselves.*

To oppose the subject to the social, or the individual to the social, is an error which is costly first of all for aesthetic theory, and then for the social. Adorno writes: 'The intervening individual subject is scarcely more than a limiting value, something minimal required by the artwork for its crystallization' (ibid., p. 167). Similarly, the living individual is merely the minimal element that life needs in order to realise itself. The conception *biologises* the social: withdraws from it, and from the individual subject, their specificity, which is their history. The *work* here becomes a metaphysical entity, endowed with the most inexplicable *need*. The social reveals itself here to be a myth, the product of a rationalist programme. Myth in so far as it mobilises, and makes a story into revealed truth. The entity of the social is thus *that which makes, almost*, the work, and which is thus present virtually before passing, thanks to the author, to the final state of *crystallisation*. Where one clearly discerns the confusion, already there in Marx, between social conditions of production and the specific production of a work – a confusion that belongs to sociologism: Raphael in *The German Ideology*. A mix of teleology and scholastics, which invents a state of the-work-before-the-work as a semi-real entity. But this supposed intervention is an invention in order to serve the cause. The subject does not *intervene*. The *desire* to reduce it, to limit it to a 'minimal element', gives, or leaves, to this *intervention* all the mystery that this pseudo-materialism would elsewhere analyse in historical terms. For *intervention* poses in its turn the whole question that the reduction should have reduced. Whereas the historicity and unicity of each life make the

---

55. Adorno, *Aesthetic Theory*, pp. 166–7.

individual subject a necessity for the social, to which the work gives shape. It is not necessary to eliminate the *author*, in order to demonstrate that they are social, historical, as well as individual, as Sartre showed for Flaubert in vol. 3 of *The Idiot of the Family*. In and through the work, the subject is not the individual. *The subject is individuation*: the labour through which the social becomes individual, and the individual can, fragmentarily, indefinitely, have access to the status of subject, which can only be historical, and social. Just as we reach, indefinitely, our mother tongue.

It is particularly important, for the critique of society, and of the subject, that theories of society be incapable of a theory of literary and artistic production. They show through this incapacity their incapacity for a general conception of the subject. And of language.

The theoretical intuitions of poets do not desocialise – on the contrary – the individual author–subject. Rhythm, prophecy, the poet, are significatively linked. The listening of the subject is as much the listening of the social as the listening of history. Everything happens as if, in an inversion of power relations, politicians and political theorists were scared both of the poet and of the unique individual – the poet being the representative, the symbol of this latter – whilst poets have no fear of the social, which nevertheless crushes them. For they cannot be subject unless they are a listening, and cannot be a listening unless they are the finest sense of the social.

Rhythm, for Aleksandr Blok in 1909, was the 'presence of a path'. It was, in his language, an 'interior "measure" of the writer', and 'The uninterrupted tension of an interior whisper, the listening as if to a distant music, are the indispensable condition of the writer's being'.[56] This rhythm, this listening are, for Blok, as much the possession of prose writers as poets. The most subjective, which is a condition for poetic expression, is drawn from the collective. Blok speaks of a distant 'orchestra' which is the '"global orchestra" of the popular soul' (ibid., p. 106). And 'As soon as rhythm is there, the work of the artist is the echo of the whole orchestra, which is to say the echo of the popular soul. The question is simply the degree of their distance and proximity from it' (ibid.). A metaphor, but is it still a metaphor, if it cannot be said otherwise? It can be situated, delimited, as specifically Russian. Placed too within a struggle of Russian intellectuals. But it is not restricted to this. Very nineteenth-century perhaps, with its social and cosmic variants, from George Sand to Victor Hugo, the 'sonorous echo'. Only that it is in its very recurrences that this metaphor becomes audible. When Blok utters that 'knowledge of *one's own* rhythm' is crucial for the writer, as well as when,

---

56. Alexandr Blok, 'Duša pisatelja' (The Soul of the Writer), in *Sočinenija* (Works), 2 vols (Moscow, 1955), vol. 2, p. 105.

from the point of view of reception, he writes, in 1919, that artists are 'bearers of a music'.⁵⁷ What is a representative writer, if not the one who best brings that song to be heard, the one who comes closest to it? Historicity, and the loss of historicity, are precisely what could lead from the metaphor to the concept, without imagining that one might ever wholly conceptualise it.

The political sense of this metaphor is to invert the rationalist myth of the *masses*, which has lent itself far too much to manipulation, invoked as a factor in progress. It is historically more precise to recognise in it, as Blok does, the 'barbarous masses', the 'people' that he sees as the 'conserver' (p. 323) of 'the spirit of music'. It is true that one cannot extract Blok's claims, which oppose 'the spirit of music' to 'civilisation', away from the thrust of the old Russian dualism, Slavophiles versus Westernisers. To approach the elementary, for Blok, is to become more 'musical' (ibid., p. 326). This does not make Blok's intuitions into false propositions, but restores a Russianness to them before having a wholly general relevance. Blok did not separate this intuition from the announcement of the 'surrounding deluge' (ibid., p. 325) – the end of a world, of a civilisation. A common metaphor at that period, and which was demetaphorised by history.

The poet is defined by Blok not as one who writes in verse, but as the 'son of harmony'.⁵⁸ Harmony being 'the agreement of the forces of the world, the order of the life of the world. Order is the cosmos, in opposition to disorder – chaos. [. . .] Chaos is primordial, elementary anarchy; the cosmos is constructed harmony, culture; from chaos, the cosmos is born; the element hides within it the seeds of culture; out of anarchy harmony creates itself' (ibid.). Whatever Blok's philosophical situation, his elements of mysticism, the intuition remains that the poet has a 'role in global culture'. Blok depicts it thus: 'first, to liberate sounds from the anarchic element in which they are born; secondly, to lead these sounds to harmony, give them form; thirdly, to carry this harmony to the external world' (ibid., p. 349). This work is, for him, a 'historical' work (ibid., p. 352). To all appearances, Blok in his turn makes the subject into an intermediary through which history passes, like the life of the species through the individual: 'My questions have not been posed by me – it is the history of Russia which posed them.'⁵⁹ But it is because the individual is this passage, which is not simply a passage of the cosmic, of the biological through them, but the passage of a history, that the individual

---

57. Blok, 'Krušenje gumanizma' (The Ruin of Humanism), in *Sočinenija*, vol. 2, p. 320.
58. 'O naznačenje poeta' (The Destination of the Poet), in 1921, speech for the eighty-fourth anniversary of the death of Pushkin, in *Sočinenija*, vol. 2, p. 348.
59. 'Stixija i kul'tura' (The Element and Culture), December 1908, in *Sočinenija*, vol. 2, p. 92.

can act upon this history. The poem, rhythm, activities of sense, are elements of transformation.

Historicity as a listening to history, indissociably subjective–collective, is what makes up the strategic character of the notion of *functioning*, as distinct from the notion of function. To analyse the functioning of a mode of signifying, of a discourse, is to take it as value-system-historicity. To neutralise in this way the opposition between an immanent reading (which encloses itself in a text so as to read it only according to its own values, from the *inside*, and renders critique impossible) and a sociologising reading. Always the inside and the outside, which replicates content and form. To consider in language various *functions* (emotive, referential, conative, phatic, poetic, metalinguistic), following Roman Jakobson, is to have recourse to structures, which are universals. In this, the assumed subject can only be the abstract subject of Kant, or the psychological subject with subliminal structures. Analysis of functions can become undeniable, the nearer it reaches its perfection, the more it empties itself of historicity. For it carries its object towards the status of a pure form.

This is what happened to Huizinga, explaining by the principle of the play-function alone 'the astonishing uniformity and limitation of the poetic mode in all periods of human society'.[60] The 'formal characteristics of play' (ibid., p. 42) can merely regain the aesthetic notion of pleasure, just as musical performance 'transports audience and performers alike out of "ordinary" life into a sphere of gladness and serenity, which makes even sad music a lofty pleasure' (ibid.). Pleasure too is historical.

7. Rhythm Before Sense

Neither copy of sense nor symbolisation, rhythm is a non-semiotic representative of the subject which is anterior to sense. Which is banalised by more than one narrative. Northrop Frye reports that the phenomenon 'is not confined to poetry: in Beethoven's notebooks, too, we often see how he knows that he wants a cadence at a certain bar before he has worked out any melodic sequence to reach it'.[61] The experience has often been observed, of the anteriority of the rhythm over the words: by Valéry with regard to 'Cimetière marin', in 'On Diction in Verse'; by T. S. Eliot in 'The Music of Poetry', and what he called 'auditive imagination' in 'The Use of Poetry and the Use of Criticism'; by Virginia Woolf, for prose.[62]

---

60. J. Huizinga, *Homo Ludens* (London: Routledge and Kegan Paul, 1949), p. 132.
61. Frye, *Anatomy of Criticism*, p. 257.
62. Cited by D. W. Harding, *Words into Rhythm: English Speech Rhythm in Verse and Prose* (Cambridge: Cambridge University Press, 1976), p. 87. Harding cites Eliot on p. 99.

Alain drew a homology between the experience of the poet and that of the reader. The reader *recognises* poetry before *understanding* it. And they submit to its effects (rhythmic, prosodic . . .) before grasping it: 'The first effect of poetry, and even before one has understood it, is an effect of grace, in all the senses of this fine word,' and a little further on: 'The poet is thus a man who, touched by misfortune, finds a kind of song that is first of all without words, a certain verse measure that is first of all without content, a future of sentiment which will save every thought there is.'[63]

Rhythm is thus a mould. The non-distinction of rhythm and metre contributes to this. Speaking of rhythm in 'Le Cimetière marin', Valéry means: the decasyllable. A rhythm-metre syncretism is chronologically anterior to the words which will fill the mould. Alain here does little more than gloss Valéry: 'The poet, thus, searches for their thoughts, not along the path of reason, but by virtue of a healthy rhythm, which waits for the words. The great affair of the poet, where they are never either too intelligent, or too wise, is to refuse anything conveniently resembling rhythm, and waiting for that miracle of words which fall in just the right place, which are of exactly the length, the sonority, the meaning, that they should be' (ibid.). Where the anteriority of rhythm is no longer anything other than the anteriority of metre. Anteriority over thought, over words: 'The poet does not start from a thought; [. . .] From this vital rhythm, he sets off, and, never letting himself get deflected, he calls forth the words, he orders them according to accent, number, sound; it is thus that he discovers its thought. And this would not be possible if there were not, in every language, hidden harmonies between sound and sense' (ibid., p. 912).

We need, then, to distinguish between two anteriorities. That of metre, and that of rhythm. Even if they are conjoined, superposed-identified, in their 'incantation' effect, they are logically distinct. The anteriority of metre is cultural. Chronological. It precedes the poet as *langue* precedes *parole*. The anteriority of rhythm is in discourse the priority of one element of discourse over another, which is words, their sense. Priority of one logic over another, and displacement of logics. The anteriority of metre, such as Alain describes it, is an explicit corollary of the sound–sense dualism. Rhythm here is a form. The anteriority of rhythm over the sense of the words is indissociable from these words, even if rhythm makes sense otherwise, partially. Being of discourse, it is not anterior to the particular discourse where it is other of sense. If there is an anteriority of rhythm, it precedes the sense of words, but not the words themselves. Anteriority only in relation to the habitual priority of sense.

63. Alain, 'L'Art des vers', in *Propos* (Paris: Gallimard, Éditions de la Pléiade, 1970), vol. 1, p. 931.

Double, this anteriority is recognised as an interiority, and the sign of a successful line of verse: 'What is most proper to the poet is to be rhythmically strong before all else.'[64] Which, however unclear the matter might be, would presuppose, for Alain, an anteriority of the individual over the social: anteriority in value, anteriority-source. Which would join up, in the ordinary sense, with a certain individualism. In the Greek tradition of the philosopher and the poet. After which there is a gift of the poem as there is, in Husserl, a gift of sense: 'His courage came to him from his poems. One song for everyone: one song is equal for everyone' (ibid., p. 1260).

Priority over thought, chronological anteriority of metre, rhythm is also, first of all, an anthropological anteriority, a prehistory within us. The archaic as a memory of oblivion, not a past but a permanence, once again the origin as a functioning. Leroi-Gourhan notes that 'rhythmic markings precede explicit figures in time', and 'We thus see that primitive art began in abstraction or even in the pre-figurative.'[65] To this Antiquity which represents, for anthropology, the 'moraines of glaciers' of which Saussure spoke regarding languages,[66] we should also include, and add, the historical ancientness of forms, and their voyages: 'The Sapphic stanza is no more the creation of Sappho or the alchaic of Alchaeus than the *Reizianum* of Reiz or the *Rufulianum* of our good master Desrousseaux. Where these rhythms come from, we do not know, some from far away, if it is true, as I believe criticism has proved, that Aeolian rhythms are very close siblings to those of India. But in any case, they are, all of them, children of the sacred dance or the solemn march, and preserve the law of the bearers of offerings or the pourers of libations.'[67] The very ancientness of rhythms, paradoxically, dehistoricises them.

Rhythms are the most archaic part of language. They are a pre-individual linguistic mode that inheres in discourse, unconscious just like the entire functioning of language. They are in discourse an element of an individual's history.

If rhythm is an element of the system of a discourse, it is bound to the history of this discourse. There is a history of Hugo's rhythms. And if there is a history of rhythm in a discourse, a particular history which can be added to the general historicity of discourse, is not this history also the history of an individual, its becoming-subject? The critique of rhythm can ask what hap-

---

64. Alain, 'La Position du poète', in *Propos*, vol. 1, p. 1259.
65. André Leroi-Gourhan, *Gesture and Speech*, trans. by Anna Bostock Berger (Cambridge, MA: MIT Press, 1993), p. 372.
66. Saussure, inaugural lecture at the University of Geneva, November 1891, in the Bouquet and Engler critical edition of *Cours de linguistique générale*, n 1.1. Reprinted in *Ecrits de linguistique générale*, English translation in *Writings in General Linguistics*, pp. 99, 121.
67. René M. Guastalla, *Le Mythe et le livre* (Paris: Gallimard, 1940), pp. 179–80.

pens to the 'atemporality of the unconscious',[68] as well as to the structuration, for Lacan, of the unconscious like a language; for this structuration appeals to rhetoric, to the theory of the sign, to the double articulation of language. And rhythm, if it is the organisation of a sense, of the sense of a subject and an unconscious in a discourse, has no double articulation, escapes the sign, its figures are neither literal nor figurative.

Before words, before the comprehension of sense, before the individual, and yet within its discourse, rhythm is the involuntary. The involuntary is a traditional attribute of the work, from Plato to Freud, whose *Moses and Monotheism* is cited by Adorno: 'Unluckily an author's creative power does not always obey his will: the work proceeds as it can, and often presents itself to the author as something independent or even alien,'[69] with regard to intentions, which present themselves in the form of 'inexorable demands' which 'appear before him as strangers'.[70] This anteriority has all the appearances of exteriority. It is particularly concerned with poetry, identified by its etymology with literary creation, which it seems to concentrate. The involuntary is not that which escapes volition, like an involuntary moment. Poetry represents, more strongly, the impossibility of willing [*vouloir*] poetry. Which is a universal of poetry. Shelley's formulation, in 'A Defence of Poetry', is exemplary: 'Poetry is not like reasoning, a power to be exerted according to the determination of the will. A man cannot say, "I will compose poetry." The greatest poet even cannot say it; for the mind in creation is as a fading coal, which some invisible influence, like an inconstant wind, awakens to transitory brightness.'[71]

The passage of the poem, and the relation of rhythm to sense, figure *par excellence* the non-unity of the subject. No more unity of the subject than hierarchy of sense. Rhythm can pass just as unobserved as the unconscious, and like this latter can show in language the emotional states of the subject. Which is to say, but with a different strategy to psychoanalysis, and with other things at stake, that language cannot be reduced to communication, to information, which are only concerned with the abstraction *speaker–subject*: 'Llanguage [*lalangue*] serves purposes that are altogether different from that of communication. That is what the experience of the unconscious has shown

---

68. Élisabeth Roudinesco, *L'Inconscient et ses lettres* (Paris: Mame, 1975), p. 25.
69. Sigmund Freud, *Moses and Monotheism: The Complete Psychological Writings of Sigmund Freud*, vol. XXIII (London: Hogarth Press, 1964), p. 104. Quoted in Theodor W. Adorno, *Philosophy of Modern Music*, trans. by Anne G. Mitchell and Wesley V. Blomster (London: Continuum, 2007), p. 162 n. 13.
70. Adorno, *Philosophy of Modern Music*, p. 12.
71. *Shelley's Prose, or The Trumpet of a Prophecy*, ed. by D. L. Clark (Albuquerque: University of New Mexico Press, 1966), p. 294.

us, insofar as it is made of llanguage, which, as you know, I write with two l's [*j'écris en un seul mot*], to designate what each of us deals with, our so-called mother tongue [*lalangue dite maternelle*], which isn't called that by accident.'[72] There is no symmetry between psychoanalysis and the theory of language. Psychoanalysis, which works only on the subject, has brought nothing to the poem. It's because psychoanalysis already had its theory of language. Like Russian dolls, it has always already (included in what it says about the subject, and of a discourse) the theory of the subject that belongs to its theory of language, the theory of language that belongs to its theory of the subject. Its practice does not allow it to criticise them.

The anteriority of poetry, and of rhythm in poetry, what Plato says about it in the *Ion* regarding the non-mastery that the poets have over poetry – and those who have mastery are not those 'who say things of great value' – this is the parable of theorising the unknown in the subject, which is what the poem, what rhythm, does. From René Char's *Hammer without Master* to Breton – 'the empire I had thus far taken upon myself seemed to me illusory' – it was up to surrealism, beyond its posturing, to have returned poetry to 'every unconscious'.

Rhythm, sense of the subject before the subject, no longer allows the old tripartite distinction, in the function of 'personae', which placed lyric in the *I*, represented drama with the *you*, and referred epic to the *s/he*. The *I* is the impersonal of the subjective, being, beyond the 'first' person, the exchange of the subject function, something quite other than non-person, the absent, the hidden, *it*. Discourse in its entirety, *I*, system of the I, rhythm, coincides, on this point, with what Lacan wrote of the subject: 'The subject is nothing other than what slides in a chain of signifiers, whether he knows which signifier he is the effect of or not' (ibid., p. 48). Passage of the subject into signifiance. With the difference that the signifier in psychoanalysis is also extra-linguistic, but the signifier rhythm, which is no longer the signifier of the sign either, remains an element of discourse. Activity of the subject, signifiance is not the subject. Lacan reminds us: 'language is not the speaking being' (p. 2). It *has* no unconscious. But rhythm, which one does not read, but which is heard in what we read and without which one cannot read, is as evident and incomprehensible as 'the dimension of life' in 'those who speak'. It is in a relation to sense, to intention, comparable to that of life to language.

Representative of the incomprehensible, rhythm is the privileged material of adventure. Visions, metaphors, are made out of it. It is the laboratory of new meanings. Thus the search can itself turn to diverse mysticisms, or

---

72. Jacques Lacan, *On Feminine Sexuality, The Limits of Love and Knowledge: Book XX*, trans. by Bruce Fink (New York: Norton, 1998), p. 138.

imitate them, or take itself as its own object, an adventure in language, instead of language being the adventure of subjects. This is Pasternak's opinion of Khlebnikov: 'I never understood what he was searching for. In my opinion, the most striking discoveries are produced when the subject, filling up and overflowing the artist, does not give the artist the time to reflect, and so in great haste they must proffer their new speech in an ancient language, without having been able to work out if this language was new or old.'[73] It is remarkable that the theme or motif that Pasternak speaks of tends towards becoming not simply homonymous but the synonymous with the subject of writing – with tenor and vehicle interchangeable – because it is what *fills* and *overflows*. The subject of writing is not the one who *searches* but the one who *finds*. They face one towards the other to the point of identifying finding with self-finding. It is then that it is found all over the place.

This out-of-control anteriority overflows the poetics of Valéry. It is perhaps what remains from it for a historical anthropology of language. For the larger part is borne by the sign. Valéry was probably the first to undermine the notion of the author: 'every work is the work of lots of other things besides an "author"'.[74] His anti-intentional poetics is famous: '*there is no true meaning to a text* – no author's authority. Whatever he may have *wanted to say*, he has written what he has written.'[75] And in 'Commentaries on "Charmes"', in 1928: 'It is an error contrary to the nature of poetry, and one which may even be fatal to it, to claim that for each poem there is a corresponding true meaning, unique and conformable to, or identical with, some thought of the author's' (ibid., pp. 155–6).

But this poetics led him, leads all those who follow him today, to a semantics of ambiguity – which resembles at once everything that is most old-fangled in Valéry, and everything that is most pervasive. This is linked to a phenomenology which places sense in understanding, in the interpreter. It's an 'affair for the reader'.[76] A negative poetics which could only ever multiply the positive: 'Now the poetic idea is at base nothing other than a representation (of some sort) satisfying conditions of psychological multiplicity – I is a clear ambiguity, presented by a fragment, on a particular point, the *resonance* of all being' (ibid., 1915, II, p. 1070). This ambiguity is lexical: a question of

---

73. Boris Pasternak, *Essai d'autobiographie* (Paris: Gallimard, 1958), p. 57.
74. Paul Valéry, 'Rhumbs', in *The Collected Works of Paul Valéry*, vol. 14: *Analects*, trans. by Stuart Gilbert (Princeton, NJ: Princeton University Press, 1970), p. 201.
75. Paul Valéry, 'Concerning "Le Cimetière Marin"', in *The Collected Works of Paul Valéry*, vol. 7: *The Art of Poetry*, trans. by Denise Folliot (Princeton, NJ: Princeton University Press, 1958), p. 152.
76. Paul Valéry, *Cahiers* (Paris: Éditions de la Pléiade, 1974), vol. II, p. 1074. The text is from 1916.

words; and lexicalist – it reduces language to words. It operates within the traditional theory, which it maintains, with its subdivisions: 'Syntax and terms must be in poetry as *precise* as possible but the sense *imprecise*; multiple, never entirely identifiable with a "finished function" of the terms' (ibid., 1916, II, p. 1078). It's a reinforcement of the dualism, which continues to think poetry as gap, and founds itself on a linguistic error: ambiguity is everywhere and is not distinctive to poetry – 'Ambiguity is the domain proper to poetry. All verse equivocates, plurivocates – like its structure, *sound + sense* – indicates (ibid., 1916–17, II, p. 1081, italics in English in original).

Valéry has thus brought the Poe–Baudelaire–Mallarmé lineage to its purest form, has contributed more than anyone else to the 'release of pure poetry' (ibid.) of which, more than the abbé Bremond, he is the author. A purity which has one variant: the idea of an involution of poetry upon itself: modern poetry – ever more poetic.

Yet there is a negative theory of the subject in Valéry. We invent because there is an unknown in the subject. He writes in his *Cahiers* [Notebooks] in 1913: 'It is what is unknown to myself within me which makes me me' (ibid., II, p. 288). His quest undoes the banal association of individual and subject: 'The individual isn't much of anything – It is the me/ego which is everything' (ibid., 1918, II, p. 295). What is at stake in poetics appears in the possibility, and the necessity, which poetics alone makes appear, of drawing Stirner, for example, away from the individualism and anarchism in which political strategies have confused and condemned him. To say *me* is poetic, and not asocial. Disaggregated from the individual, the *me* of Valéry is a function of subjects which must be the unknown of sense in order to be as much in the reader as in the poet. A theoretical intuition distinct from the proposition which would turn sense into the business of the reader: 'The true poet does not know exactly the sense that they have just had the good fortune to write. [. . .] *Verse listens to its reader.* – And likewise, when I say that I look at my Ideas, my images, I can just as well say that I am looked at by them. Where to place the me/ego, why should it be that this relation is symmetrical?' (ibid., 1916, II, p. 1078). From which he asserts that poetry – defined 'Poetry – it is to arrive at a state of perpetual invention' (ibid., 1916, II, p. 1077) – only makes the unknown out of language if it makes itself in the unknown of the subject.

But this theory short-circuits, in Valéry. It neutralises itself in propositions which turn back on themselves and are annulled. 'The most beautiful poetry has always taken the form of a monologue' in 1935–6.[77] But '*Monologue* does not exist', in 1941 (ibid., I, p. 300). It turns on the negation of the person: '*It is not someone* who *makes*' (ibid., 1941–2, I, p. 302).

---

77. Valéry, *Cahiers*, vol. I, p. 285.

Valéry is probably the most important of those who have professed that the non-person, the *it*, was the impersonal. He imagines that later, one will say: '*It* thinks, *It* wants instead of *I*' (ibid., 1921, I, p. 317). Paradoxically, behind this refusal of the *I*, he deifies the *me*, whose absence is a hypostasis: 'The abstract Idol of the perfect *me/ego* – which is to say of *self-consciousness* [English in original], the legacy of Poe' (ibid., 1945, I, p. 317). He finds the word ONE [*ON*] magical because it 'permits a proposition WITHOUT A SUBJECT' (ibid., 1931, I, p. 436). Which comes close to a fetishisation of discourse. The negative poetics of the subject leads Valéry to a refusal of the subject. Which is shown by the opposition that he sees between 'made' and 'found' verse, to which he often returns, in order to say that he would not have accepted (nor would they have arrived) certain lines of verse that he admires. Whence his notion of a 'sterility' which is not an absence of production, but a 'non-acceptance' (ibid., 1913, II, p. 1067). It is remarkable – as I will show below through other examples – that *the privilege of the metrical is the corollary of a refusal of the subject*.

It is no contradiction that the sole beneficiary of this theory of language and of the subject should be the writer, whose benefit is recognised and situated in opposition to devalued ordinary language: 'What we learn from reading a truly gifted writer is – to take liberties. The "given" language is anonymous, neutral; he has made it unique, decisive.'[78] A subtle mix of pertinence and obfuscation, where the *wanted* is not in the least bit difficult, as opposed to the given and non-intentional.

Valéry, after Baudelaire, had linked poetry to criticism – the faculty of being one's own critic and of recognising excellence: 'every true poet is necessarily a first-rate critic'.[79] The relation between theory and criticism is not clear, but both draw on life. The refusal of the subject oriented Valéry's poetics towards 'making', which mimicked the etymology of the *word* 'poetry', just as Saint-John Perse mimed the etymology of the *word* 'rhythm'. Valéry is thus one of the *authors* of a formalism quite different from that of the formalists. Russian 'formalism' is merely a polemical label planted on it by its adversaries, as is frequently the case: realism, impressionism. But the 'formal method' of the Russians was just as much a historical one. Valéry's formalism is an essentialism of poetry. The proof is in his conception of the epic: 'An epic poem is a poem that can be told.'[80] *Epic* equals *long* equals *tale* equals *non-poetry*. It is the *impure*, opposed to poetry, which is *always* pure. In 1926, in *Rhumbs*, literature: 'A poem that goes on and on is one that can be

---

78. Valéry, 'Notebook B 1910', in *Analects*, p. 131.
79. Valéry, 'Poetry and Abstract Thought', in *The Art of Poetry*, p. 76.
80. Valéry, 'A Poet's Notebook', in *The Art of Poetry*, p. 183.

"summarised". But a true poem is something that cannot be summarised. You can't abridge a memory.'[81] A strategy of its time, against literary history, led to an extreme, subtracting poetry from history, and hence from its historicity: 'Everything history can observe is insignificant.'[82] This is to posit that history and poetry are heterogeneous. Like the man *and* the work. But whilst Proust's *Contre Sainte-Beuve* is, in its theoretical intuitions, constantly a historicisation of writing, Valéry's formula becomes ahistorical, and as a result atheoretical. For, as much as history and writing are different effects of the same material, namely living subjects and non-subjects, so much is it impossible to emit a proposition on poetry, on discourse, on rhythm, which is not marked by its historicity.

8. Discourse, not *Langue*

At stake in the theory of rhythm is: the primacy of discourse, or the primacy of *langue*. Putting discourse first allows the interaction of *langue* and discourse, which putting *langue* first does not allow. Rhythm as the sense of the subject is a historicisation of rhythm, which implies the primacy of discourse. Rhythm as form presupposes the dualism of the sign, the primacy of *langue* and its consequence: the indefinite deferral of the constitution of individuals into subjects. The negation of a reciprocity between the theory of rhythm and the political can no longer fail to appear as a denial. And a censure. All the more so given that they are reinforced by the censure that is metrics. Paradoxical censure of rhythm, as well as censure of the subject. Not stepping back either in the face of the other forms of censure. As there is a solidarity of instrumentalisms, so is there a solidarity of censures.

The power relation is unequal. The theory of the sign and structuralism assure the primacy of *langue*. The theory of discourse begins. But, epistemologically, the theory of the sign and of *langue* appears to be a finite/finished [*finie*] theory. Even the infinity of variants does not seem to have to renew it. Unity–totality, it can spread, but it cannot develop. It is already steady and at its peak. Its force is political, and pragmatic. But its creativity is undermined. Inversely, the theory of discourse is only starting, not only because its concepts are recent, its epistemological terrain not yet assured and some still search for it in the precincts of Marxism or generative linguistics, where what they come away with is only ever makeshift, but also because the theory of subjects, of discourses, of poetics and of the political can never be

---

81. Valéry, 'Rhumbs', in *Analects*, p. 213. [Translator's note: the last sentence, 'You can't abridge a memory,' is a very problematic rendering of the original, 'On ne résume pas une mélodie,' which is rather 'One cannot summarise a melody.']
82. Valéry, 'Concerning *Adonis*', in *The Art of Poetry*, p. 19.

finished. From its stadium and from its status, it has both force and weakness. The weakness of its divisions mimics the theory of the multiple as the state of democracy, and what is at stake for it is linked to the stakes of democracy, just as it is at stake in democracy.

Langue is reinforced by an economic metaphor, which had currency ten years ago, devalued since, even if it still circulates. Value in language, confused with sense, was assimilated, under the pretext of materialism, with the 'exchange value of commodities'.[83] The term *work* as metaphor: 'sense is simply a product of the work of real signs' (ibid., p. 130). Between money and language, there was an 'isomorphism' (ibid., p. 199). Language [*la langue*] was a 'game' (ibid., p. 117). Hjelmslev was seen as the continuation of Saussure. And in practice Saussure was represented through Hjelmslev as an 'algebrising theory of *langue*' (ibid., p. 119). Valéry had got there first, in his first lesson on poetics at the Collège de France, in 1937.[84] It is not worth dwelling on the inanity of this analogy.[85] It nevertheless remains revealing for the primacy of *langue*.

Another metaphoric lineage, combining Heidegger and psychoanalysis, has produced entities such as the knowledge *of* language, the work *of* language: it is language which works, which knows. To the denial of metalanguage is added that of the subject. Erasure of the subject of enunciation: Heidegger's etymology replaces discourse in a poem by Trakl, its significance, through an unveiling of Old High German and Indo-'Germanic' roots. The poem is no longer anything but a palimpsest where the inscription of the one who wrote it gives way to the poem of language. Erasure of the subject of reading: the manufacturer of intertextuality, who signs, yet declares themselves absent from their product. It's that, as for Valéry, the apparent absence of the subject is its supreme magnification: it is identified directly with language. Whose greatest knowledge is the – etymological – dictionary.

Another primacy of *langue* is that of German hermeneutics. Phenomenology there brings dialogue into *langage* itself: 'language has its true being only in dialogue, in *coming to an understanding*',[86] and 'language is by nature the language of conversation' (ibid., p. 463). Humboldt, invoked by way of Heidegger, secondarises discourse: 'in language the world itself presents itself' (ibid., p. 466), and 'language is a medium where I and world meet' (ibid., p. 490). Strange fusion, which implies a continuous of words and things, and returns to take them as consciousness, since all the work of

---

83. J. J. Goux, *Freud, Marx, économie et symbolique* (Paris: Seuil, 1973), p. 127.
84. Paul Valéry, *Œuvres*, I (Paris: Bibliothèque de la Pléiade, 1957), pp. 1343–7.
85. I refer my reader to the chapter on Marx in *Le Signe et le poème*.
86. Hans-Georg Gadamer, *Truth and Method* (London: Sheed and Ward, 1989), p. 462.

language is placed within 'the one who understands' (ibid., p. 506, trans. modified), the interpreter – 'understanding and interpretation are ultimately the same thing' (ibid., p. 406). It's an illusionism of the mode of signifying, thus of signifiers, which consigns a non-linguistic status to language – takes away from it its historicity. Contemporary hermeneutics continues the theological philology of Schleiermacher. Claims it for its own.

There is an accumulation of concentrations on language, the 'weight of language',[87] through the vogue for wordplay, among psychoanalysts and those associated with them, as a substitute for epistemology. Wordplay constitutes a direct view, supposedly without intermediary subjects, and hence *without intermediary language*, on the *truth* of language. Or of any subject or object. This wordplay is a perfect imitation of all psychoanalytic knowledge about puns, slips, denial, etc. Generalised, programmed – it treats language as a subject, which tells the truth even when it lies: since all it ever does is deny, it offers up information about the truth it hides. The desire for truth being great, wordplay has no limits. As this discourse is irrefutable, but only proceeds by affirming itself, all it demonstrates is its own desire. This is the anagrammatic dissemination that gets taught to eleven-year-olds, replacing 'expressivity' with 'specific relation to language'.[88] This is the rationality, with few scruples for philology, which attributes to Yiddish the revealing particularity of presenting in denying, so much so that in this language one need not deny a negation in order to affirm.[89] Language is this super-subject only

---

87. Title of an article in the journal *TXT*, 11.
88. Bernadette Gromer, 'De l'enseignement de la poésie, ou: sur la rime', *Pratiques*, 21, *Proésies* (September 1978), p. 70.
89. Liliane Ickowicz-Zolty, 'D'une langue en plus', in *Lettres de l'École*, Bulletin intérieur de l'École Freudienne de Paris (June 1979), 25:II, *La Transmission*, pp. 49–54. Starting from the Jewish story of two travellers on a train, where one, having said to the other where he was going, is accused of lying because he said the truth, the author notes: 'This history is indeed a story supported by the Yiddish language, because Yiddish knows that the truth gives itself away *despite* what is uttered and that it is all the more evident when it announces itself by a lie or a negation' (p. 51). To arrive at this conclusion, the author identifies two – invariant – homonyms, and homographs, as if they were one word, the preposition *to* (*kein*) in 'Ikh four *kein* Warsche' (I am going to Warsaw) – from *gen* (Middle High German *gein*), 'towards', from *gegen* – and the negation, sometimes *kein* (generally double *kein-nicht*), something *night*, thus 'I am going to go'. (Whereas 'I am not going to Warsaw' would be said 'Ikh four *nicht kein* Warsche'). The language is thus itself a 'complicity in the lie'. The analyst always obtains the answer they want, since they take every yes to mean no, and every no to mean yes, as suits them. Here forcing of the discourse lies in taking the language as a stock of *words*, where a homonym is a synonym; where the grammatical function, the semantic value in the discourse, are cancelled, secondary, abandoned to sense, which is to say to the lie.

because the analyst is there to interpret. The analyst is the master of language, and language has the voice of its master. Absent as apparent subject, it is the prosopopeia of truth, God.

After the master-analyst there is the master-poet, after the knowledge of language, there is poetry as the memory of language. Language remembers itself. Jacques Roubaud, amongst others, starts from the proposition 'poetry is the memory of language', to make a montage of ancient texts.[90] The 'love of language' unifies language and poetry through the '*mezura*': rhyme and verse line interlace the 'song to language' (ibid., p. 114) 'like language/tongue is interlaced with language/tongue in the kiss', which translates Bernart Marti. Memory, love, end up making the *verse line* into rhythm. Rhythm is 'signature of verse' (ibid., p. 119). In fact, it is conflated with 'the tradition, the population of metrical examples' (ibid., p. 120). It finds itself back – in a manner wholly without paradox – with dualism. In two ways, in language and in metrics: 'one of the paradoxes of metre (which is perhaps, more generally, that of verse) is to affirm the *separate* existence of a form and a sense (ibid., p. 121), to which Roubaud adds a negation of the arbitrary which makes even more explicit, as though it were needed, what is at issue: 'to be thus a place marked by such a distinction which is besides hardly sustainable, to assure their non-arbitrary relation of reciprocal illumination . . .'. Metre represents the past, which is why it is said 'the melancholy game of metre' (ibid., p. 124). Love, memory make metre into a desire, the desire to unite with language, the desire to become equal to language (language which seems in this regard identified with a constitutive part of literature, unless it is literature itself),[91] the desire to be duration, tradition. The arithmetic of the desire that pushes the metrician, which brings them to pass through thousands of lines of verse, an entire history, which they know, make use of, in order to glorify language and its dualism. It is that metricians too find their pleasure here, because in algebrising stanzas, forms, they give the same status, the same lasting quality, as poetry, with which it is already identified, as they do to language, supposedly conceived algebraically. And through these successive identifications, metricians can love themselves.

Yet rhythm is the whole of discourse, and of all discourse, just like sense. And can only be discourse. It is a function of the smallest unit (consonantal, vocalic, syllabic, lexical) and of the greatest unity, the variable units

---

90. Jacques Roubaud, 'Le Silence de la mathématique jusqu'au fond de la langue, poésie', *Po&sie*, 10/3 (1979), p. 110.
91. Which is what assumes the *perfection* of a language, which is to say the classical notion which founds discourse in *langue*. To which Littré bears witness, in the entry *langue* (3), where it cites Voltaire.

of discourse which include that of the sentence. The primacy of rhythm, unmoored from metrics, goes back to the empirical primacy of discourse over *langue*. Georges Lote, whilst only making a study of reading aloud, reached a conclusion which overflowed his confusion between diction and verse, placing verse in discourse, not in language: '*in contemporary declaiming of verse there is no "verse" stress, but only a "sentence" stress*'.[92] 'Rhythmic combinations' (ibid., p. 261) are combinations of the sentence, and thus of discourse, as much as, in verse, metrical combinations. Passing from a discussion of a prospectus to a phrase from Bossuet, Lote wrote: 'it is thus the majesty and slowness of the discourse which determine the number and importance of resting points that are exacted by the voice' (ibid., p. 106). Poetry, essentially defined by rhythm – 'poetry only exists by virtue of the eventualities of rhythm that it represents' (ibid., p. 106) – is seen in a historicity of discourse. Lote says of Romantic verse: 'it has shown that the sentence stress reigned on its own' (ibid., p. 112).

Whilst the conception of language fixed on *langue* leads, altogether, to represent its functioning in words, in etymology, in a ludic drift [*dérive*], whilst linguists drift endlessly towards the little phrase, between two agrammaticalities, the analysis of discourse is shared between a lexicological practice and a theory which tried in vain to combine Marxism and generative grammar. Yet, the internal logic of discourse is that of Saussure, who replaced the 'traditional subdivisions' (syntax, lexis, morphology) with the double orientation of the syntagmatic and the paradigm. It is, in this sense, a primacy of the grammatical and of the system, already seen by Humboldt. This primacy inscribes in the language itself a relation between *langue* and discourse which leads to the question of the *character* of languages: is there a necessary relation between what must and can be said, written, in and through one language specifically, as opposed to other languages?

The primacy of rhythm poses this question, and indeed implies it, because it is first of all a temporality, an unequal treatment of space and time. Where rhythm, contrary to appearances, dissociates itself from metrics: because metrics *spatialises* language. This inequality is found in the very system of languages. Language is not Kantian. Édouard Pichon showed that time, in language, is not symmetrical with space: 'Time is the most intimate thing in our existence; the permanence of the I, the variance of time, this is the essential dyad which defines our existential continuity. Space by contrast appears as an empirical construction of our spirit.'[93] An unexpected com-

---

92. Georges Lote, *Études sur le vers français: l'alexandrin d'après la phonétique expérimentale*, vols 1 and 2 (Geneva: Slatkine, 1975 [1919]), p. 243.
93. Édouard Pichon, 'Temps et idiome, la voie linguistique d'exploration du problème psy-

mentary on [Apollinaire's] *Pont Mirabeau*. Regarding French: 'in no domain of the grammar of this idiom does space play an important role [. . .] in no domain of the language does space possess any sub-system specific to it' (ibid., p. 220). Faced with this psychological research, the difficulty lies in the verification of the relations between psychology, language, culture that were proposed, more prudently than their detractors would admit, by Sapir and Whorf. Pichon started from the principle that 'there is no linguistic opposition without psychological meaning, no grammatical entity which does not suppose a deep mental directive' (ibid., p. 228). The question centres around this *depth*. But being affronted [*les affrontements*] cannot not constitute a strategy. As is illustrated by the controversy provoked by Benveniste over Aristotle's categories and the Greek language.[94]

Pichon's argumentation associates historical philology with the notion of system: 'It seems, so far as one can judge from the studies thus far completed, that idioms, in the course of their development, eliminate from their grammatical systems spatial notions whereas they implant temporal notions with ever greater depth' (ibid., p. 229). Which he then demonstrates through the evolution of the declension, as Meillet analysed it: 'he has ultimately shown that the cases which are first to disappear in the cultural refining of languages were those cases expressing only spatial relations, such as the ablative, the instrumental, the locative, whilst the cases expressing also or exclusively those abstract relations called "grammatical", such as the genitive, the dative, the accusative, survived better. Ancient Greek, or contemporary High German, are the two most brilliant examples of this evolution' (ibid., pp. 229–30). Which is not a *progress* of languages, as Pichon seems to adhere to: 'the idiom of a cultured people undergoes self-improvement' (ibid., p. 233). It is not a question of languages being *perfected*. Despite Pichon's prudence, this question remains to be taken up by a historical anthropology of language, without direct psychologisation. Which is what the primacy of discourse, of discourses, can allow – that is, the primacy of language as the totality and possibility of discourse. It is not for us to 'illuminate the nature of our deepest psychological conceptions', as Pichon wrote, nor to 'prepare the path for the evolution of our conscious culture' (p. 233), with his naive opposition of the

chologique du temps', in *Recherches philosophiques*, V, 1935–6, (Paris: Boivin), pp. 196–233, pp. 199–200.

94. [Translator's note: This concerns Émile Benveniste, 'Catégories de pensée et catégories de langue', *Les Études philosophiques*, 13/4 (1958), pp. 419–29, repris dans *Problèmes de linguistique générale* (Paris: Gallimard, 1966), pp. 63–74, and the response of Jacques Derrida, 'Le Supplément de copule: la philosophie devant la linguistique', *Langages*, 6/24 (1971), pp. 14–39.]

conscious and the unconscious, which seems to establish between the two a progressive linearity, but to work at the historicity of the language–discourse relation, because this historicity is the material of our sense. It is not indifferent to the relation between sense, subject, rhythm, that language should be more organisation, rhythm of time than rhythm of space.

Value in a system of discourse, which places signifying everywhere in discourse, even into the blanks, calls into question the notion of syntax. To say *syntax* is already to enter into traditional theory, into the sign, with its consequences. The critique of rhythm is a critique of syntax. Trubetzkoy wrote to Jakobson: 'syntax terrifies me'.[95]

The syntagmatic and paradigmatic study of rhythm stands against structuralism. It restarts from where the formalists left off. These latter, in studying the relations between verse and syntax, worked, from within traditional theory, towards a critical theory. Critical of signification in verse. Critical also of syntax: 'deformed', becoming 'formative' of verse. The sentence itself, seen as 'rhythmico-syntactic event' and 'not simply phraseological, but also phonetic'.[96] What Eichenbaum called the *melodics* of verse was not sonority but the system of symmetries, repetitions, '*processes of melodisation*' (ibid., p. 333) and the 'combination of determinate figures of intonation, realised in syntax'. An analysis which tended towards syncretising different levels.

Which syntax for each poetics, which poetics for each syntax: it's the internal solidarity of the concepts proper to each which decides. For the critique of rhythm, it is notable that Benveniste escapes the separation of theories of grammar – which is dual because the sign is dual – between psychological grammars (like that of Gustave Guillaume) which move from sense to use, and formal grammars (distributional, transformational) which start from use. Both fall under the jurisdiction of the utterance, of the sentence, which they do not overcome. Grammars of *langue*. Whereas Benveniste studied the system of the verb, for example, according to its position in enunciation. Even morphology is thus conceived according to discourse, language as discourse.

A text as system imposes the strategy of discourses upon grammar: a grammar to do what? A system transforms linguistic values into values of its discourse. Thus the order-sense of personal pronouns in Éluard's *La Vie immédiate*.[97] Which is what Proust, in his own way, without technical vocabulary but with the pertinence of one who has honed their craft, indicated in

---

95. R. Jakobson, M. Halle and N. Chomsky, *Hypothèses* (Paris: Seghers-Laffont, 1973), p. 43.
96. Boris Eichenbaum, *O poezii* (Poetry) (Leningrad: Sovetskii pisatel', 1969 [1921]), p. 329.
97. Analysed in *Pour la poétique III: Une Parole écriture* (Paris: Gallimard, Le Chemin, 1973), pp. 179–274.

his letter to Thibaudet on Flaubert's style.[98] Which is not to transform grammar into stylistics, but to take it as a syntagmatics–paradigmatics that varies from discourse to discourse. And not only as the *realisation* of 'grammatical concepts', which is to say part of discourse, as Jakobson demonstrated in 'Poetry of Grammar and Grammar of Poetry'.[99]

The mentalism of Gustave Guillaume, which aims at a beyond of language, is a characteristic example of a theory of grammar that is incompatible with poetics in a historical anthropology of language. Close to phenomenology, his linguistics of position posits, as does generative grammar, a 'deep inside',[100] a 'foundation of thought' (ibid., p. 146) which is opposed to the 'visibility of direct observation' (ibid., p. 26). It places the system of language in a virtual, transcendent 'design' (ibid., p. 239). It makes discourse the traditional second – 'discourse, which comes afterwards' (ibid., p. 147). To the duality depth–surface corresponds the Aristotelean couple of 'name in force' versus 'name in effect' (ibid., p. 145). The vice of this reasoning is in the projection into an anteriority of that which is *induced* from discourse: 'Truth – masked by a typical error that consists in defining a form on the basis of its employment in discourse and not, which should always be the case, in referring oneself to operations of thinking which presided at its formation in language –' (ibid., p. 175). The very history of grammatical systems becomes, like the notion of functioning, a 'metaphysics of language' (ibid., p. 171).[101] Virtualising history, this linguistics is homologous with the dualist anthropology of 'languages which have remained primitive' (ibid., p. 26). The article is 'ignored by evolved languages' (ibid., p. 154). The 'degree of evolution' (ibid., p. 173) of languages confuses language and culture, and includes a purely metaphysical progress, a 'hominising function' (ibid., p. 22). Guillaume and his disciples see in language a 'natural history of the human spirit' (ibid., p. 21).

The discourse on language tends towards a truth-myth to the extent that, like generative linguistics, it takes itself to be the *direct* rendering of a nature, and not an interpretation: 'In the science of language we are meant not to theorise language, but to articulate the theory, very close to a philosophy,

---

98. M. Proust, 'À propos du "style" de Flaubert', *Contre Saint-Beuve* (Paris: Gallimard, Éditions de la Pléiade, 1971), p. 586.
99. Of which a complete Russian version is found in the collection *Poetics, Poetyka, Poetika* (Warsaw: Panstwowe Wydawnictwo Naukowe, 1961), and an abridged English version in *Lingua*, 21 (1968), pp. 597–609.
100. Gustave Guillaume, *Langage et science du langage* (Paris: Nizet, 1973), p. 221.
101. Guillaume belongs to those who, as Tesnière observed, 'starting from phenomena established by introspection, aspire to reach conclusions of a historical character'. Lucien Tesnière, *Éléments de syntaxe structurale* (Paris: Klincksieck, 1976), p. 38.

which it never ceases to be in its procession of structural and substructural states' (ibid., p. 27). The science and theory that are here identified *sign* the metaphysical status of discourse, in the human sciences, from Guillaume to Althusser. The most naive anteriority of thought to language is expressed naturally in the metaphor of habit, which copies exactly the spiritualist relation of body and soul: 'the mentalism of language is covered over by a physism' (ibid., p. 32). Signs would be posterior to the system!

Moreover, one finds in the psycho-mechanics of language all the attributes of metaphysics: the relation to the origin, to the cosmic. The idea that a system has a 'centre' (ibid., p. 236) with periphery and concentric circles. Finalism (ibid., p. 176) is only one aspect, inverted like the face of a card [*figure de carte*], of its geneticism: 'to study the forms in their genetic phase, anterior to their actualization in speech'.[102] Designed to be 'realising', which is 'abstractly systematic' (ibid., p. 2). To understand 'the architecture of language' takes place not through 'the social relation of man to man' but through the 'relation, which is not social, of universe to man' (*Langage et science du langage*, p. 44). This relation posits, desires an *order* of language homologous to that of the cosmos: 'How much more reasonable it would be to admit that in the mentalism of language (suspended towards a physics which it is not) there reigns an inherent order' (ibid., p. 283, n. 18).

For Guillaume as for Chomsky, but less developed, a general grammar is concerned with 'the frontier which separates human from animal' (ibid., p. 229), a strategy which orients the epistemology of language towards natural and not historical sciences. Strange descendance of Saussure, who, each time a descendant decrees themselves a disciple (here, for example, p. 221), each time (Hjelmslev, Guillaume, the structuralists) Saussure is oriented into a counterstrategy. Compared to Einstein by his disciples as Chomsky is by his.[103] Guillaume produced a school as one founds a religious sect. He has nothing to say about poetry, rhythm, and it is through this opening that all of discourse, history, enters. One cannot separate a grammar from its metagrammar.

To analyse any linguistic fact supposes a theory of language, and thus a theory of grammar. This is why a critique of rhythm is confronted with grammars, with the grammar that it implies, as with those which in turn imply the critique. We have the linguistics that fits what we want to do. But also every linguistics, like every language, is truly distinguished only by what it *obliges* us

---

102. Gustave Guillaume, *Temps et verbe*, followed by *L'Architectonique du temps dans les langues classiques* (Paris: Champion, 1970), p. 134.
103. See Guillaume, *Temps et verbe*, intro. by Roch Valin, p. xvii; Justin Leiber, *Noam Chomsky: A Philosophic Overview* (New York: St Martin's Press, 1975), pp. 18, 19.

to do, and what it *prevents* us from doing. Which it cannot itself see. It is for this reason that poetics is a critique of the sciences of language. For poetics, and through poetics, for a historical anthropology of language.

Against the generative mode, it seems to me – on the condition that we take it from the perspective of the critique of structuralism already indicated – that the only grammar with which poetics, the hold of rhythm in discourse as signifiance, can have any relation, is functional and distributional structural grammar. Its theory takes place in the empirical, which saves it from metaphysical dogmatisms. The analysis of discourses critiques the 'parts of discourse'. This is why Tesnière resists. His critique of the notion of the word – the word 'has no syntactical reality'[104] – attaches itself to what Humboldt called *inner form*. It reacts against a phonetic, morphological grammar, by positing 'the autonomy of syntax' (ibid., p. 34), but without falling into the generative scission between syntax and semantics: 'the structural expresses the semantic' (ibid., p. 42). The generativists are rediscovering him. They tend to see in him a predecessor who confirms them. They forget that his structural syntax is entirely a refutation of the general grammar 'which runs from Aristotle to Port-Royal' (ibid., p. 103). His notion of translation is inseparably functional and historical, like all of his analyses, of aspect, of the infinitive. In the tradition of Saussure and Benveniste, to whom he often has recourse, he has not separated philology from linguistics. Nowhere does he imply a deep structure and a surface structure. Occasionally, his metagrammar dates him: he remains in thrall to the notion of pre-logical mentality (ibid., p. 663), speaks of 'primitive languages' (ibid., p. 633); compares the development of languages, from parataxis to subordination, to the 'individual development of the human being' (ibid., p. 315), of the child – a comparison Humboldt recoiled from. From his anthropology there flowed a theory of translation–adaptation (ibid., p. 315). But his grammar, which tended to surpass the sentence, is a systematics which is constructed within the historicity of discourses.

Discourse is what is at stake in every grammar. Each grammatical strategy is an aspect of the conflict between *langue* and discourse, the sign and the poem, metaphysics and historicity. Poetics puts all grammatical theories to the test, like the link between metrics, grammar and rhythm. What poetics has come out of the linguistics of Guillaume? The poetics that has come out of Hjelmslev has not got anywhere. As for generative poetics and metrics, which I analyse later on, what they base themselves on prepares their collapse.

Everything happens as if rhythm – disposition, organisation of signifiance

---

104. Tesnières, *Éléments de syntaxe structurale*, p. 48.

– was an inner form of sense, as grammar is the inner form of languages. But it is only in a discourse-system that rhythm can be this system. This is why it is so important to separate rhythm in language from rhythm outside language, to demonstrate that its specificity in language only exists in discourse. What takes place elsewhere belongs to different systems. To confuse them would be to participate in the traditional strategy.

3

Metrics
Pure Metrics or Discourse Metrics

(in *Critique du rythme*, Lagrasse: Verdier, 1982, pp. 521–62)

Translated by John E. Joseph

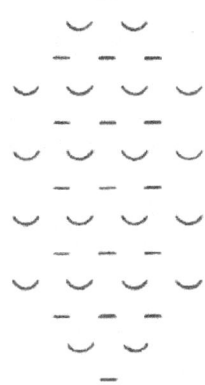

'Fisches Nachtgesang : das tiefste deutsche Gedicht'.
CHRISTIAN MORGENSTERN, *Das aufgeklärte Mondschaf*, Wiesbaden, Insel-Verlag, 1955, p. 45.

Rhythm is too important in language to be left to metrics. Metrics measures times that are no one's, because they aren't the time of meaning, the time of subjects. Only on this condition is it pure measure. Which everything in it declares. Adorno said: 'Any order which is self-proclaimed is only a disguise for chaos.'[1]

The paradox of metrics is that it is constituted in relation to a language

---

1. Theodore W. Adorno, *Philosophy of Modern Music*, trans. by Anne G. Mitchell and Wesley V. Blomster (New York and London: Continuum, 2004), p. xii.

(*langue*) but by sticking a non-linguistic order on to language (*langage*). Yet a discourse metrics is beginning to appear. It seems to me that only a discourse metrics can renew metrics.

Metrics needs to be distinguished from versification, in their relation to poetics. It isn't their object, but their methods and principles that distinguish them. Versification is descriptive, historical or normative. Metrics, covering the same domain, seems to designate a scientific descriptive–theoretical approach. Being deductive, it falls back into the normative, in a legalistic form. Metrics and versification both, like grammar, rhetoric, doubly denote an activity of language and the description of this activity. But versification is empirical, pragmatic. It describes a know-how. It registers the particularities of an observance of metrics: the versification of Baïf. Identical when versification asks, 'What is measured in verse?',[2] metrics and versification leave the technical out of meaning. The ambition of metrics, to be a science, changes nothing. Wherefore neither the one nor the other could pertain to poetics.

The procedures of metrics, its fundamental notions, are here the object of the critique of rhythm, so as to bring the technical back to the modes of signifying.

Following a strategy of historicity. The same formulation can take on quite different values depending on the project that orients it. As illustrated by this proposition of Deleuze and Guattari: 'It is well known that rhythm is not measure or cadence, even irregular measure or cadence [. . .]. Measure is dogmatic, but rhythm is critical.'[3] No resemblance could be more divergent. Yet the same combat, apparently, against the sign, and its power. But a combat situated in ethology, oriented toward the biological. It has to do with bird song. If rhythm is related to an 'autodevelopment, in other words, a style' (ibid., p. 319 [393]), it's toward an expressivity, and chaos, 'rhythm-chaos or the chaosmos' (p. 313 [385]). Toward the cosmic, not toward history. Rhythm having at stake acentrality, anti-arborescence, anti-genealogy, nomadism. What the rhizome represents. But the metaphor is extended toward the clone. The herd. Agitation. Hypostasis of liberation. Rhythm is a paradigm of insurrection, 'rhythm is the Unequal or the Incommensurable' (ibid.). Opposed to metrics as chaos is to order, as the rhizome is to the root, to the power-hierarchy tree. What's at stake with rhythm proves to be an atheory of the State. Anarchising, it reduces language

---

2. W. Theodor Elwert, *Traité de versification française, des origines à nos jours* (Paris: Klincksieck, 1965), §13.
3. Gilles Deleuze and Félix Guattari, *A Thousand Plateaus: Capitalism and Schizophrenia*, trans. by Brian Massumi (London: Athlone Press, 1988), p. 313. Original version: *Capitalisme et schizophrénie*, vol. 2: *Mille plateaux* (Paris: Éditions de Minuit, 1980), p. 385.

to the word 'order', it turns the syntactic marker into a power marker, and significance into a disease (pp. 114 [144], 117 [146]).[4] The subject is opposed to the social as in Marxism: 'There is not even a subject of enunciation' (pp. 79 [101], 135 [163]). Rhythm is directly political, with no linguistic thinking about language: 'language is a political affair before it is an affair for linguistics' (pp. 139–40 [174]). The guarantee of science that takes its place is the fundamental support drawn from Hjelmslev, a contradiction fatal to its revolutionism: it holds on to dualism, to *langue*, contrary to its search for the multiple. The refusal of centrality endangers individuation. And rhythm in language is in solidarity with individuation, each of them being historical. They have everything to lose to chaos. To chaosmic strategy.

* * *

Metrics is meaningless. In the traditional theory of rhythm, systems of versification are conventional norms that organise non-signifying units: feet, syllable count. These schemes affect only a sound substance, not meaning. The metricist works on pure rhythm. This purity is the exchange of rhythm and metre. Here language is only a building material: 'One must therefore never confuse rhythm with its matter, the rhythm frame with the linguistic scheme.'[5] Thus metrics desemanticises, says nothing about meaning, contributes nothing to meaning, because *metre is meaningless*: 'metre is essentially independent of meaning'.[6]

An organisation of discourse wouldn't be an organisation of this discourse's meaning. This dedialectisation creates the formal. The study of forms can be historical, comparative. Seeking its own universals, it necessarily works towards its own formalisation. But in discourse, rhythmic figures result from forms, endings and positions of groups of words within verse. In discourse, each verse has its particular, rhythmic, prosodic configuration. There are no longer two similar verses. Where is metrics? It defines an abstract object, outside history, outside meaning, and this desemantisation is itself a cultural operation which has its historicity. The universality of metrics is its situation.

However, convention has it that metrics should be a part of poetics. A given specialist takes it *a priori* as a relation of form to content, the historicity of which passes through metrics. But having acquitted himself of this general

4. [Translator's note: On rules of grammar being power markers before they are syntactic markers, see also ibid., p. 76 [96].]
5. Paul Verrier, *Le Vers français: formes primitives, développement, diffusion*, vol. 2 (Paris: H. Didier, 1931), p. 21.
6. George R. Stewart, *The Technique of English Verse* (New York: Holt, 1930), cited by René Wellek and Austin Warren, *Theory of Literature* (New York: Harcourt, Brace, 1948), p. 172.

remark, he describes only a history of metrical forms.⁷ In recent works on ancient metrics, the text is no longer reworked in terms of metres, as in the nineteenth century: 'The meter must be deduced from the existing text, not the text emended to fit the supposed meter. Only when we are treading on reasonably sure metrical ground are we justified in emending the text *metri causa*.'⁸ But while affirming the Aristotelian position: 'Rhythm is an essential part of any poetic creation. In Greek poetry rhythm takes the form of regular meters. Metrical studies therefore, aside from their usefulness in text establishment, are of value for their own sake as one part of the total study of Greek poetry' (ibid., p. 1), no relation is made between rhythm–metre and meaning. For reasons that remain tacit, 'There is no attempt to deal with the possible significance of metrical form in relation to content' (ibid., p. 2). This would require a leap that metrics lacks the rationality to make. Its abstention, which seems wise, is only the effect of its position within the theory of the sign. Anything to do with meaning is foreign to it.

Thus metrics recuses itself in order to follow a 'chronological development' (ibid., p. 2). Why, then, continue to present metres as an 'essential part of any poetic creation'? The variety of lyric metres and stanzas, in Sophocles, is analysed formally 'without wishing to imply any relationship between metrical form and content' (ibid., p. 191). But neither variety nor complexity is an end in itself. Yet the metricist has striven to uncover a systematicity in Sophocles. Thus these are merely 'curious facts', neither random nor signifying, such as 'Lyric anapests are lacking in *Ajax* and *Antigone*, while trochaic rhythm does not appear in *Ajax*, The Women of Trachis* and *Philoctetes*' and 'The reizianum is employed in every play but *The Women of Trachis*, the ithyphallic in every play but *Electra*. I view this as one more effort on the part of Sophocles to avoid too much uniformity in his clausulae' (ibid., p. 191). Why precisely there? And is this then a fact that modifies the discourse without having meaning or any effect on meaning? I submit that this is impossible. And if it's true that everything which modifies a discourse modifies its meaning and values, it follows that the metrical principle is untenable from the point of view of the theory of discourse.

Syllables were counted, strong and weak beats placed, for singing. This original parentage among verse, music and dance, which produced metrics, also produced a poetic myth, an origin myth. Metre 'was the sensible link' of poetry's union with 'these brother arts'.⁹ Ever since poetry was separated

---

7. Werner Hoffmann, *Altdeutsche Metrik* (Stuttgart: J. B. Metzler, 1967). Bibliographic and critical guide.
8. H. A. Pohlsander, *Metrical Studies in the Lyrics of Sophocles* (Leiden: Brill, 1964), p. 1.
9. A. W. Schlegel, *Briefe über Poesie, Silbenmaß und Sprache* (1795), in *Sprache und Poetik*, ed. by Erich Lohner (Stuttgart: Schöningh, 1962), p. 148.

from them, 'it has always had to try to bring song and, as it were, dance into discourse' (ibid.). This is the internal necessity of pure metrics. The Romantic conception of language, and of a language system, as poem of humanity, situates metrics – in the myth – as an aesthetics of language: 'Language, the most marvellous creation of man's poetic capacity, the great ever-unfinished poem, as it were, in which human nature represents itself' (ibid., p. 145). This conception is inseparable from the instrumentalism which opposes the dance to the march, the march serving merely to 'lead somewhere', as poetry is opposed to ordinary discourse, which serves merely for 'understanding one another' (ibid., p. 162). Metrics is therefore only an aspect of the metaphysics of the sign and of the origin, which says: 'Language, in its origin, is mimetic – Die Sprache ist in ihrem Ursprung mimisch' (ibid., p. 189).[10]

Corresponding to the historicity of poetic writings, and of discourses, is a historicity of metrics. Pure metrics is the law of an ordered, hierarchised, relatively fixed society. And the 'liberation' of verse ('Verse is free!') is an index of the transformation of a world. The historicity of rhythms is cultural. Pure metrics separates the history of verse from the history of poetry. Yet the metrics of poems too constitutes an 'exteriorized rhythmicity', as Leroi-Gourhan said about rocking movements of the body, 'where the creation of an artificial framework assists the individual to free him or herself from the normal operating cycle', so that 'a trance-like state is maintained', taking on the nature 'of a real escape from the environment of everyday life', with 'a dematerializing value'.[11] Metrics is a hold of the social and cultural on the individual subject. A metrics is also a collective attitude. The alexandrine is a bringing to heel. A singing parade.

This is why subjective writings have been, in the twentieth century, anti-metrical. Pound writes in *Canto* 81: 'to break the pentameter, that was the first heave'. He speaks of those who 'deform thought with iambics' (*Canto* 98). Mayakovsky writes, reacting to Shengely's book *Kak pisat' stat'i, stikhi i raskazy* [How to Write Articles, Verses and Stories], that verses have to be made 'with all one's life and not scratching tongues for iambs and trochees'.[12] His reaction is his historicity: 'But we don't need iambs and trochees. It's been a long time since anyone has written iambs and trochees, Blok's *Twelve*

---

10. In A. W. Schlegel, *Betrachtungen über Metrik* (between 1795 and 1800), in *Sprache und Poetik*, ed. by Erich Lohner (Stuttgart: Schöningh, 1962).
11. André Leroi-Gourhan, *Gesture and Speech*, trans. by Anna Bostock Berger (Cambridge, MA, and London: MIT Press, 1993), p. 287. Original version, *Le Geste et la parole*, vol. 2: *La Mémoire et les rythmes* (Paris: Albin Michel, 1964), p. 104.
12. In V. A. Katanian, *Majakovskij: Literaturnaja khronika* (Moscow: Gosudarstvennoe izdatelstvo khudozhestvennoi literatury, 1956), p. 265 (11 April 1926).

[. . .] are written in free verse. [. . .] I myself know I'm a good poet. But I've never found trochees and iambs necessary, they're foreign to me. They're strangers I have no wish to know. Iambs hold back the forward movement of poetry. The same in other cases with the combination of feet and rhymes' (ibid., p. 266).

The double meaning of metrics, as codified organisation of discourse and as description or study of this ordering, is such that to speak of the one is to speak of the other. The second meaning keeps running after the first, to identify itself with it. That is, metrics runs after its own rules, runs after its own purity. Pure sound 'is characterised by a sine wave pattern'.[13] Pure metre presents a comparable abstraction. As noted, for example, by Fritz Lockemann, in *Der Rhythmus des deutschen Verses*, when he distinguishes three types of rhythms: 'In the poem three rhythmic systems work together, in a variable way: the rhythm of the sentence, the natural rhythm, interior or situational, and the metrical rhythm.'[14] He adds: 'If we consider only the metrical rhythm in a poem, we are limiting ourselves merely to an abstraction,' and further on: 'The language of a poem is not a simple filling nor is the metre an empty frame' (ibid., p. 70).

Metrics spatialises language, by restoring music to it. In the metrical abstraction, syllables are equal, having only a value of coded position. In discourse they aren't equal. There are metrical rules. There are none for rhythm. Metrics measures. Rhythm, which participates in the risks and the unknown of a discourse, isn't measured. It's analysed in terms of discourse, terms that are not just phonic. *Metrics is imaginary*. What the notions of foot, and of isochrony, suffice to show. It's about a musical imaginary, stuck on to language, where the rigorous, numerical appearance creates the façade of fantasy. Thus in the German notation of Andreas Heusler, for the different values of syllables:

⊔	four crotchets (quarter notes)
⊔	three crotchets (quarter notes)
—	a minim (half note)
X	three quavers (eighth notes)
x	a crotchet (quarter note)
ᴗ	a quaver (eighth note)
ᴖ	a semi-quaver (sixteenth note)[15]

---

13. Alfred Tomatis, *L'Oreille et le langage* (Paris: Seuil, 1963), p. 37.
14. Fritz Lockemann, *Der Rhythmus des deutschen Verses* (Munich: Max Hueber, 1960), p. 69.
15. Andreas Heusler, *Deutsche Versgeschichte mit Einschluß des altenglischen Stabreimverses*, 3 vols (Berlin: de Gruyter, 1925, 1927, 1929, repr. 1956), vol. 1, pp. 33–4.

The syllables of discourse don't have, have never had, in any language, even ones in which length is phonological, such numerical relations, which are pertinent only for the sung.[16] Even where convention put short and long in opposition, 'the longs and shorts did not have the strictly fixed duration of crochets relative to minims of our music'.[17] Meillet said: 'There is a long syllable where the speaker feels a long, and a short where he feels a short. This is not about physics, but an action to be performed on hearers.'[18]

Metrical ideality supposes that a pattern must get realised, at least through constants, averages, and that it instils an expectation. However, the search for a metrical theory that consists of the deducible application of rules makes no sense, since no poem realises such an application empirically. The search for a theory that would take account of the non-realisations of the pattern is equally impossible, since it would come down to having a finite code generate the unpredictable infinity of discourse. Metrics doesn't cause the distortions of metrics. A discourse does. The code, as with the language, doesn't create poems. We've seen that there is poetry without metrics. Whatever the classifications into metrical types, all of them make language into an alinguistic, asemantic, adiscursive material.

Metrics occupies a schematised time that is impoverished. Thus, in the French alexandrine, it essentially retains two positions, the sixth, the twelfth. Rhythm has all twelve positions of the alexandrine, in the real time of a discourse, where rhythm is the memory of the text, not of the language, and metrics belongs to the automatisation that, in the poem, threatens the poem.

Simplification is inherent to metrics. Morris Halle, on the abstract plane of metrical models, which he reduced to the alternation WS (W: weak, S: strong), concluded that metrical structures 'are of an extreme simplicity'.[19] He was struck 'by the similarity between metrical patterns and the patterns used

---

16. This notation, despite certain criticisms, has been followed by Werner Hoffmann in *Altdeutsche Metrik* (Stuttgart: Metzler, 1967), pp. 7, 23; it is more or less standard in the German domain. German metrics has four notation systems: Wolfgang Keyser's, x́xxxx́x; Ulrich Pretzel's, xXxXxX, and for the counterstress, $\widetilde{XX}$; the classical convention, ⏑ _ ⏑ _ ⏑ _ ⏑ _ , used by Breuer and others; and Heusler's (see Dieter Breuer, *Deutsche Metrik und Versgeschichte* (Munich: Wilhelm Fink, 1981), pp. 36–8). Breuer seems to be alone, in the German domain, in criticising Heusler. He distinguishes scansion from recitation, and shows that Heusler is doing a 'metrics of recitation' (p. 75ff.), which confuses discourse rhythm with diction, by codifying the scansion of silence (p. 81). A criticism indissociable from a description of verse in its historicity.
17. Louis Nougaret, *Traité de métrique latine classique* (Paris: Klincksieck, 1948), §5, p. 3.
18. Antoine Meillet, *Les Origines indo-européennes des metres grecs* (Paris: Presses Universitaires de France, 1923), p. 9, cited by Nougaret, *Traité de métrique latine classique*, §5.
19. Morris Halle, 'On Metre and Prosody', in *Progress in Linguistics: A Collection of Papers*, ed. by M. Bierwisch and K. E. Heidolph, pp. 64–80 (The Hague: Mouton, 1970), p. 78.

in threading looms or those encountered in certain very rudimentary types of ornament' (ibid.). The simpler the model, the more the 'transformational rules' vary. The models are simple through a reduction of rhythm to metre as a set of positions, through an exclusion of prosody from rhythm, corollary of the elimination of discourse. Halle gets rid of stress, of the 'so-called prosodic features of stress, pitch or length' (ibid.). Revealing here is the role accorded to stress in French. This formalisation has no philology: 'However, it is clearly no accident that in French, *e.g.*, stress plays no role either in the mapping rules or in the rules that determine the phonetic constitution of words' (ibid., p. 79). Forgetting that the caesura is tied to stress in classical verse, as is the final position. As for the 'phonetic constitution of words', too many examples show the historical role of stress, as in *sire/seigneur*.[20] And the semantic role of prosody in pairs of the type *elle attend/elle l'attend*.[21] Not to mention Halle's failure to recognise that French stress is phrasal, not lexical.

Metrics is a metaphysics of poetry. Form, inner, outer, proportion, symmetry, unit, its categories never cease to dream of a musical transposition with no empirical counterpart in discourses. And since discourses are consubstantial with their meanings, with their values, poetry and the critique of rhythm can only overflow metrics. Whence the contradiction that metrics needs to be included in linguistics, as per Lotz,[22] because verse can't be defined by literature. In verse, units of language such as syllables are no longer linguistic units, but units of measure. The ahistoricity of metrics is an adiscursivity. Thus subterfuges intervene. In Hegel's conventionalism, metrics returns to language through a direct psychologisation of metres: 'the hexametre, through its calm swaying, lends itself to the impassive and serene unfolding of epic narratives' or 'the anapest marks the measure of a triumphant and joyous advance'.[23] Norm and deviation keep metrics on the plane of language, up

---

20. [Translator's note: *Sire* and *seigneur* are both words for 'lord', with *sire* deriving from Latin *sènior*, and *seigneur* from Latin *seniòrem*.]
21. [Translator's note: *Elle attend* 'she waits' and *elle l'attend* 'she waits for her/him/it' usually sound the same in spoken French, but when wanting to make clear that the latter is meant, speakers lengthen the [l].]
22. John Lotz, 'Metric Typology', in Thomas A. Sebeok (ed.), *Style in Language* (Cambridge, MA: MIT Press, 1960), pp. 135–49, p. 137.
23. Hegel, *Aesthetics: Poetry*, 8-I. For Greek metrics, each metre has its 'ethos'. The names of the metres tell their origin, their nature. The *iamb* is linked to satire, 'in the legend of Demeter the name of Ἰάμβη (*Iambē*) [. . .] makes the goddess laugh' (Pierre Chantraine, *Dictionnaire étymologique de la langue grecque*). The name of the *trochee* comes from τρέχω (*trekhō*) 'run'. Aristotle (*Rhetoric* 1408b) says that it's too reminiscent of the κόρδαξ (*kordax*), a dance of ancient comedy, linked to the cult of Apollo and Artemis, and considered indecent in Athens (Chantraine). The *anapest*, from παίω (*paiō*) 'to strike repeatedly', implies a step backwards. The *cretic* (_ ᴗ _) comes from 'Cretan songs accompanied by

to and including the automatisation and deautomatisation of the formalists, Shklovsky's theory of the work as 'sum of procedures'. This is a link between metrical desemantisation and the interest in Zaum.

Metrics isolates lines of verse. Grammont's examples in *Le Vers français* are mainly isolated lines. Even the statistics of the Russians, based on hundreds of lines, are based on hundreds of lines each taken in isolation, as a unit of counting. Grammont did what Becq de Fouquières did. Metrics works on examples. Metricists repeat many of the same examples. Leech admits openly that he draws on a dictionary of citations. One of them is found to conclude, Stupidity concludes,[24] that context damages the beauty of verse. Rhetoricians can even get away with extracting no more than two words, an expression, thus completing the isolation begun by metricists. But an isolated line is no longer discourse. It's an example. An extraction oriented toward the language, in the process of being returned to the language. Withdrawn from the subject, and almost from its own meaning. Tomachevsky was opposed to this isolating of verses as examples, but because he was studying 'instrumentation',[25] which can only be studied in discourse. Valéry contributed more than a little to isolating verses, to spreading the belief that a verse is a unit: 'Verse is sequence of syllables limited enough in number for this sequence to be perceived as forming a unit, aimed at a final term,'[26] and 'A line of verse is the *shortest* possible poem' (*Cahiers*, II, p. 1140). Zhirmunsky spoke of 'inner teleology'.[27] Thus were grounds provided for confusing the metrical unit and the discourse level, which is that of the poem.

Although we retain, and cite, and isolate lines of verse, the poem isn't in the line, nor even in the lines. Rather, the line, the lines, are in the poem. T. S. Eliot wrote, concerning the 'music of verse', that it 'is not a line by line

---

dances' (Émile Martin, *Trois documents de musique grecque* (Paris: Klincksieck, 1953), p. 29). The minor and major ionics (⏑ ⏑ _ _ , _ _ ⏑ ⏑) are associated with the ecstatic cults of Dionysus and Cybele, 'whose ritual dances brought about a progressive weakening of the conscious will' (ibid., p. 54). They make the rhythm 'soft, inconsistent and effeminate', according to the Anonymus Ambrosianus (cited ibid.). So too do the names of the *te'amim* speak.

24. [Translator's note: *la Bêtise conclut*: an allusion to a letter in which Flaubert wrote 'la bêtise consiste à vouloir conclure' (stupidity consists of wanting to conclude), G. Flaubert, *Correspondance I*, ed. by J. Bruneau (Paris: Gallimard, 1973), p. 338 (4 September 1850, addressed to Louis Bouilhet).]
25. B. V. Tomashevsky, 'Ritm prozy (po Pikovey dame)', in *O stikhe, statyi* (Leningrad: Priboy, 1929), p. 35.
26. Paul Valéry, *Cahiers*, II (Paris: Gallimard, 1916), p. 1124 (circa 1935).
27. V. M. Zhirmunskij, *Kompozicija liricheskikh stikhotvorenij* (St Petersburg, 1921; Munich: W. Fink, Slavische Propyläen, no. 73, 1970), p. 4.

matter, but a question of the whole poem'.[28] The line as a unit comes undone inside and out. In Arabic–Hebrew terminology, the line is a house, *bayt*, composed in Medieval Hebrew of a door leaf, *delet*, the first 'hemistich', and of a lock, *soger*. In Arabic, these are also two door leaves, *miṣ rā'an*, the first called *sadr*, 'front part, breast', the second, *'ajz*, 'rear part'.[29] But this house is open. It opens in two, inside, and it also opens, in classical Arabic poetry, toward the unit of the poem with a single rhyme and metre.

The line isn't entirely separable from the form of the grouping it's a part of. If metrical lines are something other than the repetition of metrical feet, the line paradoxically only starts to overtake the discourse rhythm with the strophe, where there is strophic poetry, and in any case in a unit that overflows that of the line, precisely in order to organise its rhythms. Rhyme, when it exists, is an element of the strophe, or of the couplet, more than of the line. In *The Composition of Lyric Poems*, Zhirmunsky deals only with the strophe, the figures of repetition extend to the poem. Lockemann remarked that both *strophe* and *verse* etymologically describe a return.[30] Rhythm is a syntagmatics that holds together line, sentence, strophe, the small unit and the large. The strophe was the metrical unit in Old Portuguese poetry.[31] The strophe, not the isolated line, is the metrical unit 'that possesses a complete idiomatic fullness' for Rafael de Balbín[32] – 'The line separated from its strophic context loses – abnormally, like a fish out of water – its communicative vitality; and it is reduced to being an inorganic segment of the phonic chain and of the linguistic sequence' (ibid.). Hence a line is polyrhythmic. Syllabism is a reduction, a scheme, not a rhythm. And a line is the sum of its possible, signifying rhythms.

A metrics that isolates lines is a statics, not a rhythmics. It turns verse into a structure, plus secondary, complementary elements. That's what Tomás Navarro Tomás and Jean Mazaleyrat do. Only the Russian formalists strove for a rhythmics. Metrics is passive, it's received. Rhythm is active, it's an activity of discourse. In the pairing passive/active, their traditional opposition reproduces the pairings *langue*/*parole*, social/individual. Thus do irregularities enter into metrical taxonomy.

For metrics, verse is fixed. Already in 1879 Becq de Fouquières wrote:

28. T. S. Eliot, *The Music of Poetry* (Glasgow: Jackson, Son, 1942), p. 25.
29. In H. Zafrani, *Poésie juive en Occident musulmane* (Paris: Geuthner, 1977), p. 230.
30. Lockemann, *Der Rhythmus des deutschen Verses*, p. 72.
31. Pedro Henriques Ureña, *La poesía castellana de versos fluctuantes*, in *Estudios de versificación Española* (Buenos Aires: Universidad Buenos Aires, Departamento editorial, 1961), p. 43, no. 1 (repr. of *La versificación irregular en la poesía castellana*, second edition, Madrid: Hernando, 1933).
32. Rafael de Balbín, *Sistema de rítmica castellana* (Madrid: Gredos, 1975 [1961]), p. 12.

'Today, verse is definitively fixed.'³³ The constant concern of metricists is to show that verse doesn't change, that nothing in what is new has modified what is old. That was Maurice Souriau's thesis in 1885: 'There is no essential difference between Racine's verse, which can be taken as the model of the alexandrine, and Romantic verse: the latter is simply the end point of an evolution which began in the seventeenth century.'³⁴ This is still the thesis of Mazaleyrat and his fellow participants in the 1966 colloquium on French verse in the twentieth century. Mazaleyrat says of Éluard: 'In its literary manifestations, the surrealist adventure is not an adventure of material forms, by which I mean rhythms, sentence structures or words.'³⁵ Whatever the pertinence of the statement, if any, metricists, by virtue of their positioning, can only see permanences. They are caught between fixity and the eternal return. Privileging the ordinal provides them simultaneously with a taxonomy and with the primacy of form. This is the source of the deep-seated unchangeability of verse found in Jacques Roubaud's *La Vieillesse d'Alexandre*. Souriau explained it when interpreting the profusion of books on verse: 'At a time when a totally new poetic school is searching for poetry outside what we are used to calling verse, a particular pleasure is felt in taking refuge in the serene mansions erected by the doctrine of sages, in finding that, in the Temple of Taste, Racine and Victor Hugo can shake hands like brothers who were too long at odds' (p. VIII). To consider in poetry only verse, and metrics outside discourse, allows and requires the stability of verse, the Romanticism of the classicists as well as the classicism of the Romantics. The fact that neither Éluard nor Yves Bonnefoy revolutionised verse is another matter. They're chosen as examples all the same.

The traditional primacy of metre in the theory of rhythm has brought with it a primacy of equalities, such that sameness dominates, as shown by the *iso-* prefix in *isochrony, isosyllabism*. Primacy of metre treated by Fraisse as natural, self-evident: 'a metrical frame is the precondition for the creation of rhythmic impulses',³⁶ and 'A metrics, a measuring system, is always the basis of all rhythmic realisations' (ibid., p. 136). Here we see the supremacy of regularity arise through the underestimating of stress and prosody, to the benefit of the syllable count: 'rhythm is created mainly through a numerical

---

33. Louis Becq de Fouquières, *Traité général de versification française* (Paris: G. Charpentier, 1879), p. 268.
34. Maurice Souriau, *L'Évolution du vers français au XVIIᵉ siècle* (Paris: Hachette, 1893), p. v, citing Souriau, *De la convention dans la tragédie classique et dans le drame romantique* (Paris: Hachette, 1885), p. 96.
35. Jean Mazaleyrat, 'La Tradition métrique dans la poésie d'Éluard', in *Le Vers français au XXᵉ siècle*, ed. by Monique Parent (Paris: Klincksieck, 1967), pp. 25–42, p. 27.
36. Paul Fraisse, *Psychologie du rythme* (Paris: Presses Universitaires de France, 1974), p. 128.

decoupage of phonemes of unequal length with an ordered succession of elementary groups of definite quantity. In this succession, the regular combinations with isochronic parts are dominant. The most classic example is the hemistichs of the alexandrine.'[37] A no less classic example of the permanence of the isochronist myth: 'In French, syllabism is tied to the principle of isosyllabism, in other words to equality, or more precisely to the non-differentiation of syllable lengths.'[38] Fraisse varied metrics by inserting the pause time of an individual phonic realisation, taken for the rhythm of the lines – the 'silence-pauses of Sarah Bernhardt declaiming these lines of *Phèdre* (length in hundredths of seconds):

Oui, prince $_{58}$ je languis, je brûle pour Thésée $_{69}$
Je l'aime $_{56}$ non point tel que l'ont vu les enfers $_{45}$[39]

This domination of sameness is the grid which makes it appear to Fraisse that there are 'four anapests' in this line of Malherbe:

Et les fruits| passeront| la promes| se des fleurs

[And the fruits will surpass the promise of the flowers] where the reality of word endings and phrase endings, prosodic relations (*passeront – promesse, les fruits – des fleurs*) and figures (*abc/acb, abc/bac*) as well as the conflict between the caesura (6/6) and the sentence, partition between noun phrase and verb phrase (3/9), instead of the pseudo-anapestic minimal metrical scansion, create the following rhythmic tension:

Et les fruits passeront la promesse des fleurs

which blurs the regularities through the effects of discourse, or rather inserts them in a real global effect.

Metrics is constituted in relation to a language, to the units of the language, but above the language. But the language acts on the metrics. A language isn't a passive material that lets itself be metrified or rhythmed. That is, in effect, to count, because as soon as there is a metrics, we count. Metres, syllables, stresses. The language imposes a rhythmic material on the verse, but not only that. It also imposes habits that have been identified with metrical

---

37. Paul Fraisse, *Les Structures rythmiques: étude psychologique* (Louvain: Publications Universitaires de Louvain, 1956), p. 111.
38. Fraisse, *Psychologie du rythme*, p. 149.
39. Ibid., p. 156. [Yes, Prince $_{58}$ I languish, I burn for Theseus $_{69}$ / I love him $_{56}$ not as hell has seen him $_{45}$]

traditions. The rhythmics of the language penetrates its metrics without the metricist knowing it.

Yet the histories of metrics and of language are often heterogeneous. The evolution of Russian verse is described by Brik as the development from a syllabic metrics foreign to the language towards the accentuation of spoken language, with metrical and linguistic stress ultimately coinciding in syllabotonic versification. In such a way that the notion of foot no longer makes sense. La Grasserie had noted that 'Turkish, Hindustani, Persian have adopted Arabic metrics, and no longer have a metrics of their own,'[40] contorting the nature of their language, whilst 'the ancient rhythms that were driven out were often preserved in popular rhythmics' (ibid., p. 32). Some languages have a double metrics, such as Czech, in which, says La Grasserie, an accentual metrics coexists with a quantitative metrics (ibid., p. 56). In Hungarian, 'accentual verse is mainly popular, quantitative verse is literary' (ibid., p. 56). Unbegaun wrote: 'To sum up then, in most European languages, modern versification is imported.'[41]

But in return, the language has an effect on the metrics. In German, the secondary stress in long words leads to a rhythmic realisation of the metrical scheme, more so than in Russian.[42] A. W. Schlegel already thought that in German 'the iamb should be the principal foot by far, and by much farther than in Greek'.[43] In English, 'deviations gradually wear away the metre, and syntactical stress tends to replace metrical stress. In consequence, English verse seems to drift steadily towards a syllabism of the French type by producing a line composed of accentual groups dominated by semantic stress. Even more than in German, differences in intensity, in quantity and also in the pitch of the stressed vowels play a part in the rhythmic pattern of English verse. Therefore, in English, much more than in Russian, the recitation of a poem is dependent on individual interpretation.'[44] The discourse rhythm creates the metre, in a process that depends on the relation between metre and linguistic rhythm. Hence, in Russian, 'Unlike binary verse, the rhythmic pattern in ternary verse is much closer to the metrical scheme. As a general rule, the two notions are even identical, which is not hard to understand. The strong syllables, in these lines, are separated by two weak syllables and the omission of a stress would result in a sequence of five unstressed syllables, a hiatus which the rhythm would hardly tolerate' (ibid., p. 46). The metre and

---

40. Raoul de la Grasserie, *Analyses métriques et rythmiques* (Paris: Maisonneuve, 1893), p. 31.
41. B. O. Unbegaun, *Russian Versification* (Oxford: Clarendon Press, 1956), p. xii.
42. See ibid., pp. 63–4.
43. Schlegel, *Sprache und Poetik*, p. 208.
44. Unbegaun, *russian versification*, p. 44.

the linguistic rhythm arrange each other. Metrical history is cultural. Ternary metres still count for only 1.5 per cent in Pushkin. Their proportion increases in the nineteenth century until they account for half the verses in Bryusov.[45]

Word stress creates metrics in which linguistic rhythm can be realised in the ordering of a metre. There are iambs, etc., in Italian. Twelve types of Italian hendecasyllables can be counted.[46] The phonology of the language regulates the mode of final demarcation of the verse. Thus Italian verse has three possible endings, on *parole piane* (like *vita*), with penultimate stress; on *parole tronche* (*levó*), and on *parole sdrucciole* (*durabile*), stressed on the antepenult. Linguistic frequency governs the types of verse. In French, both the state of the language and the habits of usage to which it has given rise mean that we count only up to the last stressed syllable. Until the sixteenth century, the counting was done differently. In Italian, a following unstressed syllable is counted. Which means that the terms for lines of verse are misleading, suggesting that the French decasyllable has ten syllables, tending to disguise its relatedness to the Italian hendecasyllable, and similarly with the 'octosyllable' and the *novenario*, the verse of 'nine'. Likewise, in Spanish, the classification of rhymes is based on the rhythmics of the language, 'rima consonante esdrújula (*válido: cálido*)',[47] rare or humorous in Spanish, as we've seen was also the case in English, but not Russian, where it is epic; the 'rima consonante llana o grave (*llanto: santo*)' (ibid., p. 65), the most common; the 'rima consonante aguda' (am*or*: ruise*ñor*)' (ibid., p. 66), distinct from the 'asonancia aguda (lug*ar*: mor*al*)', the assonance of *El Cid*.

The octosyllable is ancient, popular, autochthonous in Spain. Spanish prose is said to tend toward the rhythm of the octosyllable.[48] But is there a rhythm of the octosyllable? Navarro Tomás showed that there are sixty-four varieties of them (cited by Baehr, p. 103). According to Menéndez Pidal, it is the most 'natural (*connatural*) to the language' (p. 111). It's supposed to be the most popular metre because it's supposed to be the most linguistic rhythm.

The descriptions of Spanish verse *de arte mayor* – that is, greater than the octosyllable, *de arte menor* – are a remarkable example of the linguistic and metalinguistic nature of metrics. An ancient tradition has it that verse *de arte mayor* is based on the foot, not on the syllabic number. It is described as composed of two adonic verses (the adonic is a dactyl plus a spondee – five syllables) but the 'spondee' here is usually only two syllables, the first of which

---

45. Ibid., p. 46, taking the figures from Tomashevsky.
46. W. Theodor Elwert, *Italienische Metrik* (Munich: Hueber, 1968), pp. 61–2.
47. Rudolf Baehr, *Manual de versificación española* (Madrid: Gredos, 1973 [German edition 1962]), p. 64.
48. Ibid., p. 111.

is stressed, the second indifferent. Each adonic verse, or hemistich, consists of two accentual feet, and can be five, often six, sometimes four syllables.[49] The hemistichs could have an uncounted initial syllable, and could be treated at the start as 'two independent lines' (p. 105); and thus have between four and seven actual syllables; the second hemistich often the longer (5 + 7). Caesura at five (stress on the fifth), and able to run from eight to thirteen syllables, verse *de arte mayor* got confused with the dodecasyllable and was also said to correspond to the decasyllable 5 + 5 that Bonaventure des Périers called *taratantara* (ibid., p. 59). The relation of the sharp to the grave line or hemistich carries two considerations: the placement of the stress, and the number of syllables, which can go up to two, after the final stress of hemistich or line. This correlated play suffices to explain the variable number of syllables for the same stress positions. Before the fifteenth century and the 'invasion of Italian taste' (ibid., p. 85), in other words of isosyllabism, verse *de arte mayor* is simultaneously accentual, following the rhythmics of the language, and syllabic, following the restitution, which is metalinguistic, of a syllable (an *e* understood as paragogic (added unetymologically), and often etymological) after the stressed final. Stress shifts due to music, hiatus or not, synalepha or not – the result being a latitude in which seven equals eight, twelve equals thirteen. The rhythmic inequalities are equalised metrically.

The Spanish habit of counting a non-existent syllable in naming the verse line, 'a syllable after the last stressed one, even if it is actually missing, as happens in acute lines (*versos agudos*)',[50] illustrates the difficulty of hearing the verse of one's own language, as Henríquez-Ureña himself showed with regard to English specialists of English verse: 'we devote ourselves laboriously to complicating and falsifying our notion of verse'.[51] Not in relation to a metrical reality. The cultural–linguistic grid is the precondition of the historicity of verse, of prose, of their intermediaries, and of metrics.

Metalinguistics can go so far as to obscure linguistics. Hence the notions of prose as asymmetry, of verse as symmetry, intervene in description. The prose sentence: '*Quedamos clavados en el lugar del tope. El toro saltó como pelota, se dio vuelta sobre el lomo*' [We remain stuck in the place of the shock. The bull jumped like a ball, turned on his back][52] is analysed by Rafael de

---

49. Joaquín Balaguer, *Apuntes para una historia prosódica de la métrica castellana* (Madrid: Consejo Superior de Investigaciones Científicas, 1954), p. 119.
50. Pedro Henríquez-Ureña, *Estudios de versificación española* (Buenos Aires: Instituto de Filología 'Amado Alonso' de la Universidad de Buenos Aires, 1961), p. 15.
51. Ibid., p. 254.
52. [Translator's note: passage from the Argentinian novel *Don Segundo Sombra* (1926) by Ricardo Güiraldes.]

Balbín as presenting 'no repetition of a rhythmic nature nor any alliterative concordances',[53] even though *tope, toro, saltó* or *pelota–lomo* are just some of the links in the prosodic chain. Concerning another sentence, the 'distribution of emphatic stress' (ibid., p. 22) gives the numbers (3/1/2/3/1), a distribution that he deems '*asymmetrical*', even though the median symmetry is ostensible (*abcab*). But the very notions of symmetry, verse, prose, prevent him from seeing it. The relationship of metrics to the language isn't without dangers for the theory and analysis of rhythm.

The contradiction between metrics and discourse is perhaps maximal in the notions which seem most technical, those Zhirmunsky calls the 'structural modifiers of verse'. These structural modifiers are not only positions – the initial position, the final position, the pause. These modifiers are the combination and the conflict of alinguistic criteria and linguistic data. A combination and conflict that converge especially in the notions of *anacrusis*, the unstressed syllable or syllables which precede the first stressed one and, for the clausula, *catalexis*, a truncated final. It's a paradox of metrics, as an operation of classification (apart from studies on the origin of metres), that in studying the facts of position it studies semantic facts. Metrics, in spite of itself, hasn't stopped contributing to the study of the specific organisation of meaning by position that takes place in verse.

Anacrusis, catalexis, these notions are musical in origin, in that they presuppose for each beat a conventional and proportional duration. They aren't and can't be linguistic, since they locate their criteria in a measure, which is proper to the sung relationship of a text to music, with fixed alternations, not in language or in discourse in themselves. The anacrusis (*upbeat, Auftakt*) is defined in the Bordas *Dictionnaire de la musique* as 'note or notes which precede the first strong beat of the rhythm to which they belong'. The modern use first appears, it seems, in an 1816 treatise on German metrics. The first short syllable of an iambic verse is excluded from the metrical rhythm. The scansion of the iamb is thus made identical to that of the trochee. The Ancients distinguished rising rhythms, starting with a short syllable, and falling, starting with a long. But musically, iambic rhythm and trochaic rhythm could be converted into one another by suppressing or adding an initial short. They formed just one type, the iambic type.[54] Strong initial beat,

---

53. Rafael de Balbín, *Sistema de rítmica castellana* (Madrid: Gredos, 1962), p. 18.
54. Verrier, *Le Vers français*, vol. 2, p. 287, n. 19. This shows too, incidentally, the fragility of the psychologisations that have marked the notions of rising or falling rhythm. There is no purely perceptive, acoustic recognition of the ends of feet. Which Marijke E. Loots demonstrated in *Metrical Myths: An Experimental-Phonetic Investigation into the Production and Perception of Metrical Speech* (The Hague: Martinus Nijhoff, 1980,

trochaic rhythm-metre. *Assume the omission* of an anacrusis, you reinstate the iamb. The reverse is always true. A game without end, that metrics plays with discourse.

Anacrusis concentrates all of metrical convention, linked to the conventions of measure and foot, and leads them to the logical conclusion of their antinomy with discourse. With anacrusis, hesitation over metre begins at the first syllable. Anacrusis as 'a group of syllables preceding the first metrical stress of the line'[55] can in binary metres be single, that is to say, one syllable, as represented by Zhirmunsky:

|´— | ´— | trochaic rhythm-metre
—|´— | ´— | iambic rhythm-metre, made identical to the
                 preceding by an anacrusis

and either single or double in ternary metres:

|´— — | ´— — | ´— — | dactylic
—|´— — | ´— — | ´— — | amphibrachic
— —|´— — | ´— — | ´— — | anapestic

English and German versification makes no distinction between amphibrachs and anapests. If an anapestic sequence starts with a stress, a double anacrusis is assumed; or a single anacrusis if it starts with an unstressed. Metrics fills in the non-existent syllables. Anacrusis is the 'beginning of a gesture', said Jousse.[56]

The old and apparently basic perceptual opposition between iamb (◡ _) and trochee (_ ◡) is shaken by an alinguistic metrical principle. The iamb is only a reading of the trochee, if instead of scanning from strong beat to strong beat one scans from weak beat to weak beat. The procedure presupposes that the strong beat must be situated at the initial position of the bar. Thus the anapest has a formation 'as illogical as that of the iamb, since there the strong beat is equally at the end of the bar'.[57] The iamb and anapest are therefore only variants of the trochee and dactyl – and at the same time, 'they have no less an independent existence and distinct nature' (ibid.). Anacrusis is hence

---

p. 75). It concludes: 'metre has a long history in which no agreement has been reached on the most basic questions' (p. 131). The alternations of stress peaks depend more on the speaker, the context and the lexical structure. Intonation eliminates isochrony.

55. V. Žirmunskij, *Introduction to Metrics* (The Hague: Mouton, 1966), p. 129.
56. Marcel Jousse, *Le Style oral rythmique et mnémotechnique chez les verbo-moteurs (Études de psychologie linguistique)* (Paris: Gabriel Beauchesne, 1925), p. 16.
57. Othon Riemann and Médéric Dufour, *Traité de rythmique et de métrique grecques* (Paris: A. Colin, 1893), p. 20.

both a real syllable that allows the metre to change with one same rhythm, and a virtual additive that allows the rhythm to change with one same metre. What will be amphibrachs for Russian versification will be anapests preceded by an iamb for German and English versification. Anacrusis is the artefact *par excellence* that denounces the imaginary of metrics. With the operation, it isn't just the terms that change. The metrical idealities are transformed at the same time.

Metrics is a terminological realism. What is assonance in French is rhyme in Russian: 'bearing in mind the internal evolution of Russian verse, it seems preferable to retain the term rhyme to cover such examples of assonance'.[58] Hence: 'Certain students of Russian verse are inclined to make the term anacrusis cover every unstressed beginning of a line. For them, there are only two metres, the trochaic and dactylic. The iambic then becomes a trochaic metre and the amphibrachic a dactylic metre with a constant monosyllabic anacrusis, whereas the anapestic metre takes the form of a dactylic with a dissyllabic anacrusis. In short, there remains only the contrast between binary and ternary metres. This point of view scarcely simplifies things. On the contrary, it tends to standardize the somewhat different impressions made by the various metres upon us' (ibid., p. 59). These impressions are cultural. The frequent substitutions in the first two feet of binary lines, the relationship thus brought about between metrical stresses and rhythmic stresses (non-metrical on the initial syllable in iambic verse) are shifts of metrics toward rhythmics. Even where there are feet, there is a continuous passage to individual rhythmics, and from there to a stress-based line that can in its turn become cultural, as in modern Russian poetry. Already inside metrics 'semantic considerations alone govern the hierarchy of stress' (ibid., p. 115), and the metre can be 'shattered by semantics' (ibid., p. 116).

Anacrusis exposes how the relationship of metrics to the language is the imposition of a grid on to an object that's heterogeneous to it, the sequence of discourse: 'The enneasyllable "Dancemos en tierra chilena" figures as amphibrachic on the grammatical level and as a dactyl with anacrusis in its phonetic realisation, o óoo óoo óo.'[59] Baehr retains only the trochee and dactyl, which make the rhythmic unit start on a stress 'because the Spanish ear hears it so', and 'the iambic line is heard as a succession of trochees that begins with a monosyllabic anacrusis',[60] as in

---

58. Unbegaun, *Russian Versification*, p. 146.
59. Tomás Navarro Tomás, *Métrica española: Reseña histórica y descriptiva* (Syracuse, NY: Syracuse University, Centro de Estudios Hispánicos, 1956), §4, p. 11.
60. Baehr, *Manual de versificación Española*, pp. 27–8.

¿Adónde vas perdida?
[o] ó o ó o óo

[Where are you going, lost (boat)?] By combining anacrusis with catalexis, the field of the virtual and formal almost completely replaces the discourse rhythm. Which, in Spanish metrics, is added to the convention that a line of 7 terminating in a stress is an octosyllable, and that every syntagm stressed on the final is completed by an imaginary unstressed: *púdo subvérter* is described as — ◡ | ◡ ◡ — ◡ .[61] Here is a metrical scansion, in 'verse', from a prose sentence by Juan Ramón Jiménez, in *Platero y yo*:[62]

En la noche serena:	[oo]	óoo óo	heptasílabo dactílico
toda de nubes vagas y estrellas:	óoo	óo : óoo	óo decasílabo dactílico compuesto
se oye allá arriba:	óoo	oo	pentasílabo dactílico
desde el silencio del corral:	[ooo]	óo óo	[o] eneasílabo trocaico
un incesante pasar:	[o]	óo óoo ó	o octosílabo mixto *a*)
de claros silbidos:	[o]	óoo óo	hexasílabo dactílico
son los patos:	óo	óo	tetrasílabo

With rhythmic reality denied, anacrusis turns everything into a trochee. The iamb is described, in its Spanish use, as an 'acute trochee with an anacrusis (◡ | — [◡])'.[63] The anapest (◡ ◡ —) is an 'acute trochee with 2 anacruses (◡ ◡ | — [◡])'. The dactyl disappears entirely: *cóncha marína*, — ◡ ◡ — ◡, 'trochaic-amphibrachic clausula, is a ditrochee with the second trochee having an anacrusis (— ◡ | ◡ | — ◡)'. This trochaism is done in the name of a conformity 'to the *language*' (ibid., p. 106), which appears above all as an intra-metrical treatment of discourse. Metrics for metrics' sake substitutes its schemes for the rhythms of all groups whatsoever. The metrics of the measure cannot be syntagmatic. Only a discourse metrics can be syntagmatic. Pure metrics is entirely in anacrusis.

What makes the end of the verse is a demarcative. Whatever form it takes, a demarcative is a signal of the end before the end. For example, *en*, a syntagmatic demarcative in French, which opposes the open syntagm *j'ai fini de* . . . (I'm done x-ing) to the closed syntagm *j'en ai fini* (I'm done with it). The end of the line breaks the rhythm. A break in the rhythm is a reminder of the rhythm. This reminder has an anthropological role: 'if we bear in mind

---

61. Oreste Macrí, *Ensayo de métrica sintagmática* (Madrid: Gredos, 1969), p. 130.
62. Francisco López Estrada, *Métrica Española del siglo XX* (Madrid: Gredos 1974 [1968]), pp. 62–3: 'In the serene night: all vague clouds and stars, there is heard above: from the silence of the barnyard: an incessant passage: clear whistlings: these are the ducks.'
63. Oreste Macrí, *Ensayo de métrica sintagmática*, pp. 64–5.

that in all cultures many unusual motor or verbal phenomena occur as a result of individuals being "transported" to a mental state other than their normal one, we must acknowledge that disturbances of the rhythmic balance do play an important role'.[64] The end of the line, in Russian versification, is marked by a 'special treatment of the final foot, which can be either truncated by one or two weak syllables, or lengthened by several unstressed syllables'.[65] The line can end on a stress, *zanemóg*; the group bearing the final stress can be disyllabic, *túči*; trisyllabic (dactylic), *vórotom*; rarely, tetrasyllabic (hyperdactylic), *závoronka*; pentasyllabic, *očaróvyvajuščij*. There can be a syllable too many, elided with the following line, as in the hypermetre verses of Virgil.

What appears truncated in relation to full realisation of the metre is called catalectic. The term is from ancient metrics. The final foot is shortened. It has 'undergone a *catalexis* (κατάληξις: abrupt termination)'.[66] The full realisation is called acatalectic. The iambic tetrametre is complete in the second line of *Eugen Onegin*:

x ╱|x ╱| x ╱|x ╱
Kogda ne v šutku zanemog

[when he fell ill for real] but the trochaic tetrametre is catalectic in

x x|╱ x|x x |╱
Nevidimkoju luna.

[the invisible moon]. The linguistic perception of the verse is, as with anacrusis, at odds with metrical calculation and expectation. Calculation, expectation, proper to music, where a pause, a silence, can be considered as proportional to the other elements. Which, linguistically, it isn't. Bely wrote: 'Everything having to do with the catalectic has a meaning that is not rhythmic, but metrical; on the contrary, the life of anacrusis influences rhythm.'[67] Both catalexis and anacrusis are metrical fictions: they have a metrical, a uniquely metrical, reality. Expectation, disappointment, signal take place only in relation to a measure. The indifferent final syllable was a demarcative criterion, as noted by St Augustine (*De Musica*, IV, I, 1). Similarly in the

---

64. Leroi-Gourhan, *Gesture and Speech*, p. 284. Original, *Le Geste et la parole*, p. 99.
65. Unbegaun, *Russian Versification*, p. 71.
66. Nougaret, *Traité de métrique latine classique*, §22, p. 9. The same verse line, the Saturnian, can be taken as a catalectic iambic septenary or a headless trochaic septenary, if taken in quantitative metre as in written Latin, or as an accentual trochaic senary if it is spoken Latin (cf. Ernst Pulgram, *Latin-Romance Phonology: Prosodics and Metrics* (Munich: W. Fink, 1975), p. 216). Metrics is not devoid of the spirit of juggling.
67. Andrei Bely, *Ritm kak dialektika i 'Mednyj vsadnik'* (Moscow: Federazija, 1929), p. 92.

Greek and Latin hexametre, in relation to the contradictions of the first four feet between quantity and accent, the coincidence of the metrical rhythm and the stress rhythm, in the clausula formed by the fifth and sixth feet, the last of them catalectic.

In French, lines with 'feminine' endings are not considered to be full lines, nor are lines with 'masculine' endings considered to be catalectic. An effect of the language as well as of metrical habit. If the line is oxytonic in Spanish, it is counted for a syllable more than it actually has because the paroxyton that accompanies it has the stress *on the same position*: the '7' is an '8' because the '8' has the stress on the seventh. What counts in Spanish is the syllable that doesn't count in French. Not the place of the stress that enables this syllable count, and that is bound up with it. Final homophony seems to be second, historically, after isosyllabism, in medieval Latin liturgy. The line ending first placed the rhyme, before the rhyme passed for a signal of the line ending. There is in each case a linguistic and cultural inflecting of metrical idealities. Whence the non-correspondence, language to language, of syllabic values, and of bars.

Caesura is the third of the structural modifiers of verse. More than anacrusis and catalexis, which are exclusively metrical, caesura is the major meeting point of the metrical with discourse. It has a double function which is transposed by the double interpretation of its meaning. Traditionally caesura is the metrical breaking of long lines, which some call compound or complex, Zhirmunsky defines it as 'a division in the rhythmical movement, prescribed beforehand as a general rule of the verse structure, as an element in the metrical scheme'.[68] Etymologically, *caesura* means *cut*. Which the vulgate repeats. Tobler defined it as a cut, a break 'after a set number of syllables'.[69] But Lote defines the caesura as a *stress*. This stress determines a 'suspensive pause', according to the fourteenth-century *Leys d'Amors*, as opposed to the 'final pause'. The caesura 'is a stress placed in the high notes of the voice, as rhyme is a stress placed in the low notes, the latter doubled by a homophony'.[70] Which excludes, it seems to me, taking the first hemistich, which ends at this caesura, as the end of a line, rather than as a principal metrical stress, fixed or mobile, the second after that of the line ending.

Ronsard, in his *Abrégé de l'art poétique français* of 1565, said that alexandrines are 'composed of twelve or thirteen syllables, the masculines of twelve,

---

68. Žirmunskij, *Introduction to Metrics*, p. 136.
69. Adolphe Tobler, *Le Vers français ancien et moderne*, trans. by Karl Breul and Léopold Sudre (Paris: F. Vieweg, 1885), p. 106. [Orig. German publ. 1880.]
70. Georges Lote, *Origines du vers français* (Aix-en-Provence: Annales de la Faculté d'Aix, 1940), p. 195.

the feminines thirteen, and always have their rest on the 6th syllable',[71] a rest which he also calls 'resumption of breath' (ibid., p. 1007). He recommends 'if possible (for no one ever practises what they preach), that the first four syllables of the common verse line [decasyllable], or the first six of alexandrines, be fashioned with an incomplete meaning, without borrowing it from the following word. Example of a common verse line with a complete meaning in the first four syllables: *Jeune beauté | maitresse de ma vie* [Young beauty mistress of my life]. Example with an incomplete meaning: *L'homme qui a | été desur la mer* [The man who has been on the sea]' (ibid., p. 1008). Port-Royal considered the caesura as a 'rest that breaks the verse in two'.[72] Banville too saw it as a 'rest'.[73] Corneille distinguished more acutely, in a reply to Scudéry, between caesura and rest: 'You have peeled the verses of my play to the point of accusing one of them of lacking caesurae: if you had known the terms of the craft in which you are meddling, you would have said that it lacked rests in the hemistichs.'[74] The French tradition has all but made the caesura the centre of metrics, such is the importance accorded to it. Which Roubaud still does. That's taking Malherbe's side without knowing it, as Souriau showed with regard to the verse of La Fontaine (p. 214), foregrounding the mute *e*'s. He cited Faguet: 'The mute *e*'s are the strong caesurae of French verse' (ibid., p. 217).

Only as a stress could the caesura constitute an articulation of discourse. Whence, in Greek hexametre, its non-coincidence with the foot ending: their coincidence would have undone the verse as a structure by giving too much importance to the foot. Whence, also, in French, until Verlaine, the obligation to end a word, if not a phrase, at the caesura. Sometimes with the presence of normally unstressed words, as cited by Becq de Fouquières, whom Lote repeats, in Hugo's *Légende des Siècles*:

> *Conjunction*: Il teint sa dague **avec** du suc de mandragore [He dyes his dagger **with** mandrake juice]
> *auxiliary*: A pris forme et s'en **est** allé dans le bois sombre [Has taken shape and **has** gone away into the dark wood]
> *pronoun*: Les dieux, les fléaux, **ceux** d'à présent, ceux d'ensuite [The gods, the plagues, **those** of now, those of later].

---

71. Pierre de Ronsard, *Œuvres complètes* (Paris: Gallimard, Éditions de la Pléiade), vol. 2, p. 1006.
72. Cited by Souriau, *L'Évolution du vers français au XVIIe siècle*, p. 150.
73. Théodore de Banville, *Petit Traité de poésie française* (Paris: Bibliothèque de L'Écho de la Sorbonne, 1872), p. 10.
74. In Souriau, *L'Évolution du vers français au XVIIe siècle*, p. 156.

It is the tension between the virtuality of the caesura as metrical element and the syntagmatic reality of the pauses which creates the intensity, the very energy of the caesura, as is proven by the projections that are the *rejets* and *contre-rejets* at the caesura. Returned to the plurality of possible real pauses, the caesura acts simultaneously as metrical virtuality and as reality of discourse. By virtue of the pauses after mute *e* Becq de Fouquières distinguished fifteen rhythms in the Romantic alexandrine.[75] Souriau found still others, in La Fontaine.[76] And, also in La Fontaine, the decasyllables 4-3-3, 4-4-2, 2-2-6, 1-3-6, 2-5-3. And nineteen ways of breaking up the octosyllable.[77] But all these rhythmic divisions could be metrically caesuraed at the sixth position of the alexandrine. Rhythmically, they can be 'caesurae stronger than the hemistich' (ibid., p. 447). But the caesura is metrical, not rhythmic, in itself. Its effects are what's rhythmic.

The caesura has more effect through its transgressions than by the realisation of its order. It might be claimed that even its elimination doesn't eliminate it, since it has possible value only by relation at least to the memory of it, and this memory is inscribed in the history of the alexandrine: that is, *in all its uses*. Thus the elimination of the caesura at the sixth syllable (of the possibility of a stress on the sixth syllable of the sixth caesura) in the alexandrine doesn't produce a new metre, but still and always a counter-alexandrine within the alexandrine.

The caesura is, in French at least, the only metrical ideality that has such important linguistic effects in the verse, apart from the rules of elision. Whence the excessive importance that's been accorded to it. Benoît de Cornulier notes how Jacques Roubaud reduces the critique of metrics, 'by simply identifying the 6th caesura with the alexandrine, then the alexandrine with the social order'.[78] It suffices to note, amongst the structural modifiers of the verse, the virtual absence in French metrics of anacrusis and catalexis, in order to understand that there is no podological metrics in French, and that anapests in French are only metaphorical.[79] Effect of the caesura, as of the clausula: the fifth, seventh and eleventh positions of the alexandrine are as strong as the sixth and twelfth, through the avoidance of consecutive stresses

---

75. The divisions: 1: 4.4.4.; 2: 3.5.4; 3: 3.4.5; 4: 4.3.5; 5: 5.4.3; 6: 5.3.4; 7: 4.5.3; 8: 2.5.5; 9: 5.5.2; 10: 5.2.5; 11: 2.6.4; 12: 4.6.2; 13: 3.6.3; 14: 1.6.5; 15: 5.6.1; The 3) and 10) were refused by Souriau, because there the caesura falls in the middle of a word.
76. The divisions 1.3.8, 1.8.3, 1.4.7, 1.7.4, 2.7.3, 3.2.7, 4.8, 3.9, 2.10.
77. Souriau, *L'Évolution du vers français au XVIIe siècle*, pp. 220–3.
78. Benoît de Cornulier, *Problèmes de métrique française* (PhD thesis, Faculté de Science de l'Université d'Aix-Marseille, 1979), p. 335.
79. Another metaphorism: even verse lines and numbers assimilated to iambic rhythm, and odd ones to trochaic.

in these positions in the classical canon, and the practice of stressing these positions in the battle against this canon. Another effect of the caesura: on the syntax of inversion, inside the small number of combinations that the twelve syllables permit.

The caesura is also the only metrical position that retains the trace of a stress system, not fixed by syllabism, in the caesura called epic (epic, lyric caesura: terms invented by Diez in the nineteenth century for French and Provençal verse), and that the theoreticians of the fifteenth century called 'the pass',[80] a supernumerary unstressed final, as on *France* in

> *Quant vient en mai* || *que l'on dit as lons jors*
> *Que Franc de France* || *repairent de roi cort*

[When it happens in May, called the time of long days / that the Franks of France return from the king's court] a system maintained until different dates in Spanish, in English. Claudel assimilates caesura and rhyme to 'a dominant and a tonic'.[81] The caesura is the passage from metrics to rhythmics. The caesura is of the whole line. Anacrusis and catalexis rely only on the notion of foot.

The foot is the pure metrical idol. A unit of measure that includes a marked beat and an unmarked beat, regardless of the number of syllables in each beat, the foot is determined across, or above, word endings. The foot presupposes scansion, scanning. To scan a line is 'to "march" it rhythmically while tapping the foot to the strong beat of each foot following the placing of the 'longs' and 'shorts' of that foot'.[82] I won't insist on the metrical obsession that exists in French for saying *foot* for *syllable*. The foot implies the isochrony of feet: 'The foot is *essentially* an *equal breaking up of time*.'[83] It is the dominance of Greek and Latin that has created isochrony in French, that of 'tetrametres' and 'trimetres'. Heterochronism is 'frequent in Arabic and Sanskrit metrics' (ibid., p. 85). To say *foot* is to say 'equal intervals that separate strong beats'.[84] Equality of beats, of which this is an example. In

> *Jamais | mon triste cœur* || *n'a recueilli | le fruit*

[Never has my sad heart gathered the fruit] 'As much time will need to be put into pronouncing *jamais* (two syllables) as into pronouncing: *mon triste cœur*

---

80. Lote, *Origines du vers français*, p. 195. Also in Georges Lote, *Histoire du vers français*, part 1: *Le Moyen Âge*, vol. 1 (Paris: Boivin, 1949), p. 208.
81. Paul Claudel, *Mémoires improvisés: quarante et un entretiens avec Jean Amrouche* (Paris: Gallimard, 1954), p. 54.
82. Marcel Jousse, *L'Anthropologie du geste* (Paris: Éditions Resma, 1969), p. 156.
83. de la Grasserie, *Analyses métriques et rythmiques*, p. 70.
84. Riemann and Dufour, *Traité de rythmique et de métrique grecques*, p. 16.

(four syllables).'⁸⁵ The *will need to be* denotes the normative in the metrical principle.

The foot, a metrical ideality, has been superposed on to accentual (stress-based) rhythmics to the point of leading us to speak of metrical stress alongside word stress and sentence stress. But there is metrical stress only in verse, or rather in and through metre. Only word stress and phrase stress, sentence stress, have a proper linguistic existence. Not the foot. Add to that, specifically, the secondary cultural effect that leads us to speak of iambs, of anapests, in French. Even in ancient Greek poetry, in the iambic trimetre, the unit was not the foot (an iamb) but the dipode ᴗ — ᴗ — , where the first syllable could also be long, called 'irrational', denoted |X — ᴗ —|. What Bely brought back into Russian rhythmics.

The foot is only metrical. Its convention is radically heterogeneous to language – to words, with their stress or quantitative form, their length, their position, not to mention phrases and sentences. The caesura is the only metrical fact in which the word ending takes precedence. As soon as there is accentual verse – the Russian *dol'nik* – the number of unstressed syllables between each stress not being counted, there are no longer feet. Metrics minimises the word endings and privileges feet. The superposition of the foot and the word ending produces a 'spasmodic' effect.⁸⁶ It valorises feet at the expense of the line. Unbegaun noted that 'Two lines with an identical stress pattern but with a different division into words may produce a slightly different rhythmic effect' (ibid., p. 129). But 'Accentual verse could scarcely adapt itself to such practices. Depending solely on stress, it thereby makes the word emphatic' (ibid., p. 131). The conventional nature of metrics, on which it is founded, prevents it from treating language as arbitrary, in other words as radical historicity. Discourse, and not word.

So long as a metrics maintains the notion of foot, it maintains the original measure and music. Leech tried to distinguish the measure, which 'invariably begins with an accent',⁸⁷ from the foot, which can start with a stressed or unstressed syllable. But, even while trying to constitute a 'linguistic guide', he can't get out of the relationship between verse and music. He compares enjambment with syncopation (ibid., p. 123). He reckons that the two rhythms, iambic and trochaic, can be distinguished only by an arbitrary decision: because he privileges the measure. He notes as follows the relation between the measure and the foot for this line:

---

85. de la Grasserie, *Analyses métriques et rythmiques*, p. 100.
86. Unbegaun, *Russian Versification*, pp. 127–8.
87. Geoffrey N. Leech, *A Linguistic Guide to English Poetry* (London and Harlow: Longman, 1969), p. 112.

measure: *The | ploughman | homeward | plods his | weary | way*
foot: x   /   x   /   x   /   x   / x   /

The anacrusis is recognisable. Leech rightly recalls that a literary tradition has stuck a theoretical metrics on to the linguistic rhythm of English.

Thus, in the popular prosody of nursery rhymes, metrics is inadequate. Here is how Leech scans the following nursery rhyme, where |Λ| marks a 'silent stress (Λ), which sometimes has an entire silent measure to itself' (ibid., p. 114). Which is only pertinent for music, or the sung, not for a linguistic rhythm:

Old Mother Hubbard	| / x x | / x
Went to the cupboard	| / x x | / x
To give her poor doggy a bone.	x | / x x | / x x | / | Λ
When she got there	| / x x | / x
The cupboard was bare	| / x x | / x
And so the poor doggy had none.	x | / x x | / x x | / | Λ

His entire commentary hinges on the anacrusis that his notation shows: 'The important metrical fact about this rhyme is that it is written in three-time throughout, all measures internal to a line having three syllables. But operating with traditional feet, one would feel obliged to scan lines 1, 2, and 4 in terms of "falling rhythm" (dactyls and trochees) and lines 3, 5, and 6 in terms of "rising rhythm" (iambs and anapests), and thus obscure the regularity of the pattern. Here, and in countless other cases, traditional scansion forces one to over-analyse, by introducing distinctions which are irrelevant to the metre' (ibid.). To free himself from one convention, Leech introduces another, stuck on to the rhythmics of discourse, which is not better treated by the notion of three-beat measure than by classical metrics. Linguistically, *Hubbard, cupboard* are two syllables; *there-bare*, one syllable. It's in order to preserve the measure that Leech, who wants to speak here as a linguist, invents three anacruses.

The rhythmics of the nursery rhyme seems simpler than these artifices. It consists of two lines with two stresses followed by a line with three, two times. With constant internal intervals of two unstressed. There are here two variants of the two-stress line: with unstressed ending, 'feminine'; with stressed ending – the stress falling each time on the same position. The initial unstressed doesn't seem to play a determining role in the stress count, nor in the rhythmic pattern: lines 3 and 6 have the same one.

Leech's 'silent stress' allows him to reduce the odd lines to even metres: 'A pentametre can be regarded as a hexametre with one stress silent, and so on' (ibid., p. 115). The metrical consciousness prefers even numbers. So the nursery rhyme is rewritten thus, putting the two short verse segments on one line (the subscript marks the segment ending):

| / x x | / x₁ | / x x | / x₁
x | / x x | / x x | /₁ | Λ
| / x x | / x₁ | / x x | /|
x | / x x | / x x | /₁ | Λ

Leech is trying to show 'a regularity obscured by the normal line-by-line arrangement' (ibid., p. 116): 3 and 4 stress lines. But he inserts a caesura, transforming simple lines into complex ones, since the intervals are of two except at the junction of the former short lines, where he masks the demarcative effect of rhyme as well. This would be a stress-syllabic verse. It seems to me that there is instead here an accentual metre, concerning which Leech later reminds us that it's the metre of the oldest Anglo-Saxon poetry, which has survived in popular poetry. Measure and regularity can only conceive irregularity, at the risk of admitting, faced with a text, that 'the irregularity becomes the rule' (ibid., p. 128).

The problem of the relationship between metrics and language is how to get rid of the notion of foot. Already metrics comes closer to discourse by taking as its fundamental unit the line, no longer the foot. Thus, relating Spanish word stress and feet, Rudolf Baehr specified that metrical denominations can't be used in classifying Spanish verse, because 'it is rare that a line or a series of lines is systematically composed of clearly identifiable feet, given that in Romance poetry it is not metre that is the unique basis of the rhythm, as in the metrics of the Ancients, but the entire line'.[88] So long as the metrical unit is the foot, metrics can only stand outside meaning. If the unit becomes the line, one must go beyond the line in order to find the linguistic discourse units.

For the Russians, the unit is the line, while keeping the feet, even though, through the numbering, the formal maintenance of the notion of foot actually leads to the notion of *position* in the line.[89] That is, to the introduction of time in metrics, time which is something other than pure succession. The Russians have developed, through the systematic inventory of positions in verse, the study of personal rhythms, the study of the historicity of metrics, and of rhythmics. As witnessed by the quarrel of the pyrrhic (two shorts), counted as a distinct foot, whereas it is in fact an unrealised place for an iamb:

---

88. Baehr, *Manual de versificación española*, p. 27.
89. The unit is also the verse for Wolfgang Kayser, in 'Vom Rhythmus in deutschen Gedichten', *Dichtung und Volkstum*, 39 (1938), pp. 487–510.

the non-realisation of the second foot in the iambic tetrametre is a figure that appears at a certain period, and breaks a classical scheme. Yesenin, for example, goes toward rhythms 'that imitate the intonation of conversation'.[90] Yesenin 'proposes rhythmic solutions that differ profoundly from period to period. The solution of the classical type, in accordance with the design of rhythmic inertia, which tends to load foot 2 and unload foot 1 and especially foot 3, appears at first as the preferred solution. But, around 1916, different tendencies appear: foot 2 more often unloaded, foot 3 more often loaded increase the proportion of asymmetric realisations, which give [the iambic tetrametre] a modern allure. The inventory of the growing and shrinking number of rhythmic figures, the statistics established by Taranovsky for comparing the number of stresses realised at various periods, and finally the positioning strategies for long words allow us to measure the importance of the evolution that Yesenin underwent over several years' (p. 48). An example of what can be done with the relationship between the rhythmics of the language and metrics, producing rhythmic rhymes, dactylic rhyme. This is a first attempt at a discourse metrics.

One of the paradoxes of metrics is that this search for discourse – rare, and in its early stages – which is the only possibility for a modernity of metrics, for a renewal of its relationship to rhythm, can be observed, to my knowledge, in discussions of ancient Greek verse. A study on the metrics of Aeschylus and Sophocles integrates metrics with poetry, not by limiting itself to declaring that an 'intelligent appreciation of poetry is impossible without some understanding of metrical organization' and that 'efforts to understand the formal structure of the tragic trimetre are required'.[91] Many studies make similar declarations, then practise a formal metrics that indefinitely defers the relationship between poetry and metrics. To renew this relationship required not only passing from laws to tendencies, but essentially suppressing the notion of foot.

This Paul Maas began to do,[92] by renouncing the terms *arsis* and *thesis*; by renouncing feet, πόδες, χῶραι; and by replacing them, for the trimetre, with twelve elements, divided into three basic sequences 'or iambic metra, with caesura after the fifth and/or seventh element'.[93] But Seth L. Schein widens the method's scope and interest by ridding it of dipodes, and adding: 'For

---

90. Jacques Veyrenc, *La Forme poétique du Serge Essénine: les rythmes* (The Hague: Mouton, 1968), p. 79.
91. Seth L. Schein, *The Iambic Trimetre in Aeschylus and Sophocles: A Study in Metrical Form* (Leiden: Brill, 1979), p. 1.
92. Paul Maas, *Greek Metre*, trans. by Hugh Lloyd-Jones (Oxford: Clarendon Press, 1962). [Original, *Griechische Metrik*, Leipzig and Berlin: B. G. Teubner, 1923.]
93. Schein, *The Iambic Trimetre in Aeschylus and Sophocles*, p. 2, summarising Maas, *Greek Metre*, pp. 38–9, 66.

the metron really is the same sort of entity as the foot. Metron boundaries are arbitrary; unlike colon boundaries, they coincide with word-end only infrequently, except at the end of the line, and to consider them as elements of metrical organization is the same kind of systematizing error made, e.g., by editors who analyse Pindar's periods into metra which are often unrelated to the colometric structure of the text printed beneath the analysis' (ibid., pp. 2–3). These are no longer formal fictions that are the metrical units, but 'the position and shape of words in the line' (ibid., p. 3). The elements of the iambic trimetre are numbered from 1 to 12:

```
1   2   3   4   5   6   7   8   9   10  11  12
ṷ   —   ṷ   —   ṷ   —   ṷ   —   ū̆   —   ṷ   —
```

where ṷ designates a greater frequency of the long than the short, and ū̆ the opposite: 'Thus, I would describe *Persae*, 249,

ὦ γῆς ἁπάσης Ἀσιάδος πολίσματα,

as having word-end at positions 1, 2, 5, 8 and 12, or, more simply, at 1, 2, 5, 8 and 12. A scheme for this line would be:

```
  1   2       5           8
— | — | ṷ — — | ṷ ṷ ṷ — | ṷ — ṷ —.
```

A schematic description of the 'word-shape' of ἁπάσης would be ṷ — — 5 ' (ibid., p. 3, n. 16).

This is the inventing of a relationship between metrics and language previously misunderstood in so many ways. Statistical study finds a rigorous basis to it: the new study of the relations between metrical position and word form. The differences noted, between texts, are then indeed 'useful criteria for literary criticism' (ibid., p. 4), going as far as the attempt at a relative chronology – which, in this same domain, was challenged by Pohlsander. *Prometheus Unbound*, on account of the frequency of its enjambments, is dated as the last play of Aeschylus, close to the metrics of Sophocles (ibid., pp. 62–3). Here we have the wherewithal for renewing modern metrics, and amongst other things the study of French verse.

Thus the trimetre of Aeschylus has the following structure (ibid., p. 18):

```
    2  3     5     7  8      10
 ṷ — | ṷ ⁝ — ṷ | — ṷ ⁝ — ⁝ ū̆ — | ṷ —
```

with word-ending at the fifth position at the minimum in 76 per cent of cases. From which are deduced two *cola* or structural units: ṷ — ṷ — ṷ 5 and — ṷ — ū̆ — ṷ — 12. The analysis allows what feet didn't allow: the study of the interaction of the metre and the meaning. The author speaks of 'metrical mimesis' (ibid., p. 21). The image of Prometheus in his bonds is created, in *Prometheus Unbound*, verse 113, by the form of the meaning, the length of the words, the position of their endings:

ὑπαιθρίοις δεσμοῖς πεπασσαλευμένος

[riveted in fetters beneath the open sky], and '*Persae*, 501,

στρατός, περᾶι κρυσταλλοπῆγα διὰ πόρον,

[(when our host had made an end of its fervent invocation of the gods) it ventured to pass across the ice-bound stream] is another striking example of the interplay of metre and sense' (ibid., p. 21, n. 12). Seth Schein thus localises lengths, word forms, according to parts of speech, and syntax. The localisation of proper names always turns out to be the same. An '*explication de métrique*' (ibid., p. 30) is then provided, for eleven lines of *Agamemnon*. It's the beginnings of a discourse metrics. The caesura appears as a 'word-end [which] occurs within the line much more frequently than would be expected *ceteris paribus*'.[94] Scarcities and frequencies replace rules, which themselves weren't laws. In Sophocles, there are 44 per cent more trimetres than in Aeschylus: 44 per cent of dialogue, which explains 'why we often feel that Sophocles is more "dramatic" a poet than is Aeschylus' (ibid., p. 35). More words, more monosyllables, more particles in Sophocles. More enjambments, between trimetres and between *cola*. These are the effects of context on metrics. Where this or that metrical and rhetorical particularity is staked out to mark a character, such as Clytemnestra (ibid., p. 50). The method's linguistic gain is also a poetic gain.

No one knows what a verse or a line is: its why, its how. Why it goes just to there. The syllables have been counted. It's not enough to count the syllables. Is syllabism a structural modifier of verse? The tradition of delimiting lines of verse isn't an explanation but a pragmatics. It is simultaneously imperative and vague. It trained the French to the alexandrine's twelve. It isn't exempt from illustrious misunderstandings. That of the English metricists and poets of the eighteenth century, regarding their accentual verse, which they took to be syllabic. Prisoners of these linguistic–cultural habits, as were the Spanish metricists. As for the French, some believe in anapests, others are content to assure readers that French verse is 'syllabic, rhymed et caesuraed',[95] thinking they've said all there is to say.

---

94. [Translator's note: Howard N. Porter, 'The Early Greek Hexametre', *Yale Classical Studies*, 12 (1951), pp. 3–63, p. 10, cited by Schein, *The Iambic Trimetre in Aeschylus and Sophocles*, p. 7, n. 7.]
95. Pierre Guiraud, *La Versification*, 'Que sais-je?' (Paris: Presses Universitaires de France, 1970), p. 11.

In word-stress versifications, there isn't necessarily isosyllabism, a fixed number of syllables for a rhythmic unit. French verse seems to be based on syllable count. But this count doesn't explain their rhythmic structure, which Paul Verrier called 'half-accentual'.[96] The alexandrine is then a verse line of twelve with two fixed metrical stresses, the others being rhythmic, mobile. The alexandrine has even passed for entirely accentual verse.[97] The syllabic, quantitative, stress-based principles can be unopposed to one another at certain moments of coincidence between the linguistic and the cultural. They can combine, as in the *rhythmi* of Cisalpine Gaul in the fourth century, in *lingua romana rustica*, and already in this soldiers' song of the third century that Verrier cites (ibid., vol. 1, 19):

Mille, mille, mille, mille / mille decollavimus.

[A thousand, thousand, thousand, thousand / thousand heads we cut off.]
The syllabic principle is stable, but it is insufficient.

Syllabism is ambiguous from its origin, by its very name, *rhythm*, in opposition to *metre*, which designates the classical quantitative principle. *Rhythmus* 'served to designate verse in the terminology of the Middle Ages'.[98] Ever since Quintilian, in the first century, '*rythmi, id est numeri*' (cited ibid., p. 40 [33]), which Lote appears to translate as number of syllables.[99] What a text by a fifth-century grammarian seems to make explicit.[100] The origins

---

96. Verrier, *Le Vers français*, vol. 2, p. 18.
97. Albert Thibaudet, *La Poésie de Stéphane Mallarmé* (Paris: Gallimard, 1926, p. 254) wrote: 'The alexandrine, I remind the reader, is made up not of twelve or thirteen syllables (that is a consequence or an accident) but of four spaced stresses, one of which has its position fixed, at the rhyme, one with it approximately fixed, at the caesura, and two with it almost optional, within the body of the hemistichs.' Cited by Benoît de Cornulier, *Problèmes de métrique française*, p. 64. Thibaudet confused metrical and rhythmic, in addition to replacing a historical theory of verse with a vague notion.
98. Lote, *Origines du vers français*, p. 21; *Histoire du vers français*, part 1: *Le Moyen Âge*, vol. 1, p. 17.
99. In their *Dictionnaire étymologique de la langue latine* (Paris: Klincksieck, 1932), Alfred Ernout and Antoine Meillet relate *numerus* to ἀριθμός, 'numerus oratorius, measure, rhythm', 'grammatical number', 'crowd, number'. Which validates a slip from ῥυθμός to ἀριθμός. A founding pun. But Latin *numerus* also designated metrical cadence, and rhythms in poetry as in prose, or the 'regulated movements of athletes', right down to merging the rhythm proper with the talent proper – that is to say, the very confusion of metre and of rhythm proper to traditional theory. So it isn't at all certain that *numeri* in Quintilian is simply the number of syllables.
100. 'Rhythmus quid est? Verborum modulata compositio non metrica ratione, sed numerosa scansione ad judicium aurium examinata, ut puta veluti sunt cantica poetarum vulgarium'. What a sixteenth-century French author rendered as: 'It appears that Rhythms resemble Metre: in that it is a harmonious composition of words, not by measure and

of French verse, for Georges Lote, are in 'the syllabism of liturgical Hymns' (ibid., p. 60 [50]). But this syllabism is tied to the accentual nature of these Latin poems, even if the theoreticians don't talk about the stresses.[101] Therefore Lote's conclusion – 'In all these texts, it is not a matter of stress, quite the contrary' (p. 41 [34]) – proves only the absence (still uncertain, on account of the *tones*) of stress in the descriptions, not its linguistic absence. Arabic serves to illustrate how a non-description and a non-awareness of stress don't prove that there is no stress. Accentual rhythm is, in sum, invisible in syllabism, as it has been since Virgilius Maro Grammaticus, in around 600, wrote about *prosi versus, prose verses*, in the liturgical sense (cited ibid., p. 94 [78]), where each syllable has the value of a spondee – long beat – for church chanting. Only chant, in the sung, eliminates linguistic stress. The equivalence of Greek *rhythmus* and Latin *numerus*, bearing only on liturgical chant, leaves intact the ambiguity of syllabism, as support and order for the music, which says nothing about linguistic stress, which occurs but doesn't enter into its order, and is thus neither codified nor described.

Syllabism, for French verse, is both a frame and a mask. As Spanish metrics shows clearly. This is what's interesting for the theory of rhythm in the non-syllabic metrics of the *Poema de mio Cid*, confronted with the syllabics of the *chansons de geste*. French verse as seen by a Spaniard is as follows: 'at first, poems written in verses of 5 + 7 syllables (*decasyllable*, by the French way of counting) are more numerous than those written in verses of 7 + 7 (*alexandrine*), whereas starting from the second half of the thirteenth century, the alexandrine alone is used'.[102] Spanish verse shows two things about French verse, about its syllabism and about its isosyllabism. The verse of the *Poema de mio Cid* is anisosyllabic. It allows appearances to be reversed. Menéndez Pidal wrote that the question isn't why Spanish epic poetry, which is the more archaic, doesn't count syllables, but instead 'why the French *jongleurs* (minstrels) count syllables? It is they who constitute the exception' (p. 40). Menéndez Pidal counts the verse of the *Chanson de Roland* as 5 + 7. Its lines are, Spanish-style (the last two with 'epic caesura', following the French count):

> fixed order such as that which is kept in the composition of Metres or verses, but by numbers of syllables, as it pleases the ears. And such are the Hymns of the vulgar Poets' (cited in Lote, *Origines du vers français*, pp. 36, 38; *Histoire du vers français*, part 1: *Le Moyen Âge*, vol. 1, pp. 30, 31). Where *modulata* designates a melodic accompaniment, and *scansio numerosa*, apparently, the syllable count.

101. Lote discounts the admittedly obscure evidence in which *tones* are mentioned (*Origines du vers français*, p. 41; *Histoire du vers français*, part 1: *Le Moyen Âge*, vol. 1, p. 34).
102. Ramon Menéndez Pidal, *De Primitiva Lirica Española y Antigua Épica* (Madrid: Espasa-Calpe, Austral series, 1977 [study from 1933]), p. 39.

(4 = 5) + 6	*Sire Rollant, e vos sire Oliver*	v. 1740
(4 = 5) + 7	*Franceis sunt morz par votre legerie*	v. 1726
5 + 6	*Li arcevesques les ot cuntrarier*	v. 1737
5 + 7	*Mielz valt mesure que ne fait estultie*	v. 1725.

[Sir Roland, and you Sir Oliver; Franks died through your carelessness; The archbishops heard them dispute; Better moderation than recklessness.] But there are also 'too long' lines, as Bédier said, and other 'too short' ones:[103]

5 + 8	*Ja cil d'Espaigne ne s'en deivent turner liez*	v. 1745
6 + 7	*Dès ore cumencet l'ocisiun des altres*	v. 3946

[Those from Spain shall not return happy; Then shall begin the massacre of the others] and with 'lyrical caesura' (*escheles* means 'battle corps')

(3 = 4) + 7	*Treis escheles ad l'emperere Carles*	v. 3035

[Three divisions has the emperor Charles.] The counts aren't neat. This is because the position of the stress, and the unstressed that does or doesn't follow, influences the number of syllables.

Even within the framework of isosyllabism, in the eight-syllable verses of the romances, the even verses had assonance, as in English and German ballads; they could be seen as a single line of sixteen:

Durmiendo estaba el amor,   los celos lo despertaron;
por un caminito estrecho   a los ojos lo sacaron.[104]

The role of stress is what syllabism hides. Now, unlike in France and Italy, where poetry became isosyllabic very early, there is a long 'ametrical period'[105] in Spanish poetry, eliminated in learned poetry in the fifteenth to sixteenth centuries, and surviving in popular poetry.

Spanish ametricality is not merely an anisosyllabism,[106] an instability, which causes epic verse to oscillate between ten and twenty syllables. This ametricality puts syllabism into question as a structural principle, in an

---

103. Joseph Bédier, *La Chanson de Roland* (Paris: Piazza, 1947 [1912]), p. VII.
104. Ramón Menéndez Pidal, *Los Romances de América* (Madrid: Espasa-Calpe, Austral series, 1972 [1939]), p. 32, 'Love had fallen asleep; jealousies awakened him; in a narrow little path they plucked out his eyes.'
105. Baehr, *Manual de versificación española*, p. 153.
106. Henríquez-Ureña (*Estudios de versificación española*, p. 121), using the term 'irregular versification', then 'fluctuating verse', all the while postulating an accentual versification opposed to syllabism, says nothing about the metricality of the *Poema de mio Cid*, and deals essentially with mixed verses, where he distinguishes four types: anapestic cadence, predominance of nine (= the French octosyllable), seguidilla, free schemes.

essential way. This is why the definitional difficulties, as with the verse *de arte mayor*, are the theoretical ground *par excellence* for the conflict between the accentual and the syllabic.

The critique of the structural modifiers of verse, in pure metrics, which is the category of the technical separated from meaning, is only the search for the relations between metrics and meaning. But to postulate or try to elaborate a discourse metrics is not to introduce discourse into metrics. It is the reverse which can displace, transform metrics: to lead it toward discourse, and discourse rhythmics. To introduce discourse into metrics is to reconcile the two, to return to psychologism doubly, by injecting expressivity into metrics, and bringing individual phonic realisation into it.

When metrics postulates a relationship with meaning, without changing anything about itself, it draws the meaning, through expressivity, from a content. It makes itself interpretative, by a leap it can't justify. Thus: 'The trochee: *Dämmerung senkte sich von oben* [Dusk dropped from above] is interpreted by its content. It appears here dragging and heavy, because it is linked to the representation of falling.'[107] Although opposing this reading to a historical interpretation of verse structures (ibid., p. 30), the author maintains: '*Der Inhalt deutet den Rhythmus* [The content interprets the rhythm]' (ibid., p. 68). With Arno Holz, 'The content interprets the rhythm [. . .] as expression of solitude and emptiness' (ibid., p. 102). One sees in the 'undifferentiated rhythm of Dehmel the annihilation of the individual in the technological world' (p. 136). In relation to minimal, asemantic metrical scansion, introducing the rhythm of meaning is introducing discourse. Whence the following two scansions, for a verse by Rilke, the first purely metrical:

Hinhalten, Niemals-Gebenkönnen, Dastehn

[To stop, never to be able to give, to stay there], following the scheme (ibid., p. 75):

x | x́ x | x́ x | x́ x | x́ x | x́ (x)

then semantic stresses (*Sinnakzente*), and sentence rhythm (*Satzrhytmus*) are introduced. The scheme becomes:

─́ | x́ ᴗ Λ | x́ x | x́ x | x́ ᴗΛ | ─́ | ─́

---

107. Hartwig Schultz, *Vom Rhythmus der modernen Lyrik: Parallele Versstrukturen bei Holz, George, Rilke, Brecht, und den Expressionisten* (Munich: Carl Hanser, 1970), p. 13, who here cites Herbert Lehnert, *Struktur und Sprachmagie: Zur Methode der Lyrik-Interpretation* (Stuttgart, Berlin, Cologne and Mainz: Kohlhammer, 1966), p. 11.

Where the signs Λ, ⋏ denote measures of silence: Λ, a 'quarter-pause', in other words a crochet (quarter-note) rest; ⋏, an 'eighth-pause', a quaver (eighth-note) rest.[108] This measure combines the confusion of language with musical codification, and that of discourse rhythm with phonic realisation. Whence the remark: 'The rhythm x́.⋏ | x́.⋏ is essentially indistinguishable from the rhythm — | —, since there is always a short pause between two syllables' (ibid., p. 66). Thinking one is borrowing rigour, one ends up transposing vagueness. But the notation has the virtue, by being situated in discourse, of trying to denote the rhythmics of the sentence, and of the situation, in addition to the metre. Rhythming a verse by Stefan George (ibid., p. 20) as follows

Du nur mir bist und alle so mir blühn . . .
—́ | —́ | —́ | x⋏ ᴜ | x x | x x | —́

[You are mine alone and all are flourishing for me.] Where it appears that looking for a discourse metrics leaves traditional metrical feet in ruins. This is the *modern* solidarity between poetry and the theory of rhythm.

Discourse doesn't codify silences. But such a codification is what Brecht sought in his 1938 essay 'Ueber reimlose Lyrik mit unregelmässigen Rhythmen' [On Unrhymed Poetry with Irregular Rhythms]. He denoted thus the *reading* of one of the quatrains of his *Deutsche Satiren*: 'How should it be read? We next place an irregular rhythm over it:

‒ ᴜ ‒ ᴜ‒ ᴜ‒   ᴜ ‒   ‒   ᴜ
Ja, wenn die Kin der Kin der blie ben, dann

— ᴜ‒ ᴜ   ‒   ᴜ ‒   ᴜ ‒ᴜ ‒   ᴜ ‒   ᴜ ‒ ᴜ ‒ᴜ
Könn te man ih nen im mer Mär chen er zäh len

‒ ᴜ ‒ᴜ   ᴜ ‒ ᴜ   ‒   ᴜ
Da sie a ber äl ter wer den

—   ᴜ ‒ ᴜ‒ ᴜ —
Kann man es nicht.

When saying the missing feet they must be taken into consideration by a lengthening of the foot to come or by pauses.'[109] An attempt more like theatre, and directing the actor, than like a discourse rhythmics, because

---

108. These signs are borrowed from Heusler, *Deutsche Versgeschichte*, cited above.
109. Bertolt Brecht, *Ueber Lyrik* (Frankfurt am Main: Suhrkamp, 1964), cited by Schultz, *Vom Rhythmus der modernen Lyrik*, p. 23. 'Yes, if children remained children, then / we might always tell them fairy tales / but as they grow older / we cannot.' Brecht's essay is examined in detail in Klaus Birkenhauer, *Die eigenrhythmische Lyrik Bertolt Brechts* (Tübingen: Max Niemeyer, 1971), p. 76.

its notations of silences can't have linguistic rigour, and some of its marks (stresses on *die* [könn] *te*, [Mär] *chen*) are effects of a-linguistic pedagogical overmarking, in the sense that they deviate from normal accentuation. But Brecht's attempt remains one of the modes of relationship between metrics and discourse.

The most systematic attempt at a discourse metrics I'm aware of, in the French domain, on the theoretical level, is the metrics of Benoît de Cornulier.[110] Studying the metrics of the alexandrine in Mallarmé, Verlaine, Rimbaud and Yves Bonnefoy, Cornulier distinguishes himself from previous metricists because he doesn't try to 'inventory "irregularities" (in relation to a more classical metrics)', but to 'detect an internal regularity'.[111] Which is enough to oppose him to Roubaud's method. This is no longer the search for entities with a vague historicity, such as the 'ordinary alexandrine'. But, from a discourse, which is a work, is undertaken metrics, which thus becomes a contribution to a rhythmics. This is no longer the isolation of verse outside discourse, as in Grammont and the whole French school, 'the manipulation of a mixture of verse lines of Verhaeren, Aragon, Moréas and Verlaine, grouped, as in treatises of versification, into a sort of limited liability corporation'.[112] Nor is this any longer the fiction *foot*, the phantasm *anapest*, the spirit *iamb* that haunt the house of verse. It is the linguistic study, which Cornulier terms metricometry, of 'the distribution of certain well-defined properties: which syllable boundaries follow a feminine syllable, which precede such a syllable, which divide the masculine part of a word, which detach (with consonants or feminine *e*'s) a proclitic or an enclitic from its base' (ibid., p. 273).

Thus is sought a sort of metrical grammar of a particular discourse: for example, 'The hypothesis that a ternary break *can*, in Verlaine, detach a proclitic or a preposition like *à* or *de*, allows us to perceive a total regularity that would not appear in the contrary hypothesis' (ibid., pp. 133–4). The aim, in Verlaine: 'to render in verse the varied inflections of the voice' (ibid., p. 134), leads to integrating 'a chanted diction associated with an emphatic accentuation', not as an individual phonic realisation, but as organisation of discourse, as rhythmics, in '*Et la tigresse épou-vantable d'Hyrcanie*' (ibid., p. 202 [And the frightening tigress of Hyrcania]). Like Seth Schein on Aeschylus and Sophocles, Cornulier speaks for the 'metrical violence' (ibid.,

---

110. In *Problèmes de métrique française*, cited above, fragments of which have appeared as 'Métrique du vers de 12 syllabes chez Rimbaud', *Le Français moderne*, 2 (April 1980), pp. 140–74; *Théorie du vers: Rimbaud, Verlaine, Mallarmé* (Paris: Seuil, 1982), and numerous articles.
111. Cornulier, 'Métrique du vers de 12 syllabes chez Rimbaud', p. 143.
112. Cornulier, *Problèmes de métrique française*, p. 139.

p. 284) of 'metrical onomatopoeia' (ibid., p. 332, n. 7). On Verlaine, and his way of 'dissociating the measure from the rhythm of writing', 'his metrics presupposes (so can aim to suggest) a very unacademic, very "unliterary", very "ungraphic" diction of the sentence; besides which, the word "diction" or "recitation" is unsuitable; it is *parole*, speech' (ibid., p. 379). Wherein the caesura in the middle of words takes on a discourse value: '*De cette science in + truse dans la maison*' (ibid., p. 199 [Of this science, in + truder in the house]).

In discovering the specificity of a rhythmics, a discourse's metrics discovers this discourse's historicity, and its own historicity. Across the internal chronology of works (ibid., pp. 185–203), Cornulier establishes that Verlaine distances himself from the classical 'through the importance of the discordances which he admits not only at the binary break, but also at the ternary breaks', more than Mallarmé does (ibid., p. 378). In so doing he re-establishes, very concretely, that the verse of Rimbaud's *Mémoire*, and of the *Vers nouveaux et chansons*, is 'critical verse, sometimes at least antimetrical rather than simply free of any measure' (ibid., p. 326). It aims to '*kindle the instinctive search for isometry the better to betray it*' (ibid., p. 327). In poetry it's always war.

In metrics too. Polemical poetry inspires polemical metrics. The uncertainties of metrics are shown as grid effects masking what other hypotheses put into action. Against Roubaud and Lusson who read[113] the negation of the caesura, and so a division into three, in Baudelaire's line[114]

A la très belle, à la très bonne, à la très chère

[To the very beautiful, to the very good, to the very dear.] Cornulier writes: 'Without a binary caesura, this line would have been quite simply lame for the author of the *Fleurs du mal*: it is almost certainly necessary to suppose this caesura, justifying a fervent stress on *TRÈS bonne*' (ibid., p. 58). The suspension on *la* (*à la-très bonne*) makes for a stronger reading than the ternary, which simply follows the syntax. By a *rejet* at the caesura. So too with all the sixth-position examples 'on a proclitic or on an insignificant monosyllable' in Baudelaire, gathered by Cassagne. Cornulier too shows, contrary to the tradition that has made Mallarmé the emblem of modernity, that 'metrical emancipation' applies to less than 1 per cent of his lines (ibid., pp. 60, 74), 'Mallarmé never wrote the "emancipated" lines that he thought he did' (p. 107).

---

113. Pierre Lusson and Jacques Roubaud, 'Mètre et rhythme de l'alexandrin ordinaire', *Langue française*, 23 (September 1974), pp. 41–53, p. 50.
114. In this line from 'Que diras-tu ce soir ...' the three instances of *très* are, following the orthography of Baudelaire's day, joined to the following adjective by a hyphen.

French verse is uniquely syllabic, for Cornulier: 'the fundamental role attributed to stress in French verse is sometimes purely illusory, sometimes simply secondary' (ibid., p. 379). The effect of stress 'is simply an automatic consequence of the fact that the hemistichs and lines are rhythmic groups or are syntagms' (ibid., p. 380), and 'French verse lines are really defined in terms of *syllabic number*: one cannot get away from that. In so far as the method of observation and the metrical analyses here proposed have managed to steer clear of the notion of stress, and in so far as they result in a better understanding of the metrics of Mallarmé, Verlaine and Rimbaud, one can consider that they contribute to refuting the idea that French verse, notably by these poets, rests *essentially* on stress. Conversely they demonstrate the pertinence of the exact syllabic number' (ibid., p. 380).

Which is perfectly pertinent, except for the fact that the caesura, the importance of which Cornulier has shown when it was transgressed, *is a stress*, before being a suspensive pause, and playing a suspensive role. Likewise the constant recourse to notions of feminine or masculine *e*, or the notion of syllable boundaries, of syntagm endings, presupposes stress and stress position. What arises from this is the relationship specific to French between syllabism and stress. It is because French verse is syllabic that it is accentual, in the French sense of phrase stress. Verlaine, and Rimbaud in the *Derniers vers*, have laid bare this relationship whilst exploiting it. It is also the rigour of metrics, in Mallarmé, Rimbaud, Verlaine, that Cornulier uncovers, as against the weak metrics of those who have forgotten the tension of metre and rhythm. They thought they were collaborating in the liberation of rhythm, being modern with their ternary scansion (which Cornulier denounces) of this line (ibid., p. 382),

> *Grêle – parmi l'odeur fade – du réséda*

[Thin – amidst the bland smell – of reseda] which was limp scansion, masking the rhythmic counterstress, the summit of the line, not to mention the properly prosodic effects that bind the line together

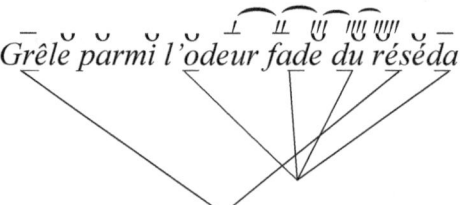

Caesura and counterstress are inseparable in the metrics of French, where they show, emblematically, that syllabism is an aspect of stress grouping, as stress is an aspect of syllabic grouping.[115]

Can a metrics be invented? But first, can a metrics be understood? Does an imposed order suffice to make a rhythm? If there are no semantic effects, it isn't a rhythm, and perhaps not a metrics. These are questions that metrical borrowings lead us to propose, such as that of the tanka in French, sectioning by syllable groups of 5–7–5–5–7. All the testimony of the poets points in the direction of a rhythmics, more than of a metrics: 'The musical and metrical expression of emotion is an instinct, and not an artifice.'[116] Generally, metrics is a starting point, not a destination. In the relationship between metrics and poetic writing, does a metrics have to be created? Cassagne remarked that Baudelaire, 'although a superior artist, is however not the creator of a new metrics.'[117] We speak of Corneille's, Racine's, Hugo's verse. The Russians speak of Pushkin's metrics. They didn't create a metrics, but a rhythmics. Through the impression of a rhythm which is the poet's own, we get the impression of a specificity which is that poet's own. It's felt empirically. It isn't theorised. It's a discourse–subject. The same, fundamentally, in verse or in prose, in Hugo.

Syllabism alone can't be a structural modifier, for the simple reason that there isn't, and can't be, in French at least, syllabism alone. Syllabism appears only in relation with meaning groups, which are rhythmic groups, which are therefore stress groups. If you programme arbitrary syllabisms, outside the rhythmic group, whether they're borrowed from Japanese or fabricated through some numerical principle or other, you can only, through artifice, constitute new accentual groups. The effect will be what meaning they make. Here too subversion cannot become a routine.

---

115. Other metrical theses of Benoît de Cornulier lie beyond the scope of my research, through their psychological or genetic aspects, which I can't discuss here, such as his opposition between 'simple lines', up to eight syllables, and 'complex lines', 'complex or indirect' (ibid., p. 26), from nine up. I wouldn't venture to justify, or to establish, as he does, this limit of *eight* on the basis of the psychology of perception. Nor however will I criticise it. Is the psychology of form a theoretical and historical territory, for metrics? I would limit myself simply to observing that it is the Spanish demarcation of verses *de arte menor* and *de arte mayor*. The *eight* is a demarcative, traditionally, for Henríquez-Ureña (*Estudios*, p. 38, n. 1). It's again a matter of understanding the tradition. Necessity, without compromise, of a critique.
116. Coventry Patmore, 'English Metrical Critics', *North British Review*, 27 (August 1857), pp. 67–86, p. 70, cited by Georges Faure, *Les Éléments du rythme poétique en anglais moderne: esquisse d'une nouvelle analyse et essai d'application au* Prometheus Unbound *de P. B. Shelley* (The Hague: Mouton, 1970), p. 26.
117. Albert Cassagne, *Versification et métrique de Charles Baudelaire* (Paris: Hachette, 1906), p. 122.

The problems of metrics, all the way down to its technicalities, in so far as they affect rhythmic groups – and they can't fail to do so – with their form, their endings, are still and always problems of meaning, hence problems of discourse. But the musical history of metrics, and what remains of music within it, consists in turning away from discourse. That is why the most novel transformations constitute a critique of traditional metrics. In and towards language, that is to say, exclusively with linguistic notions, they're the start of discourse metrics.

4

Sign
Not the Sign, but Rhythm

(in *Critique du rythme*, Lagrasse: Verdier, 1982, pp. 705–15)

Translated by Pier-Pascale Boulanger

Rhythm is irreducible to the sign. But it exists in language. Prose, or verse, with the fusion, depending on the culture, of the notions of prose and verse-poetry. Relativity reveals historicity. In addition to Hebrew, Arabic, Chinese, examples can be found in Malaysian, Yoruba, Gaelic, Bantu.[1] Rhythm, as value, inherent within value, organises discourse. Unlike the status of things within the sign, rhythm, contained in discourse, all the while being language, is the sole effect and the activity of the non-language that is the body. With its particular status, through sense, it slips by the sign, which does not see it. Rhythm is the discourse of signifiers. Not an intermediary between body and language, because language could never share a border with anything out of language. Individual, collective, indissociably, rhythm is the radical dissident of sense, according to the sign. But for a historical anthropology of language, rhythm is the constant matter of sense, each and every time ordinary and unique.

Rhythm is thus more than for the ear. It is for the entire subject. Rhythm, a subjective–collective organisation of a discourse, is its orality. More than some formal device. Where, in written works, to disoralise rhythm is to decorporalise, desocialise, in other words to desubjectivise, and dehistoricise. Which can be seen in certain discourses.

A critical anthropology of voice, and of orality, can no longer support the traditional opposition between scholarly literature and popular literature, written literature and oral literature. It too resulting from the sign and a Western way of thinking gone adrift. Prose or verse, all enduring works are

---

1. Examples are taken from Ruth Finnegan, *Oral Poetry: Its Nature, Significance and Social Context* (Cambridge: Cambridge University Press, 1977), pp. 26–7.

oral, have their orality, from Homer to Rabelais, from Hugo to Gogol, from Milton to Joyce, from Kafka to Beckett and others. Each specificity reinvents orality. It is neither primitive nor ancient: 'it is a normal part of our modern life as well as that of more distant peoples.'[2]

Ruth Finnegan has described, in her capacity as a sociologist of literature, a mode of production called oral, as opposed to written. The category she describes is sociological, not literary: a mode of production, in which transmission can be included, as well as a mode of representation. But the absence of writing in the processes of production and transmission that would seem to characterise orality, as is commonly thought, paradoxically conceals orality. It leads us to believe that orality is the absence of writing, that orality is opposed to writing.[3] The criticism of definitions and the efforts made to characterise orality are proof that orality goes beyond oral literatures.

As a sociologist, Finnegan has to concentrate on performance. Orality cannot be trapped in the simple opposition to writing. Orality overwhelms 'oral poetry'. Even when bringing rhythm down to repetition, the rule of 'the style of oral literature', Finnegan finds this rule in all poetry, or in 'much of the better known written poetry in English'.[4] This rule, which is supposed to differentiate poetry from prose, is limited however by the overlaps between prose and poetry. I have shown that parallelisms are not specific to biblical 'poetry', as has been said, and is said again by Finnegan (ibid., p. 99). Discourse, through its rhythmic organisation, is not the basis on which orally produced and transmitted texts can be distinguished from other texts. A formulaic style is not a proof of oral composition (ibid., p. 70). Nor can orality be defined statistically according to the number of *formulae* (ibid., p. 69). This is why the definition remains sociological. And orality not defined within its specificity.

Finnegan notes Jousse's 'biological reduction'. The scope of her information allows her to establish that rhythm is not a concept that is 'physical but cultural and relative' (ibid., p. 91). In particular, she shows that the simplistic view that opposes oral and written poetry is the same that opposes modern, industrial societies, societies with writing, and 'the supposedly far-different world of non-literate, "traditional" or "developing" peoples' (ibid., p. 272).

---

2. Finnegan, *Oral Poetry*, p. 6.
3. Again this is the *ethnological* notion of orality. But the theory of language imposes an anthropological notion of orality, one which would hold together rhythm and the historicity of all discourses. Literature plays a critical role here. Against the general tendency to privilege writing. Antoine Meillet notes that certain cultures, such as the Gauls, have voluntarily avoided writing, especially where religion is concerned (*Aperçu d'une histoire de la langue grecque*, Paris: Klincksieck, 1975, p. 151).
4. Finnegan, *Oral Poetry*, p. 132.

A model of literature reveals a model of society. Poetry is essential to anthropology, because 'it is through poetry – not exclusively, certainly, but surely pre-eminently – that people create and recreate that world' (ibid., p. 274). The critique of rhythm reveals the theories of society.

The reason is that rhythm is a marker of subjectivity, its system, the history of a subject through his or her discourse. Rhythm is what is intimate, not private. The movement of enunciation. What is situated and situating. More so than any other signifier, it is a signifier for all other signifiers. Through rhythm the subject is manifest as incompletable, as a function of the individual, who can only be whole and fragmented in the subject. In other words, reading is, in the most ordinary way, no more than accessing subjectivity.

Rhythm situates the theoretical error of the criteria of subjectivity. In particular that of Marxism. Poetics and politics stand together. For whatever poetics is worth, and politics follows suit. Rhythm and subjectivity, inseparable, show the absence and impossibility, in Marxism, of a theory of rhythm and of the subject. Marcuse criticised the Marxist notion of 'bourgeois' subjectivity in the name of a 'liberating subjectivity', through which 'art remains a dissident force' and 'represents the ultimate goal of all revolutions: the freedom and happiness of the individual'.[5] Subjectivity alone creates value. Which is what Adorno said. Because it creates 'sympathy'.[6]

But the critique of the Marxist critique of subjectivity keeps – as did anarchism with the Marxist theory of the state – the same notions as Marxism. Only the value is reversed. Subjectivity is no longer 'bourgeois'-condemned. It is revolutionary-valued. But this very association between artistic revolution and social revolution, which wants to save revolution-through-subjectivity, ends up losing it. Like the doctrine it thought it was criticising. Because to associate artistic revolution with social revolution necessarily pushes artistic revolution into a conceptuality that does not recognise it, through its constitution and history, for the same reason that it does not recognise the theory of language. The only way that it could generate a historical and dialectical history of language is by criticising itself. Which is impossible because of its theory and politics.

The critique of rhythm can thus merely criticise Critical Theory, and what comes out of it. Marcuse remains in dualism the same way he remains in Marxism. His 'aesthetic dimension' is a form. It eludes being opposed to content by a simple sleight of words, where 'form becomes content and vice

---

5. Herbert Marcuse, *The Aesthetic Dimension: Toward a Critique of Marxist Aesthetics*, trans. and rev. by Herbert Marcuse and Erica Sherover (Boston: Beacon Press, 1978), p. 69.
6. Theodor W. Adorno, *Noten zur Literatur* (Frankfurt am Main: Suhrkamp, 1958, p. 80), in Marcuse, ibid., p. 61.

versa'.⁷ Hence all it does is speak of subjectivity, always opposed to a mass, as being the individual of individualism. Marcuse keeps the Marxist notion of the *autonomy* of art: 'The work of art can attain political relevance only as autonomous work' (ibid., p. 64). He keeps the Hegelian logic of *Aufhebung*: 'The utopia in great art is never the simple negation of the reality principle but its transcending preservation (*Aufhebung*) in which past and present cast their shadow on fulfilment. The authentic utopia is grounded in recollection' (ibid., p. 83). He keeps *reflection*, a pseudo-relation of causality between art and society. He sees change in art as 'anticipating or reflecting substantial changes in the society at large. Thus, expressionism and surrealism anticipated the destructiveness of monopoly capitalism, and the emergence of new goals of radical change' (ibid., p. 11). Naivety and vagueness coalesce into the simplified and unprovable movement from art to society, which has led to the well-known scholasticism. Not only does Marcuse stand these grounds, but in doing so he also contradicts his own proposition: 'The political potential of art lies only in its own aesthetic dimension' (ibid., p. 12). From sociologism to formalism, Marxism, even if critical, remains trapped in the dualism of the sign. Which, in Marcuse, dual entities, Eros and Thanatos, Dionysius and Apollo, further mystify.

Change in art is not an object other than its subjectivity, its own relation to the collective, in other words a semantic of historicity. The very object of the critique of rhythm.

As nothing is hidden in language, the subject-effect is manifest, in that no work can fill in for another one. The body of a text, when there is one, is merely the specificity of a discourse that is its own unit of significance, where rhythm is the main signifier. As obvious as it may seem, it was not before rhythm came along. Thus a poet is a creator of rhythms and a breaker of rhythms. Using metrics or not. This is what was difficult with fixed forms. They suggested that rhythm was ready made. Empirically, adjectives derived from authors' names, with the vague precision of *je ne sais quoi*, designate, without asking why, these denied subjects that become evident, such as Apollinairean, Baudelairean and all the others. T. S. Eliot wrote that 'a man who introduces new rhythms into the language "enlarges our sensibilities"'.⁸ The prevalence of certain sense-forms in each culture is proof of this. It can range from groups such as the octosyllabic cinquains in Apollinaire's *La Chanson du mal-aimé* to the way two words are used together. They are shifters, parables of rhythm and of the subject.

7. Marcuse, *The Aesthetic Dimension*, p. 41.
8. Cited by William McNaughton, 'Ezra Pound's Meters and Rhythms', *Publications of the Modern Language Association*, 78/1 (March 1963), p. 138.

The unit has the same variable extension. It can have a cultural role that biblical episodes play separately. The unit is that which has no units: the poem, the subject. Not the verse. Mandelstam considered the entire *Divina Commedia* as a 'stanza', or 'a crystallographic figure, that is, a body'.[9] The poem is the transitory moment of an I-here-now. But because it is situated, it gives, in the sense of Max Jacob, the impression that it is closed, all the while being an open unit.

The poem, and no longer the verse, is the unit of the poem. That is why the historic notion of free verse dissolves in the notion of free poem. Not only in European poetry but also in very strong formalist traditions, such as Arabic poetry.[10]

In this tradition, the verse comes first, not the poem. Poetry is a 'rhythmic and rhymed discourse'.[11] The poem has an 'ordering function', the one of a 'general thematic operator'.[12] Ibn Kaldhûn also said this: 'Each verse, with its combinations of words, is by itself a unit of meaning. In a way, it is a clause in itself, and independent from what precedes it and what follows it.'[13] A definition promoting a cult of the fragment, anthologies and rhetoric, as noted by Vicente Cantarino.[14]

But metrical formalism cannot support its own postulate. Further on, Bencheikh writes this: 'it is not metrics that created poetry, but poetry that suggested metrics'.[15] The Arabic monorhyme poem forbade enjambment on the grounds of metrics. But in practice *rejets* and *contre-rejets* were frequent, as Bencheikh shows, so much so that 'the discourse is intelligible only when the poem is read as a whole: the verse extended to the extreme' (ibid., p. 153). The very frame that Bencheikh seems to have adopted in order to keep with Arabic tradition, the 'metrical balance sheet' is an 'admission of powerlessness' (ibid., p. 203). Elements that Bencheikh lists as 'cohesive devices' belong to discourse, not to metrics: 'ligatures in language, narrative organisation,

---

9. Osip Emilievitch Mandelstam, *Interview on Dante, III*, in *Sobranie Sočinenij v Treh Tomah* [*Collected Works in Three Volumes*], ed. by Gleb Petrovič Struve and Boris Andreevič Filippov, vol. 2 (New York: Meždunarodnoe Literaturnoe Sodružestvo, 1971), p. 415.
10. Against the unity of the classical couplet, Adonis writes that 'the poem must be *whole* as is a painting', in Kamal Kheir Beik, *Le Mouvement moderniste de la poésie arabe contemporaine* (Aurillac: Publications orientalistes de France, 1978), p. 88.
11. In Vicente Cantarino, *Arabic Poetics in the Golden Age: Selection of Texts Accompanied by a Preliminary Study* (Leiden: Brill, 1975), p. 44.
12. Jammal Eddine Bencheikh, *Poétique arabe* (Paris: Gallimard, 1989), p. 148.
13. Muhammed Ibn Kaldhûn, *The Muqaddimah, An Introduction to History*, trans. by Franz Rosenthal, vol. 3 (Princeton, NJ: Princeton University Press, 1967), p. 773.
14. Cantarino, *Arabic Poetics in the Golden Age*, p. 53.
15. Bencheikh, *Poétique arabe*, p. 230, n. 4.

thematic tension' (ibid., p. 163). Even metrically, the single rhyme turns the poem into a unit. The interior rhyme pushes the poem-as-unit one degree closer to the verse-as-unit. Right into the verse, discourse takes precedence over the metre, since the metrical pause at the hemistich 'very often' occurs 'precisely within a word' (ibid., p. 178) and 'does not prompt a semantic pause' (ibid., p. 181), whereas the metrical and semantic limits coincide at the median line. Bencheikh concludes by saying that rhythm 'cannot be differentiated without any trick or danger in the grammatical and stylistic organisation' (ibid., p. 248). There could not have been a better way to show, unknowingly, the incoherence of a poetics based on the verse as 'unit of the poetic discourse' (ibid., p. 147), the inability of keeping to its own terms. In fact the verse signals the primacy of a cultural code. The poem signifies the primacy of discourse. There is no need to ignore metrics any more than verse already ignores it. But there is a need to situate the poem in discourse. The poem is no more made of verse than discourse is made of words.

The units of language are variables, more than universals. Verses are not everywhere, the same way words are not everywhere. The unity of the unit is eroding. The internal plurality of the unit, of the subject, of rhythm, is what the critique of rhythm aims for. This historicity becomes apparent when a non-Indo-European linguistic tradition is contrasted, such as that of Japan. In Japanese, the notion of word has no correspondence, between *go* which designates morphemes, simple and complex, and *bunsetsu*, or phrasal unit, which is related to the clause.[16] Poetics and theories of language stand together. The relation between poetics and linguistics is situated within this solidarity.

The transformation of the notion of unit, which is revealed through poetry, means the transformation of a language relation between the subject and the collective, the transformation of the notion of the individual. It implies violence, and is no more separable from an ethics, from a relation to the political, than from a theory of sense.

The verse is a dialectic of metre and rhythm, similar to that of the collective and the subject. But each of these four terms contains the others in specific ways. Thus to conceive of rhythm as breaking away from the constraint of culture is to dedialecticise it. As the unit of the poem is the poem,

---

16. Vladimir Mikhailovich Alpatov, 'Ob Osobennostjah Japonskoj Lingvističeskoj Tradicii', *Voprosy Jazykoznanija* (*Topics in the Study of Language*), vol. 4 (1978), pp. 76–81. Alpatov identifies four non-Indo-European linguistic traditions: Indian, Arabic, Chinese, Japanese. The importance of writing, along with features specific to languages, the closing of traditions on to themselves, are in large part constitutive of the irreducibility of these traditions.

the unit of the verse is the verse, where what delimits the syntagma and word is the only rhythmic notion that is linguistic. Figures generate a semantics, paradigms, a logic, that are still not entirely free of ancient aesthetics of the futile, archaising, isolating. Meanwhile, a cultural history and typology of dictions remains to be done – a part of historicity which is poetry.

The history of the poem will send the opposition between prose and verse back to the pile of antiquated ideas on poetry which Jakobson has been repeating, adding free verse in between: 'free verse is an attenuated *form* of verse, a *compromise between poetic* and *ordinary language*' in 'the universal coexistence of two poles of language: verse and ordinary prose', thus mistaking prose for ordinary language as did Monsieur Jourdain.[17] The verse is a variable of variables. Its rules are in the subject, who is always historical. Free verse will have been the theoretical stripping of the subject's work, which has always taken place.

The critique of rhythm is nothing but the meeting of poetic and theoretical lineages that define the possibilities of a subject, of a moment. The passage from a metrics to a rhythmic is situated. The broadening of its stake, by which its tension is created, is such that adventure necessarily overwhelms it. Theory is all the more necessary because it is ruled by the multiple.[18]

It is kinship that links the poem and theory, as the poem links, against tradition, popular poetry and learned poetry. From Russian formalists to contemporary semioticians, typology has insisted on what opposes them.[19] The critique of rhythm retains what they have in common, which Montaigne had already done: 'The vulgar and purely *natural poetry* has in it certain proprieties and graces, by which she may come into some comparison with the *greatest beauty* of *poetry* perfected by art.'[20] Continuity that one sole cultural tradition has occulted. It is true that it is more in evidence at certain moments. Mandelstam wrote, on Blok's poem: 'The poem *The Twelve* is a monumental and dramatic popular verse.'[21] Henríquez-Ureña has shown the

---

17. Roman Jakobson and Linda Waugh, *The Sound Shape of Language* (Bloomington: Indiana University Press, 1979), p. 216. Meschonnic refers to Molière's *Le Bourgeois Gentilhomme*.
18. *Nam qui facit, quod non sapit, deffinitur bestia*, according to a verse by Gui d'Arezzo cited by Théodore Gerold, *La Musique au Moyen Âge* (Paris: Champion, 1932), p. 353, in prose, a sequence where syllabic-accentual lines all end with an 'a', echoing 'alleluia': the presence and praise of God are in knowledge.
19. For instance, Solomon Marcus, *La Sémiotique formelle du folklore: approche linguistico-mathématique*, trans. by Hélène Combes (Paris: Klincksieck, 1978), p. 3.
20. Michel de Montaigne, *Works of Michel de Montaigne*, vol. 1 (New York: Derby & Jackson, 1859), p. 451.
21. Osip Mandelstam, *Collected Works, Sobranie Sočinenij* (New York: Inter-Language Literary Associates, 1967–9), vol. 2, p. 316.

close relations between popular poetry and '*culta*' poetry, in Lope de Vega, Tirso de Molina and Góngora.²² The distinction was not made before the fifteenth century. The play of prosodic and accentual figures (where identical vowels in crossed schemes were accentuated), which Henríquez-Ureña did not live to see, was both a repository of verse and a reservoir of modernity.²³ But also, paradoxically, anonymity is the most powerful exposure of the subject. Its maximum poetic and theoretical fulfilment. More than a different prosody or metrics, popular poetry engages the subject. It is why rhythm cannot be reduced to mnemonics. Memorisation is as much the effect of a vision as of a figure.

The theory of orality shares the risk of orality. Theory and poem stand together. Theoretical poem. Theory as well as the poem bear the allegory of their own path, a discourse behind discourse, as rhythm organises its values through sense. It is what rhythm does not say – through which it eludes any voluntarism – and what theory also does not say. That which it cannot see nor grasp. *Going with the way of the wind.* Alain, though so very dependent on tradition, had a sense for it. In every poem he saw an epic: 'Yet the poem takes us away, and such is the sense of the epic.'²⁴ In the sense, overwhelmed but precise, where formal typology is overwhelmed, such that: 'Epic is not knowing where one is going.'²⁵ To the sense of the poetry's allegory which is in every poem, Alain added: 'The poem awaits; the poem is insatiable. Such is the epic movement, which resembles epic action. Thus there is something epic in every poem, or else it is nothing' (ibid., p. 1278). By setting the term adrift, Alain sets discourse adrift, returns to etymology and continues the commentary on orality: 'It is then that the song of proverbs is heard. And for my part I have come to hear the song of epic in every peasant story, and finally everywhere the song of birds in man.'²⁶ Beyond his historical designation, generic, which is neither simple nor reducible to something simple, the notion of epic stands originally and functionally together with orality. Perhaps more so than with the notion of narrative [*récit*]. Northrop Frye uses the term '*epos*' to describe works whose mode of address is oral.²⁷

22. Pedro Henríquez-Ureña, *Estudios de Versificación Española* (Buenos Aires: Universidad de Buenos Aires, 1961), pp. 193, 195, 198.
23. José María Alín, *El Cancionero Español de Tipo Tradicional* (Madrid: Taurus, 1968), p. 107.
24. Alain, *Vingt leçons sur les beaux-arts* (Paris: Gallimard, 1931), p. 517.
25. Alain, *Propos*, vol. 1 (Paris: Gallimard, 1956), p. 1277.
26. Alain, *Histoire de mes pensées* (Paris: Gallimard, 1936), p. 148.
27. Northrop Frye, *Anatomy of Criticism: Four Essays* (Princeton, NJ: Princeton University Press, 1957), p. 248. Whereas Cecil Maurice Bowra, in *Heroic Poetry* (London: Macmillan, 1961 [1952]), limits epic to 'the pursuit of honour' (p. 3), heroes and grand actions

The epic is an intimate relation with the unknown. It is why it is manifest in certain stories. But more than journeys, exploits or the grandeur of heroes, it is, like sense, history, rhythm, what ceaselessly eludes the self and which, through intersections, exchanges, new beginnings, indefinitely fulfils, like the past with the future, its *métissage*.

* * *

The theory of rhythm is political. The empirical, not monism, is what is being opposed here to the dualism of the sign. Rhythm overwhelms the partition of the sign. It is the empirical in its historicity, irreducible to the whole in two. In the empirical where language is I find myself, the multiple, the infinite. The empirical, not empiricism. Dualism opposes language to life, prefers its own order, which acts as its frame and truth. This is why it cannot grasp rhythm. And along with rhythm a sense of sense and of subjects where dualism cannot go. It is what this book risks.

The theory of language and of history is also a poetics, the poetics of society. Without it, there is no theory of creativity, no relation through which the individual and the collective construct one another. The effect of this lack can be seen in Marxism, psychoanalysis, generative grammar, for instance. Pragmatics and 'cognitive' science. Through the analysis of what this lack means, the critique of rhythm is given a place and a role in the social sciences. And in or against philosophy.

Speaking of rhythm, I am speaking of you, it is you who is speaking, the problems of rhythm are yours. The critique of rhythm has no conclusion. It opens on to the historicity of language, of literature, of theory. Not on to applications, but on to experience. Poetry is present in theory as part unsaid. It is the rhythm of the critique of rhythm, since theory, like poetry, can only be done through the unknown.

belonging to a 'curious kind of past' (p. 25). A traditional definition, which sought mainly to differentiate the epic, as a human adventure, from the supernatural.

PART 2

POETRY AND POEM

The following text, *The Rhythm Party Manifesto*, has already been published in English translation by David Nowell Smith in the online journal *Thinking Verse*, I (2011), pp. 161–73. It is the concluding and summarising chapter of the volume *Célébration de la poésie* (Lagrasse: Verdier, 2001). This book is a reflection on what a poem is and does. But as every reflection, it is situated. Meschonnic attacks his contemporary French intellectual scene, particularly the philosophers, and its representation of poetry – what he considers not only a use and abuse of poetry, but also a misunderstanding based on a wrong conception of language.

He also shows that the traditional complaint about a lack of interest in poetry is mistaken, since, in reality, what happens in poetry is of interest to everybody because it is there that the sense of language and the sense of the subject are negotiated.

Meschonnic explains here, in manifesto form, his definition of the poem as opposed to a fixed idea about poetry. The title of the book, *Celebration of Poetry*, is ironic since Meschonnic insists on the uniqueness and unforeseeability of a poem. As soon as we believe we know what poetry is, there cannot be poetry any more. Consequently, by celebrating it, we have preconceived ideas and miss what makes a poem a poem. For this reason, Meschonnic also prefers the term *poem* to *poetry*. The poem, for him, is not necessarily the literary form but an activity of transformation of a form of life into a form of language, and reciprocally a form of language into a form of life. The poem is the manifestation of the fact that we do not 'use' language. The rhythm-poem is the maximal subjectivation of discourse: that is, in the poem, a subject forms itself. Meschonnic's compound *forme-sujet*, translated as *subject-form(er)*, brings together that which forms a subject, and the form a subject takes.

Hence, in this understanding, the poem as transformation and subject-form(er) not only occupies a central position in literary studies, but is the activity of thinking itself and thus of central concern to all the humanities – and to what it means to be human altogether.

5

The Rhythm Party Manifesto

(in *Célébration de la poésie*, Lagrasse: Verdier, 2001, pp. 291–303)

Translated by David Nowell Smith

A manifesto, because it is necessary, in order to be a subject, to live as a subject, to make a place for poems. A place. What I see around me being called 'poetry' for the most part tends – strangely, infuriatingly – to refuse a place, its place, to what I call a 'poem'.

There is, particularly in a French-style contemporary poetry, and for reasons not foreign to the myth of the genius of the French language, the institutionalisation of a cult devoted to poetry which involves a concerted absence of the poem.

There have always been fashions. But this fashion exerts a pressure, the pressure of several accumulated academicisms. An atmospheric pressure: the air of the times.

Against this suffocation of the poem by poetry, there is a necessity to demonstrate [*manifester*],[1] to make manifest the poem, a necessity that some of us sense from time to time, in order to emit a speech suffocated by the power of literary conformisms that do nothing except to aestheticise schemas of thought which are in fact schemas of society.

An idolatry of poetry produces voiceless fetishes which pass themselves off as, and are taken as, poetry.

Opposed to all poetisations, I say that there is a poem only if a form of life transforms a form of language and if reciprocally a form of language transforms a form of life.

I say that it is only in this way that poetry, as an activity of poems, can

---

1. [Translator's note: Meschonnic's use of *manifester* here involves a verbal punning central to his argument. It is at once to 'demonstrate' (as in, to follow a political demonstration), to 'render manifest' and to put in a 'manifesto'.]

live in society, can do to people that which only a poem can do – people who, without this, will not even know that they are being desubjectivised, dehistoricised, until they are no longer themselves but rather products of the marketplace of ideas, the marketplace of feelings, of behaviour.

Instead of the activity of everything that is poem contributing, as only this activity can, to constituting people as subjects. No subject without the subject of the poem.

For if the subject of the poem is lacking from the other subjects of which each one of us is the result, there is at the same time a specific lack and an unawareness of this lack, and this lack impacts on all other subjects. The baker's dozen of subjects that we are. And it isn't the Freudian subject that will save you. Or that will save the poem.

Only the poem can unite, hold affect and concept in one mouthful of speech which acts, transforms our manner of seeing, hearing, feeling, understanding, talking, reading. Translating. Writing.

In this the poem is radically different from the story, from description. Both of which name. Which remain within the sign. And the poem is not of the sign.

The poem is what teaches us not to use language. It alone teaches us that, contrary to appearances and to habits of thought, we do not use language.

Which does not mean that, as an unthinking inversion of terms would have it, language uses us. Something which, curiously enough, would have all the more relevance, providing this relevance is delimited, is limited to typical forms of manipulation, as we find incessantly in operation in advertising, propaganda, mass communication, non-information, and all forms of censorship. But then it is not language which uses us. It is those who manipulate, who pull the strings of the puppets who we are in their hands – it is they who use us.

But the poem makes of us a specific subject-form(er).[2] It exercises in us a subject that we would not be without it. And this, through language. It is in this sense that it teaches us that we do not use language. But we become language. One can no longer be satisfied simply to say, if other than as a somewhat vague presupposition that we are language. It is more accurate to say that we become language. More or less. A question of sense [*sens*].[3] Of the sense of language.

2. [Translator's note: *Forme-sujet*: Meschonnic's compound brings together both that which forms a subject, and the form a subject takes.]
3. [Translator's note: The French word *sens* is another which Meschonnic employs in its semantic fullness, to encompass 'direction', an individual 'meaning' and a more generalised 'meaningfulness', and also the 'senses' themselves. Particularly noteworthy here is that *sens du langage* can mean a sense *for* language, a sense *of* language, but also 'sense' such as it takes place *in* language and languages.]

But only the poem that is poem teaches us this. Not that which resembles 'poetry'. All made up. In advance. The poem of 'poetry'. This poem encounters merely our culture. Itself variable. And, to the extent that it tricks us, in making itself pass for a poem, it is harmful. For it muddles both our relation to ourselves as subjects and our relation to ourselves as we are in the process of becoming language. And the two are inseparable. This product tends to make and remake us into a product. Instead of an activity.

This is why critical activity is vital. Not destructive. No, constructive – constructive of subjects.

A poem transforms. Naming, describing, are worth nothing to the poem. And to describe is to name. That is why adjectives are revealing. Revealing of our confidence in language – and this confidence in language names, does not stop naming. Look at the adjectives.

This is why to celebrate, which has so often been taken for poetry, is the enemy of the poem. For to celebrate is to name. To designate. To pick out substances like beads of the rosary of that sacred taken to be poetry. At the same time as accepting it. Not only accepting the world as it is, the ignoble 'I have only good to say of it' of Saint-John Perse, but accepting every notion of the language through which it is represented. The unthought link between the genius of place and the genius of language.

A poem does not celebrate, it transforms. This is what I take Mallarmé to be saying when he states: 'Poetry is the expression, through human language brought back to its essential rhythm, of the mysterious meaning of aspects of existence: in this way it gifts authenticity to our time on earth [*séjour*] and constitutes the only spiritual task.' Where some believe that it's out of fashion.

For the poem, I want to hold on to the decisive role of rhythm in the constitution of language-subjects. Because rhythm is no longer, even if certain philistines haven't realised it, the alternation of the tick-tock on the cheek of the metronomic metrician. But rhythm is the language-organisation of the continuous of which we are made. With all the otherness which founds our identity. Come in, metricians, it merely requires a poem for you to lose your footing.

For rhythm is a subject-form(er). The subject-form(er). That it renews the meaning of things, that it is through rhythm that we reach the sense that we have of our being undone [*défaire*], that everything around us is made out of its own unmaking [*défaire*], and that, approaching this sensation of the movement of everything, we ourselves are part of this movement.

And if the poem-rhythm is a subject-form(er), rhythm is no longer either the weak fusional notion of which phenomenologists are so fond (watch your language), or a formal notion – form itself is no longer a formal notion, a notion of the sign – but a form of historicisation, a form of individuation. Down with the old couple of form and meaning. Poem is all that, in language, realises this recitative that is a maximal subjectivisation of discourse. Prose, verse or line.

A poem is an act of language which only takes place once and which restarts ceaselessly. Because it makes subject [*faire du sujet*]. Does not stop making subject. Making you. When it is an activity, not a product.

This is a manner more rhythmic, more language, of transposing what Mallarmé called 'authenticity' and 'time on earth'. 'Time on earth', a term still too static to express instability itself. But 'the only spiritual task', yes, I'd say once more yes, in this world swept away by the vulgarity of conformisms and the market of the sign, or else one must abandon the attempt to be a subject, a historicity in progress, in order to be just a product, an exchange value among other commodities. What the technicisation of mass communication merely accelerates.

No, words are not made to designate things. They are there to situate us amongst things. To see them as designations demonstrates the most impoverished idea of language. And the most common. It is the combat, but as it always has been, of the poem versus the sign. David versus Goliath. Goliath, the sign.

This is also why I believe that one would be wrong to attach, once and for all, Mallarmé's 'the absent of all bouquets' to the banality of the sign. The sign as absence of things. Especially when one opposes it to the 'true life' of Rimbaud.[4] One remains within the discontinuous of language opposed to the continuous of life. Mallarmé himself knew that on a stone 'pages will only close again with difficulty'.

It is here that the poem can and must beat the sign. Must devastate the representation that is agreed upon, taught, canonical. Because the poem is the moment of a listening [*écoute*]. And the sign merely brings us to see. It is deaf, and it deafens. Only the poem can put into voice, make us move from voice to voice, make of us a listening. Give us all of language as listening. And the continuum of this listening includes, imposes a continuity between the subjects that we are, the language that we become, the ethics in action that is this listening, whence the politics of the poem. A politics of thought. The 'rhythm party'.

Whence also the derisory quality of the interminable refrain by poets of ivory-tower poetism, in Hölderlin, of 'poetically man dwells upon this earth'. No. Man dwells semiotically on this earth. More than ever. Not that I'm

---

4. [Translator's note: Rimbaud, *Une Saison en enfer*: 'La vraie vie est absente. Nous ne sommes pas au monde.' In *Œuvres complètes*, Paris: Gallimard/La Pléiade, 1972, p. 103.]

taking issue with Hölderlin. No, I'm taking issue with the Hölderlin-effect, which isn't the same thing. The chain link essentialisation of language, of the poem (with the neo-Pindarism that comes out of it, and which also is fashionable), of ethics and of politics.

Poetism is the alibi and the preservation of the sign. The prayer-mill of poetisation.

It is against this that we need poem, again poem, always poem. Rhythm, again rhythm, always rhythm. Against the generalised semiotisation of society. Which some poets have believed (or given that impression) they could escape through the ludic. The love of poetry, instead of the poem. Digging their own grave with their rhymes. Poetic distress more than time of distress.

What remains to be thought is the clarity of the poem. What is at stake, through the poem, is the subject in each of us. And the necessity of extricating Mallarmé from the interpretations that continue to push him down upon the sign, again and again isolating over the last forty years the same words, the 'elocutionary disappearance of the poet'. But never 'the poem, enunciator'. The subject, through the poem; the poem, through the subject. Mallarmé-symptom. Reduced merely to questions of meaning. Which allows him to continue to be seen as a difficult poet, the poet of 'difficulty'. The obscure. No change, or very little, since Max Nordau. Always the imbeciles of the present.

In pushing Mallarmé back into his epoch. Doubly closed in, Mallarmé: in the sign, and in symbolism.

What is at stake – if we are to render audible Mallarmé's orality and clarity – is the poem. Against the wise idiocy of the sign.

Now, contrary to those who no longer believe in Mallarmé's words on 'the orphic elucidation of the earth', I would say that the poem, the very smallest poem, a Spanish 'copla', is the stand-in for the challenge of the 'modern Odyssey' in Mallarmé himself, and in all the voices that have been their own voice.

Because, with each voice, Orpheus changes, and starts anew. An Odyssey starts anew. Pay heed to it, oh men of little voice.

With a poem, it isn't a product of the visionary that is at work, as an entire tradition, initially poetic, later poetising, believed. But 'the only task of the poet', to start off again from Mallarmé – for initially there is one, and only the poem can give us what is its alone to do – is to listen to everything that you don't know you are hearing, everything you don't know you are saying, and everything one doesn't know how to say, because you think that language is made of words.

Orpheus was one of the names of the unknown. A vulgar and common error is to believe him stuck in the past. Instead of seeing that what he designates continues in each and every one of us.

And 'The Odyssey', the 'modern Odyssey' Mallarmé speaks of, another gross error has been, and still is, to confuse this with voyages and their stories, with the decalcomania of epics and the received ideas that we had of them. Just like confusing the monumental and the unwieldy. The poem demonstrates that the odyssey is in the voice. In all voices. Its voyage is listening.

And if listening is the voyage of the voice, the academic opposition between lyric and epic is thereby abolished.

In a new sense, each poem, if it is a poem, an adventure in voice, not some sort of reproduction of the poetry of the past, has something of epic within it. And let's leave to the museum of the arts and traditions of language the notion of lyricism that some contemporaries have tried to reintroduce into the taste of the times, by making it say a rosary of traditionalisms: the confusions between the 'I' and the 'me', between voice and singing, between language and music, in a common ignorance of the subject of the poem. Confusions that poetry's own history has helped to bring to life.

But the poem gives signs of life. What resembles it, because it wants to be poetic, to have the air of a poem even if not to be one itself, gives signs of being a book.[5]

A poem is made out of what we are going towards, which we do not know, and what we draw back from, which it is vital to recognise.

For a poem, one must learn to refuse, to set to work on an entire list of refusals. Poetry does not change unless we refuse it. Just as the world is changed only by those who refuse it.

Amongst my refusals I put: no to the sign and to its society. No to that overblown impoverishment that confuses language in general with an individual language [*le langage et la langue*], and speaks only of a language [*langue*] without knowing what it is on about, of the memory of a language, as if a language was a subject, and of an essential relation between the alexandrine and the genius of the French language. Don't forget to breathe every twelve syllables. Have a metrical heart. A mythology that is doubtless no stranger to the return to fashion of the ludic in academic versification. And if it was meant to make us laugh, it didn't work. Aristotle had already pointed his finger at those who write in verse to hide the fact that they've nothing to say.

No to the sign-consensus, in the generalised semiotisation of the world of communication. No, one does not get to the things themselves. For one does not cease to transform them or be transformed by them, through language.

No to the poetising phraseology that speaks of a contact with the real. To the opposition between poetry and external world. Which leads poetry

---

5. [Translator's note: Here Meschonnic is punning on *vivre* [to live] and *livre* [book].]

merely to speak about. To enumerate. To describe. Again – to name. It isn't the world that is there, it is the relation to the world. And this relation is transformed by a poem. And the invention of a thought is the poem of thought.

No, poetry is not within the world, within things. Contrary to what poets have said. A linguistic imprudence. It can be nowhere but in the subject who is subject to the world and subject to language as the meaning of life. We have confused the feeling of things and the things themselves. This confusion instructs us to name, to describe. A naivety quickly punished. The proof, if such was needed, that poetry isn't within the world, is that non-poets are in the world just as poets are, and do not make this world a poem. A horse goes around the world and is still a horse.

To live is not enough. Everyone lives. To feel is not enough. Everyone has feelings. Experience isn't enough. The discourse on experience isn't enough. For there to be a poem.

No to the illusion that living precedes writing. That to see the world modifies the gaze. When it is the opposite: the need for a sense that isn't there, and the transformation of sense by all the senses that changes our relation with the world.

If living precedes writing, life isn't anything except life, writing nothing but literature. And that's evident. At least one must learn to recognise this. This is what teaching should be.

No to seeing taken to mean hearing. Some poets have believed that they spoke of poetry in staking everything on seeing, on the gaze. What is lacking is a sense of language. The revolutions in the gaze are effects, not causes. A manner of speaking which hides its own unthought. The strong opposition lies between thinking via received ideas, and thinking one's voice, having one's voice in one's thinking.

No to the Rimbaudism that sees Rimbaud-poetry in his departure outside the poem. Like Mallarmé in his Book which he did not write.

No to when one opposes inside and outside, imaginary and real, that apparently unquestionable self-evidence. It prevents us from thinking that we are nothing other than the relation of the two.

No to metaphor taken as the thought of things, when it is simply a means of circling around them, being pretty, instead of being the sole way of saying.

No to the separation between affect and concept, that cliché of the sign. Which makes not only the fake poem, but also the fake thought.

No to the opposition between individualism and collectivity, that social effect of the sign, that unthought of the subject, thus of the poem, which treats literature, poetry like a board game, that old-fangled tune [*rengaine*] of the 'renga' – those would-be poems that one makes in teams.

No to the confusion between subjectivity, that psychology, in which lyricism remains trapped, those metres that get sung, and the subjectivisation of the subject-form(er) that is the poem.

No, no to the convenient opposition between transgression and convention, invention and tradition. Because there has been for a long time an academicism of transgression just as there is an academicism of tradition. And because, in both cases, one opposes the modern to the classic, in merging the classic with neo-retro, and in both cases one has misrecognised the subject of the poem, its radical invention which has always made the poem, and which returns these oppositions to their confusion, to their unthought, masked by the dictates of the market.

No also to the ease which opposes the easy and the difficult, transparency to obscurity, because it identifies the easy with habits of thought. No to clichés on hermeticism. The sign has a lot to do with this, irrationalising its own unthought, which it indeed renders obscure. It is its clarity which is obscure. Like French clarity [*la clarté française*]. But the poem, one shouldn't play that old trick on it again.

No to poetry as the aim of the poem, for straight away it becomes an intention. To poetise. Which can't therefore create anything but literature. The poetry of poetry being no more poetry than the philosophical subject is subject of the poem.

To demonstrate [*manifester*] is not to give lessons, nor to predict. There is a manifesto when there is something intolerable. A manifesto can no longer tolerate. That is why it is intolerant. The soft, invisible dogmatism of the sign does not itself come across as intolerant. But if everything in it were tolerable, there would be no need for a manifesto. A manifesto is the expression of emergency. Even if it just comes across as incongruous. If there were no risk, there would no longer be a manifesto. Liberalism does not show that it is the absence of liberty.

And a poem is a risk. The work of thinking also is a risk. To think what a poem is. What makes a poem a poem. What a poem must be to be a poem. And for a thought to be a thought. This necessity, to think value and definition inseparable. To think this inseparation as a universal of poem and thought. Their historicity, which is their necessity.

Even if this thinking is particular, it has in principle taken place in a practice, it will necessarily always be true. It is thus in no way a lesson for that which is called the century to come. No more than the academy's summing-up of the century. This effect of language, the temporality-effect of the sign. The discontinuous of centuryism.

To summarise, the poem demonstrates and what the poem must demonstrate is the refusal of the separation between language and life. To recognise this as an opposition not between language and life, but between a representation of language and a representation of life. Which resituates Adorno's alleged interdiction (that it is barbaric and impossible to write poems after Auschwitz), which some people wish to invert with Paul Celan in the role of the inverter, whilst they remain in the same unthought, as Wittgenstein shows through the example of pain. It cannot say itself. But then, a poem does not say. It does. And a thinking intervenes.

These refusals, all these refusals are indispensable so that a poem should come – to be written, to be read. So that living should transform itself into a poem. So that a poem should transform living.

To cap it all, if this also seems somewhat paradoxical, this is because it is merely a question of truisms. Misrecognised. This is the comical in thinking.

But it is only through these refusals, which are the heartbeats of thought, so as to breathe in the unbreathable, that there have always been poems. And that a thinking of the poem is necessary to language, to society.

PART 3
RHYME AND LIFE

The following three texts are chapters from the essay *La Rime et la vie* [Rhyme and Life] (RV), in its reviewed and expanded edition (Paris: Gallimard, Folio series, 2006 [1989]). As always, Meschonnic combines general reflections on poetics with detailed analyses of poets and the literary and theoretical situation in France. In this volume, he focuses on the relationship of language and poetics to life. The book takes its title from Marina Tsvetaeva, who is in a sense the tutelary figure of the essay, being a central example of what Meschonnic means by orality and of the ethics of art.

The first of the texts has the same title as the entire volume, *Rhyme and Life* (pp. 247–73 in RV); it was initially written as a foreword to a book on Marina Tsvetaeva by Ève Malleret, but in the end did not appear there. It was published in an American translation by Gabriella Bedetti in *Critical Inquiry* (15/1, 1988). Meschonnic identifies life with poetry, since in poetry everything becomes life through language, and at the same time language becomes life. This shows, as also underlined in Part 2, that poetry, or the poem, for Meschonnic, is not necessarily the literary form but more generally an activity, a process of transformation.

In the second text of this section, *Orality, Poetics of the Voice* (pp. 310–40 in RV), based on a paper given at the Research Centre on Orality at the Institut National des Langues et Civilisations Orientales in Paris on 28 April 1987, Meschonnic positions these reflections in his overarching critique of the sign that opposes language and life, as well as the oral and the written. For him, however, orality – a central focus of the book – is not part of this duality of oral and written. He constructs a tripartite constellation of the written, the spoken and the oral. Meschonnic defines the oral as the mode of signifying characterised by a primacy of rhythm and prosody in the movement of sense.

Since the poetic subject of enunciation transforms discourse and is subject through this discourse, this primacy of rhythm and prosody implies an interdependency of subject and orality. This is the historicity of language and the mutual transformation of subject and discourse. The oral can be speech or writing, but literature would be the maximal orality since it is most attentive to rhythm. Orality is hence a key notion of Meschonnic's theory, impossible to separate from rhythm and the continuous.

In the last short chapter, *The Subject of Writing* (pp. 366–70 in RV), based on an intervention at an encounter of psychoanalysts and writers in Toulouse on 28 January 1989, Meschonnic draws a connection to the subject and criticises the psychoanalytical reduction of subject and language.

6

Rhyme and Life

(in *La Rime et la vie*, Paris: Gallimard, 2006, pp. 247–73)

Translated by Andrew Eastman

Poetry makes everything life.[1] It is that form of life which makes everything language. It comes to us only if language itself has become a form of life. That is why it is so untranquil. For it never ceases to work on us. To be the dream of which we are the sleep. A listening, an awakening which passes through us, the rhythm which knows us and which we do not know. It is the organisation within language of what has always been reputed to escape language: life, the movement of what no word is supposed to be able to say. And indeed words do not say it. That is why poetry is a sense of time more than the sense in words. Even when its course is ample, it is in what passes from us through words. Its time is not that of glaciers or ferns. It speaks a time of life. Through everything it names. Even its haste transforms. Because it is a listening which compels one to listen.

Traditionally, however, poetry is subject to the effect of the separation between the order of language, and the order or disorder of life. For the order in which the thinking of language is found is an order against chaos. The fabulous is not in chaos. It is in order. A mythical conception of language is charged with maintaining order. And so there is an unbreachable gap between poetry in terms of life, and the language, the forms of poetry. Its metres and its rhymes. This is what it is up to us to think. Through and for poetry, language, life. Against sentimental poetisations of poetry, and of life. As much as against formalisations.

---

1. An American translation of this text by Gabriella Bedetti appeared in *Critical Inquiry*, 15/1 (autumn 1988). This text was initially intended as the foreword to Ève Malleret's work on Marina Tsvetaeva (*Tentative de jalousie*, Paris: La Découverte, 1986), but did not appear there.

If forms of language have a sense for life, poetry shows this and hides it at the same time. That poetry has come, so often that a universal principle has been seen in it – but mistakenly, as we have only recently learned – through a metrics, an ordinance, an ordination of language, this is not what could bring metres and rhymes any closer to the sense of life. Because this principle did not even bring them any closer to the sense of words. Was not in itself a principle of sense. To the original separation of language and life was added the separation between the reason of language, and the formalisation of poetry. Cutting poetry off doubly, from language, and from life. Confining poetry within the forms of poetry, doubly deprived of sense. The paradox in this procedure is that the most formalist of all is what least appears so. It is sense. After beating out the measure with their feet, poets counted on their fingers. And rhyming dictionaries are drawers of syllables comparable to the ones used for playing with the letters of words.

A deeply ingrained notion, which passes for the nature of things, opposes language to life as the abstract generic to the concrete particular, words, which do not bark and cannot be eaten, to things and to the living. Language is thereby included in the schema which opposes life and death. On the side of death. And if it is not death, it is dead. A variety of tomb, cenotaph, monument. The old Greek pun proved it through language itself: *sôma–sêma*. It showed a physical equivalence between the body, *sôma*, and the sign, *sêma*, also tomb. The sarcophagus of the voice. The voice, yes, being on the side of life. This entire mortuary anthropology of language continues to be called upon in order to oppose the letter – which kills or is dead – mortally to the living spirit. This radical cut passes not only between language and life, but also within language. The convention of rhyming doubles the conventionalism of the sign – that stand-in for things. What separates the sign and life separates rhyme and reason. The rational and the irrational, the discontinuous and the continuous, prose and poetry, lined up in double file. The chain effects of dualism.

But poetry is a flaw in the sign. The sign does all it can to hide it, to ignore it. Poetry never ceases to reappear. For it belongs, like life, to the irrational continuous. It is in the words, but it is not the words. Which is what can be understood as signifiance, a mode of signifying which is not to be confused with sense or with signification. The side of the body, and of life, which bursts forth elementally. Thus the cut within the sign, which constitutes it, between a signifier and a signified, the cut which makes for the unlimited power of the sign and the reign of the signified, its transcendence of languages, which is that of reason, and which philosophy stands by, is complicit in, and benefits from – this cut situates at once the possibility of poetry and its incomprehension. For the sign. Poetry's celebrated banishment. Politics against rhyme.

Poetry is intolerable for the sign, for its rationality, which is technical reason and the reason of state. Which is why it dwells in the ghetto of the signifier. Being body which gets through to the sign, life which makes it lose its senses. According to the sociology of the sign, whose theoretical effect is the dualism of the individual and the social, poetry is the private which explodes the model of the sign. Overwhelms it as the subject overwhelms the individual. Shows the state of decomposition which the sociology and the politics of the sign have arrived at, no less than its theory of language. No, signs [*signes*] cannot understand swans [*cygnes*]. All the attempts at co-opting poetry which we are witness to will not prevent the sign from being overwhelmed by life.

Poetry makes a critique of the sign which brings language back into life. Poetry, so weak and so implacably hunted down, whose compensatory adulation is only the corollary of its misrecognition, turns this misrecognition back against traditional theory, a misrecognition which is that of language as a whole. Because it is a misrecognition of the empirical. And consists in the double exclusion which makes for the internal solidarity of the sign: that of poetry from ordinary language, that of language from life, which is also ordinary.

If Monsieur Jourdain's master of philosophy reminds us that we do not speak in rhymes, to answer him, we must accept that we have to take certain circuitous routes. For the apparently simple, natural oppositions are here, precisely, but effects of theory.

Rhyme and metrical forms, both associated with poetry, are to be grasped – if one seeks to understand them, and poetry, in relation to each other – through poetry. Not poetry through rhyme and metre. For this latter take is what constitutes traditional theory, where the reciprocal heterogeneity of form and sense makes rhyme senseless. Rhyme-residue.

It is through de-rhymed, de-metrified modernity that one may best understand rhyme. The reason for its relation to poetry. And for the transformations of this relation.

Understanding rhyme supposes that we cease opposing poetry and ordinary language. For the same reason that we must cease opposing language and life. Not that poetry would be the language of life. Only poetisation, that fake, holds such views. But, if language takes place only through and between subjects, language is in life. And poetry is too. Being one of the languages of language.

It is not sufficient to cite music and dance (nor, as a fallback, that paltry surrogate, mnemonic technique) to account for poetry's feet and rhymes. If these cadences are an origin, they cannot be reduced to survivals. A state of affairs which has been extinct for centuries. Which rhyming poetry supposedly goes on repeating up to the present day. An origin is not the sense of something, much less the whole sense, even if it is a part of it.

If everything in language is the play of sense, which is necessarily so, since nothing of what is in language can be without an effect on sense, then not only rhymes have sense, and metres, but each consonant, each vowel, all the seen and heard materiality of words which is a part of sense. Which organises it. The effect being in this organisation, not in any of the terms taken separately. Rhythm is this organisation which makes sense. Working through prosody. And, in spoken language, through the body. A body which is social as well as individual, historical as well as biological. Through which passes all of what the formalism of the sign excluded from sense like a residue. Deprived of sense because this formalism denied it any sense. This organisation never ceases for an instant in all of language. That is why poetry is ordinary. The only exceptions, to a maximal degree, are technical and scientific discourses, and the dictionary.

It would not be stretching a point to bring together poetry and life, because poetry is one of the languages of life as it is one of the languages of language. But it is a regulated organisation of it. And thus rhyme – whose etymology like its mode of functioning condenses and symbolises all metrics – no doubt makes audible in language a very old cosmology. Rhyme is not only an echo from word to word, but also the echo of an echo which is its model. Ordering for ordering, the order of language having become an order within language, evokes and mimes a cosmic order. As rhyme rhymes, it accomplishes this order, corresponds to it, is accorded with it. Perhaps, from afar, it acted upon it. But, in any case, rhyme and metre were a form of praise. An indirect theology. A doing as well as a meaning. This meaning only working through this doing. Even if, as it happened, it was no longer anything but an echo of it. The responsory. Medieval poetics stated this clearly. Shelley knew it, and restated it. And rhymes know it for all those who have forgotten it.

But poetry itself ended up forgetting the sense of its forms. When it began to imitate itself, for form's sake, it ceased to have a sense. This is what people said in the eighteenth century, a century thought to be a-poetic. When the metamorphoses of prose were matched by an academicism of verse. And then poetry sought to justify itself. It found life. In this way poetry became a critique of poetry, a critique of verse and rhyme, in the last century. Seeking new reasons for itself, it sought other forms. Forgetting the sense of the old forms drove it towards the form of its sense. Its historicity, without which it is merely an imitation. Its historicity is its only constraint. Its historicity is all that poetry has to answer to. Historicity has transformed rhyme, as it has transformed poetry's relation to itself, and its relation to the world. The cosmos, today, is the subject, and the subject's history.

Which makes for a new relation between rhyme and reason, rhyme and language, rhyme and life. Not one of these terms escapes with its former traditional sense. That is the consequence of this history. Whoever would refuse to recognise this metamorphosis would show not only that they understand nothing about poetry, but also that while clinging to a rationality whose disastrous consequences they refuse to see, they are deaf to language, being of those abstractors from life whose ideas have stopped, whereas poetry, language, life never stop.

In appearance, the transformations of poetry include an abandoning of rhyme. A break with traditions. Rather, however, and according to a cultural plurality which avant-garde militantisms have simplified, these transformations have accomplished a laying bare of the device. And not only in Mayakovsky's punning-rhyme. It is rash to conclude that free verse, in France and elsewhere, has dispensed with rhymes, and with rhythms of recurrence. Those which were called metrical, when verse was opposed to prose. As though poetry were verse, and prose, ordinary spoken language. Poetry rhymed because lines of verse rhymed.

Modernity is not so much the end of rhyme as the end of certain ideas about rhyme, prose, language. It is only according to a traditional vision that traditional rhyme is defunct. But poetry's task has not changed: to discover itself. Its rhymes, and what rhymes – it is up to poetry to discover it. To imitate the manner in which poets of the past understood and heard rhymes is nothing. But we continue to listen to them, as we listen to Mozart. They are present to us. It is we, if we were to repeat them, who would not be.

Except for those whose poetry goes on snoring away, we no longer perform the 'terrible concert for donkey's ears', as Éluard wrote in *Premières Vues anciennes*.[2] But the drums and violins which he opposed to 'one must speak a musical thought', only caricatured poetry because they had issued from it. Codified for so long, they are the culture's Muzak. For that matter, the place where the donkeys' concert brays the loudest, where rhyme works the streets, is in advertising. The echo is instant proof. It shows that the magic is eternally young there, an archaism only in the fictions of reason.

Codification, the culturally sanctioned – this is what poetry has moved away from. Not at all times either, as is well known. At moments of collective emergency, historicity once again belonged to rhyme. But more generally, it is not the disappearance of rhyme which characterises modern poetry. A disappearance which would be comparable to that of punctuation, which

---

2. Paul Éluard, *Œuvres complètes* (Paris: Gallimard, Bibliothèque de la Pléiade, 1968), vol. 1, p. 540.

at times visualises a mental theatre, at other times a primacy of rhythm, a liberation of orality.

If modernity really consisted in such a break with rhyme, it would be a break with the very act of listening to language, evoked by Baudelaire in his projects for a preface to *Les Fleurs du mal*: 'Why any poet, who does not know exactly how many rhymes each word has, is incapable of expressing any idea whatsoever.'[3] The symbolist moment practised a prosody in which the saturation of rhyme made of this very saturation the second prosody[4] of its ideas about music. It raised the echo to an excess which was an appeal and a listening. Expressionism, and the Futurisms, but Claudel as well, consonantised poetry. Modern poetry has generalised, diffused rhyme to the whole mass of the saying and the said. The disappearance of rhyme at the end of the line is a passage towards the rediscovery of rhyme. For poetry and for all of language. The rediscovery, without knowing it, of a sense and a reason. In sum, pure rhyme, disentangled from the recorded couplings listed in the dictionary. It is not rhyme which has come to an end, but a convention.

Rhyme is coextensive with the whole of language. A specific mode of signifying consists in showing this: poetry. A figure of language, in that it appears only if it accomplishes this generalised listening. By doing so it produces a signifiance which is indefinitely coming into being. A rhythmic, prosodic semantics. Which overwhelms the sign with the body, includes vision in listening, in the understanding which passes under the words or through the words but is not in any word. What poetry makes audible, when it is this listening, psychoanalysis has recognised a small part of.

Poetry is not poetry unless it invents, or discovers, new rhymes. In this way it transforms reason. Each new rhyme modifies reason. Near or distant rhymes, clangorous or muffled scandals, uproars latent in language.

One of the ways of breaking with routine is exacerbating it. Driving rhythm to a level of tension such that it suppresses the intervals – Hopkins's *sprung rhythm* – , the writing of speech, the intensity of what is spoken through the body. Driving rhyme to invade, or to interrupt, the word. And the line. Putting drama into doggerel. Identifying the counting song with destiny. Rhymes so close to each other that they interpenetrate. Responses

---

3. Charles Baudelaire, *Œuvres complètes* (Paris: Club du Meilleur Livre, 1955), vol. 1, p. 915. ['Pourquoi tout poëte, qui ne sait pas au juste combien chaque mot comporte de rimes, est incapable d'exprimer une idée quelconque.']
4. [Translator's note: In referring to a 'second prosody', Meschonnic is apparently making a parallel with French rhetorical treatises focusing on the composition of vernacular poetry, called 'rhétorique seconde', or 'second rhetoric' (as distinguished from treatises devoted to composition in Latin); one of the first of these was Eustache Deschamps's *L'Art de dictier* (1392).]

coming so close upon the questions that language no longer has time to catch your breath. Haste as poetry and as poetics. Elsewhere, in other forms of life, in better accorded, less dissonant times, poetry could take another course. But poetry cannot choose its rhymes. We know that poetry happens only when it doesn't have the choice.

Order was thus the first rhyme, the first principle of rhyme. Metrical poetry responded to the world. Then it responded to itself. Then poets began to notice it was saying the same thing over and over. Old granny rambling on again.

Violence has become a rhyme, a principle of rhyme. A reason. Those who made rhyme the reason of poetry knew what they were saying. Even in their academicism. Even to the point of no longer understanding the tragic side of rhyme, and its humour, in the works of the Grands Rhétoriqueurs. The loss of the sense of poetry can be measured by the opposition, so sure of itself, between rhyme and reason. But it is a question not only of holding on to what words mean, but also of reinventing what they say. This is what poetry, the thinking of poetry, the poetry of thinking do and have always done.

Play at etymology as you wish. True and false, derived from *rim* or *rythme*, it tells you the same truth. That rhyme organises something made through its own unmaking. That it gathers together. The coupling is only a particular case, which in our culture has hidden the rest from us. Rhyme heaps up. It hoards. It shuffles the words and turns over the one you were expecting, the one you weren't thinking of. In both cases, you lose.

Because rhyme cheats. It shows you a word in another word. The truth of one word in the truth of another one. It partakes of paronomasia. Which only its restrictive identification with a final position in the line masked. Rhyme cheats as destiny would cheat if it played cards. Because it would know in advance. Rhyme knows in advance. It is that relation in the words which knows of them before they do, not what you want them to say, but what they say of you. What they show of you.

Because rhyme is a principle of listening. Listening to language passes again and again through rhyme. Whose figures are much more numerous than metrical codification allowed one to see. The analysts' evenly suspended attention is a rediscovery of rhyme, a way of approaching it. It is not surprising that analysts are so fond of puns, and of making them, as others are obsessed with spoonerisms. They have rediscovered one bit of rhyme, and they endlessly replay this scene, in their exhilaration at renewing what they rightly see as a reason. But they make a repetition of it.

The distance between rise and fall, between casting and reeling in, makes the rhythm of rhymes. What is called prose – odd singular, one should say *proses* as one says, in French, *les vers*⁵ – is only another mode of memory, another rhythm of the responsories language makes to itself.

This multifariousness of the modes of rhyme situates the difference, which seems manifest, irreducible, between poetry and prose. And there are poetries which can differ as much in their relations to certain fixations and conventions of rhyme, as verse to prose. Some closer to their prose than to our verse. Their confrontation is one of the passages of modernity. Where poetry and translation also work through each other.

Inventing itself, French poetry has turned away from its recognised forms. It has broken them to rediscover itself. Steeped in its past, it has turned this past back against itself. With the help of a few notorious aliens, it finally took to pieces the national verse line, the alexandrine. That supposedly finished perfection, which is to say, that ruin, starts to look like a flag each time an imbecile lifts it up again. Immediately crushed by the historical monument. This misfortune happens only to the deaf. Or in moments when one is deaf. To those who cannot understand that one does not write an alexandrine with impunity, whether deliberately or not. Because the cultural form is so powerful that one is then written by the tradition. Rather than inscribing oneself, or writing oneself, into it.

Rhythmically speaking, irreversibility exists. There is even nothing else but. Modernity is not simply a minor metrical infraction. A bad patch for the traditional-minded. Until time in its wisdom puts things back in order. It really does seem, after almost a century of non-metrical, or differently metrical, poetry, that the alexandrine, along with end rhyme, are things of the past definite. Perfectives. Perhaps the forms of poetry live only in the imperfective.

If one asks why such a finished form might no longer serve, when so many poets have each time made something different out of it, each time their own thing, and why now – after a great many poems, after all. The answer is in the relation between rhyme and life. The alexandrine was a way of relating to the world. It is this relation which is finished. Because that world is also finished. Pretending to go on with it, or not hearing that it no longer responds to anything because it responds to something bygone, writing alexandrines, has meant, since then, saying, in addition to what is being said, a resumption, a betrothal, a harmony – a metrics which is not only verbal, but social. An accord with the social order, the distant echo of an accord with the cosmic. Fortunately we continue to take pleasure in it. Or to

---

5. [Translator's note: The contrast Meschonnic is making here does not work for English. French *vers* refers to a line of verse and is used in this sense in the plural; English *verse* functions like a collective noun (similar to *prose*); when used as a count noun, *verse* means a stanza or group of lines.]

play on it. Just as we listen to early music, as we continue to look at paintings which remain paintings. But we can no longer compose such music. No more than we can paint in the past. Those modern poets who have kept the alexandrine have set themselves up in pre-furnished beauty – and already Nerval spoke ironically of Hugo's 'fine' verse, and Hugo said: 'I don't like verse, I like poetry.'[6] The neo-classical. Or mockery, bravado. In the 1880s-style. The old metres are lost crafts.

Apart from those who mistake the history of poetry for poetry, poets have taken risks. Apollinaire, Reverdy are emblematic heroes of risk-taking. Of poetic atheism. Against free verse, the traditional-minded have not known what to invent to protect themselves from formlessness. Showing thus that rhyme and metre were for them poetry's reason. Opposed all the more to reason itself. They were mistaken about form because they were mistaken about sense. Leaving the prose poem to the prose of the world, they concentrated their polemics on free verse. Their arguments, the same for a hundred years, on the contradiction in terms between *free* and *verse*, have never grasped that it is the poem, and poetry, which are free. Poetry is indifferent to calculations, because it can just as easily favour them with its presence as desert them. You cannot catch it with numbers. You cannot settle accounts with it. Poetry plays. Not you. As for those who hide behind machines – poetry laughs. I've seen it.

Nostalgia for old forms is thus a private matter. A matter of opinion, of feeling. Not of the historicity of poetry. That each new craft produces its own academicism is another matter. But the practice of poetry, and the idea of poetry, taken as a whole, have moved away, even in serial productions, in group styles, from classical verse.

Translating has followed. Within the confused relation between translating and writing, a relation muddled by the translator's referring to the concepts of the language [*langue*] and of science, rather than to discourse and its poetics. The traditional discordance between translation and the poem is that of a passivity versus an activity. The whole aestheticised, moralised as fidelity and transparency. Sense, versus rhyme and life. But it is by holding together rhyme and life that translating becomes writing.

The paroxysm of their contradiction, the utmost of difficulty, paradoxically, can lay the ground for an encounter between poetry and poetics. For this tension makes poetics necessary. Poetics shows where the language sciences [*savoirs de la langue*] fail. By their very nature, these are so completely included in the sign that not only do they not see its limits, but they take their

---

6. Victor Hugo, *Le Tas de pierres, moi* (1839–43), in *Œuvres complètes* (Paris: Club Français du Livre, 1968), vol. VI, p. 1146.

ignorance for the totality of the text. Their incapacity is the ground of their self-satisfaction.

This paroxysm occurs especially when poetry in another language proceeds according to another idea of poetry, another relation to its past, another relation between rhyme and convention. Between rhyme and life. Translating then finds itself in an apparently insoluble contradiction. The case is particularly clear with the difference between French poetry and Russian poetry. A translation is obliged to show this difference, or to conceal it. It is in a false position in both cases. The traditions, and their non-relation, confer on this situation an exemplary status.

Modern Russian poetry continues to rhyme the rhyme-convention. It writes metrically, more or less. Translating it according to the characteristics of modern French poetry would be transposing the continuous into the discontinuous. Preserving its rhymes, counting its syllables metrically, would be mistaking versification for poetry, a past for a present. Producing a fake, working in neo. But free-versing it, would be breaking up its principle of organisation, its language, its relation to its own nineteenth century.

The reciprocal situation is treated otherwise. Russian translators put rhymes back in where the line ends had none, a metrics where the French poet wasn't counting any more. To make it poetic. When French Surrealist poetry is translated it is reconstituted according to a sort of anamorphosis which aims at rectifying its decadence. It would be difficult to mistake each other more completely.

This failure has a history. It seems that it cannot be viewed outside of the dissymmetry in the relations between Russian and French poetry. A cultural dissymmetry. French is spoken in *War and Peace*. But not Russian in Balzac or Zola. Yet this current of history is not sufficient to explain things.

The myths of language and literature play their part. Just as they muddle the relation between rhyme and life, they muddle the relation between popular poetry and learned poetry. Between the practice of poetry and the thinking of poetry.

The practice and the invention of poetry do not preserve us from the myths of language which underlie the notions of the genius of languages, and interfere with poetry. Marina Tsvetaeva, who nevertheless produced a genuine writing in French, thought, according to the common cliché (but it has a history) that French – this is what she wrote to Rilke – is 'very far from that poetic language', the poet's 'maternal' language, which German is 'much closer to'. This on the subject of Rilke's poems in French. To the genius of languages corresponds, for her, an anteriority, a transcendence of poetry with respect to languages: 'Writing poems is already translating, from one's mother tongue into another, no matter whether it is French or German.

No language is a mother tongue. Writing poems is a rewriting. That is why I do not understand people speaking of French or Russian poets, etc. A poet may write in French, he cannot be a French poet.'[7] It is true that she adds, letting the contradiction stand, 'Nevertheless, each language has something of its own, which makes it what *it* is.' The comparison, always the same since Mme de Staël, between German and French, leads her to suppose German as 'deeper than French, fuller, more extended, *darker*. French: a clock without resonance; German: a resonance rather than a clock (its strokes). German the reader constantly, endlessly transposes; French is there. German – *becomes*, French *is*. An awkward language for the poet, that's precisely why you chose it. An almost impossible language!' (ibid.). Which is followed by a third contradiction: the French of Rilke's French poems is in reality German: 'You (*Vergers*), you write in German – you write yourself, you, the poet' (ibid.). French is so evidently coldness itself, and a metaphor of a-poetic language, that speaking of some German poet, whom she finds cold, she says: 'Platen writes in French.' Yet her own practice of poetry says nothing of the sort. Does not speak through clichés. And Marina Tsvetaeva's poem in French, 'La Neige', is a true poem by Tsvetaeva. Her whole poetics is to be found there. Or should one say that it speaks Russian?

The cut which separates rhyme and life, rhyme and history, popular poetry and learned poetry just as well, a cut which is particular, each time, to a language-culture – in Spain it is not what it is in France – has a particularly pernicious effect in the commonly held representation of Russian poetry. A consensus as a-historical as it is unshakeable situates its beginnings in the eighteenth century. And even then Lomonossov's verse line was borrowed from German. The whole of epic poetry (the *bylines*) and popular song, medieval forms which so remarkably neutralise the opposition between prose and verse, all of that is consigned to folklore. And yet Pushkin did not make this distinction. Neither did Nekrasov, Tyutchev, Blok or Mayakovsky. A comparable cliché – but which doesn't have the same effects – attributes the inaugural role in France to Villon. And even then Villon is an isolated figure, and French poetry as taught in schools only begins in the sixteenth century. Such ideological dummies make it apparent that a strategy lies behind these pseudo-histories of poetry.

To the cliché youth-of-Russian-poetry corresponds that of its openness.

---

7. Rilke, Pasternak, Tsvetaeva, *Correspondance à trois, été 1926* (Paris: Gallimard, 1983), p. 211. Letter of 6 July 1926. [Translator's note: English translation: Boris Pasternak, Marina Tsvetaeva, Rainer Maria Rilke, *Letters Summer 1926*, second edition, ed. by Yevgeny Pasternak, Yelena Pasternak and Konstantin M. Azadovsky; trans. by Margaret Wettlin, Walter Arndt and Jamey Gambrell; foreword by Susan Sontag (New York: New York Review of Books, 2003). The translation given here is based on the French version.]

As opposed to French poetry, supposedly closed to outside influences. The latter, however, from the sixteenth century onward, has successively absorbed (besides classical Antiquity) Italy and Spain, England and Germany, then the Far East . . . But not Russia. As for Russian poetry, it has drawn more from Germany than from France. After Pushkin's receptiveness to a variety of sources, Annensky and Brioussov looking towards Baudelaire, Verlaine, Mallarmé – there were the duos of Tyutchev to Schelling, Fet to Schopenhauer, Alexis Tolstoy to Heine. The only vector moving in the opposite direction has been René Ghil. And Russian poetry has continually drawn on itself.

No French equivalent of the way Rilke was marked by Russian poetry. But Rilke could read Pushkin and Lermontov in Russian. He wrote poems in Russian.[8] Going in the other direction, Rilke's effect on Pasternak, or Tsvetaeva, has French analogues. From Mérimée to Gide, it is the Russian short story and the Russian novel which have come through. Not poetry.

Conversely, when Mayakovsky came to Paris, it was the painters, not the poets, he was interested in. Admittedly, he did not know French. But Marina Tsvetaeva lived around Paris from 1925 to 1939, as a Russian isolated from Russians, and even more so from French poets.

In the magazines of the French poetic avant-gardes one finds no trace of any living Russian poet. In *Sic* (January 1916 to December 1919), Diaghilev, Larionov, Gontcharova, Mussorgsky, Stravinsky appear. . . . Dance, painting, sculpture. Not one poet. In *Nord–Sud*, nothing. In the tract *Erutaréttil*, from 1923, Lermontov.[9] In the 'Liquidation' of *Littérature*, number 18 (March 1921), the only Russians are Dostoyevsky, Tolstoy; Lenin, Trotsky; Chagall and Stravinsky. The only one to receive a good mark is Dostoyevsky. Not one Russian work is mentioned in *Littérature* (March 1919 to August 1921; March 1922 to June 1924). Not one poet in *La Révolution surréaliste*, from 1924 to 1929. Nor in *Minotaure* from 1933 to 1939. Only Mayakovsky appears, with a few poems, in *Le Surréalisme au service de la révolution* (number 1, July 1930), and this is in response to the controversy brought about by his suicide. A few passing allusions to Gorki and Ehrenburg do not count. At the end of 1931, in the tract *Lisez . . . ne lisez pas* [Read . . . do not read], on the 'Lisez' [Read] side: Mayakovsky. The only good Russian poet is a dead Russian poet.

Mayakovsky's corpse dispensed with, what is said of the 'Russian émigrés' situates clearly enough the absence of any relation with the only Parisian Russian poet whom the Surrealists could have known and recognised, Marina

---

8. *Correspondance à trois*, p. 19, p. 24.
9. *Tracts surréalistes et déclarations collectives* (1922–39) (Paris: Le Terrain Vague, 1980), p. 12.

Tsvetaeva. She does not appear to have encountered them either. She could read them. They did not understand Russian. Éluard had begun translating Blok with Gala in 1918. They did not get very far. Only Elsa Triolet could not be unaware of Tsvetaeva. Who had poems in the *Anthologie de la poésie soviétique* (1918–34) published by Gallimard in 1935. Among these was 'La Neige', probably written by her directly in French.[10]

But also she and the Surrealists were separated not only by a political ideology. Rhyme, and life, separated them. Housework and poverty on one side. Bibliophiles, art collectors, dealers in manuscripts on the other. And as to their poetics, everything opposes them. A poetics of rhythm, from prosody all the way to metaphor and syntax, on Tsvetaeva's side. For the Surrealists, the image and the theory of the image masking the problem of rhythm. Almost a single key, the noun plus noun complement construction, to open the locks of all metaphors.

This non-relation does not foreclose possibilities. The delayed arrival of a message in a bottle. Non-contemporaneity is no doubt a minimal condition for relations between one poetry and another. Today, in Russian, those who are closest to Western poetics are non-Russians, Aygy, Suleimenov. In French, everything seems to suggest that poetry had no need of this relation. And was unaware of it. French poetry invented, exported. Like impressionism in painting. It is only in the last twenty or thirty years, often much more recently, that Russian poetry has been translated. And it is not enough for it to be translated. It must come to something more than information without a voice. Up to now discovery in French has never come about through Russian. And when we began to hear Khlebnikov, the effect already seemed to have been borrowed from Joyce, or Michaux.

Marina Tsvetaeva only truly begins to speak in French forty-five years after her death.[11] It is true that even in Russian her works have only recently been made available.[12] She is still in part unknown. But she has not gone unrecognised.

10. She says herself, in response to a questionnaire, in 1926, that she has written poems in French and in German (*Correspondance à trois*, p. 74; cf. ibid., p. 141).
11. After a translation by Elsa Triolet, unrhymed and as conventional as is her presentation of the poet's suicide: 'Tsvetaeva could not endure the misfortune which had descended upon her country,' in *Marina Tsvétaeva, poèmes traduits par Elsa Triolet* (Paris: Gallimard, 1968), pp. 9–10.
12. 'It is only in the second half of the 1950s that her work began to filter through surreptitiously, and in fits and starts, in *samizdat* publications and in the press,' Lidia Chukovskaya, 'L'Avant-mort de Marina Tsvetaïeva' [The Fore-death of Marina Tsvetaeva], *Passé Présent*, 3 (1984), p. 131 (trans. by Ève Malleret). A two-volume Soviet edition of a selection of her works appeared in 1984.

Marina Tsvetaeva is perhaps the only poet, along with Mayakovsky, to escape from the customary opposition between rhyme and life, between the Russian mode of rhyming and Symbolist rhyme, then the diffusion of rhyme as signifiance, and the clash between the Russian and French traditions. Tsvetaeva even more so than Mayakovsky. For she took excess so unbearably far that Mayakovsky, who had the tragic sense of the Grands Rhétoriqueurs, appears like a humorist in comparison. Because she brought traditional poetic procedures to a dizziness that spreads to the whole discourse. Rhyme eats the words. Far from being a liberation from tradition through rejection, it is an overwhelming of tradition through exaggeration.

Ève Malleret found a way to translate this violence, succeeded in translating it.[13] A violence of rhyme because it is violence which makes rhyme. Just as signifiance carries and miscarries sense. This is why her translation is a writing. A test of what one must call, without really understanding what one is saying, an affinity. A recognition and a creation of oneself in another. Through which this poetry achieves a presence, that is to say, a future.

Because she translated Marina Tsvetaeva, Ève Malleret has succeeded better than anyone else up to now in recognising her: by placing herself at the point where rhyme and life are one. Which is illustrated, for example, by her observation that Tsvetaeva, from the time of her exile onwards, never lived anywhere but in suburbs. She accords thereby its full value to a motif of the poems. She holds together poetry and the subject, the parable of an existence given over to the suburbs of life.

It is by recognising the centrality of rhythm in the poetics of Tsvetaeva that Ève Malleret avoids repeating the mystified readings which she denounces – those effects of the sign, from its poetics to its politics.

Tsvetaeva's poetics, and the poetics of the translation, accorded in what they both hold together, resolve one through the other the paroxysm of rhyme and the difficulty of translating. The tension is the song. The tune carries the words. When they are separated, nothing comes through but the words – the snare of sense.

It is by bringing rhyme to an extreme where, in short lines, short words, densely charged with consonants, often, it becomes almost the whole of the saying and the said, almost a single continuous–discontinuous rhyme in certain passages, that Marina Tsvetaeva raises rhyme itself to the status of an allegory. As she does with violence in language.

---

13. In Marina Tsvetaeva, *Le Poème de la montagne, le poème de la fin* (*Poema Gory, Poema Konca*), trans. and intro. by Ève Malleret (Lausanne: L'Âge d'Homme, 1984), and in Marina Tsvetaeva, *Tentative de jalousie & autres poèmes*, trans. from Russian and intro. by Ève Malleret (Paris: La Découverte, 1986).

Through rhyme, language partakes of the cry. It allows us to hear that rhyme is not simply a responsory. Rather, through the echo of language with itself, another echo comes, of something inarticulate, beneath sense, and which however has never ceased speaking itself through all rhymes, *amours–toujours*, *ténèbres–funèbres*, *ombre–sombre*: that rhyme – nascent stage or dying stage, but indefinitely renascent – is something in the nature of a cry. No doubt it could be heard, at certain moments, beneath sense and even beneath significance, in the spoken language of conversation, as one hears it in dreams, or in language games for oneself or for others. But poetry makes it audible more than elsewhere. Which makes of poetry not an opposite to or deviation from ordinary language, but its very figure. It is when poetry draws from ordinary language all of its rhymes that it becomes the latter's truth and fable.

Mayakovsky's punning rhyme succeeded in reactivating the poetic principle of the pun. On the side of significance against the sign. Like the proverb. Both having undergone the same social effect of rejection in the classical period, the age of reason and of the State. The pun declares that something is rotten in the state of the sign. Its incongruity, an unveiling of the signifier, and of its force, likewise partakes distantly of the cry. Even if it is through laughter. But Hamlet's puns are no laughing matter.

Tsvetaeva's rhyme is not a pun. It aims directly at the cry. Pasternak compared Tsvetaeva to Marceline Desbordes-Valmore.[14] Elsewhere, speaking of *The Ratcatcher*, he connects her language to *zaum*, the far side of reason, with the 'rage of rhythm rebelling against itself' (ibid., p. 188). Tsvetaeva herself says: 'by dint of crying, jumping, rolling, I make my way to *sense*' (ibid., p. 208).

Her poetics of the cry is a poetics of orality. Aside from sense. In a notebook (26 September 1940): 'My difficulty (in writing verse and perhaps for others, understanding) is in the impossibility of my problem, for example, with words (that is to say, thoughts) to say a groan: a-a-a. / With words, thoughts to say a sound. So that in the ears only a-a-a remains. Why such problems.'[15] Nadezhda Mandelstam, remembering Tsvetaeva, recalled her 'voice, so similar to the verse' (ibid., p. 10). Her poems were written 'for voice'.[16] She sometimes writes spoken forms, instead of standard spelling. For example, in *Mólodets* (The Swain): *što* instead of *čto*.[17] The splitting up

14. *Correspondance à trois*, p. 64.
15. In Ellendea Proffer, ed., *Tsvetaeva, A Pictorial Biography* (Ann Arbor: Ardis, 1980), p. 35. [Translator's note: the translation given here is based on Meschonnic's French version of the Russian text.]
16. *Correspondance à trois*, p. 144.
17. Marina Tsvetaeva, *Stixotvorenija i Poemy v 5 Tomax* (New York: Russica, 1983), vol. 4, p. 143.

of words, frequent with her, partakes of the cry. Thus in the *Poem of the End – 7 –*, the word *poslédnij*, 'last', is cut *po-slédnij* – 'For the last time'. A critic has written: 'The unit of her discourse is not the sentence, not even the word, but the *syllable*.'[18] Violence does not leave the word intact. Tsvetaeva to Pasternak: 'There are minimal divisions of words. It is out of these, I think, that *The Swain* is composed.'[19] Whether it is said to be Expressionist or Futurist, vague cultural terms, violence is an oralisation of language.

Rhyme is a cry because it cries out a truth. Tsvetaeva makes *žizn'*, 'life', and *lžívo*, 'with lie', rhyme: *Žízn', ty části rifmúeš s: lžívo*, – 'Life, often you rhyme with lie.' Which she immediately follows with (just as Éluard after 'La terre est bleue comme une orange [Earth is blue like an orange]'[20] wrote: 'Pas une erreur les mots ne mentent pas [No mistake words don't lie]') the line *Bezošíbočen pévčij slux*, 'Without lie the sound of the song'.[21] This extraction of truth makes of paronomasia an etymology, to make words say more than they say. Out of a rhetoric Tsvetaeva makes a writing.

In prose as in verse. Thus, in 'Art in the Light of Conscience', the immediate juxtaposition *iskússtvo-iskús*,[22] 'art-test', in which *iskús*, an outdated word, designating the probationary period of the novitiate, alludes to a priesthood. The whole being included in the signifier itself. It is a thinking through rhyme, from rhyme to rhyme. In 'Rain of Light', her 1922 article on Pasternak, she passes from *byt*, 'ordinary life', to *byk*, 'bull', to *dub*, 'oak'. In her notebook of June 1941, a two-word sentence condenses, like a proverb: '*Doživát'-dožóvyvat'*',[23] which Ève Malleret translates, or rather rewrites: 'Il faut marcher jusqu'au bout – mâcher jusqu'au bout' [one must walk to the bitter end – chew to the bitter end].[24] Tsvetaeva's writing is the same, whatever the language. In German, in her letters to Rilke: *Augenblick – Augenblitz*.[25] In French in 'La Neige'.

Rhyme ends up being not only the matter, but the subject of the poem.

---

18. V. Orlov, in his introduction to Marina Tsvetaeva, *Izbrannyje Proizvedenija* (Selected Works) (Moscow and Leningrad: Sovetskij Pisatel', 1965), p. 45.
19. *Correspondance à trois*, p. 125.
20. Paul Éluard, *L'Amour la poésie* (Paris: Gallimard, 1929), VII.
21. Quoted in Orlov's introduction, p. 43.
22. Marina Tsvetaeva, *Izbrannaja Proza* (Selected Prose), 2 vols (New York: Russica, 1979), vol. 1, p. 395.
23. In Proffer, *Tsvetaeva, A Pictorial Biography*, p. 35. *Doživát'*, imperfective of *dožít'*, 'survive', 'live until'; *dožóvyvat'*, imperfective of *doževát'*, 'finish chewing', which is *ževát'*, but *ževát'*, a colloquial word, also means 'do something without interest, go on repeating' – and evokes *živat'*, frequentative of *žit'*, 'live'.
24. In 'L'Avant-mort de Marina Tsvetaïeva', p. 137.
25. *Correspondance à trois*, p. 103.

Lba – i lba.	Front et front	Front and front
Tvoj – vperiod	Le tien touche	Yours touches
Lob. Gruba	Presque. Affront –	Almost. Affront –
Rifma: rot	Rime: bouche.	Rhyme: mouth.[26]

and towards the end of the *New Year Letter*:

Ráiner, rádueš' sja nóvym rífmam?
Ibo právil'no tolkúja slóvo
Rifma – čto – kak ne – tsélyj rjad nóvyx
Rifm – Smert'?
       Nékuda: jazýk izúčen.

Rainer, des rimes nouvelles – content ?
En effet, comprendre correctement
Le terme *rime* – qu'est-ce d'autre hors
Plein de rimes nouvelles – la Mort ?
Car pas d'issue: la langue est épuisée.[27]

Rainer, new rhymes – pleased?
Indeed, to understand correctly
The term *rhyme* – what else is it but
Plenty of new rhymes – Death?
For no way out: language is spent.

Tsvetaeva is a figure of poetry where rhyme and life have merged in one and the same matter of language.

Which situates a famous remark of Tsvetaeva's, in which she opposes herself to specialists of poetry – '*My* speciality is life.' She is the first to recognise, in her own writing, 'that frequency of the word: *life*'.[28] But she also wrote, in the litany of her poverty, after saying that she has no clothes, no room, no time for writing: 'I do not like life as such, for me it only begins to signify, that is to say, to take on a sense and a weight – when it is transformed, that is to say, in art.'[29] There is the 'frequency of the word: *life*', and there is also: 'In general, I suffer from an atrophy of the present.'[30] The words which

26. Marina Tsvetaeva, 'Popytka Kómnaty – Tentative de chambre' ('Attempt at a Room'), in *Stixotvorenija i Poemy v 5 Tomax*, vol. 4, p. 258; trans. by Ève Malleret.
27. 'Novogódneje, lettre de nouvel an' ('New Year Letter'), in ibid., vol. 4, p. 277; trans. by Ève Malleret.
28. *Correspondance à trois*, p. 241.
29. Marina Tsvetaeva, *Pis'ma k A. Teskovoj* (Letters to A. Tesková) (Jerusalem: Izd. Versty, 1982) (reprint of the Academia edition, Prague, 1969), p. 37 (letter of 30 December 1925).
30. *Correspondance à trois*, p. 193.

surround the poetry often say something else than what they designate: 'soul', 'feeling'. They are already in themselves allegorical.

It was on the subject of Pasternak's book *My Sister Life* that Tsvetaeva wrote this remark about life. On the subject of poetry. Presupposing thus that poetry resolves in and by itself the usual antinomy between life and book, valid everywhere else. But where life, *žizn'*, was distinguished from *byt*, 'ordinary life', no less than from aestheticism. Of Pasternak's book, she wrote: 'It is human – *durch.*'[31]

Rhyme-rhythm appears as a form of life. The surprising thing is not the solidarity between rhyme and life. The surprising thing is the surprise which this solidarity elicits, and which derives from the dominant point of view: the sign, from which we look at the poem.

If, instead of looking at the empirical through the cultural grid of the sign, one tries to recognise the empirical of modes of signifying, the empirical of the poem, one is not mechanically inverting things, not viewing the sign from the poem, rather the critique of the sign brings us back to that fundamental ordinariness which, for us, makes of life, forms of language, and of language, forms of life.

The usual antinomy is both dismissed and maintained by Tsvetaeva's remark, in her article of 1922. She opposes a technicity to an essence. In *My Sister Life*, 'the line is the formula of its essence. [. . .] Wherever there can be a superiority of "form" over "content", or content over form, – there essence never spent even a single night. – [. . .] Of the demonstrable riches of Pasternak's poetry (rhythms, metre, etc.), others will speak in their turn – and capably – paying no less attention than I do to the indemonstrable riches. / That is the business of poetry specialists. *My* speciality is life.'[32] Which is to say, in her terms, the essence of *My Sister Life*. Poetry and life in an indistinction anterior to their separation, and which yet works through the technicity of language.

Life-rhyme makes of life a listening. It is the continuity with Blok and with Verlaine, – explicitly – in the value of *sound*: 'Word-creation [*slóvotvórčestvo*], like all creation, is only walking on the traces of natural and national sound. A walk to sound. *Et tout le reste n'est que littérature* [*And all the rest is only literature*].'[33] That this sound is more than the phonic matter of

---

31. Marina Tsvetaeva, 'Svetovoj Liven'', 'Rain of Light' (Berlin, 1922), in *Izbrannaja Proza*, vol. 1, p. 142.
32. Marina Tsvetaeva, '*Eto delo Spetsialistov Poezii. Moja že Spetsial'nost'* — *Žizn'*, in *Izbrannaja Proza*, vol. 1, p. 136.
33. In '*Iskusstvo pri Svete Sovesti*' ('Art in the Light of Conscience'), (*Izbrannaja Proza*, 1932) vol. 1, p. 396. The sentence in italics is in French in the text. [Translator's note: Allusion to Verlaine's 'Art poétique', which contains the line 'Et tout le reste est littérature'.]

words, and something other, something like the tune Apollinaire hummed to himself, or Blok's 'music', appears from what she adds further on:

> This sound is not allegorical, although it is not physical. It is to such a degree non-physical, that in general you do not hear a single word, and if you hear, you do not understand, as though half asleep. The physical sound is either sleeping, or it does not carry, covered by another sound. / I do not hear the words, but a sort of noiseless chant in my head, a sort of line of sound – going from allusion all the way to command, but it would be too long to go into that now – it is a world of its own, and to speak of it – is a task of its own. But I am convinced that here, as in everything, there is a law.[34]

The relation between rhyme and life removes poetry from aesthetics. It takes poetry into another world than that of the sign, where the discourse of aesthetics holds forth. Rhyme is an ethics. Which is shown by 'Blok's cruel remark about Akhmatova's first poems: – Akhmatova writes verse as though a man is looking at her, and you must write them as though God sees you.'[35] The article 'Art in the Light of Conscience' ends on Mayakovsky's suicide: 'For twelve successive years Mayakovsky the man killed poet-Mayakovsky in himself, but in the thirteenth year the poet rose up and killed the man.'[36] Poetry, for Tsvetaeva, forbids any other politics but that of poetry itself, any other party but the party of rhyme – of life.

This is what, eternal beginners in life, and in poetry, we can perhaps begin to understand, and to do, better than before. What Marina Tsvetaeva, a Russian, brings to us, to French poetry. Or rather to poetry, to one's idea of it, and to one's practice of it, whatever the language.

But multiplicity, the integration of languages and forms of life from all sides, as Stockhausen describes it for contemporary musics, this circulation of poetries presupposes a recognition of signifiers which itself takes place through a poetic circulation from language to language. There was certainly no poetry before Babel. But, in language, rhyme and life have the same future.

---

34. Ibid., vol. 1, p. 402.
35. Ibid., vol. 1, p. 394.
36. Ibid., vol. 1, p. 406.

7

Orality, Poetics of the Voice

(in *La Rime et la vie*, Paris: Gallimard, 2006, pp. 310–40)

Translated by Andrew Eastman

What is at issue[1] is establishing an interaction between the ethnological conception of orality and a poetics of orality. To do so, it is necessary to situate practices of orality in relation to the theory of language operating in ethnology. Necessary to register the negative viewpoint – the negative definition of orality which results from it.

The analysis of the different ways of speaking of orality and the voice may be undertaken with new possibilities if one places oneself within a theory of rhythm as organisation of discourse and the subject. The confusion of the voice and the phonic is closely dependent on the confusion which identifies rhythm with the phonic. Towards a definition of the voice which is no longer physiological or psychological but cultural, historical and poetic, one passes from the duality oral/written to a triple distribution: the written, the spoken, the oral. The debate is the very question of the specificity and the historicity of language.

Orality as a Problem to be Disentangled from Empiricism

One cannot use the existing definitions, of rhythm, of orality, as points of departure unless one is to repeat indefinitely the established notional order. No more can one start with the received definitions in order to understand what epic or lyricism, prose or poetry is today. Words which are eternally lagging behind actual practice. They aren't the only ones.

My starting point is *Critique du rythme*, and 'Qu'entendez-vous par

---

1. Written on the basis of a talk given at the Centre de Recherches sur l'Oralité [Center for Research on Orality], at the Institut National des Langues et Civilisations Orientales in Paris, 28 April 1987.

oralité?'² Work which itself starts from the article by Benveniste on 'The Linguistic Notion of Rhythm'.³ Which re-establishes the forgotten distinction, operative in Heraclitus, between *schema*, organisation of what is fixed, and *rhythm*, organisation of what is moving.

Not that thereby all becomes clear. It is rather a matter of ridding oneself of false clarities. Those offered by the paradigm of the sign. Within it, the oral is a syncretic term, fusing together an unknown element, which one may continue to call *oral*, and a known element, which is the *spoken*. The voice being the place of production and the matter of it. Inseparable from language, but in an asymmetrical relation with it, since language can be written, but not the voice, and it may remain without the voice. In the order of the spoken, there is still language in the silence of the voice, since there is no silence (of speech) outside of the voice, of the possibility of the voice. To be silent, as Heidegger pointed out, is not to be mute. Even less is it to be without language.

The absence of sound which bears the same name of silence is something else entirely, being neither the intermittence, nor the disappearance of the human voice. There are almost two homonyms here. Nature does not keep silent. The silence we put there resembles us, just as much as language does. The silence of the world is a metaphor. We are better off not forgetting that a metaphor is a metaphor.

As we know from common experience, there is voice in silence, and silence in the voice. Always sense. Or rather signification. For with language there is no outside of language. Silences are part of it. Furthermore, we make them speak.

This is shown by *L'Art de se taire* [The Art of Keeping Silent] by Father Dinouart,⁴ recently republished. The authors of the foreword show that he belongs to a 'rhetoric of the body' (p. 18), to an 'art of facial expression' (ibid., p. 41). The action which Cicero spoke of, discussed in the article *Action* in the *Encyclopédie*.

Something we have long known about, but which has no poetics. Only a pragmatics and a sociality of the body-in-language, which brings the gaze into language, language into the gaze.

Orality, designating the whole set of properties which characterise what is

---

2. This appeared fragmentarily in *Langue française*, 56 (December 1982), then complete in *Les États de la poétique* (Paris: Presses Universitaires de France, 1985).
3. Émile Benveniste, *Problèmes de linguistique générale*, Paris: Gallimard, 1966 [*Problems in General Linguistics*, trans. by Mary Elizabeth Meek (Coral Gables, FL: University of Miami Press, 1971), pp. 281–8.]
4. Abbé [Joseph Antoine Toussaint] Dinouart, *L'Art de se taire, principalement en matière de religion* (1771), preceded by Jean-Jacques Courtine and Claudine Haroche, 'Sciences du langage, langages du visage à l'âge classique' (Grenoble: Jérôme Millon, 1987).

oral, and which passes through the mouth, is only apparently tautological. It remains to be seen, as with *modern* and *modernity*, whether the morphological link between the words does not hide a subtle decoupling. The abstract word accords the status of an entity to an apparently obvious fact which hides what is to be sought: what happens and what is at stake in the relation between language and voice, speaking and writing.

As Benveniste does, one must draw from an empirical set and its empiricist presentation (which contents itself with data which are apparently ready-made and naturally present) the problem buried under its solution. The problem of the masking of rhythm, of discourse, of the subject by the sign as mode of representation of language. Within a transformation now taking place, and proper to modernity, of the relations between the voice and the visual, between writing and the visual. Mayakovsky has the typography of his diction, the diction of his typography. Jankélévitch noted that music is invisible and that all that can be shown of it is 'lateral'.[5] What one sees of it is dance, where rhythm brings the body into play. In the same way, voice is invisible, rhythm is invisible, but they call for a visualisation, a notation.

With orality, as for any language event, sense is in question. Or rather modes of signifying. That is what makes the treatment of punctuation in textual editing, or translation, and the functioning of literature in general and of poetry in particular the touchstones of the theory of language. Thereby the status of orality is itself a critique of all theory. As Paul Zumthor says, orality is 'the term: but what idea benefits from it?'[6]

The state of the question reveals a double impasse: that of traditional theory which identifies orality with phonation and provides, where literature is concerned, only a negative, purely sociological definition of it; that of oral-formulaic theory.

The living voice; the written, dead. From Plato to Derrida and to Barthes, such is the undisputed representation: 'We have embalmed our speech like a mummy, to preserve it forever.'[7] And 'what is lost in transcription is quite simply the body' (ibid., p. 5). Barthes had in mind the appeals and incertitudes proper to the function of contact, and saw the proof of them in the passage from parataxis to subordination: 'the sentence becomes hierarchical'

---

5. Vladimir Jankélévitch, 'Corps, violence, et mort' (1975), in the journal *Quel corps?* (Paris: Maspero, 1978), p. 54.
6. Paul Zumthor, *La Lettre et la voix* (Paris: Seuil, 1987), p. 9.
7. Roland Barthes, *The Grain of the Voice, Interviews 1962–1980*, trans. by Linda Coverdale (Berkeley: University of California Press, 1991 [1985]), p. 3. [Translator's note: subsequent quotations are from this translation.]

(ibid.). Two characters, according to him, being proper to writing, besides subordination: parenthesis and punctuation.

But the argument hardly holds. Parentheses may very well be made in speech. One can even say that we never stop making them, we do not close them, and speech has its own punctuation: intonation and pauses. Barthes confuses the parenthesis *function* and the punctuation *function*, which are elements of the rhythmics of sense, and of its set of gestures, with the graphic signs which symbolise them. A confusion which verges on a display of wit, or on a play on words.

Barthes arrived at a tri-partition: speech, the written, writing. The written being the transcribed, and writing 'properly so called, the kind which produces texts' (ibid., p. 6) having 'a separate subject each time' (ibid., p. 7). Only the writer being then a subject. There are as many modes of 'punctuation' as there are subjective rhythms. But by doubling the written, Barthes's tri-partition maintains the duality of the oral and the written, the confusion between the spoken and the oral remaining unchanged. Barthes accomplishes one of the effects of the sign, its instrumentalism, by isolating writing outside of ordinary language. Isolation, deviation which coincide with the idea of the 'useless' writer (ibid., p. 235), represented as a 'pervert who lives his activity as a utopia' (ibid.). Any theory is a self-portrait.

The term of *orature*, recently proposed to characterise oral literature,[8] a neologism which may have passed for a stroke of inspiration, and the recognition, the revaluing of a specificity, on the contrary blocks the question by substituting for it an answer, a realism of the word, which does not fill up the gap between the oral and the written, but pretends not to see it any longer.

Historically, one does not observe a radical heterogeneity. Paul Zumthor has shown, for the literature of the Western Middle Ages, that the 'letter' and the 'voice' are not opposed but converge towards each other. Before the fifteenth century, '*Oral* no more signifies *popular* than *written* signifies *learned*.'[9] But Zumthor is speaking here of the circumstances of emission and execution of works, not their poetics in so far as they are texts.

I take orality as a rhythmic practice defined at once linguistically, culturally and as a subject-form(er), which places literature and the spoken in a relation of solidarity, rather than separating them. Not in an indifferentiation which would misrecognise them, but as sharing the same means and organising them otherwise, according to a plurality of modes of signifying. Field work by ethnologists, who study the categories of discourse as African

---

8. I refer the reader to *Les États de la poétique* (Paris: Presses Universitaires de France, 1985), p. 123.
9. Zumthor, *La Lettre et la voix*, p. 132.

peoples, for example, understand them, with their own terms, in their culture, here takes its place.

The written would then be, besides the transcribed – the spoken being the phonic with all its own registers – defined as comprising the forms in which the (linguistic or social) codes are dominant, the mass of discourses where the language [*langue*] is understood and produced as the use which is made of it by an individual, a creature of social relations and grammatical constraints. Not an enunciation by which a subject comes into being.

The language–subject is thus double. There is the linguistic subject of enunciation, in Benveniste's sense. Which, already, modifies Saussure's individual *speech* [*parole*], which itself, it must be noted, *neutralises* the opposition between the spoken and the written. Being the individual act of language. Neutralising as well any distinction between the individual and the subject. And there is the poetic subject of enunciation, such that discourse is transformed by this subject and the subject attains the status of subject through this discourse. Which only happens through the primacy of rhythm and prosody in the organisation of sense. Which places the subject and orality in a relation of essential solidarity.

The oral would then be the set of modes of signifying characterised by this transformation. Their index. In the written as much as in the spoken. There is a voice of orality in the spoken. Just as we do not have the same voice when we read as when we speak. No orality without a subject, no subject without orality. A continuous of the subject, from the subject of discourse in Benveniste's sense to the subject of the poem. The oral belongs to the continuous – rhythm, prosody, enunciation. The spoken and the written belong to the discontinuous, the discrete units of language.

The two axes proposed by Saussure for the study of the functioning of language, the associative (the structuralist paradigmatics is a considerable impoverishment of this concept) and the syntagmatic, thus make possible the functional analysis of discourse and orality, whereas the 'traditional divisions' (lexicon, morphology, syntax) not only are no longer appropriate but prevent one even from seeing.

The relation between the concepts of analysis and their object no longer then has anything of that homogeneity with language which results when mimetism and the denial of metalanguage programmed a fantasmatic identification with writing, that 'pleasure of the text' which so many sheep-like followers have dreamed of. By losing oneself in the text. A fusion of the written and of writing. And an after-effect of the formalism of structures, which has turned some former structuralists sentimental. From pseudo-rigour to pseudo-emotion. The sign in a nutshell.

Critical homogeneity consists in the recognition of modes of signifying through the critique of the sign, something which literature and empirical language do already without being aware of it.

Any grasp of discourse which does not include its orality returns unknowingly to a discourse analysis using the concepts designed for the study of a language [*langue*]. This does not prevent one from making pertinent observations on points of detail, ingenious ones even, but the study remains essentially logicised.

As rhythm is no longer reducible to sound, to the phonic, to the ear, nose and throat sphere, but brings into play a respiratory imagination which concerns the living body as a whole, in the same way the voice is no longer reducible to the phonic, for the energy which produces it also brings into play the living body with its history. Thereby rhythm is at once an element of the voice and an element of writing. Rhythm is the movement of the voice in writing. With rhythm, one hears, not sound, but subject.

The Oral as Voice of the Body, but What Body?

If one listens to etymology, the oral concerns the mouth. But in the voice the ear plays a crucial role: 'It is thanks to the ear that a subject can control the various parameters of his or her voice.'[10] Thus the wordplay of the association cited by Zumthor, between *oral* and *aural*. A family tie likewise associates *vox* and *vocare*, 'call', from designation to vocation, and to convocation, and reminds us that from the beginning listening, as well as calling, is a part of the voice.

But the point is to listen to the voice, not to the *word* 'voice'. As Heidegger does in German, passing from *Stimme*, 'voice', to *Stimmung*, 'mood', and to *stimmen*, 'be in agreement with'. From this it is deduced that the voice 'produces an affection',[11] that the voice is '*the essence of affectivity*' (ibid., p. 30). This, à la Heidegger, is the realism of the voice.

A vocal body schema has been spoken of.[12] The voice is a biological sum in movement. But Mauss, in his study of the practices of the body, showed that the body is historical, cultural.

The body, 'as set of social relations',[13] is only opposed to a 'subject–body' according to the dualist schema of the sign, which opposes the individual to society. And shows that it confuses the individual and the subject. A subtle

---

10. Guy Cornut, *La Voix* (Paris: Presses Universitaires de France, 1983), p. 83.
11. Daniel Charles, *Le Temps de la voix* (Paris: Jean-Pierre Delarge, 1978), p. 29. Daniel Charles eliminates from his reflection the 'language-voice' ['*voix-langage*'] in order to study the 'music-voice' (p. 11), but he cannot separate one from the other.
12. Cornut, *La Voix*, p. 39.
13. 'Pour un corps de classe!', *Quel corps?*, p. 7.

way, now you see it, now you don't, of eliminating the subject. As does a Marxism denouncing the 'bourgeois legal perspective' (ibid.) which criticised the instrumentalisation of the body but 'in the name of a new instrumentalisation' (ibid., p. 9), according to a Hegelian 'unity of contraries' (ibid.), seeking to think 'the primary source of the process of metaphorisation, idealisation and irrationalism which is taking over contemporary discourse' (ibid., p. 12) – the body.

Michel Foucault wrote in 1975 that in 'calling into question the equation Marxism = revolutionary process, an equation which constitutes a sort of dogma, the importance of the body is one of the important, if not essential, elements'.[14] As an extension of this, I posit that for calling into question the equation the sign = only theory of language, which still constitutes a sort of dogma, orality as organisation of the subject is essential.

It is a question of 'stripping the problem of all that is purely physiological' as Saussure said.[15] Because a biologism is an instrumentalism. All biologisations of language reinforce the instrumentalism of the sign. The larynx is described as an instrument.[16] The voice is treated as an instrument: 'tool of self-expression', 'tool of self-affirmation' (ibid., p. 52). For the singing voice, 'the voice is treated so to speak as a musical instrument' (ibid., p. 64). And 'Any other tool besides the voice can be repaired, any other instrument can be replaced. Once a voice is lost it will not come back, broken, it cannot be remade.'[17] Instrumentalism, or meta-instrumentalism: 'the language-voice takes over structures and an anatomico-physiological mechanism which "serve other purposes" – for example, breathing.'[18] The comparison of the voice with an instrument is a very old one. And it is *natural*. One finds it in the article *Voix* [*Voice*] in the *Encyclopédie*: 'The organs which form the voice make a sort of wind instrument.'[19] Two centuries later, this comparison hasn't budged. The article *voix* in the *Encyclopedia Universalis* begins: 'The voice, the first of instruments, allows thought to change into sung or spoken structures.'[20]

---

14. Michel Foucault, 'Pouvoir et corps' [Power and Body], *Quel corps?*, pp. 2–5. English translation in Michel Foucault, *Power/Knowledge, Selected Interviews and Other Writings*, ed. by Colin Gordon (New York: Pantheon, 1980), pp. 55–62.
15. Michel Godel, *Les Sources manuscrites du 'Cours de linguistique générale' de Ferdinand de Saussure* (Geneva: Droz, 1957), p. 30.
16. For example, in Cornut, *La Voix*, p. 36.
17. Alain Arnaud, *Les Hasards de la voix* (Paris: Flammarion, 1984), p. 26.
18. Charles, *Le Temps de la voix*, p. 11.
19. *Encyclopédie*, vol. XVII (Neuchâtel: Faulche, 1765), p. 428.
20. *Encyclopedia Universalis*, vol. 16 (Paris: Société d'édition Encyclopædia Universalis, 1968), p. 968. The article bears primarily on the singing voice.

But the voice is no more an instrument than language is an instrument. Of communication. Or an institution. To instrumentalise one is to instrumentalise the other. These two instrumentalisations are really one and the same. One and the same reduction. Which has been denounced by the anthropology of language. Starting with Humboldt. But first of all by orality itself, paradoxically unheard, unperceived in the concert of instruments.

Just as the poem is not that prolonged hesitation between sound and sense, which Valéry spoke of, metaphorically, from within the sign, no more is the voice an oscillation 'between the body and language'.[21] This is the implicit solidarity between the discourse on the voice and the theory of language. It is up to poetics to make it explicit.

Voice and the Subject, Voice and Language

The perturbations of the voice are the well-known marks of emotional disturbances and, more significantly, of an 'appeal which cannot be expressed by words but is expressed by the voice'.[22] From this we get, not only professionals dealing with the voice, but a psycho-sociology of the voice, and its cultural characteristics: 'The falsetto voice, for example, is practically never used in Europe by men for it is associated with a pejorative connotation whereas in Northern Africa, its use is much more frequent' (ibid., p. 56).

At once 'vital energy', 'neuromuscular function' and 'sound message' (ibid., p. 111), the voice is the *exterior intimate*. Which accounts for the metaphor of the voice for writing, and for the writer. Act of language, act of the subject.

A shift from voice to diction and from voice to text is apparent in this reflection of Valéry's:

> The human voice seems so beautiful to me in its interiority, and taken as close as possible to its source, that professional reciters are almost always unbearable to me, they who claim to *highlight, interpret*, whereas they overload, debauch the intentions, distort the harmonies of a text; and they substitute their lyricism for the song inherent in the combined words. Is not their profession, and their paradoxical expertise, that of leading us momentarily to mistake the most negligent verse for something sublime, while making ridiculous, or annihilating, most works which can stand on their own?[23]

---

21. Guy Rosolato, 'La Voix: entre corps et langage', *Revue Française de Psychanalyse*, 38/1 (January to February 1974), pp. 75–94.
22. Cornut, *La Voix*, p. 94.
23. Paul Valéry, *Le Coup de dés* (1920), in *Œuvres*, I (Paris: Éditions de la Pléiade, 1957), p. 623–4.

This shift from a voice of a professional reciter to a voice of the text implies the existence of a poet's diction which would be nothing other than, precisely, the voice of the words. Not a toneless voice, but an interior voice. The actor theatricalises, emphasises. Tends to be entirely on the outside. The opposite flaw is found among some poets, that of not bringing out their voice. Which must be this contradiction held and maintained, to remain wholly interior, yet come forth.

The metaphor of the voice for writing shows that both are interiority. A banal metaphor. Seemingly self-justified, so often does it reel off its story as though it were simply an obvious fact. One could make an anthology of such instances. I quote at random:

> Literature only begins at that moment, at the moment when I hear a singular voice [. . .] there is no literature if there is no voice, thus a language which bears somebody's mark. It requires a style, a tone, a technique, an art, an invention [. . .] the author must impose his presence on me; and when he imposes his presence on me, he imposes his world.[24]

The problem of poetics is not to criticise this metaphor, but to understand where it comes from, and how the voice–subject and the subject–voice pass through the writing of orality.

If sense is in words, significance in rhythm and prosody, signification can be in the voice. Through the voice, signification precedes sense, and carries it. Words are *in the voice*. Just as a relation precedes and carries its terms. Which is what intonation does. Paradoxically, understanding precedes sense. And this goes for children: 'Education tends to teach children to express through words and sentences what they expressed before through their voice.'[25] The specific work of the poem is perhaps to retransform words and sentences into voice. The *a-a-a* which Tsvetaeva speaks of.[26] This is why poetry is a critique, and an allegory, of understanding.

There is an eroticism of the voice, since there is a sex of the voice, which does far more than its denomination as a secondary sex characteristic would suggest, personalised and everywhere mixed with signification. A continual relation which voice and inflexion have with speech. Charm, or repulsion.

For the politician's voice, it has even been maintained that 'it is the voice,

---

24. Simone de Beauvoir, *Que peut la littérature?* (1965), quoted in Francis Vanoye, *Expression communication* (Paris: Armand Colin, 1973), p. 151.
25. Cornut, *La Voix*, p. 48.
26. See 'Rhyme and Life', [in this volume, p.]

much more than the ideas expressed, which wins the audience's support'.[27] The examples being Hitler, Léon Blum, Pétain and De Gaulle.[28]

Is there voice without language? With music, the voice tends to go out of language. But the 'music-voice', as Daniel Charles says, is perhaps only this tension, in the *Sprechgesang* of Schoenberg, or the effects of voice in Berio. A certain kind of musical experimentation really makes of the voice an instrument, with the various registers, voices, musical modes, mixing it with the synthesiser, bringing it back to the cry, to babble or to opera singing. Contradiction of a semiotics without a semantics, music, and a semantics without a semiotics, the work. The voice without sense.

The absence of sense is an allegory of sense in language. The absence of sense still speaks of sense. This is an irony of language. As much a parable of the end of sense as of the beginning of sense. Language has these margins, where the voice is on the verge of going out of language, apparently. In fact, it remains within, as is shown by the variants of onomatopoeia and counting rhymes found in different languages.

Performance poetry, lettrism, sound poetry are analogous offshoots of dualism. Going, occasionally, so far as to separate the voice from language. Until they are nothing more than a pure rhetoric, that of spectacle.

For all that, the voice is not something irrational opposed to the rational in language. Which is what a lyrical representation makes of it: 'But the voice is madness, unreason, heedlessness of the moment, ignorance of the future, [. . .] wandering is its home.'[29] Which is nothing else but the lyricising of the sign, the very schema of signifier and signified. The irrational of the signifier, analogous to its madness, opposed to *logos*. And here is speech: 'Speech is the beginning of wisdom. It speaks of sense, [. . .] it speaks to the future' (ibid.). An opposition which does not see that all of language, like the voice, can only be placed in the tension between reason and unreason if one opposes language and life. From which we get the specious truism: 'Writing the voice, an impossible wager' (ibid., p. 87). For that is what writing, each time in a unique manner, does. The novelesque and the poetic of the voice is what the novel, the poem write. And that is what makes a poetics of the voice necessary.

In the same way that Julia Kristeva made of the *chora* in Plato the feminine irrational of rhythm, opposed, in *Powers of Horror*, to the masculine-rational-Jewish-and-God-the-Father, 'voice's very indeterminateness, an indeterminateness which might well be its very fabric' (ibid., p. 102), this

---

27. Cornut, *La Voix*, p. 54.
28. Analyses by Jean-Loup Rivière, 'Le Vague de l'air', *Traverses*, 20, 'La Voix, l'écoute', (November 1980), pp. 17–25.
29. Arnaud, *Les Hasards de la voix*, p. 85.

indetermination–feminisation reproduces the stylistics of deviation, that of the sign: 'In its voluble, volcanic, fusional force – *chora* –, the voice maintains intact the gap which separates it from thought attempting to close it, taking in all its discourses, docile to all its influences, but not recognising itself in any and exceeding them all' (ibid.). The clausula taken from Wagner (ibid., p. 105)

> in the universal stream
> of the world-breath –
> to drown,
> to founder –
> unconscious –
> utmost rapture![30]

comes back to the eternal return à la Nietzsche, the return of nature in the matter of language.

This irrationalisation is a desubjectivisation. The desubjectivisation of the voice is a spatialisation. As with language, the body is 'put into space by means of the voice' (ibid., p. 28), and the voice 'traces in the space which it invades innumerable figures, moving, ungraspable, which it endlessly combines, entangles and disentangles' (ibid., pp. 46–7).

Desubjectivised, spatialised, the voice is dehistoricised. It is the voice of anti-historicity:

> Freed of all determination, effaced in its inexhaustible movement, having thus conquered an eternity which wounds me but calls on me, it waits for me, accompanies me, precedes me, requiring of me nothing but a fascinated compliance, an unreserved obedience, the entrance into its darkness where my disappearance, consented to, is assured. Through it, in it, I accede, even to the point of fusion with it, 'to something of nature in space'. (ibid., p. 103)

The essentialisation of the voice, and that of language, involve the same indefinite withdrawal out of sense, out of the empirical. And have the same consequences.

The Oral and the Written in Ethnology

The sign is what makes for anthropological dualism. This old opposition, rejected, persistent, self-ashamed – scratch the surface slightly and you will

---

30. [Translator's note: Richard Wagner, 'Tristan und Isolde', trans. by Dmitry Murashev, available at <http://www.murashev.com/opera/Tristan_und_Isolde_libretto_English_German> (last accessed 19 February 2018).]

find it – between the civilised and the savage, the logical and the prelogical, the rational and the irrational, us and the others. Paul Zumthor said it was the 'original flaw' of ethnology.[31]

The opposition between the oral and the written seen as two types of literature and culture is shown concretely in the question: 'How far is translation possible?' which Ruth Finnegan posed in 1982.[32] The creole tales of Réunion, as they are edited and translated on site by linguists who replace the spoken language, and its rhythms, with a written language which doesn't give the slightest idea of it, are an example of this. No linguistic constraint requires this. The only constraint is that of the preconceived idea which consists in this very opposition. It is remarkable that translation is what makes this appear.

The oral, in *oral literature*, is defined by the 'multiplicity of variants' for Veronika Görög-Karady (ibid., p. ii), who is concerned to define genres in relation with social functions. But this is only a secondary variation on the fundamental notion designated indifferently by 'oral literature', 'oral performance', 'oral communication', 'oral delivery' (p. iv). The difference between the French and the British seen as the opposition between a study of texts and an empirical study, abstract structural themes rather than local ones, continental linguistics and on the other side a narrower ethnography. Secondary distinctions, recognised as stereotypes, within the same dual anthropological and semiotic definition – that of the sign.

But the criterion of oral variations may be otherwise interpreted. Jean Derive, at the same Oxford conference, noted: 'when there is a written reproduction it is almost always with the explicit aim of saying something else', and 'on the contrary, when there is a reformulation in oral literature, it is almost always in order to say the same thing' (ibid., p. 15). Necessarily, it is a question of performances: 'the oral text no longer exists as soon as it is uttered, except in memory, and its existence can be maintained only by successive realisations' (ibid.). But this opposition between the written and the oral involves a play on the word reformulation: execution–representation in an oral situation; assimilation to variations on a theme (Antigone, Faust, Don Juan) in written literature: 'it happens fairly frequently that creation is based on culturally significant works of the past' (ibid., p. 14). In which case one is

---

31. Paul Zumthor, *Oral Poetry: An Introduction*, trans. by Kathryn Murphy-Judy (Minneapolis: University of Minnesota Press, 1990), p. 29. [Translator's note: Subsequent references are to this edition; translations modified.]
32. In the foreword to the collection *Genres, Forms, Meanings: Essays in African Oral Literature*, ed. by Veronika Görög-Karady, with a foreword by Ruth Finnegan, *Journal of the Anthropological Society of Oxford* (1982), p. vi.

dealing each time with *another* work, with what is unique to it, historically: Molière's Don Juan and Milosz's. The project cannot be defined simply by a 'subversion of the sense of that culturally significant element' (ibid.). The literariness of the written work is not faced up to if one culturalises it and if one secondarises it as literature of literature, as is shown by all the prefixed terms (metatext, paratext, hypotext) by which a certain post-structuralism reduces literature to reproduction or parody. Retaining rhyme, leaving out life.

A schematic idea of written literature sees it in terms of a 'binary problematic where certain elements are considered as models and others as reproductions' (ibid., p. 18). What is revealed when the notion of variant is brought into play is the sign-separation between a signifier and a signified. The signifier, reserved for the types of texts which are transmitted integrally ('learning by heart'); in the case of a paraphrase, the text is seen 'on the side of the signified' (ibid., p. 15). The very conditions which make a poetics impossible. The reference to the automatic discourse analysis practised by Pêcheux confirms this – the notion of transformation, borrowed from generative grammar, already implying a denial of significance, through the distinction between linguistic transformations and discursive transformations. The recording of variants according to whether they are 'given by a woman, a man, a child, a master, a slave' (ibid., p. 16) belongs to sociology.

The importance which the notion of genre appears to take on is an effect of the sign. Undermined by literary modernity, the genre was a privileged object of structuralist taxonomy. Here the only fruitful consequence consists in the interest taken in taxonomies of cultural self-designation. Towards a socio-linguistics.

The European specialists of oral literature focus on the status of communication. Performance and transmission. Seeking to recognise how the non-written is designated: 'Apparently the oral has an autonomous existence only through the status of the sender; otherwise the oral is determined by the written,' and 'the written text enters the process of communication only through reading, just as the oral text exists only by being uttered.'[33]

This is what makes designations in the original language worth noting. For example, in the Anufo language spoken by the Chakosi of Togo, notional distinctions show that the saying and the said depend on the conditions of enunciation: depending on whether speech takes place at night or during the day, by whom, to whom. A sociology of speech and song: 'At night, women can only sing' (ibid., p. 11). A metalinguistic study: 'The verb form *di* designates the action of eating food as well as other acts among which that of

---

33. Diana Rey-Hulman, 'Pratiques langagières et formes littéraires', in *Genres, Forms, Meanings*, p. 3.

telling tales: "to eat the sex of a woman": to copulate; "to eat the judgement": pronounce a judgement; "to eat the kingship": to be enthroned as king; "to eat the market": go to the market; "to eat poverty": to be poor' (ibid., p. 13, n. 3). This orality of speech is a devouring.

The tale is treated as a document. Without underestimating the enormous work of collection and transcription, and the interest of analyses like the one made by Geneviève Calame-Griaule, at the same conference, of the tale 'The Young Girl Looking for her Brothers', analyses all made with reference to psychoanalysis – there is no poetics of the tale here. No poetics of orality.

The Oral, the Written in Linguistics

The oral taken for the spoken is the rule among linguists. As, for instance, in the issue of *Langue française* entitled 'L'Oral du débat'.[34] This number continually refers to the 'structuration of oral French', the 'graphic transcription of the oral' (p. 3). The identification of the oral with the spoken is never a matter of any doubt, as in the article on 'The notation of the oral', which begins: 'Though the primacy of the spoken language over the written language has long been affirmed, [. . .] linguistic or grammatical analyses [. . .] have, until recently, always focused on written language documents' (p. 6), and, further on: 'The disdainful negligence which the oral language has suffered from for centuries has at last come to an end, but only recently and not without difficulties and struggles' (p. 6). *Spoken language, oral language*, these variations attest to a semantic non-differentiation: 'work on an oral reality' (p. 7), 'phonetic reality' (p. 7), 'oral discourse' (p. 18). Where furthermore *language* [*langue*] and *discourse* are mixed up. The written being, partially, the transcribed: 'pay close attention to features of orality which could not have been transcribed' (p. 8).

Of course it is not a question here of contesting the long negligence of and condescendence towards the spoken, and the studies it calls for, but rather of making a critique of the confusion of the oral and the spoken. Evidently, the idea of distinguishing between the two seems never to have crossed anyone's mind.

Punctuation thus continues to be understood as 'specific to the written' (ibid., p. 9), a confusion of graphic signs with the notion of punctuation itself as a syntactic–semantic–rhythmic function. For it is in so far as punctuation is supposed to be proper to the written that it is said to have a 'syntactic role', like the 'grammatical symbols'. Only through transcription do they acquire a

---

34. *Langue française*, 65 (February 1985), edited by Mary-Annick Morel, Centre de Recherche en Morphosyntaxe du Français Contemporain, Paris III.

'slightly distorted value', that of 'prosodic markers'. Double misconception: of the history of punctuation in its theatricality and its orality; and of the interrelation between syntax and rhythm.

A rediscovery of prosody remains confined to the oral–spoken. Except when there is an invention of prosodic signs, as for the pause (not marked in writing by a comma, according to the logico-grammatical punctuation in general use) between subject and verb, noted by Charles Bally: 'La vie: est courte' [Life: is short], 'Le soleil: éclaire la terre' [The sun: shines on the earth]. But Bally added: 'subjects are not conscious of these interruptions, they do not count in phonology.'[35]

As for the philologists who prepare editions of texts, for whom only the written exists, the misconception of the oral appears in a completely different form, in the denial of historicity which leads them to modernise punctuation, even as, out of historicist motives, they conserve old spellings. There is no point in revisiting that here.[36] But we must have a look at what pedagogy does with science.

The Pedagogy of the Oral, the Written

The opposition between the oral and the written, where French is concerned, goes as far as envisaging 'two languages – *written French* and *spoken French*', and 'the two languages have neither the same morphology, nor the same grammar, nor the same expressive means.'[37]

Here no more than above does the objection I am making bear on the well-known differences between the spoken, *the various forms* of the spoken, and the written, *the various forms* of the written. It bears on the conception of language which filters through the sciences.

The use of the term *language* [*langue*] is indicative of the outdated predominance of communication, code and information in the theory of language.

Oral and *spoken* are interchangeable here: '*spoken French*' (ibid., p. 40); 'in writing' opposed to 'orally' (p. 42); 'oral communication' (pp. 43, 159) opposed to 'written communication' (p. 43); 'written language' and 'spoken language' (p. 44); 'oral message' (p. 44). The commonplace identification, supposedly a specifically linguistic one.

Then, with no explicit warning, the value of the opposition changes:

---

35. Charles Bally, *Linguistique générale et linguistique française* (Berne: Francke, 1965 [1932]), §72, n. 1. Quoted in *Langue française*, 65, p. 45.
36. See Henri Meschonnic, 'Oralité et littérature', in *La Rime et la vie* (Paris: Gallimard, 2006 [1989]), pp. 287–309.
37. Francis Vanoye, *Expression communication* (Paris: Armand Colin, 1973), p. 41.

'the style of oral presentation' (p. 174) is defined 'by a sort of compromise between the spoken language and the written language'. A new distinction, but a muddled one: symptomatic of a pragmatic behaviourist attitude, which reserves the same treatment for group communication techniques, expressive techniques, content analysis and the grammar of the spoken.

Structuralism and semiotics, in their effects on school curricula and pedagogy, have reinforced this identification–confusion, which is masked by the moral satisfaction of fighting the good fight to accord the spoken, in the teaching of 'the language' ['*la langue*'], an importance it never had, given the value traditionally attributed to the written.

The book *Pratiques de l'oral* begins: 'The oral is now taught from the elementary school to the university and, beyond, in numerous continuing education workshops. The capacity to communicate orally is an educational objective emphasised by most official educational programmes.'[38] A pedagogy of the oral: it will necessarily lump together the descriptive and the normative.

Oral, orality, linked unproblematically: 'the oral is a socialisation of individual experience', and 'something is at stake, in orality, which has to do with exchange, sharing, and relationship' (ibid., p. 9). But among 'oral settings' (p. 10) and in what is denominated 'oral language' (p. 10), the heterogeneous domains of 'the teaching situation' – 'chit chat' (p. 56) – and 'acting', 'theatrical expression' and the situation of the story-teller are lumped together, along with the simple prior sense which designated the spoken in general.

To the linguistic analysis of modes of speech is added, or substituted, one is not sure, a rhetoric of expression. In itself multiple. Theatrical expression, with an allusion to the *jongleurs* of the Middle Ages and to story-tellers, oddly merging a distant past with the present, 'was specifically oral. Oral in two ways: it was never based on a written text but proceeded from a verbal and gestural improvisation; it was steeped in orality, nourished by traditional folk narratives, myths, in short, by a collective speech transmitted from generation to generation' (ibid., p. 12).

A double separation takes place: the oral is no longer simply the spoken, and *orality* is given a value which is more literary than linguistic – it now only corresponds to a part of the *oral*. Contradiction between the element of backward-looking archaism implied by the reference to the *jongleurs*, and the pragmatism of expressive techniques.

To this is added a politicisation of the terms, drawn from a text by Walter Benjamin, *The Storyteller*, from 1936, and enlarged upon by Michel de Certeau: '"Progress" is scriptural. [. . .] What does not work towards progress

---

38. F. Vanoye, J. Mouchon, J.-P. Sarrazac, *Pratiques de l'oral: écoute, communications sociales, jeu théâtral* (Paris: Armand Colin, 1981), p. 9.

may be called "oral", reciprocally what separates itself from the magical world of voices and the tradition may be called "scriptural". With that separation, a borderline of civilisation is drawn' (cited ibid., p. 52). Whereby, 'in the face of an ostracism of this sort', a reaction: 'the oral – more precisely, here: orality – possesses several magic and saving virtues matching its rarity' (ibid.). A confirmation of the difference between oral and orality, and a programme for 'lending an ear to what remains of orality in our society' (p. 53).

The search for 'pedagogical efficiency' results in a syncretism where behaviourist psychology overrides linguistics and poetics. Brings out into the open the political character of the sign. With ecology in the voice.

It remains for us to give an account of how structuralism, the most recent of science's spectacular scenarios, analyses orality, and what ensues.

The Structural Poetics of Orality

Paul Zumthor asks: '*is there a specifically oral poeticity?*',[39] and responds with the dual opposition of the voice and the written. On one side, the 'human voice', 'phonation', 'living speech' (ibid., p. 4) which has supposedly 'died out' in our societies. Which revives the old anthropology. A dual anthropology. On the other side, 'the universe of signs'. There is thus for him a poetic definition of 'oral poetry' (ibid., p. 5). Zumthor describes the 'presence of the voice' as the primordial matter existing before language, at 'the origins of all oral poetry' (ibid., p. 10).

Orality, then, 'cannot be reduced to vocal action' (ibid., p. 153), it includes gesture, resides in performance. All the impasses of traditional theory. To escape from it, excessive importance is accorded to sound poetry (ibid., p. 228).

If the voice is 'the instrument of prophecy' (ibid., p. 225), it is not only as phonic substance and performance, but as prosody and syntax, vision of the voice, words becoming vision. Which is explained by Maimonides: the vision works through 'the *name* of the thing seen',[40] which alludes to a homonym, 'which is also one of the species of allegory'.

Ruth Finnegan, in *Oral Poetry*,[41] demonstrated the impossibility of founding a distinction between oral poetry and written poetry, poetically.

---

39. Zumthor, *Oral Poetry, An Introduction*, p. 3.
40. With examples like that of *makkel schaked*, 'an almond staff' (Jeremiah 1: 11 and 12), an allusion to *schoked*, 'vigilant'. Maimonides, *Le Guide des égarés* [The Guide for the Perplexed], second part, ch. XLIII, ed. by S. Munk (Paris: Maisonneuve & Larose, 1970), vol. 2, p. 327.
41. Ruth Finnegan, *Oral Poetry: Its Nature, Significance and Social Context* (Cambridge: Cambridge University Press, 1977). I refer the reader to *Critique du rythme*.

With the well-known criteria only a sociological distinction remains. But Zumthor persists in seeing a 'poetic orality' in the 'facts of oral culture'.[42] That is to say, in popular cultures, characterised by their 'slow foundering' (ibid., p. 15) between the sixteenth and nineteenth centuries. A *de facto*, if not *de jure*, identification of *popular* with *oral*.

The consequence of this folklorist definition: the (remarkable) inventory of orality is the inventory of a 'decline' (ibid., p. 53).

The phonic sense attributed to orality, as well as the discussion of the relations between *oral* and *popular*, is what leads to equating poetry and song, 'the record and the radio' (ibid., p. 17), 'all this poetry of often mediocre quality' (ibid., p. 48). A critique, and at the same time the neutralisation of critique, through the priority given to sociologism. That widespread ambiguity, which places Brassens among the 'poets of today', and sees Jacques Brel as a 'great poet' (ibid., p. 100).[43] As though the love of poetry must lead to this demagogy of confusing everything.

It is not sufficient to reject the 'negative' definition (ibid., p. 17) of orality as the absence of writing. The position which considers as 'oral any poetic communication in which transmission and reception at least pass through voice and hearing' (ibid., p. 23), even if one distinguishes between 'oral *transmission* of poetry' and 'oral *tradition*' (ibid.), does not change anything in the traditional situation. It brings with it a confusion between *poetic communication* and *poetry*. Nor is it innocent to say *verbal communication* for language. The sign, information, behaviour. To say nothing of its implied separation, equally questionable, from non-verbal communication.

A distinction, taken from Jousse, between the spoken which passes through the mouth, and an oral defined as an 'utterance formalised in a specific manner' (ibid., p. 23) and 'mediated by tradition' no better suffices to get out of the sign. The 'MacLuhan perspective' where Zumthor places himself even aggravates the 'Orality/Writing dichotomy' (ibid., p. 25).

Invoking rhythm is no more helpful, if the notion of rhythm retains its traditional sense. Zumthor speaks of oral 'poetic art' as a 'predominance of rhythms' (ibid., p. 98). But *rhythm* here designates 'architecture of being, symbolic articulation, image, mirror, denomination, participation in what animates the universe' (ibid., p. 101). Ritual overvaluation, which one finds in poets like Hölderlin, but which remains within the lexicon of philosophy, with an allusion to ontology. Thought rooted in the sign, number, order.

The 'four ideal categories' of orality confirm all that they proposed to

---

42. Zumthor, *Oral Poetry: An Introduction*, p. 13.
43. [Translator's note: 'Poets of Today' is the name of a French series of books presenting modern poets.]

'reduce', the negative character of orality. Primary or pure orality remains 'without contact with "writing"' (ibid., p. 25); coexistent, mixed or secondary, and 'mechanically mediated' – these adaptations are once again social in character. All of this leads to a contradiction: setting aside the 'criterion of quality' (ibid., p. 27) – a structuralist, sociologising approach (structure knows nothing about value) – while seeking, at the same time, a 'poetics of orality' (ibid., pp. 80, 97).

For poetics is a theory of value. There is neither specificity nor historicity without value. A misuse, or rather a deficiency, of language, led people to believe there could be a structural poetics. The two terms *poetic* and *structural* clash with each other. The confusion arises from the structuralist identification of *structure* with *system*.

Finally, regarding the fragmentary character of the texts, Zumthor writes that the oral text 'cannot, in so far as it is a *text*, an organised linguistic sequence, differ essentially from the written' (ibid., p. 41). This Ruth Finnegan showed, and it nullifies Zumthor's whole argument: '[f]rom the linguistic point of view, a text – be it oral or written – remains a text' (ibid., p. 97). At once the postulation of a poetics of orality, and its failure.

For there is a vagueness about the very notions of text and poetry. The text is defined linguistically as 'total meaning', and at the same time '[T]he poem is the text' (ibid., p. 60). Poetry includes the 'cries of street vendors, poetry of a centuries-long tradition' (p. 67), 'chatter' (p. 68), lullabies (p. 69), the 'hit songs' of mass-market 'youth culture' (p. 70), Christmas carols (p. 73), drinking songs and funeral songs (pp. 73–4). Implicit conjunction of the notion of poetic function, borrowed from Jakobson, and the sociological approach, along with a touch of youth-oriented demagoguery, in order to lump together all that plays the role of poetry. The latter loses in intension what it gains in extension.

As for epic and the oral-formulaic style, it is well known that research on the formal criteria of orality has not yielded convincing results: 'the commonly held opinion today leans, by reaction, towards scepticism and tends not to recognise the formula as a sure mark of orality' (ibid., p. 97). I add biblical parallelism to this. And its structuralist extension by Jakobson and others. Formulism undergoes a double defeat: as a criterion of epic, as a criterion of orality. The non-formal definition of epic by 'the exaltation of the hero and of the exemplary exception' (ibid., p. 95) is not pertinent for modernity. It thus contributes to making epic appear like a form of the past. Cutting off orality from modernity. And epic then becomes the mainstay of 'oral tradition'.[44]

44. Paul Zumthor, *La Lettre et la voix, de la littérature médiévale* (Paris: Seuil, 1987), p. 34.

The paradox of a structural poetics of orality – and yet its internal logic as well – is to combine an appearance of rigour with vagueness: 'oral poetic language, such as it is and in every circumstance – does it not carry with it a fundamental tendency to complicate structures of discourse?'[45] Yet nothing could be simpler than a copla. *Complicate*, *structures*: these two terms are at once a tautology and an absolute superlative.

Written poetry supposedly has at its disposal 'more freedom in the choice of means', but all the features mentioned (ibid., p. 110), the insertion of elements devoid of sense or in a foreign language, the litany, refrains, recurrences, are found everywhere. What is said of poetry in general relates as much to written poetry as to oral poetry (ibid., p. 213), independently of uncertainties about its metrical or non-metrical character (ibid., pp. 135–6). To a double modality (the spoken, the sung), Zumthor opposes a triple distinction between the 'spoken voice', 'measured recitative or psalmody', and 'melodic song' (ibid., p. 142). The distinction is entirely pertinent. But these three modalities are all modalities of the voice. They don't tell us anything about a poetics of orality. They remain within the duality of the oral and the written. As does the distinction between oral tradition, across time, and oral transmission, as performance.

Preferring 'to the word *orality*, that of *vocality*', Zumthor confirms that traditional theory remains enclosed in its contradictions, and opposes 'the voice and the written'.[46] A way out of the impasse is sought in the aesthetics of reception, that of Jauss, thus moving from the opposition between the oral and the written to the opposition between the constitution of the text and its reception. Once again nothing has changed as far as the poetic problem is concerned. Reception belongs to the sociology of literature. Meanwhile the question of the production of a text without writing is lost sight of, since the orality is situated in the performance. Which leads even to searching for marks of orality in the self-referential designations included in the oral text (ibid., p. 39) or in external attestations.

Paul Zumthor's constant aim is to situate poetic acts in their 'temporal conditionings' (ibid., p. 312). Literature no more exists in itself than orality does. It is not certain that 'mass culture' (ibid., p. 322) fosters it.

Historicity is not simply the trace of the conditions of emission or execution. Poetic historicity is a historicity of texts in their very saying. The task of poetics is to recognise it.

Structuralism brought to this task the buzz of a certain era. That buzz, today, has turned to a conceptual silence.

---

45. Zumthor, *Oral Poetry: An Introduction*, p. 101.
46. Zumthor, *La Lettre et la voix*, pp. 21, 26.

Psychoanalysis and Orality

For a problem like that of orality, it would be odd if there were nothing to learn from psychoanalysis. But here I will make only a short, risky, fragmentary incursion.

If one looks in the direction of the psychoanalytical theory of language, it is remarkable that hysteria was what spurred Freud's interest in language. And perhaps it has not been sufficiently taken into consideration up to now what these works on hysteria may continue to teach us, not only about language, but in particular about orality.

Metaphorically, and this metaphor has become a contemporary cliché, the body is language, language is of the body. One speaks of the 'embedding of discourse in the body'.[47] Roland Gori writes that 'the body can be a language' (p. 33) and, more precisely, that 'somatic conversion is apparently a language and one organised according to the linguistic model of symbolisation. Speech infiltrates the body and the body relays it, replaces it in its message, this is the whole problem of hysteria' (p. 34). But here it is a question of speech in the 'analytic situation' (p. 7), not the speech of the poem, and in place of the body there is 'the very structure of unconscious representations, of the fantasies of which the body is the object' (p. 7).

The 'malleable nature of the material of speech', which Freud speaks of in *Delusions and Dreams in Jensen's* Gradiva,[48] which makes of words 'sounded things',[49] is inseparably that they are produced as *words* and as *voices* (which Spanish, preserving the Latin, says with a single word), just as Aristotle, in the *De Interpretatione* (16a), spoke of τὰ ἐν τῇ φωνῇ, 'the things which are in the voice'. If words are in the voice, one may also say that there is voice in words.

Hysteria, as it was studied by Freud, makes possible a way of seeing discourse which is of importance for the theory of language and particularly for that of literature. For it highlights an effect of language on the body, an aspect of the relation between language and the body in which *there are no more metaphors*: the metaphors are realised.

Hysteria shows the power of language over the body, and just as well its

---

47. Roland Gori, *Le Corps et le signe dans l'acte de parole* (Paris: Dunod, 1978), p. 10. This relation is approached in multiple ways in the collective work by J. Nadal, M. Pierrakos, M. Secco Bellati, M. F. Lecomte-Emond, A. Ramirez, R. Vintraud, N. Zuili and M. Dabbah, *Rêve de corps, corps du langage* (Paris: l'Harmattan, 1989).
48. Sigmund Freud, *Delusions and Dreams in Jensen's* Gradiva, Standard Edition of the Complete Psychological Works of Sigmund Freud, vol. 9 (London: Hogarth Press, 1959), p. 85.
49. Gori, *Le Corps et le signe dans l'acte de parole*, p. 17.

bodily character. Hence, one could propose that something bodily is necessary for language to have power. Activity, *energeia*.

In hysteria, the symptom replaces speech when speech is demetaphorised. Speech dissolves the symptom by making its metaphorical character evident. Perhaps one could say that orality is present when it is language which becomes hysterical. Not the speaker. Orality intervenes as a counter-hysteria, a form of hysteria which would put *the body into language*. The maximum possible amount of body, and of its energy. As rhythm. The rhythm as subject-form(er). Whereas hysteria, working the opposite way, puts *language into the body*. And makes the body mime it.

Orality would then be, not a discharge, but a maximal instinctual charge. Not a pathology, like hysteria, but its opposite. The same force, but turned from the body towards language instead of being turned from language towards the body. And thus the maximal efficacy of language.

Of this rhythmic–subjective continuum, one may well understand that the sign understands nothing. Thus rhythm is irrationalised. The old metaphor of the magic, or the alchemy of the word. Of the Word, that theo-linguistics with its capital letter which is another designation made from the point of view of the sign. Viewed from the poem, this alchemy is demetaphorised in its turn. It is for the sign that figures, and a rhetoric, exist. The poem is the moment when metaphors are realised.

Thus words are no longer the placeholders of things, as in the sign. That is to say, signifieds, carried by signifiers which have no relation to them. A strange conception, the absurdity of which is masked by habit. But rather, the matter and the continual labour of the generation and the physicality of sense. Which is discourse, the point at which the double articulation which belongs to the point of view of language [*langue*] ceases to be pertinent.

This is what orality shares, surprisingly, with hysteria: it is no longer a saying, nor something said, but a doing.

An aspect, and a fragmentary one, of orality. It may appear a bit mad. Because orality overwhelms our concepts, and we come to it from the sign. A paradoxical situation, because nothing is more commonplace than orality, which belongs to everybody's experience, and to each instant.

Orality appears to be an origin, being first of all in the voice. But, as Saussure showed for what passes in language for origin, orality is, not an origin, but a mode of functioning. It is only through the critique of received ideas that one gains access to it.

Writing, translating are truly realised only if they are a practice of orality. And no doubt one can be a writing only if one is the invention of one's own orality.

8

The Subject of Writing
(in *La Rime et la vie*, Gallimard, 2006, pp. 366–70)

Translated by Andrew Eastman

Psychoanalysis has nothing to tell us about the subject of writing.[1] The poem and the theory of language – both act the subject. Through the subject, through language, the poem and theory encounter psychoanalysis. Psychoanalysis itself traverses them, invokes them, convokes them. Yet the relation between the practice of writing, the theory of language, and psychoanalysis appears marked as much by necessity as by a contradiction.

The necessity has to do with the concepts and the methods of discourse analysis which Freud produced empirically. From which, a grasp of language that has become a part of our reading.

For some, this part has absorbed all. They lay a book down on a couch. This grasp has become a part of our writing. Through the science it carries along with it, going so far as to programme practices which mime their own science. They do what they know. They know all of what they do. Rashly counting on realising dreams. This effect, though widespread, is minor. It is a kind of parlour game.

More insidiously destructive is the absence, in psychoanalysis, of a theory of what it is continually doing: listening. The absence of a theory of rhythm and discourse which might be the theory of its own listening. Psychoanalysis, born in the era of philology, in some cases an imaginary philology (that of Abel), has lived on to the age of structuralism. The sign, language [*la langue*]. It has rushed to embrace aphonic, asubjective, ahistorical structures. And, as

---

1. Written on the basis of an intervention at an encounter between psychoanalysts and writers, organised by the Entretoile association, in Toulouse, 28 January 1989. This reflection presupposes the analyses presented in *Le Signe et le poème* (Paris: Gallimard, 1975), pp. 305–25.

a compensation, nature-as-origin. The dualist myth continues to govern the dominant thinking on language. Psychoanalysis makes do very well with this. It has ensconced itself in it. It sustains it. Traditional theory. And in this way it makes itself deaf to discourse, to the poem, and, thereby, partially, to the subject.

This evenly suspended deafness takes the form of metrics. All of what poetics, as theory of rhythm, makes a critique of. The resistance of psychoanalysis is that of the sign. The master's voice is deafening. A critical theory would require poetics and psychoanalysis to listen to each other.

The difficulty of the relation to science thus makes it that one can only speak around the subject.

And yet, recognising the *I* seems to be the very question of modernity. The *I* passes only when free of any referent, an empty word, as Benveniste showed, full only each time of the person who utters it, who utters herself or himself. It is the surprising yet certain tie between subjectivity (first in the linguistic, and then in the poetic sense) and modernity. Thereby modernity is no longer the old opposition between the modern and the new.

If poetic writing, more than any other, affords knowledge of the subject, it is by revealing that the subject is its ordinary function, and that it is itself an ordinary function of the subject.

Poetic writing allows us to see, then, that its historicity is a part of the history of individuation, so that we may cease confusing, as sociologists do, the subject and the individual. It allows us to recognise, when it takes place, the Sainte-Beuve operation: which is at once the amalgamation of the-man-and-his-work, and its apparent opposite, the dissociation between the man, the thought. As we have just seen with the spectacle of the recent Heidegger affair.[2] For these two figures know only the individual. Fusion or fission – the two extremes of one and the same polarity. The psychologism remains unchanged. Proust's *Contre Saint-Beuve* has lost none of its relevance.

This lumping together of the two notions of individual and subject is remarkable. For the individual is at once empirical and utopian. Exalted by certain doctrines yet also misunderstood. Precisely because of its opposition to the social. Individualism or careerism is all that one has succeeded in making of it, aside from psychologism and subjectivism. Max Stirner, as a result of powerful strategies, like Marxism, continues, it seems to me, to be misread. Perhaps for the same reason which would associate him with Baudelaire. Art for art's sake, that other sense of the unique, has also been

---

2. [Translator's note: The French publication, in 1987, of Victor Farias's book *Heidegger and Nazism* sparked controversy in France.]

mistaken, through a self-serving and now commonplace misconstrual, for aestheticism.

Drawing on the utopian part of the individual, the subject, that unstable, intermittent function, is superlatively a utopia within a utopia. The generally accepted notions make little room for it. Even if, recently, we have begun to speak of it again, we do so thinking that the individual is coming back after the impersonal era of structure.

This is why, before pretending that we know what we are talking about when we are talking about the subject, giving it a good slap on the back, it is necessary to take a few elementary precautions.

The first is to postulate that a reflection on the subject is an integral part of the theory of language, lacking which such theory inevitably devolves to the sign, either on the side of psychologism, or on that of sociologism. At the same time, this postulation consists in keeping a firm grip on language's irreducible specificity. No longer simply a 'chess game' but also a 'river', to recall Saussure's metaphors. And this implies a critique of the sign through rhythm. A critique of semiotics in its ubiquitousness. It seems as if semioticians had never really heard the critiques made by Benveniste in 'Sémiologie de la langue'. They go on semiotising with a deaf ear. Cinema, painting, literature. They leave their sign everywhere. Pedantry masks imprecision. I am quite sure it will all dissipate along with the present day and age.

Another precaution, which consists in taking specificity and historicity as two aspects of the same contradictory status. A contradiction held and maintained between the result of the forces and sciences which make up a situation, and the unpredictable transformation not only of the present but of the future, since it endures.

The specificity–historicity of a writing immediately situates the specificity–historicity of poetics, in relation to psychoanalysis as much as to philosophy or linguistics, rhetoric, stylistics or literary history. The search for it presupposes the reciprocal implication of language, ethics and history.

This is why any conception of language must be viewed as a strategy. Poetics is a critique of sense. For example, of the notion of sense in hermeneutics. Or of realism, that ghost of the subject.

Hence the revelatory effect of pursuing an enquiry into the situation, status and treatment of language, and of poetry in particular, in the discourses on thought, art, society. Poetics broadened into a historical anthropology of language. The revelatory effect of the treatment reserved for Saussure, Benveniste. Humboldt. The effect on contemporary philosophers of their ignorance of linguists. Or historians' wilful ignorance of questions of discourse.

From beginning to beginning, analysing the perverse effects of the sign, or of the origin, confronting the interiority of art as seen by painters or poets with the poetisations of a few philosophers, poetics may discover, working against the today of philosophers, a new relation between language and time. This is an adventure of the subject.

From indirection to indirection, the subject on the tip of the tongue is not a word or a sentence that one can say. It is the tune of the words which have no sense without this tune, which we are the only ones to hear, and which we try to write.

─── PART 4 ───

TRANSLATING

The following three texts deal with translation and translation theory, a field where Meschonnic, himself a translator of the Bible and author of many texts on translation theory, is of particular influence and importance. Already in *Pour la poétique II* from 1973, he focused on this issue; after many articles and substantial prefaces to his own translations he published a full monograph in 1999, *Poétique du traduire*, followed in 2007 by *Éthique et politique du traduire*. This latter is also his only book available in English so far, and was translated by a member of the translator team of this Reader, Pier-Pascale Boulanger.[1] As early as 1975, George Steiner quoted Meschonnic in one of the three epigraphs to his ground-breaking *After Babel: Aspects of Language and Translation*, and Meschonnic's influence in this field is indirectly present too in the work of Antoine Berman, his student, and, among Berman's followers, Lawrence Venuti.

As befitting someone so insistent on understanding language as *activity*, Meschonnic's own experience of translating the Bible, and a very particular understanding of meaning-making procedures in biblical Hebrew, in fact establishes the basis for his theory. The exposure to the semantic accent system of biblical Hebrew allowed Meschonnic to develop a theory of language which saw meaning as residing not only in linguistic reference but in what he called a 'serial semantics': motivated forms of verbal patterning, chains of signifiers, prosodic contours, distributions of and connections between speech sounds and motifs across a longer text. To translate merely the 'sense' of the words would be to prioritise one element of meaning over the others, and

---

1. Henri Meschonnic, *Ethics and Politics of Translating*, trans. by P.-P. Boulanger (Amsterdam: John Benjamins, 2011).

struck him as insufficient to explain the functioning of this particular textual language or, for that matter, language as such. This way of translating also necessitates a model of language which outstrips the sign, but also underpins his claim that it is most of all the *poem* that shows the limits of the sign.[2]

The following three texts complement Meschonnic's book *Ethics and Politics of Translating*. Translation is one of the main fields of application of his theory of rhythm.

The first text chosen here, *Translating, and the Bible, in the Theory of Language and of Society*, was published in *La Rime et la vie* in 2006 (Lagrasse: Verdier), pp. 420–41, in a revised edition of the original 1989 publication, and was republished in *Nouvelle Revue d'esthétique* 1/3 (2009), pp. 19–25. Meschonnic attacks the hierarchy between so-called original works and translations, and is hence a precursor to later developments in translation studies, such as foreignisation, as promoted by Lawrence Venuti, and Clive Scott's recasting of translation as experimental writing. Meschonnic positions his translation theory within his critique of the serial binary of signs which keeps us from thinking language – translating uncovers these insufficiencies in sign-thinking. He posits that, more than what a text says, it is what a text does that is to be translated: its force. The lever for getting out of the standard practices of translating is the particular accent system of the Hebrew Bible. Meschonnic states that the Hellenisation of Hebrew in our tradition has marked our way of thinking language and thus erased rhythm.

The second text consists of extracts from *Un Coup de Bible dans la philosophie* (Paris: Les Cahiers du Peut-être, Association des Amis de l'Œuvre de Claude Vigée, 2016 [Paris: Bayard, 2004], pp. 19–21; 113; 117–23; 174–92). This book elaborates on the importance of biblical Hebrew and explains how this particular accent system functions and what the consequences are. This book deals principally with Meschonnic's formative experience of translating the Bible and how this informed his theory of language. Thus, in a way, it is Meschonnic's third monograph on translation theory. This experience is at the origin of his theory of rhythm since it made him understand, through the *te'amim* (literally meaning 'taste'), which are the accents in biblical Hebrew, the body-in-language. This organisation of the movement of speech in biblical Hebrew shows how rhythm, in a serial semantics, contributes to meaning – against the logic of the sign.

Meschonnic therefore demands that we re-Hebrewise the Bible, in

---

2. Cf. for his translation theory my articles 'Traduire le poème, avec Henri Meschonnic', in Marcella Leopizzi/Celeste Boccuzzi (eds), *Henri Meschonnic, théoricien de la traduction* (Paris: Hermann, 2014), pp. 191–204; and 'Translation and Poetic Thinking', in *German Life and Letters*, 67/1 (2014), pp. 6–21.

French, and in any language, in order to demonstrate the general rhythmisation of language and as a model that allows for a better understanding of what takes place in language. But in order to achieve this, the traditional translations that do not take this rhythm into account need to be revised; he calls them 'effacers'. Translating can thus overcome an insufficient theory of language.

Meschonnic hence wants to embible translation to make everyone recognise a functioning of language such that the whole of thinking is changed by it. The sign and its notion of sense are overwhelmed by listening to this rhythm.

The third text on translation then offers a demonstration of how Meschonnic applies the continuous of his theory of language to a text: in this case, Shakespeare's *Hamlet*. The chapter Le Nom d'Ophélie [*The Name of Ophelia*] is taken from his book *Poétique du traduire* [*Poetics of Translating*] (Lagrasse: Verdier, 1995), pp. 245–57. Meschonnic shows the effect of using words with the same vowels or consonants in the vicinity of the name of Ophelia. Like communicating vessels, these elements of paronomasia are full of sense: they establish the sense of the name within this play. This is a powerful demonstration of *signifiance*, the way sense is established beyond the meaning of the words, and what that means for translating.

9

Translating and Society
Translating, and the Bible, in the Theory of Language and of Society

(in *La Rime et la vie*, Lagrasse: Verdier, 2006 [1989], pp. 420–41)

Translated by John E. Joseph

> '... I have great news to tell you: I have just published Horace.'
> 'But,' said the geometer, 'Horace has been published for two thousand years.'
> 'You misunderstand me,' replied the other: 'it is a translation of that ancient author that I have just produced: I have spent twenty years doing translations.'
> 'What! Sir,' said the geometer, 'you have gone twenty years without thinking? You speak for others, and they think for you?'
>
> Montesquieu, *Persian Letters*, Letter 129.

I open with this quotation from Montesquieu's *Lettres persanes* because it still speaks for most of our contemporaries today, according to the opposition and hierarchy that everyone seems to accept between what are called original works and translations.

And it's my pleasure, which I shall do my best to share with you, to shatter this cliché in order to think freely. To recognise these mouth toads – you recall the toads that jump from the poor girl's mouth in Perrault's tale *Les Fées* – and the clichés that jump from our mouths when we talk about translation are those toads, the ones which say that translations age and original works do not. Have a look at a *Dictionary of French Literature*, all those supposedly original works that died with their epoch. And the cliché which says that to understand is to translate, and that to translate is to traduce, hence that translating is meaningless, not even realising that the notion of meaning prevents us from understanding language. But luckily these clichés are quickly caught by other clichés which compensate for them, and which say that a work is the sum of its translations, and that to translate is to write. When observation shows that, on the contrary, in the immense majority of cases, to translate is to unwrite.

The problem is that the sign doesn't know what a poem is. And that we imagine we're thinking language, but are thinking sign.

For this traditional opposition between original work and translation is constructed within and according to the sign, which passes for the nature of language, this linguistic model of form and content, of sound and meaning, of signifier and signified, following the accepted terminology, and which is actually made up of a relationship between the two of such a sort that translation alone can reveal it: the signified takes the place of everything, and the signifier remains hidden away and at the same time maintained.

And this schema is reproduced six times: according to the linguistic paradigm; according to the anthropological paradigm of the *viva voce*, the living voice, and of the letter that is dead or that kills; according to the philosophic paradigm of words and things, of conventionalism and originism (the origin of language and languages is sought after because it isn't understood that, as Saussure said, when we seek the origin, we find the functioning); and there's the theological paradigm of the Old Testament and the New, in which the Christian theology of prefiguration marvellously brings about the hiding away of the signifier by offering it as the signified, the *Verus Isräel*; then comes the social paradigm of the individual opposed to society; and finally the political paradigm of the relationship between minority and majority, which constitutes the aporia of democracy.

It is this entire serial binary that constitutes the sign, according to the opposition of body and soul (or mind), and of affect to concept.

And it is this binary that translation reproduces, by opposing the departure language and the arrival language, the source and the target, sourcerers and targetists, a cross-eyed vision with one eye turned toward the departure language placed on the side of form, and the other eye toward the arrival language pointing toward the content, in the opposition between identity and otherness. Literalism, supposedly oriented to otherness, to form; and fluent translation. What the master thinker of the dominant and globalised cliché, Eugene Nida, terms formal equivalence, which he opposes to dynamic equivalence.

Where translating the Bible, a sacralised religious text, plays the precious role of showing how standard translation chases after its clientele: each time, one Christian more.

It is all these dualisms, all these oppositions between heterogeneous pairs, it's the totality of all these couplings that constitutes the sign, and configures it in a totalising and dogmatic conception of language.

All these dualisms come together in the representation of the discontinuous that governs the heterogeneity of the categories of reason. This is no longer anything but a dresser with drawers. That we open and close one after the other.

In language, it's the language system [*langue*] in opposition to discourse. The paradox of the notion of language being that it prevents us from thinking discourse. Hence the notion of *language system* and the notion of *meaning* paradoxically prevent us from thinking language. Which is confirmed by all the structuralism of the twentieth century, adding its scientism to the cultural heritage of the previous 2,000-plus years – since Plato – with the confusion maintained and still taught between Saussure and structuralism, whereas I count nine misinterpretations that radically oppose structuralism to Saussure. And which make up the consensus, the culturally dominant opinion. In order to think language, to think the poem, we have to break this cliché. But the cliché is firmly entrenched. In what is called the general public. As also among the learned.

This is why we must never stop denouncing this misinterpretation, given the maintenance of order that governs knowledge and its teaching. Thus I count:

1. when Saussure says *system*, a dynamic notion, structuralism says *structure*, a formal and ahistorical notion;
2. when Saussure proposes that with language all we have are points of view – a crucial notion: representations – structuralism with the sign presents itself as describing the nature of language;
3. and Saussure constructs the notion of point of view according to an entirely deductive (rational–logical) internal systematicity, whereas structuralism created descriptive (empirical) sciences of language;
4. and Saussure thinks the unity of *langue* and *parole*, language and speech, in discourse, but structuralism disjoined as two heterogeneous entities a linguistics of *langue* and a linguistics of *parole*;
5. also, in Saussure, the theory of language postulates and presupposes a poetics, whereas structuralism only managed to oppose the rationalism of the *Cours* to the madness of his notebooks on anagrams[1];

1. [Translator's note: The *Cours de linguistique générale* was put together after Saussure's death by his colleagues Charles Bally and Albert Sechehaye from his manuscript notes and the notebooks of students who attended his lectures at the University of Geneva, and was published in 1916 (Paris and Lausanne: Payot). The *Cours* contains the essence, though not the whole, of Saussure's teaching; hence Meschonnic's remark in point 6. The ninety-nine notebooks that record his search for hidden anagrams in poems, mainly in Latin but also in Homer, became known through articles by Jean Starobinski, starting in 1964 and culminating in his book *Les Mots sous les mots: les anagrammes de Ferdinand de Saussure*

6. and Saussure, as even the text of 1916 shows, opposes the associative, which is multiple, to the syntagm, when structuralism managed only to practise the binary opposition of the paradigmatic to the syntagmatic[2];
7. and for Saussure the radical arbitrariness of the sign implies a radical historicity of language, of languages, of discourses (when we seek the origin we find the functioning), but in structuralism arbitrariness was understood as a conventionalism;
8. also, for Saussure, diachrony and synchrony together are history, and structuralism taught that diachrony was history, in opposition to synchrony, the state of language;
9. with the result that Saussure thinks the continuity of language and criticises the traditional divisions (lexicon, morphology, syntax), whereas structuralism was the triumphalism of a scientism of the discontinuous, following the dichotomies of the sign.

Whence – I was mistaken to stop at nine, it's the illusion of counting – arises a tenth opposition: now we can recognise the continuity between Humboldt and Saussure, against the received idea that opposes the one to the other.

This effect of theory emerges powerfully from the recently published manuscripts of Saussure.[3]

But the very heterogeneity of the categories of reason according to the sign is what dominates in received cultural opinion, and in what are called the scholarly disciplines, in line with regionalisms and compartmentalisations that are so many obstacles to thinking about the relationship between language and society, between language and the language arts, between language and life. This heterogeneity of the categories of the dominant reason ironically situates what is to be thought as a utopia, or a prophecy, against the maintenance of order.

(Paris: Gallimard, 1971); English version, *Words upon Words: The Anagrams of Ferdinand de Saussure*, trans. by Olivia Emmet (New Haven, CT: Yale University Press, 1979). Saussure never published this research, but abandoned it after failing to convince himself that the anagrams he was finding were deliberately constructed by the poets and not the result of chance.]

2. [Translator's note: in the 1930s the Danish structural linguist Louis Hjelmslev (1899–1965) rechristened Saussure's 'associative' axis as the 'paradigmatic' axis, implying, for Meschonnic, a closed paradigm, as opposed to an indefinite web of associations.]

3. Ferdinand de Saussure, *Écrits de linguistique générale*, ed. by Simon Bouquet and Rudolf Engler (Paris: Gallimard, 2002). [English version, *Writings in General Linguistics*, trans. by Carol Sanders and Matthew Pires, with the assistance of Peter Figueroa, Oxford: Oxford University Press, 2006.]

Now this effect of theory strongly affects the relationships between rhyme and life.

For the discontinuity of the sign, this thinking of the totality that prevents us from thinking the relationship between the infinity of history and the infinity of meaning, produces collateral damage.

In the permanent conflict between the sign and the poem, we can start with the fallacious opposition between verse and prose. For there are metrics of prose: they have been known since Antiquity. The Latin *cursus*, for example. Not to mention that prose works like those of Saint-John Perse don't cease to metrify. But above all, this apparently clear and undiscussed opposition triggers another, even more fallacious opposition, between poetry and prose. A problem that exposes the crumbling of any formal definition of poetry starting with the prose poem and poetic modernity.

And here we reach the poetic universal enunciated by Mallarmé, who displaces the poetic problem toward the opposition between *naming* and *suggesting*. Which is not an outdated symbolist relic.

If we start again from Saussure, and particularly from what is shown by his manuscripts published in 2002, with his two major concepts of point of view and internal systematicity, we reveal the sign and all its effects as being, not the nature of language, but a representation of it; and, what is more, we can displace the representation of language toward the continuous, understood as a body-in-language continuum.

And this continuum obliges us to think the poem, in order to think the multiplicity of the acts of language. The poem is no longer the sign's weak link, but the starting point for the entire theory of language.

A paradox: no longer to oppose *poetic language* to *ordinary language* (two real essences, which, funnily enough, signifies that they don't exist and that we don't know what we're talking about), but to start from the poem to think the entire theory of language as a relation of interaction amongst language, poem, ethics and politics.

By poem I mean the transformation of a form of language by a form of life and the transformation of a form of life by a form of language. Four times the word 'form', but not at all according to the sign, as opposed to meaning. No, form in the sense of organisation and invention of a historicity, configuration of a system of discourse. Its force. The force is not opposed to meaning in the way form is opposed to content: the force carries the meaning and dominates it.

Which is immediately tied to a new conception of rhythm, no longer as alternation of a same and a different (that is rhythm according to the sign – an aspect of the formal and that's what all the dictionaries say), but as the organisation of the movement of speech within language, and specifically within the writing of the poem.

Which in turn immediately has a double effect. One is to transform the notion of orality: in the sign, the oral is opposed to the written; in the continuous, orality is subject which is heard. The subject of the poem.

At once, the other effect is to transform the notion of the subject, no longer the dozen subjects that diversely constitute the culturally dominant conception of *the-question-of-the-subject*. And I count, again: philosophical subject, psychological subject, subject of the knowledge of others and subject of the domination of others, subject of the knowledge of things and subject of the domination of things, subject of happiness, subject of law, subject of history, subject of language, subject of discourse, Freudian subject.

None of these has written a poem. And if it reads a poem, it isn't the poem that it reads but itself projected into the poem. Where the concepts borrowed from psychoanalysis say nothing more than what a grammarian can say, who can see only verbs, subjects, objects. Not the poem.

That's why rhythm as the organisation of the movement of speech in discourse leads us to postulate a subject of the poem. And I call *subject of the poem* the maximal subjectivation, integral to discourse. Which becomes a system of discourse.

As Péguy said: 'It's signed in the very fabric. There isn't a thread of the text that isn't signed.'[4]

The body-in-language continuity is then the sequencing of the rhythms of position, initial and final, of inclusion, conjunction, rupture, lexical repetition, syntactic repetition, prosodic series. It is a serial semantics.

So, and before even envisaging the other effects of sequencing and interaction with the ethical and political representations of society in its acts of language, it appears inevitably, from the poem's point of view, that to translate can no longer be the activity conceived within the sign as it's usually practised.

And all that precedes was the prerequisite needed to situate and transform translating, transform the thinking of translating, transform the practices of translating, transform the social and poetic evaluation of translating.

In other words, more than what a text says, it's what it does that is to be translated. More than the meaning, it's the force, the affect.

So it's no longer a language that is to be translated but a system of discourse, not the discontinuous but the continuous. Elementary, Dr Sensible, Dr Formalin.

---

4. Charles Péguy, 'Un Nouveau Théologien, M. Fernand Laudet', §280, *Œuvres en prose 1909–1914* (Paris: Gallimard-Pléiade, 1968), p. 1034.

This unquestionably transforms the entire theory of language.

But the link between language and literature? In what way does the continuous transform the theory of literature?

First, the continuous works outside of or against the notions of literary genre: poetry, novel, theatre, essay, philosophical text.

If the continuous is the subjectivation of a system of discourse by a subject that invents itself through and in its discourse, that invents a new historicity, the continuous of the poem ignores the differences among genres. From this point of view there is a portion of poem in a novel, a play or even a so-called philosophical text if there is this invention of the subject, this invention of a historicity.

It is the non-separating of affect and concept that makes the force and the invention of meaning.

It's even in so far as there is poem in it, in the sense I define it, that a novel is a novel and not airport fiction, and that a philosophical text is an invention of thinking and not a discourse about philosophy.

This point of view immediately works against the heterogeneity of the categories of reason that makes our scholarly disciplines (with country-specific cultural variables): language for linguists and the autonomy of translation theory, consigned in fact to hermeneutics, hence to the sign; literature for literature specialists; philosophy for, I won't say philosophers, reserving this term for the inventors of thinking, but philosophy specialists, themselves separated into ethics specialists, aesthetics specialists, philosophy of science specialists, political philosophy specialists. Even if some of them build bridges. And we need to see how.

But the point of view of the continuous also works, inside what is called poetry, against the traditional division between lyric and epic. An essentially semiotic and thematic division.

Because if the continuous first lets us hear in orality no longer sound but subject, poetry is a history that attains a voice, that is heard in a voice.

Which immediately leads us to recognise that poetry, all poetry, whether self-centred or narrative, is epic, or isn't poetry at all.

It's also the point of view of the continuous that leads to the critique of the multiple confusions that make the word poetry into a cacophony that culturally we aren't even aware of.

Thus there are grounds for ceasing to confuse poetry with verse, and secondarily for ceasing to oppose poetry with prose; for ceasing to confuse poetry with emotion, whether aesthetic or sentimental, the emotionalist confusion that describes feelings; for ceasing to confuse poetry with the etymology of the word poetry, an etymologism oriented either to a mystery of creation, hence an indefinable essence, or to fabrication and formalism, whereby the ludic and experimentalism are taken for poetry. But then it isn't the subject of the poem that makes the poem, it's the philosophical or psychological subject, which knows what it's doing and so does what it knows. This is no longer a poem, but poetisation, the love of poetry taken for poetry.

There are grounds for recognising – disentangling from the received ideas of the culturally dominant opinion – two distinct senses of the word poetry: a descriptive sense which is that of the corpus of written poems, I call it the *stock*, in other words Italian poetry, French poetry, Russian poetry, etc.; sixteenth-century poetry, twentieth-century poetry, etc.; the poetry of Ronsard, Hugo, Leopardi, Ungaretti, Mayakovsky, each poet separately, and poetry in this sense is at the same time totality and infinity, knowable and unknowable; and the other sense of the word poetry, its functional sense – which purposely appears here last, after the received ideas have been cleared away, and it is the condition, the foundation of all the others, and in particular of the stock – is that poetry is the activity of a poem, a poem being what invents and reinvents poetry, when it is the transformation of a form of language by a form of life and of a form of life by a form of language.

Which allows us no longer to confuse poetry and the love of poetry, the celebration of poetry.

For if the poem to be made, and the poem to be read and translated – that is, to be recognised as a poem – is oriented toward poetry, in the sense of the stock, it necessarily reproduces its successes and its criteria, and thereby, at the same time, it is not a poem but poetisation.

So it is necessarily the case that the poem to be made and the poem to be read, to be translated, constitute themselves in the paradoxical situation of a disappearance, of a loss of criteria. Criteria that can only be those of known poetry, the mass of poems that already exist.

Which literary history itself shows abundantly, through the difficulties of contemporary reception, since necessarily, always and everywhere, the contemporary is made of three presents, which have an extremely unequal social force.

For I propose to recognise that there are, at one and the same time, a past of the present, a present of the present and a future of the present. To extend the intuition of Saint Augustine who posits, in his *Confessions*, that there aren't simply past, present, future, but three presents: a present of the past, when I think of it, a present of the present, and also a present of the future, when I think of it, in my now. I propose that there are not only these three presents, but also three pasts and three futures. Future of the past, think simply of Maurice Scève and Jean de Sponde, for instance; past of the past, Raymond Poisson, ultra-famous in the seventeenth century; past of the present – all that is outmoded, even from shortly ago, and that continues:

the sign is in the past of the present; future of the present, which is not yet received in thinking and in culturally dominant opinion. Humboldt, for example, has more future than past.

One understands why certain contemporaries will never meet: those who are in the past of the present, and those who are in the future of the present.

And this transformation of point of view on language and literature, on the relations between identity and otherness, on the relations between the continuous of rhythm and the discontinuous of meaning-according-to-the-sign is the effect of the empirical and theoretical lever that is the activity of translating.

Yet anyone can see that the standard practices of translating are inscribed in the sign, and perfectly accommodated to the cultural representation of language. This is why I propose calling them *des effaçantes*, effacers, erasers.

To get out of them, to get out of the bowl where we little fish are trapped, mistaking our bowl for the vast sea, it will take outside support, otherwise we can have neither the thinking nor the means of getting out of the sign.

As it happens, in a completely empirical way, my experience as a translator, tied to my work of writing poems, leads me to propose such a lever.

This theoretical lever is the functioning of rhythm in the Hebrew Bible.

This functioning is such that it is of the order of the continuous. It is radically outside and irreducible to the Greco-Christian model of thinking and of the practice of language in which we have been immersed for around 2,500 years. Since Plato. Which is why there is a need to de-Platonise thinking about rhythm.

The all-rhythm of the Bible, in Hebrew, does not include the difference that is familiar to us between verse and prose. It is neither verse nor prose. Which is hard for us to think, so much have we been modelled by this opposition.

From this a triple effect is triggered.

One is that paradoxically this situation matches the very situation of modern poetry, ever since the mid-nineteenth century prose poem. Poetic effect, which is why I place it first, because it is generally invisible.

Historically, chronologically and conceptually, the first situation is theological–political, theological–philological, theological–poetic: it is the Christian refusal of the rhythmics of the Bible passage, from the fact that the written notation of this rhythmics came late. In fact, it was constituted between the sixth and ninth centuries of our era, and the first entirely vowelised and rhythmised manuscript dates from the tenth century. A notation reputed to be inauthentic and unauthoritative by Christian science. A refusal fundamentally caused by Christianity having been founded on the Greek translation of the Septuagint, in the third century before our era, and not on the Hebrew text. Translation of a lost original.

Where it appears that the second effect is Christianisation–Hellenisation. And that the work to be done to recuperate the rhythm is a de-Christianisation and a de-Hellenisation, and at the same time a desemiotisation.

For, starting with Flavius Josephus, in the second century, on the model of the poetry in Homer, poetic beauty being necessarily metrical, the idea prevailed that there are hexameters in the Bible. Hence for centuries the search for a Greek metrics, and starting from the Middle Ages the search for an Arabic metrics. Without success. Then, in 1753, Robert Lowth's postulation of substituting a rhetoric for an unfindable metrics, the theory of biblical parallelism, which is still the received idea.

And the Hellenisation of thinking language is the erasure of rhythm, not only in the Bible but for all thinking language. For it is a metrification of rhythm that reigns.

Now, without entering into details, but recalling that biblical anthropology has also shown that the Hebrews were ignorant of the very notion of poetry, and knew only the opposition of the sung and the spoken, it is imperative, from my point of view, to recognise, for general thinking about translating, language and literature, and after answering the theological–philological objection, that the pan-rhythmic of the text, in the Bible, which installs a poetics of the continuous, is a parable and a prophecy of language, going well beyond its particular case, with relation to the globalised reign of the sign.

Parable, because it is a particular with the value of a universal; prophecy, because it is a refusal of received ideas that are in power.

The answer to the objection of the lateness of the notation has to do with constituting a will to transmit what previously had only an oral nature: the vowels were unwritten, the alphabet having only twenty-two consonants; the rhythms of reading were unwritten, being made up of melodic lines and gestural indications by the hands. The names of these accents testify to this, which necessarily presupposes their anteriority relative to their written notation.

Moreover, the term that designates the rhythmic accent, constitutive of the Bible passage (the notion of passage being attested from the second century) is by itself a parable of the body-in-language: it is the word *ta'am*, plural *ta'amim*, which signifies the taste of what one has in the mouth, the flavour, this flavour being the reason for saying, and this is the very meaning, and the first meaning, of orality. What comes from the mouth. Orality is a buccality, in all the physicality of language.

Whereby the taking sides that translates certain passages in the Bible as verse and others as prose is immediately put in its place, as ideologism, Christianism in the way one says solecism.

But above all, and this is what overflows the case of the Bible as a particular example, the lesson of rhythm that emerges from it, and it is the strongest lesson, the *lectio difficilior* as philologists say (relative to the *lectio facilior* that is Hellenisation), is that to translate the poem, in the specific sense in which I propose to take it, is to translate the continuous and the force of discourse, and no longer just what an utterance says. What the words say.

Thus the third theoretical effect is what I call a generalised *ta'amisation*, from the term *ta'am*: rhythmising all translating, and not only Bible translation, rhythmising all thinking about language. For then there is cause to translate the enunciation as inseparable from the utterance,[5] to take note that the notion of meaning (in which hermeneutics is confined) is an epistemological obstacle to thinking about language. So to translate a serial semantics that overflows the traditional objection according to which what is done in the phonology of a language obviously cannot be redone with the phonology of another language.[6] What Ezra Pound, in his *ABC of Reading*, called melopoeia. Because it is not language that is to be translated, but what a poem has done to its language. So there is a need to invent discourse equivalents in the arrival language: prosody for prosody, the same as metaphor for metaphor, pun for pun, rhythm for rhythm. Poem for poem.

Thus, what translating the continuous puts to the test is no longer an opposition between an identity and an otherness, but work by which an identity comes about only through an otherness.

This is the lesson of general poetics to be drawn from rhythm in the Bible.

But there are two more. One is the triggering of a sequence, of a chain reaction that reveals the simultaneous thinking and active interaction of language with the poem, with the ethical and with the political. For if the poem is the activity of a subject of the poem, it's first of all an ethical act, and if it's an ethical act, because it concerns all subjects, an ethical act is a political act. So a poem is an ethical and political act. Which makes poetics a poetics of society, in so far as every society and all thinking about society are judged by their theory of language, and by what they do with language.

5. [Translator's note: 'enunciation' and 'utterance' translate *énonciation* and *énoncé*, key terms of the linguistic theory of Émile Benveniste (1902–76). Both indicate a perspective on language that starts from the speaker or writer rather than from the linguistic system, with *énonciation* being the general activity and an *énoncé* a particular product of the activity.]
6. [Translator's note: Pound divided poetry into three types, *melopoeia* (poem as music), *phanopoeia* (poem as image or picture) and *logopoeia* (poem as idea or argument). It is unclear how phanopoeia applies in this context; possibly it is a slip, and *melopoeia* is what Meschonnic intended.]

The other lesson, for a poetics of society and for a poetics of life, and this is perhaps the major paradox, starting from the religious text that is the Bible, is a distinction to be made, and that I'm making, between the sacred, the divine and the religious. And this is an observation that I draw from my Bible translation work, work in progress. It is what I observe in *Genesis* and what I haven't found said in any religious commentaries, of whatever religion. I observe that the religious confounds without distinction the sacred, the divine and the religious. And to work to deconfound them is what I call a detheologisation. No offence to the religious.

For the text itself shows clearly that there is first the *sacred*, I mean by that the fusional bond of the human to the cosmic and to the animal: the serpent speaks to Eve, and Saint Augustine asked concerning *Genesis* 1: 3 (And God said, Let there be light), 'what language did God speak?', then he answered that this wasn't a human language, but a figure of His will. Where we also have to distinguish the sacred, and nostalgia for the sacred.[7]

Then there is the *divine*: it's the principle of life and its realisation in all living creatures. And in *In the Beginning*[8] there isn't yet the religious.

And even the stone tablets that Moses holds, when he comes down from the mountain top, and that he breaks upon seeing the golden calf, bear the ten words of an ethics that is the ethics of the divine. Not yet the ethics of the religious, because there isn't yet a religious. An ethics of life.

The religious comes later, in *Exodus* and especially in *Leviticus*, with its prohibitions, prescriptions and religious calendar. In other words, the religious is the socialisation and the ritualisation of life that appropriates to itself the control and the very emission of the sacred and the divine. It becomes the emitter of ethics. To separate the divine from the religious is intolerable to the religious. This is what Spinoza did. And he remains excommunicated.

This amounts to saying that the religious is almost at once the theological–political. History shows that this is a catastrophe that happened to the divine. Against the pseudo-etymological definition of Lactantius, who ties *religio* with *religare*, ties men to God, and Durkheim continues it by positing that religion binds men to one another. But against this idea of the religious, the history of religions itself, and history generally, show that religions are murderous, and that they kill in God's name. Check your daily newspaper.

---

7. The confusion between the two is exactly what is shown by 'Heidegger language' – as I have shown in *Le Langage Heidegger* (Paris: Presses Universitaires de France, 1990), which displeased the Heideggerians.
8. Henri Meschonnic, *Au commencement*, translation of Genesis (Paris: Desclées de Brouwer, 2002).

In so far as I translate the significance of the continuous in the Bible, I translate atheologically. And it is according to this internal systematicity of the poem that I de-Christianise the Bible in order to make hearable in it again the Hebrew of the poem and the poem of the Hebrew.

This is the very coherence of poetics as recognition of functionings and historicities, in order to get out of the sign, its received ideas and its power effects, which necessarily create the current condition of the inferiority of translating and translations in relation to the writing and the reading of the poem.

Poetics is an atheology because theologisation is a semiotisation. I detheologise because I desemiotise. At the same time as I deacademise. For the truth of the religious acts like the sign, like meaning: it produces a residue, form. That is, an inclusion in the sign, which is not even seen as a representation, historical, cultural, situated and limited.

This is what the knowledge of the exegetes doesn't know. And what has taught me that each knowledge produces its ignorance, a specific ignorance, and doesn't know that it doesn't know what it doesn't know. By which it prevents it being known. And becomes the maintenance of order.

Whence this continually surprising and continually verified challenge, of the casualness, or the deafness of sectarian Bible translations to the signifier, precisely because they are sacralising. Wherein they don't know that they're idolatrous, too, in Maimonides's sense: they worship a human creation. This – whatever the sect, and this is what makes them weak compared to the force of the poem.

I offer here just one example, choosing the simplest there is, unrivalled by other passages, which are difficult. It is in what are called the Psalms, which I call *Glories*.[9] Two words, in poem 120, verse 7: *ani shalom*, where *ani* = 'I', *shalom* = 'peace'. The verb *to be* in the present tense being implicit: thus, 'I am peace', and these two words joined by a hyphen, a conjunctive accent that welds them together in a single affect group. I have translated, to render this strengthening: *moi je suis la paix* (literally, 'me, I am the peace').

This strong formula is what the erasing-translations have applied all their cleverness to watering down, have competed with one another to trivialise. Here are the French translations, in chronological order: Le Maistre de Sacy: *j'étais pacifique* 'I was pacific' (the past tense is uncalled for, the formula of the text is necessarily in the present – but what one wanted to make pass as a beautiful translation only translated the Vulgate: *eram pacificus*, which reproduced the Greek of the Septuagint: *êmên eirênikos*); Ostervald in 1722

---

9. Henri Meschonnic, *Gloires*, translation of the Psalms (Paris: Desclée de Brouwer, 2001).

said: *je veux la paix* 'I want peace', repeated in the Synodal version of the French Biblical Alliance in 1965; Samuel Cahen, in 1830: *je suis pacifique* 'I am pacific' and Segond in 1877: *je suis pour la paix* 'I am for peace', the discourse of a political tract, reproduced by the version of the *Saintes Écritures, Traduction du monde nouveau* [Holy Scriptures, New World Translation]; the Rabbinate of 1899: *je suis, moi tout à la paix* 'I give myself all to peace'; Crampon: *quand je parle de paix* 'when I speak of peace'; Dhorme: *moi, j'incarne la paix* 'I embody peace'; the Jerusalem Bible: *moi si je parle de paix* 'if I speak of peace'; Osty: *je suis tout à la paix* 'I give myself all to peace'. Only Chouraqui, with *moi, je suis paix* and the TOB [Traduction œcuménique de la Bible, Ecumenical Translation of the Bible] with *je suis la paix*, are here, with slight variants, and unequal success (the absence of the definite article in Chouraqui's version is unfortunate and cacophonic), close to the text.

In other European languages, to give some examples, the situation is identical, the problem general. In English, the King James Version has 'I am for peace', like Segond in French; the American version of 1939 (*The Complete Bible, an American Translation*, Chicago) repeats 'I am for peace', the *New English Bible* of 1970 says 'I sought peace', the translation of the American *New JPS* (Jewish Publication Society), from 1985, says 'I am all peace'. In Spanish, the *Santa Biblia* (antigua versión de Casiodoro de Reina, of 1569, revised in 1960 by the Sociedades Bíblicas en América Latina) says *yo soy pacífico* 'I am pacific' and the *Biblia del Peregrino* of Luis Alonso Schökel (Bilbao, 1995): *Yo estoy por la paz* 'I am for peace'. The Italian version directed by Dario Disengi says, in 1967: *Io ho intenzioni pacifiche* 'I have pacific intentions'. The German of Luther in 1545 says: *Ich halte Friede* 'I keep peace'. Only Buber says the text: *ich bin Friede*.

I have tried to be, in very relative terms, exhaustive in order to showcase the obscene and denounce it: the religious is what profanes the text that it calls sacred. And of course it doesn't know it. This is the theological–poetical aspect of the theological–political. And this is what the translation of a religious text teaches us. It is another aspect of the war between the sign and the poem. It is why it partakes simultaneously of the obscene and the taboo, an aspect of the war of the religious against life, with the large-scale participation of a whole philosophy devoid of any theory of language, opposing language to life as affect to concept. Accomplice and beneficiary of the sign.

Experience helps in recognising – the poem being a form of life, and even the maximum of the relation between language and life – that theologisation is at the same time the major enemy of the poem and the major enemy of life. It is for poetics to reveal the scandal. As for the culturally dominant opinion, its role is to suppress it.

And when I say 'life', for the relation of the poem between language and life, I say it in the sense of a maximal, radical historicisation of life. The sense in which Spinoza, in the *Political Treatise*, speaks of a 'human life', two words about which it isn't anodyne to recall that they form the title of the posthumous piece by Uriel da Costa, *Exemplar humanæ vitae*, which implies and presupposes a battle against theology bringer of death. This is the allusive value of these two words in Spinoza. And Spinoza defines it, this human life, not by biology, but by 'the true virtue and life of the Mind'.[10]

All the internal systematicity that makes the poem rhyme with life.

---

10. *vitam humanam intelligo, quæ non solâ sanguinis circulatione, & aliis, quae omnibus animalibus sunt communia, sed quæ maximé ratione, verâ Mentis virtute, & vitâ definitur*, *Theological–Political Treatise* (V, 5) – 'I am speaking of human life, which is defined not only by the circulation of blood and other things which are common to all animals, but above all by reason, the true virtue and life of the Mind.' Where *virtue* has the sense of 'force'.

10

Translating and the Biblical
A Bible Blow to Philosophy

(extracts from *Un Coup de Bible dans la philosophie*, Paris: Les Cahiers du Peut-être, Association des Amis de l'Œuvre de Claude Vigée, 2016 [Paris: Bayard, 2004], pp. 19–21; 113; 117–23; 174–92)

Translated by Pier-Pascale Boulanger

Language

Language being that in which, through which, we think and we live a *human life*,[1] and in the sense that, as Benveniste says, 'language serves for *living*',[2] I posit as a principle that if we do not think language, we do not think, and we do not know that we do not think. We go about our business.

And that if in language we think and know only the sign, this representation both familiar and academic, which an entire tradition portrays as the whole of language, we do not think language, we think sign, believing that we are thinking language. Its totalisation, rather than its infinite. An essentialisation, rather than its historicities. The evil genius of languages sees to it.

Many things depend on this situation, so banal that it seems normal, including the notion of sense, interpreting and translating. The effects of this can be felt. But this very tradition that shapes us culturally does not let them

---

1. In the sense that Spinoza speaks of (in *Tractatus Politicus*, V, V): '*Cum ergo dicimus, illud imperium optimum esse, ubi homines concorditer vitam transigunt, vitam humanam intelligo, quae non solâ sanguinis circulatione, & aliis, quae omnibus animalibus sunt communia, sed quae maxime ratione, verâ Mentis virtute, & vitâ definitur.*' I translate: 'as we have said, that the best State is the one where men spend their life in harmony, I mean a human life, which is not defined by the sole circulation of blood, and other things, that are common to all animals, but especially by reason, true virtue and the life of the Spirit.' I refer to my book *Spinoza: poème de la pensée* (Paris: Maisonneuve et Larose, 2002), p. 173. Virtue meaning force, of course.
2. Émile Benveniste, 'La Forme dans le langage' (1966), *Problèmes de linguistique générale 2* (Paris: Gallimard, 1974), p. 217.

show. Thus the thought of language depends more on its unthought than on that which it knows how to think.

Inasmuch as thinking language aims to recognise this unthought, it is in relation to the chain reaction of the reasons of the sign and its entire paradigmatic, a counter-coherence that has to be recognised, revealed under the generalised semiotisation of thought and society.

This unthought is the entire chain of the continuous in language, the body-in-language continuous which is necessarily the rhythm–syntax–prosody continuous, the chain of signifiances covered with the dualism of the signified and the signifier and their radical heterogeneity, and thereby the continuous of language transformed by the poem, as the invention of a new historicity, the poem transformed by ethics and radically historicising ethics, ethics in turn historicising the political. Rather than the heterogeneity of the categories of reason.

This chain reaction necessarily transforms the entire thought of language, interpreting, and translating. We do not think language if we do not think the continuum in language, the rhythm-continuous, the subject-continuous, with the discontinuous of the sign, and against it.

It is to this extent, and to this excess, that the things of language tackle philosophy. This false singular and false plural. At least under a certain aspect. Of complacency and convenience. To be evasive.

And it is through this movement of the continuum in language that what takes place in the language of the Bible tackles philosophy.

I posit that the major cultural paradox here, precisely for the reasons that prevent us from thinking it, is that what we call the Bible must act as a theoretical lever to transform the entire thought of language, of rhythm and of translating. Hence a critique of hermeneutics, a critique of translations. First of biblical hermeneutics, and of the translations of the Bible. But more generally of all of translating. And of all of hermeneutics. Which is where we tackle philosophy.

And we do not think the Bible if we do not think its language. I am only stating a truism. Or what should be one. Let's say, a commonplace in the future.

Because the Bible is more than a specific case, even with its importance culturally, and rightly so, as a religious text. Where the religious has this strange effect of concealing language. The Bible, through the movement of speech in its writing, and because it is a pan-rhythmics which does not know and dismisses the relevance of the opposition between verse and prose, constitutes a problem such that, still exacerbated by its concealment, it makes a parable of the role of rhythm in language. Of its theoretical effect. Utopia and prophecy of language all in one.

There is a Bible blow inasmuch as these things of language in the Bible are concealed by the very history of reading, by the very history of the thought of language, by the very history of translating.

A blow. And a toll. *To*: in this biblical case, a preposition also meaning *against*.

This matter cannot not be a battle. The *for* of rhythm and of the poem against the reign of the sign. The historicity of the poem against the theologico-political of the sign, theologically programmed philology. And everything in what we call philosophy stands with and benefits from the sign. The sign is a liar and a thief.

This paradox, standing high up on this sacred mountain of paradoxes, is that language and rhythm in the Bible battle the theologisation of thought.

Thank goodness there is a comical of thought. The state of things cannot be separated from the work needed to change things. Rhythm as the organisation of the movement of speech 'must confront *doxa* and idolatry'.[3]

To embible translating, means, through listening to the rhythm in the Bible – recognised above all for transforming the translation of the Bible –, recognising in it a functioning of language such that step by step the whole of thinking is changed by it.

To embible translating, means giving back to thinking language, to the thinking and practice of translating the subject-continuous that it is missing. To work at this precisely through its maximum effacement, the Bible.

Where what is at stake in translating is the need to transform the entire theory of language. To historicise it radically.

It is a question of showing that the main and even the sole problem of translation is its theory of language. Unknowingly, when we believe that we are translating a text, it is its own representation of language that we are showing, and which gets between the text to be translated and the translator's intention. If we place ourselves in the discontinuous of the linguistic sign to translate a poem, we do not translate the poem, we only translate from one language into another language. In other words, we do not know what we are doing. It follows that the entire theory of language depends on its theory of literature, that any translation depends on its theory of language, that any theory of language depends on its theory of rhythm, that the discontinuous depends on the continuous, thus that the entire theory of language depends on its theory and practice of translation, just like translation depends on its theory of language. Which, immediately, shows the major role of transla-

---

3. Marc de Launay, 'Nous creusons la fosse de Babel', in Pierre Bouretz, Marc de Launay and Jean-Louis Schefer (eds), *La Tour de Babel* (Paris: Desclée de Brouwer, 2003), p. 129.

tion for the entire representation of language, and society, as any society depends on its representation of language and is revealed through it. And this role far exceeds that of relayer of messages assigned to translation by the representation of the sign, which is the common representation of language. Translation is thus what is at stake in a true cultural revolution.

Rhythm is the Prophecy and the Utopia of Language[4]

1. Ta'amising French, Ta'amising Translating, Ta'amising All Languages, Ta'amising Thought

Because *ta'am*, plural form *te'amim*, which is usually translated by 'rhythmic accent', is rhythm, in the Bible, but such that there is no verse nor prose, nothing else but rhythm, a generalised rhythmisation of language.

Rhythm, then, but in the Bible. The rhythm of the Bible. Which is to say in a radical irreducibility to the Greek categories of the thought of language that we live by. Those of dualism – the sign. Those of Monsieur Jourdain's master of philosophy. Those of the deafness of exegetes, all ecumenically united in a same and another non-listening to rhythm. In the ignorance produced by their very science as exegetes, as erudite exegetes. And the more eruditissimus they are, the more deafissimus to rhythm they are.

Even though Someone said 'Listen . . .'

A never-ending battle between the sign and the poem.

The Bible as parable and prophecy of the rhythm in language. Parable because, while being a particular example, it pertains to all languages, all texts and all times. Prophecy, because it is, on the rejection of the common representations of language, the postulation of an unthought which has yet to be thought, against all traditions, against the entire theologico-political: yes, a cultural revolution. A silent one, since no one, or almost no one, can hear it. Which intensifies its urgency. And the comical of thought.

Where there is a specificity, a unicity, a historicity of the functioning of language in the biblical text. In Hebrew. And such that for a good seventeen centuries it has been denied by hermeneutics, which dominates the studies of the religious text. Bunched together with the notion of the religious.

Yet the Hebrew biblical text works within the rhythm–syntax–prosody continuous, following a serial semantics. And such that it does not know the opposition which is familiar to us between verse and prose. Nor does it have the notion of what we call 'poetry'. Not knowing that we do not know, most of the time, what we mean by this word.

---

4. This is a reworked version of a text published in *Palimpsestes*, 15 (2004).

The Hebrew biblical text is thus a semantic rhythmics of the continuous. Yet we think language according to the terms of Greek dualism, of the semiotic. According to the terms of a radical heterogeneity and a binary, and confused, opposition between verses and prose, between poetry and prose.

And for seventeen centuries Christian hermeneutics has denied this organisation, and Jewish hermeneutics, which does know it, only sees in it, aside from the liturgical music of cantillation, punctuation with phonetic and logico-grammatical effects.

This goes to show that no one can see that this organisation of the movement of speech in writing, in the sense of the written language, but also in the sense of the poem, is the prophecy and the utopia of the thought of the body-in-language in language, and of the continuous between language, poem, ethics and politics.

Prophecy converging practically with the notion of utopia, in the sense of a lacuna in received ideas, a rejection of received ideas, as well as an imperious intimation to think what is not thought.

For the Bible above all, in the way it is understood and translated. But also for the entire conceptuality of language, in general, no matter the languages and their cultural relations, once it is no longer only a question of the meaning of words, but also of the power and the continued activity of a text. And thinking power is different from thinking meaning.

This is the complete opposite of reducing language to meaning. Where, as useful and indispensable as it may be, hermeneutics has always been blocked, and continues to block the thought of language.

From this, urgency and power arise as a twofold effect: the necessity to think the poem in order to think all of language, all the activities of language, including of course all that are not those of the poem. Because what is thought depends on what is unthought, because sense depends on the movement of sense.

The urgency and power also consist in giving, or giving back, to translating, its role as a tester of theories and practices of language. To bring to light that the first and sometimes the only thing that is translated is not the text but the representation of language at work in the act of translating. All the more unknown that the reduction of language to *langue*, to the sign, is sure of itself. Wherein lies precisely the arrogance of philology, and hermeneutics. Both overconfident underachievers.

Once we understand that what should be translated is what a text does to its *langue*.

And it is the functioning of rhythm in the biblical text that leads to changing the canonical and universal notion of rhythm as the alternation between a same and a different, this duality allied to the internal duality of the sign, both reinforcing one another to fuse together the seeming common sense in the notion that sense is opposed to form with all the endorsements of linguistics and philology.

Where considering the text as religious confirms and aggravates the duality of the sign through that of the truth producing the same residue as the notion of sense, and thoughtlessly partaking of the sole notion of *langue*.

But the rhythm in the Bible forces us to change this representation of the discontinuous in recognition of the continuous – of the organisation of the movement of speech.

This is where a chain reaction starts that nothing can stop.

If the theory – which is a reflection on the unknown – of rhythm changes, the entire theory of language changes. If the theory of language changes, the entire perception of the power in language shifts from seeing to listening. If listening becomes the sense of language and power, then the way we translate changes as well, or will change, along with the way we read. And write.

Thus the critique of the sign that those who are deaf see as a destructive attitude appears as the very act by which to construct a thought of the multiple and infiniteness of sense, and its power, in language.

It is true by the way that thought is eager to shatter the patter of translation, and of the common representation of language.

Nothing new here. This is always how ideas have changed. The additional paradox – it adds comedy to thought – is that this imperious intimation to think the unthought of language is seen as violence. Whereas the brutal reduction of language, which is altogether discontinuous and continuous, to the discontinuous is not seen as violence, being in the guise of companionable common sense and science.

In emblematic terms, while I will return to it further on, or elsewhere, to think language, we must leave Descartes for Spinoza, we must leave canonical semiotism for the thought of Humboldt, for whom the categories of *langue*, represented by grammarians and dictionaries, were but the 'dead skeleton of language'.

It is thus a question of transforming radically how we think.

To recognise the differences better, usually muddled, and devoid of any stakes, between the sacred, the divine and the religious.

This will detheologise what we call thought. Detheologise ethics too. To acknowledge in it the necessity of thinking within it a radical historicity of values. The paradox here being that it is the divine that opens the infinity of history and the infinity of sense.

Which thus reveals the religious as a catastrophe that has happened to the divine. As is shown by the theologico-political especially. But also the loss of power in semiotising denominational translations.

Here, poetics being an integral part of listening to the ways of the power of language, appears immediately as irreducible to the prevailing commonplaces in philosophy.

To translate specificity is the absolute opposite of prevailing hermeneutics, which is represented in the commonplace view of phenomenology. Such that, for instance, after and like so many others, Michel Deguy has repeated it: 'Everything is translation,' according to the lesson learned from Heidegger.[5] Hence: 'Translating is hermeneutical' (p. 106). In which all that can be heard, as always, is the sign, *langue*, thus from *langue* to *langue* 'to make German heard in French*, for instance, which is ultimately strictly impossible' (p. 108). This kind of sleeptalking passes off as philosophy.

Whereas listening to the continuous shows that it is not, it is no longer Hebrew that must be translated, when we translate the Bible, but what the Bible has done to Hebrew. In the sense where it is not Hebrew that has made the Bible, but the Bible that has made, and continues to make, Hebrew.

Yes, one day we should donate to the Museum of Commonplaces on Language (yet to be created), to the collection of dinosaur skeletons, the idea that we translate thoughts into words, this confusional conception, which muddles the specificity of the language act that is translating with the general act of understanding.

Which is only a language play really, a play on the word transposition, *Übersetzung*, which Heidegger deploys by separating *über* from *setzung*, to get something to cross to the other side.

A wordplay that so many translators are fond of as they see themselves ferrying words across languages, unknowingly confusing Charon for Saint Jerome, the patron saint of translators, who knew what allusive value was, carried over as they are by this ferry tale, when what they have carried over is nothing more than dead bones.

Thus it is time to uncover what is at stake here.

Which is imposed by the rhythm in the Bible, and listening to it, as a starting point for another way of thinking language, and this is precisely why rhythm, as I have redefined it, is a prophecy of language, it is an operation which may seem painful to some but it is necessary. And which can only lead to the discovery of the text's force and beauty. The poetics of the divine, stripped of its rhetoric of the religious.

This work calls for stripping. Old paintings covered in layers of grime can be stripped. Here it is a matter of several cultural layers.

---

5. Michel Deguy, *La Raison poétique* (Paris: Galilée, 2000), p. 103. It is always interesting to note in Hegel how the things of language, the things of poetry and the things of religion seem to mix together, and hold one another.

We must de-Christianise, de-Hellenise, de-Latinise, desacralise, I would also add, in a sense that requires an immediate explanation, to de-Frenchify what is presented to us as translations of the Bible in French.

By 'de-Frenchify' I mean that we must denounce this feeble and unconsciously condescending pact in the way it seeks out current, basic 'ordinary French'. Not to mention that it instrumentalises the text for the purpose of converting. To my knowledge, this is done in French, in Spanish, in English.

This practice determines two audiences, with two types of translation: style is added for a supposedly literate audience. The others presumably do not need it. Which is encapsulated in a sentence that Eugene Nida quotes from a native living in the forests of the Amazon as proof of this triumphant method: 'I never knew before that God spoke my language.' And there you are, one more Christian.

And by 'de-Frenchify' I also mean upsetting this canonical inanity opposing so-called poetic language to so-called ordinary language. Two real entities – that is, two illusionisms. We should listen to what Montaigne said: 'I would have a power of introducing something of my own,' or Aragon who, in *Traité du style*, in 1928, wrote: 'I trample syntax because it must be trampled. Like grapes. You see my point.'[6]

To de-Frenchify means to decurrentify, to decurrentfrenchify – this cowardice and trickery, because the poem of Hebrew, or of any other language for that matter, is not written in an ordinary language any more than it is in a poetic language: it is the maximum of the relationship between language and life. Which has nothing to do with the opposition between easy words and complicated words, between simple syntax and scholarly syntax.

In other words, the task to be considered and carried out is to be considered and carried out for every language, and it is an ethical task: to show clearly that the separation between a text for the literate and a text in current French for the vulgar, the linguistically correct, is ignominious ethically and politically, and poetic poverty. A human defeat: a defeat of the human for a victory of the theologico-political. From this point of view, the poetically correct is an accomplice.

All this work of stripping seeks nothing other than to have the Hebrew of the poem heard again, as well as the poem of the Hebrew. For the Bible. No longer the 'Lord of armies' [*Dieu des armées*], but rather the God of multitudes of stars [*Dieu des multitudes d'étoiles*]. Where we recognise at once the multisecular ideological mass which ends up opposing, in Hegel, a religion of hate to a religion of love.

---

6. Louis Aragon, *Treatise on Style*, trans. and with an intro. by Alyson Waters (Lincoln, NE: University of Nebraska Press, 1991), p. 17.

We could not have shown more clearly, with this tiny example, that the stakes of the poem are ethical and political.

Thus, to re-Hebrewise the Bible. In French. And in every language in which a translation was done. In which translation is done. After centuries not only of language dilution and annexation, but also of ideological perversion.

And because the rhythmic accent is called *ta'am* in Hebrew, 'the taste' of what is in one's mouth, a metaphor of the mouth, the body, which speaks to the physicality of language, I say that the poetic, ethical and political aim is to *ta'amise French*, to rhythmise it. *To ta'amise* all languages. And the way of thinking language.

A task which belongs precisely to the poem, and which shows, like a parable, that a poetic act is ethical and political.

Translating the Taste, that is the War of Rhythm

1. Untangling Problems

Let's face it. Translating the Bible, this ancient activity, and translating while transforming how we look and listen, is a matter that can still stir passions. That's rather a good sign. For the potential topicality of a thing as ancient, and venerable.[7]

But precisely because of its potential it is the object of multiple appropriations. Touching it is like stepping into a minefield. It is touching the sacred. And the sacred, it must not be touched.

Yet, the entire interpretative chain shows how uninterrupted and diversified the attempts have been. Along with the stakes and strategies. Interests. Translating, even more so than commentary, reveals these stakes, these strategies. To a point that it has become a subject of reflection itself, in order to shed light on what we show unknowingly.

This dispute is an excellent revealer of ideologies. Of the theologically planned lag of the messengers of the biblical in contemporary thought on language, which entails the discovery that *langue* is not all, there is discourse, and more than *langue* it is discourse that must be translated, and especially so when this discourse is a system of discourse, an invention of its own activity as it carries on as an activity. Which is infinitely more than a message. It is the poem of thought.

The general problem of translation is both exacerbated and concealed – unthought – since with the Bible we are dealing with a text that *is* religious, and *is considered* religious. Two different things. If I translate the Bible as a

---

7. A previous version of this paper was published in *L'Infini*, 76 (autumn 2001).

poem, I do not violate its religious character. The paradox is that if we treat it as a religious text, we desecrate it.

The attitude of religious proselytism is reductive. Its main concern is delivering a *message*. The term is preset in the dualism of the sign. Sense, and a residue, form. A dualism exacerbated by implicit behaviourism. Through *message*, a *behaviour*, a *response* is to be achieved and elicited. And *sense* is also already split in two: a stimulus for a response. A stimulus that is preset so as to elicit the desired response.

No, it is no coincidence that it is through biblical texts that scandal erupts. I know that I have already said it. But I am saying it again. Because it is necessary. And this scandal must be recognised, analysed. Certain outrages serve as symptoms. Obligingly providing the opportunity to clarify more than confusion.

Criticism by no means consists in condemning ancient translations, but rather in recognising what a text does, and what a translation does. There are many attitudes towards language. Each has its own effect. All can be judged on their results. It is always a matter of thinking the unthought. In order to situate products according to the sense of language that they show.

What makes the biblical domain particularly interesting, and sensitive, is how concentrated the issues at stake are. So much so that everything within it, every term, is significant. Thus 'Sacred Texts', because this expression deoralises what the word *miqra*, in Hebrew, means: reading. And covers Hebrewism with Christianism. It is a Christianism, in the same way one says solecism: a mistake in the grammar of the divine. And this domain is filled, overflowing, with such mistakes.

There is an enormous problem, far from clear, that calls for clarity, and it is found in the Hebraic Bible. It is only from a religious, cultural, Christian point of view that there is an Old Testament and a New Testament. For now, the problems I see have to do with that specific brand of Hebrew, which is, once again, as Buber said, neither Old nor Testament. The main problem, refuted at that, is that the foregrounding of the 'religious' in the Testament makes it impossible to think language. Which is instructive, and edifying, to show. Enlightening indeed. To reflect on this is not intended to vex anyone, but only to draw the attention to a cultural deafness, which is an oddity that could very well be found in a cabinet of horrors.

It is thus necessary to untangle what is tangled up. So that the stakes and tactics become clearly apparent. Problems, I see a long series of them. Which we should take it upon ourselves to discern. Otherwise we will not even see the burning bush.

I have already mentioned the cultural fact that, in the West, our founding texts can be read only in translation. And that these translations are effacers.

In addition to this there is a problem specific to the New Testament: there is manifestly a fullness of Hebrew underneath the Greek. In the Acts of the Apostles 21: 40, Paul 'prosephōnēsen tē Hebraidi dialektō', or 'spake unto them in the Hebrew tongue'. And Bernard Dubourg has shown extensively that the Hebrew lies *under* the Greek.[8] Grammar, lexicon, puns, coded numerical equivalents. Hebrew, not Aramaic. But Matthew (27: 46) cites the beginning of Psalm 22 in Aramaic, though it is in Hebrew. Thus for centuries, from Hebrew to Greek, from Greek to Latin, from Latin to modern languages, we have been reading translations of translations of translations.

Quite distinct, on the Bible market, because the Bible has a market, are the Jehovah's Witnesses' very widely spread translations, *Les Saintes Écritures: traduction du monde nouveau*, 1971, translated from English.

Of a completely different order, the translation recently undertaken of the Septuagint, clearly a translation of a translation, but which is justified, considering the importance of the Septuagint, and its specific problems, which made it a second original.

Let's not forget this one detail, another thing worth pointing out again, that during the long period when translation was done from the Vulgate alone, the psalms, in the Vulgate, were '*juxta Septuaginta*', meaning from the Septuagint. The translations in vulgar tongues were thus, for this part of the Bible, translations of translations.

Then came the problem of the long Catholic tradition that restricted readings to the Vulgate, proclaimed to be the sole 'authentic' version by the Council of Trent in 1546. Pope Clement VIII in 1596 continued to oppose 'the purchase, reading and possession of Bibles in vulgar scriptures'.[9] Because there were medieval translations, from Latin, as early as the thirteenth century, the Book of Psalms being the first one.

It was to prevent, in the name of the 'Holy Inquisition', heresy. In that respect Montaigne was against vulgar versions. In 1580:

> God ought not to be commixed in our actions, but with awful reverence, and an attention full of honour and respect. The word or voice is too divine, having no other use but to exercise our lungs and to please our eares.[10]

Montaigne was referring to the psalms, 'the sacred and divine songs which the holy spirit hath indited unto David' (ibid., p. 378). In 1588,

---

8. Bernard Dubourg, *L'Invention de Jésus: l'hébreu du Nouveau Testament* (Paris: Gallimard, 1987), p. 75.
9. Pierre-Maurice Bogaert (ed.), *Les Bibles en français: histoire illustrée du Moyen-Âge à nos jours* (Turnhout: Brepols, 1991), p. 101.
10. Michel de Montaigne, *Essayes of Montaigne*, vol. II, trans. by John Florio; ed. by Justin Huntly McCarthy (London: David Stott, 1889), §56, p. 378.

Montaigne was even more hostile to this divulgation: 'They have heretofore beene accompted mysteries, but through the abuse of times they are now held as sports and recreations' (ibid., p. 379). And he went on to write:

> It is not a study fitting all men, but only such as have vowed themselves unto it, and whom God hath, of his infinit mercie, called thereto. The wicked, the ungodly, and the ignorant, are thereby empaired. It is no historie to be fabulously reported, but a historie to be dutifully reverenced, awfully feared, and religiously adored. Are they not pleasantly conceited, who, because they have reduced the same into the vulgar tongues, and that all men may understand it, perswade themselves, that the people shall the better conceive and digest the same? Consisteth it but in the words, that they understand not all they find written? Shall I say more? By approaching thus little unto it, they go back from it. Meere ignorance, and wholly relying on others, was verily more profitable and wiser than is this verball and vaine knowledge, the nurse of presumption and source of temeritie.[11]

It is definitely an appeal for obscuration, a rejection of the vulgar.

This restriction, wholly theological, to the Vulgate, was accompanied by the multicentennial motif of Jews as counterfeiters of the original Hebrew text, a teaching that was perpetuated all the way into the biblical criticism of the nineteenth century, and still for Renan, among others, hostile to the Masoretic text (established, vocalised, rhythmicised by the Masoretes – from 'masorah', transmission – Jewish philologists between the fifth and ninth centuries). Another problem. Which must also be hammered: the 'scientific'.

In Spain, in Italy, the Church forbade translations into vulgar tongues until 1757. As for official Catholicism in the nineteenth century, the Holy See repeatedly expressed 'reservations about the Scriptures in vulgar tongues'.[12] Pope Pius IX in his 1864 *Syllabus* condemned Bible societies and especially translations done by non-Catholics. It was in 1943 that the *Divino Afflante Spiritu* encyclical of Pius XII liberated Catholic exegesis and approved translations of the Bible from the originals.

In Catholicity, translation was done from the Vulgate for a long time. Jacques Lefèvre d'Étaples translated the New Testament in 1523 from Latin, as well as the Book of Psalms in 1524, all of the Old Testament in booklets from 1528 to 1532 and in folio format in 1530. And André Frossard too translated from the Latin Vulgate, *En ce temps-là la Bible*, from 1969 to 1972 (ibid., p. 226). And that Latin passed for an elegant Latin, but it was full of Hebrewisms.

---

11. Ibid., pp. 379–80.
12. Christian Cannuyer, in Bogaert, *Les Bibles en français*, p. 190.

The breakaway from this submission, through the Reformation, and Robert Olivetan, in 1535, brought another problem, it too concealed by a certain triumphalism, as if going back to the Hebrew text sufficed. And the breakaway was not as pronounced as was generally believed. It was the start of a strange trend of revisions and revisions of revisions, on both the Catholic side and the Protestant side. Which gave the impression of a renewal, especially in the second half of the twentieth century. Problem.

On top of this, the acceptance of different types of translation. For different audiences. Problem. I will return to this.

Two problems arise here. Which only look technical: one which is exposed by the rejection of the Masoretic text as late and inauthentic, in the quest for a lost original text; while rare and fragmentary ancient manuscripts contain consonantal writing only and thus say nothing about the rhythmics of it; hence, there are problems not only with sense, that varies according to this or that vocalisation, but particularly with the wholesale denial of rhythmic accents, marked only by the Masoretes, who invented diacritical signs to notate them.

Signs were invented to indicate the pronunciation of vowels (above and below the writing until then only consonantal), it would be absurd to think that vowels were invented as a result. But signs were a method of preserving 'the correct pronunciation of the Scriptures [that] risked being lost in the Diaspora'.[13] And the graphic signs of the accents, used to notate 'both punctuation and melody', were invented at the same time by the 'transmitters' (the meaning of Masoretes) whose 'close attention' consisted in, for these sacralised texts, 'a unique kind of loyalty in the history of literature' (ibid., pp. 65–6). Between the sixth and the eighth centuries.

As for the 'unification of the consonantal text', it has been dated to 'the time of Rabbi Aqiba whose exegetic method requires an attention to every scriptural detail' (ibid., p. 64). In the second century, that is: he died in 135 (ibid., p. 128).

The Christian theologico-philological rejection of the Masoretic text, wholesale throughout history, then fragmentarily revised, especially targeted *te'amim*. Rhythmic and cantillation accents. The poetic anthropology of the Bible, by showing that certain *te'amim*, through their very names, recall a cheironomy (hand movements that guide reading), reveals how old this organisation of the movement of speech is. The written notation came afterwards.

But because it is a pan-rhythmics, which knows neither verse nor prose,

---

13. Mireille Hadas-Lebel, *Histoire de la langue hébraïque: des origines à l'époque de la Mishna* (Paris and Louvain: Peeters, 1995), p. 51.

it could not and still cannot be reduced to the Greek representation which is still with us today: verse, prose, and 'everything that's not verse is prose.' For professorissimus Monsieur Jourdain, that is. From Flavius Josephus to biblical criticism. Where the so-called *scientific* is but the alibi of the crypto-theological. Double problem: of detheologisation, and of poetics.

Hence the problem of a Hellenising reading, in terms of metrics and prose. Through the organisation of the text in a way that conforms to metrical theories. This old-fashioned thing tends to be accepted.

Another problem on top of this, the doctrine of parallelism as the criterion of repartition for a definition no longer metrical but rhetorical of poetry opposed to prose. Still commonplace today. With metrical mixes.

The wonder of awe is reached, seeing how this indescribable mixture that is the science of philology, stylistics (the illusion of discussing what is understood as *poetry* and what is understood as *prose*) and the history of the Christian appropriation through its anti-Masoreticism, with the theory of parallel members, how this entire tangle is commonly accepted right down to the history of the Hebrew language. A triumph of the Christian theologico-political is what this consensus is: 'Biblical poetry is characterised by what is called parallelism.'[14] Immediately adding 'that no classical norm applied to this poetry in which there is no prosody, no metrics, no regular rhyme scheme. All that matters is the rhythm of signification, logical structure, most often presented in parallel members' (ibid., p. 75).

Where once again consensus only proves consensus.[15]

Once again, the absurdity of a formal definition of poetry, both as verse, and as the best of verse but without verses: 'However, it would be an error to believe that the use of pairs of synonyms is restricted to poetry. Probably due to the influence of poetry, literary prose also sees it as a form of elegance.'[16] And 'these pairs of synonyms as well as numerous others are common to poetry and prose'.[17]

In short, no formal definition of 'poetry' nor of what is called 'prose'. A traditional confusion between poetics and rhetoric. Where it appears as usual

---

14. Hadas-Lebel, *Histoire de la langue hébraïque*, p. 75.
15. This opinion is as prevalent in Benjamin Hrushovski's chapter 'Note on the Systems of Hebrew Versification', in *The Penguin Book of Hebrew Verse* (New York: Viking Press, 1981), pp. 57–72, as it is with Hadas-Lebel. Or with Chaim Rabin. I maintain that this is *lectio facilior*, a Hellenisation–Christianisation made invisible through consensus. And here I refer the reader to my essay *Critique du rythme* (Lagrasse: Verdier, 1982), pp. 457–78, and to my preface to *Gloires* (Paris: Desclée de Brouwer, 2001).
16. Hadas-Lebel, *Histoire de la langue hébraïque*, p. 77. On the formal definition of poetry, I refer the reader to my *Célébration de la poésie* (Lagrasse: Verdier, 2001).
17. Hadas-Lebel, *Histoire de la langue hébraïque*, p. 77.

that we do not know what we are saying when we use the terms 'prose' and 'poetry'. In general, for one.[18] In particular, also, when the Bible is discussed. But because we have not yet noticed, we carry on.

In this entire presentation of the history of the systems of vocalisation and vocabulary ('stylistic' overview), not one word on *te'amim*. They are absent, due to the discontinuous. To the unthought of the continuous.

This received idea has a transhistorical permanence. In the eighteenth century, the Jews 'from the Talmudic era "enemies of Christians, have altered the Holy Books [. . .] in order to settle sense in accordance with the prejudices of their sect"'.[19] Through the notation of vowels imposed as vowels. For Richard Simon, in 1678, it was time to 'repair the Hebrew text'.[20] To repair this contradiction between 'the Holy Scripture [. . . which] is entirely the word of God', and vowels 'the invention of men' (ibid., p. 146).

Yet again Maurice Olender in 1989, when discussing bishop Robert Lowth, it is only to mention a 'poetry of the sublime'.[21] And he cites the bishop, for whom, in 1753, one was no longer obliged 'to follow "blindly those blind guides, the Jewish doctors"' (ibid., pp. 30–1). No criticism whatsoever. Lowth wanted to save the vocalisation of the text from 'hermeneutic distortion' through a 'philology of the sublime' (ibid., p. 31). The doctrine of parallelism is accepted in the same historicist movement that evidently does not make a distinction between the language system (in which there necessarily were vowels) and consonantal writing, which did not notate them. And the notation of *te'amim* is dismissed in one broad sweep.

Hence the war of rhythm.

All of this leads to the main problem of translation into French today, and which also has a part to play in the religious market: the literary challenge of producing in French a Bible that has the poetic power of the King James Version of 1611 and that of Luther in 1545. The last edition. Of his lifetime. With the problem caused by the blur between poetic power and cultural power. Each sponsoring its own candidate: Lemaistre de Sacy, for Catholics; Segond, for Protestants.

---

18. And Cicero knew this: '*Est autem etiam in dicendo quidam cantus obscurior*' ('There is moreover even in speech a sort of faint singing'). *De Oratore*, §18.
19. Olender is citing *Le Journal des sçavans* [The Journal of Erudites], 16 May 1707. Maurice Olender, *The Languages of Paradise: Aryans and Semites. A Match Made in Heaven*, trans. by Arthur Goldhammer [1992] (New York: Other Press, 2002 [1989]), p. 21.
20. Richard Simon, *A Critical History of the Old Testament*, trans. from French by anonymous [1682] (London: Walter Davis, 1685 [1678]), p. 356.
21. Olender, *The Languages of Paradise*, p. 28.

A problem that is blurred even more by biblical paraphrase as a specific genre. When it is passed off as translation.

Yes, all this lacks rhythm.

2. The Bible and not the Bible

First, let's repeat, for reassurance, a few truisms. But – oddly enough for truisms – some are unknown.

The first one, with regard to translation, is that a text is a text. But that a translation is a translation. A specific speech act. The authors of the very first bilingual word lists in the Ancient Near East, 5,000 years ago, already knew this. The proof is in their lists.

Therefore, if you read Dante in French, you are not reading Dante. But a translation. Of Dante. The proof of this is that there are several versions. But there is only one text by Dante. And this goes for any text. Even the Bible.

And if you are told, in French, here is THE Bible, you are being fooled. And you are taken for a fool. And there is more. You are turned into a fool. Don't let that happen.

Only then will it be possible to have a look. Which is to say a close look. At the bluff and its effects.

Thus no translation of the Bible is the Bible. Obviously. And there are several translations, some so different that it is hard to believe that they come from the same text. What is more, as we know, the Bible is the text with the most translations.

But a text is not necessarily – here is another masking effect – the sum of its translations. A trendy idea. Unless we reduce the poem purely to transmitting messages: the poem reduced to the sign, to a meagre sociology. Or pretend that translating is writing. And here precisely lies the entire problem, which we also complacently believe to be solved. Because the relation between a text and its translation cannot elude, at least not indefinitely, the relation to its activity as a translation. In relation to what a poem is. And that is why, precisely, we have believed that translations become outdated.

No. Not more so than works. Because ordinary experience shows that translations-poems last, they *age*. Which is the only way to last. The same way originals do. Texts that are considered mere artefacts of their time, originals and translations, are the ones whose activity does not last. Because they were merely *products*. And not *activities*. Which are said to age.

Here lies the whole poetic challenge. Which puts translations and works on an equal footing.

Hence what follows must be clearly understood.

That every translation is a specific speech act and as such ineffaceable. A translation that presents itself as inexistent and as transparently showing the text of which it is the translation is a sham, or a sign of ignorance of one's practice, which is no better. And also comes down to a sham.

That being said, the common, and ingrained, ideology of translation as being effaced so as to give way to the original shows a naivety almost as enormous. Because it does not seem to know that the more translators believe they are effacing themselves, out of modesty, the more they show, unknowingly, the entire collection of ideas they have on language, literary objects and what translation can and cannot do, so much so that this collection ends up being more visible than the translated text, and even covers it. It's obscene.

Basically, this leaves translations that know and show themselves as translations, and in so doing show linguistic, poetic, historical and cultural alterity. Instead of effacers showing their identitarianism. And whenever effacers strive to look natural, the best they look is artificial. They lose everything.

This is the effect of the cultural.

And equating, naively enough, translations with translated texts, is quite common. It also endorses the erasure of translations as translations, as speech acts and interventions that are specific and particular. It is exactly what George Steiner does at the beginning of his preface to the King James Version: 'What you have in hand is not *a* book. It is *the* book. That, of course, is what "Bible" means.'[22] A play on language, one might say, on this double identity: it is the 'Hebrew Bible' – originally – but under the guise of its English translation.

A play on language which itself is doubled when, for its symbolic role, Steiner calls it *the* book, whereas the exact meaning of the Greek word βιβλία, as everyone knows, is the plural form of 'books'. The idea of 'a book of books' has such a strong symbolic value that it has eliminated everything that may have happened in the move from one language to another, and especially from one language practice to another.

In fact, with this play on language comes a classic sleight of words. The Bible, and then suddenly the Great Code. Any problem with languages or translation has disappeared. The cultural has taken over, automatically taken for language itself. The very bulk of translations (into 2,010 different 'languages', according to Steiner (ibid., p. 43)) negates translation.

Pointing out again that it is the book with the most translations only negates the poetic problem even further. And the 'weight of knowledge' that Steiner likes to enumerate only reinforces the received ignorance of rhythm – more specifically when he states the conventional opinion, this theologico-rhetorical veneer, which leads him to speak of the psalms: 'Nowhere else are the parallelisms, the admixture of prose and verse, the use of metrical

---

22. George Steiner, *No Passion Spent: Essays 1978–1995* (New Haven, CT, and London: Yale University Press, 1996), p. 40.

prodigality more accomplished' (ibid., p. 73). So many false claims and absurdities. But uttered with utmost seriousness. Because in the Bible there is no prose or verse, hence no metrics, and the doctrine of parallelisms was invented precisely to fill in for this missing metrics.

This, without any connection whatsoever with the cursive notation in the 'Masorah or "tradition" of vowel signs, accentuation and marginal notes, [. . .] is the product of this collective medieval recension' (ibid., p. 46).

The invisible comical here is that in many cases when Steiner praises the Hebrew original, he refers to the King James Version – and he does the same thing as Nida, as if the 1611 version were in reality the original.[23] What is more, he does not read Hebrew. His French translator mentions that the canonical order that Steiner observes is the Christian one and not that of the 'Hebrew Bible' (ibid., p. 56). Which renders Steiner's very title 'A preface to the Hebrew Bible' ambiguous. And spurious. In reality it is a preface to the King James Version. And it is not the same thing: he sees the song of songs as a 'rapturous rebuke of the Qoheleth', because in the King James Version the Song of Solomon comes after Ecclesiastes, whereas in the Hebrew Bible, *šîr haš·šî·rîm*, the song of songs comes before it (ibid., p. 75). Steiner's translator carefully notes that the Christian Bible 'moved the Prophets based on apologetics' (ibid., p. 125).

And Steiner, because he is 'no Hebraist', rehashes clichés, about *davar*, as 'thing' or 'speech' (ibid., p. 59). But he does not forget to include prefiguration, the 'virgin' instead of the 'young woman', a theology that erases the '*Biblia Hebraica*' (ibid., p. 63). And he reproduces the list of various 'authors', Yahwist, Elohist and so on. Reworded with much exaltation that serves to cover the banality of it all. It is the discourse of the cultural. Which is probably why the cultural is all hail: it identifies with it.

3. It's the Ear that Sees, the Eye is Deaf

In so far as we see the world through what we hear of language, in a language, with the narcissism of minor differences, as Freud said, depending on languages, the sign is overwhelmed, sense is overwhelmed.

The sign semiotises visually. To see is commonly intended to mean to understand. You see? But language uses the physical senses. The mouth, the lip, the tongue, turn speech into chewing. The prophet sees with his ear. Maimonides proved it.

It is relevant that what is usually translated by rhythmic or cantillation accent is *taʿam* in Hebrew – plural *teʿamim* – or *taste*. The taste of what we

---

23. See Bogaert, *Les Bibles en français*, p. 102.

eat, the taste of things. The sense of taste. I take this metaphor (medieval Hebrew considers it as *ratio*, raison d'être and rationality) as designating the affect. And it is therefore the affect that makes the *ratio* of language: the movement of sense. Much more than a logico-grammatical punctuation, much more than the melodic value of accents in liturgical cantillation.

There is a triple paradox. The first one is that the very relation believers have with the texts that are holy to them prolongs Christian philological anti-Judaism (which denies accents as inauthentic) by separating language in two, truth and a formal residue. The second paradox is that if translation means listening attentively to taste, then the rhythmic grasp of the poem captures discourse in all of its power, which bears affect and concept together. And translating must then be *anterior* to interpretation. Because the poem is bearer and borne, but a translation that is posterior to interpretation is only borne.

The third paradox, the most incredible one: no translation, none, in any European language (as far as I know) has taken as its benchmark the taste of biblical texts.[24] I am only stating a fact.

Which, of course, does not mean that no translations of Hebrew have been done. But only of the idiom. In fact, Hebrew shifts, it is the taste of language that is *all Hebrew* to the specialists.

Again, simply stating the facts.

Yes, as monumental as it seems – but it is precisely because it is monumental that it goes unnoticed – there has *never* been a translation of the Bible with its rhythm, as rhythm. So long as translations were from the Vulgate, this effacement, itself effaced, was understandable. But ever since translations have been done from the Hebrew text, from Olivetan to contemporary translations, absolutely all of them translate the Hebrew language, but not the rhythmic organisation of the biblical text.

The reasons are easily identifiable. The result is there all the same. And *inaudible*.

With regard to the considerable number of practices related to the translation of the Bible, I am obliged to reaffirm that to *ta'amise* French, to embibelise translating, engenders a radical transformation in comparison to *all* the other practices, all of them, in the systematised attention to the tastes of the text which are literally the *te'amim*, a term usually rendered as 'accents'.

None so deaf as those who will not hear of it. Deafer yet those who compare my work to André Chouraqui's translation, thinking they are

---

24. This is what I have set out to do since *Les Cinq Rouleaux* (Paris: Gallimard, 1970), *Jona et le signifiant errant* (Paris: Gallimard, 1981), *Gloires* (2001), *Au Commencement* (2002) and *Les Noms* (2003) (all three Paris: Desclée de Brouwer).

similar, when they have *nothing* in common. Etymologism and word-as-units in Chouraqui, against unity of the continuous, rhythm–syntax–prosody. In other words Chouraqui translates a language. I translate a system of discourse. Rhythm–syntax–prosody. Just like all the other translators, Chouraqui does not render the *te'amim*. He does even worse. With his uneven lines, he poetises, and his line breaks muddle the difference between conjunctive and disjunctive accents, weak and strong, so much so that he distorts rhythm even more so than if he had written his translation in prose, as, for instance, the Rabbinate has done, since he seems to pretend to render rhythm precisely where he consistently betrays the true *taste* of the text. So much so that the 'flavour' he claims to have rendered is but a linguistic calque. Moreover he has toned down, like the others, outbursts of syntactical violence.

Thus going directly back to the Hebrew text does not suffice. Neither Olivetan nor Segond has the beauties of the language of the King James Version and Luther, and it is not due to culture or society. I will return to this further on.

But another paradox is still that neither the King James Version nor Luther renders the tastes of the text. Although in Luther's 1545 edition slashes are used in an original way as punctuation.

Rhythm reveals that even more so than linguistic knowledge, or knowledge of the specific relation between two languages, translating has to do with the culture of the poem.

The rhythm in the Bible is thus a parable, and a prophecy of language. Taste is to be translated more so than sense. Sense as it is usually understood as the meaning of words in a language. Sense taken as units, the word as a unit. And etymologism that tries so hard to reinforce the effect, of sense, only reinforces the discontinuous: the harder the etymologising calque wants to hit, the more its speech act becomes a form of poetic suicide.

But taste is not opposed to sense. On the contrary it bears sense within it, because it is the very movement of sense, and not in any one word taken individually. It is what moves from one word to the next, and as such a serial semantics. Hence it is inseparably pausal rhythm, syntax and prosody. The recitative of language, which says infinitely more than the narrative.

Rhythm, in the sense of the continuous, is the great encompasser in language: not in the traditional sense that is the alternation between a same and a different, but in the sense of a subject-form(er), in the sense of a body-in-language, and of a continued activity which makes rhythm into one single and inseparable unit of language–poem–ethics–politics.

In this sense, there is a war of rhythm, the war of the poem against the big semiotic giant, that knucklehead who sees everything double in his schizophrenia: sense and sound, content and form, oral and written, things and words, individuals and society. The social contract of language.

The 'flavour', orality, is not there where, some time ago, a noisy advert claimed it was. The poetic problem here has nothing to do with the 'renaissance' of Hebrew in Israel. And it is not a language problem. The poem cannot be created within the unit of the sign. The jabber of the literary market does not replace a poetics.

Thus it is not the word that is the unit, even less so its etymology. The poem cannot be created within the discontinuous of language. But in the continuous. The organisation of taste, in the Bible, is also the parable of this.

4. Taste and Verse

The unit of language in the Bible is the verse. In other words the unit is not grammatical. It is not the sentence, it is the verse, and the verse is a unit of rhythm. A verse is called *pasuq*, which is the past participle of 'cut'. The final accent, which marks the end of the verse, is called *siluq*, which means 'separation', or *sof pasuq*, 'end of the verse'.

The accent that is the strongest and acts as a caesura is *atna'h*, meaning rest. But caesura does not mean that there are hemistichs. Segments on each side of the caesura can be very irregular. There may be no *atna'h* accent, or it may be on the first word of the verse (as in Genesis 34: 31 or Ezekiel 34: 79). Certain verses have only three words, even two. I render *atna'h* by an indentation inside the verse and a capital letter on the first word of the second segment.

Next, there are two levels in the hierarchy of dominant accents, called *melakhim*, meaning 'kings', or *sarim*, 'princes'. The main accent is *zaqef*, 'raised', and when two of these follow one another, the first one is the strongest. Which is what happens to the voice crying (in Isaiah 40: 3): the voice is not crying in the desert, it is crying that in the desert the way be open for Adonai. Because of deafness to tastes, this was not heard. As typographical equivalents, for strong accents, I put a large blank space.

There is a third group of tastes that separate, within what is left to be separated, such as *tevir*, 'broken'. And I put a small blank space.

This is quite simplified of course, compared to complex sequences, but their diversity is mainly musical. It is their hierarchy that indicates their pausal and semantic value. I render the hierarchy using various blank spaces systematically. Which have nothing to do with those used by Mallarmé or Claudel.

As for conjunctive accents, called *meshartim*, 'servants', which put two words in one bite, their presence is signalled by the absence of blank spaces. And in no way are these non-marks: *eli éli* (*Gloires* 22: 2) '*mon dieu mon dieu*' [my god my god], with an accent rising on the second word to indicate the end of the group, is without a doubt a mark of affect on sense, and if this mark changes nothing in the sense of the words, it does a lot to the mode of signifying.

Each of these accents has a name. Three categories emerge from these names. There are those that refer to the graphic form invented by Masoretes: *segolta* ('cluster'), *shalshelet* ('small chain'); those that enunciate a melodic line: *revi'a* (to hold a note) or *tevir* ('broken'); those that designate a hand movement: *zaqef* ('raised' finger) or *tif'ha* (the width of the hand). The latter category bearing the trace of ancient cheironomy, hand gestures. Necessarily anterior to the invention of diacritical marks. I therefore consider their ancientness as authenticated. That too must be repeated.

This is what had to be shown, against the theologically programmed deafness, and has been known for a long time.[25] It was at stake in a problem that was not one of translation per se, but decisive for the status of rhythm, and its relation to translating.

If further illustration had to be provided to show that the notion of *prose* is foreign to the Bible, it would be an opportunity to mention once again that there is both a graphic and a melodic difference between the books of Job (*Iyov*), Proverbs (*Mishle*) and Glories (*Tehillim*) and the twenty-one other ones said to be 'in prose'.[26] But because the difference does not affect the internal hierarchy, and since only the pausal-semantic rhythmics affects discourse, it is the only one I listen to when I translate.

But then, for the poem of the Bible, it is no longer possible or acceptable to allow these two attitudes that efface, both of which for different reasons, the taste of its language.

The first attitude is that of traditional Jewish hermeneutics: music makes it impossible to hear rhythm in language – in other words to hear language at all.

The effect is classic. But concealed by language, which metaphorises both ways: musical phrase, music of the poem. It's the same old song.

The second attitude, to be looked at closely, in order to appreciate how it works, is religious appropriation by Christians. Very subtly. Very quietly. All the more insidious for being done discreetly, and hidden behind the 'scientific'.

---

25. Cf. William Wickes, *Two Treatises on the Accentuation of the Old Testament: On Psalms, Proverbs, and Job. On the Twenty-one Prose Books* (New York: KTAV, 1970 [1881]).
26. The number of accents differs, eighteen disjunctive and nine conjunctive for the 'books of prose', compared to twelve and nine respectively for the three other books. Where evidently the meaning of term 'prose' is not the commonly accepted one.

5. Cantillation Without Rhythm

David Banon, in his history of the edifying Jewish commentary, does not once encounter or mention *te'amim*. All the while noting, after the separation from Judaism, 'the polemic and rejection' from the moment when Theodosius, in 380, made Christianism 'the sole authorised religion'. The beginning of the theologico-political.[27]

A Samaritan hymn is mentioned, without any commentary on metrical organisation, although the hymn is typeset in a versified format.

Re-retold stories, parables, prescriptions and a collection of legends, the history and the description of the corpus strictly focus on content. They summarise the two elements that make up the commentary, the *halakah*, 'the way', and the *aggadah*, 'the tale'. The book is about sense, stories, themes – in short, exegesis (ibid., p. 62).

But the commentaries are presented 'verse by verse' (ibid., p. 66), such as for the late sixth-century Midrashim. Which means, *the verse being the unit of rhythm*, that, long before the notation by the Masoretes, the verse was known and acknowledged as a unit. This is apparently so obvious that it is not even pointed out. It is typical of Jewish hermeneutics. It did not bother, it seems, to respond to the Christian denial of the *te'amim*.

David Banon does mention 'cantillatory marks' once, but he mixes them with everything else, and as he says, only for cantillation (ibid., p. 74).

Even the distinction between the eye, vision, in philosophy, and the ear (speech and voice) in the Midrash completely omit the *te'amim* (ibid., pp. 92–5). It is about 'listening to speech' (ibid., p. 116). The sense, the sign. Which remain what they are despite the call for 'Derridean *"deconstruction"*' and Paul Ricœur's 'narratological hermeneutics' (ibid., p. 126). All is normal: it is a hermeneutics.

Things that have to do with the theory of language, the theory of rhythm, and how they affect one another, evidently do not interest the historians of Jewish exegesis. Maurice-Ruben Hayoun, in his presentation of Jewish exegesis, when discussing Yehuda HaLevi, does not once touch on the importance HaLevi gives to rhythm in his *Kuzari*.[28] As for the passage on Abraham Ibn Ezra, where he mentions that 'the four categories of biblical exegesis are similar to the Christian theory of the quadruple sense of the Scripture',

---

27. David Banon, *Le Midrach* (Paris: Presses Universitaires de France, 1995), pp. 38–9. This book is not the Midrash. It is a presentation of the Midrash. It is a document because it is a discourse-on.
28. Maurice-Ruben Hayoun, *L'Exégèse juive: exégèse et philosophie dans le Judaïsme* (Paris: Presse Universitaires de France, 2000).

again nothing on the importance that Abraham Ibn Ezra, the only one apart from Yehuda HaLevi, placed, for any exegesis, on the *te'amim* (ibid., p. 53). It is strictly about theology and nothing else. At no point, concerning Maimonides, is there a mention of what is said, in what we know as *The Guide for the Perplexed*, about the role that hearing plays in prophecy.

Just an observation, incidentally, on the 'Averroism' of Ibn Rushd's 'Latin commentators who seem almost always to work on translations of translations (from Arabic into Hebrew and ultimately in Latin)' (ibid., pp. 73–4).

Nothing on the *te'amim* in Mendelssohn's translation. Everything is centred on the history of 'rabbinic sermons' (ibid., p. 123).

That is how history is written – the history of exegesis, the history of thought: in the total absence of any thought on language, in the absolute absence of rhythm and orality. Strange omission of the inaugural commandment: 'Listen . . .' Granted the rest of this injunction is strictly theological. But let's keep in mind that theology is a *logology*. Language speaks of language.

As for the Karaites, whom one would expect to be sons of hearing, it is interesting to see that it is not how they are presented. They are said to be *qara'im*, or *ba'ale miqra* (the masters of the *miqra* – reading), or *bene miqra* (the sons of reading) because they limit themselves to the 'reading of the biblical text'.[29] Compared to the *ba'ale mishnah*, – or the 'Rabbanites' – who interpret the Bible using oral lessons, the Mishnah (repetition), the Midrash (research) and the Talmud (study) (ibid., p. 9).

Compared to Protestants (the Protestants of Judaism) by Richard Simon, for their hostility to the Talmud, 'the target par excellence of Christians' (ibid., p. 34). 'Mystiquery and rabbinage', said Richard Simon in his 1678 *Histoire critique du Vieux Testament* [*Critical History of the Old Testament*], which made him paradoxically sympathetic to Karaites.

Jewish to some, non-Jewish to others: Catherine II and even Hitler. But the very nature of the conflict is entirely theologico-practical. Rites and rules of behaviour. Through which the relation to texts is seen in terms of content. Thus in the division between content and form.

Islamicised, Turkeycised, no kabbalah, no mezuzah, no tefillin, no shofar, 'in the grief of the destroyed Temple', all of this pertains to the ritualisation of religious life and the interpretation of certain biblical texts (ibid., p. 112). Contrary to what could have been expected, nothing on the rhythm of the Bible and nothing on the way it affects the theory of language.

To take another example, from the translation of the American Jewish Publication Society, which 'was made directly from the traditional Hebrew

---

29. Emanuela Trevisan-Semi, *Les Caraïtes: un autre Judaïsme*, trans. from Italian by Simone Kauders (Paris: Albin Michel, 1992), p. 15.

text into the idiom of modern English', and which after a historical account, presents its own methodology, all that is discussed concerns sense and the difficulties it poses.[30] The translation is said to be 'based on the traditional Hebrew text – its consonants, vowels, and syntactical divisions – although the traditional accentuation occasionally has been replaced by an alternative construction' (ibid., p. xx). Aside from that, not *one* reference to the *te'amim*. But there is mention of the 'poetry of Psalms' and of 'thought units' (ibid., p. xxi). It is the traditional effacement. Greco-Christian. Liturgy covers the sound of rhythm.

---

30. Jewish Publication Society, *Tanakh: A New Translation of the Holy Scriptures According to the Traditional Hebrew Text* (Philadelphia: Jewish Publication Society, 1985), p. xv. 'The committee's translation of *the Psalms* appeared in 1973; of the *Book of Job*, in 1980' (p. xxi).

11

Case Study of Poetic Translating
The Name of Ophelia

(in *Poétique du traduire*, Lagrasse: Verdier, 1995, pp. 245–57)

Translated by Chantal Wright

Roman Jakobson, in his 1960 conference paper 'Linguistics and Poetics', in order to illustrate what he called the poetic function, used the following examples intentionally drawn from outside the domain of poetry:

> 'Why do you always say *Joan and Margery* yet never *Margery and Joan*? Do you prefer Joan to her twin sister?' 'Not at all, it just sounds smoother.' In a sequence of two coordinated words, and as long as there are no issues with hierarchy, the speaker perceives, in the precedence given to the shorter name and without having to provide any justification, the best possible configuration of the message.
>
> A girl used to talk about 'the horrible Harry'. 'Why horrible?' 'Because I hate him.' 'But why not *dreadful, terrible, frightful, disgusting*?' 'I don't know why, but *horrible* fits him better.' Without realizing it, she clung to the poetic device of paronomasia.[1]

This was immediately before he embarked upon his famous analysis of the slogan *I like Ike*. From outside the domain of poetry, but alluding to a study by Dell Hymes on a 'dominant nucleus' in particular sonnets by Keats. There might be something analogous when we encounter, in *Hamlet*, the collocation *fair Ophelia*. Beauty (and blondeness) itself.

Roman Jakobson's observations were of course situated within his rejection of the arbitrary nature of the sign in Saussure, which he conflated, like all structuralists, with conventionalism. On the assumption of a natural relationship between language and nature.

---

1. Roman Jakobson, 'Linguistics and Poetics', in *Selected Writings III* (Berlin: Mouton, 1981), pp. 25–6.

But the example of *Joan and Margery* illustrated only the mark of rhythm within discourse, which tends to place the shortest word first and finish on the longest. The cultural rhythm of discourse, which has nothing of a poetics about it, but which comes from a rhetoric of rhythm.

So too *horrible Harry*, which is certainly paronomasia, is of the order of rhetoric. And it is discourse that constructs the effect of naturalness: the partial reflection in the mirror of the signifiers of one word by the signifiers of another. When it is a proper name accompanied by a word like an adjective, discourse establishes a sort of partial equivalence, whence the effect of sense. Leaving aside all common sense.

But there is mystery in paronomasia. Why it allows the truth of a word to speak through the discourse of another, sense cannot tell us. Paronomasia is of the same order as rhyme, which is made greater use of today in advertising than by poets. It must therefore have an efficiency that goes beyond our current sense of sense. And it is true that it can augment the effect of naturalness. It is a demonstration, without it being clear how or even exactly of what. That is something.

This is exactly what, without going into an endless anthropology of poetry, the name of Ophelia demonstrates in *Hamlet*. And Ophelia is fair, and sweet, the text tells us over and over again. It therefore seems *natural* that *fair* should be associated with her name, if only through its sense. And *fair* more than *beautiful*, just like *horrible Harry*. But there is something else.

Reading and rereading *Hamlet*, I noticed that *each time* the name of Ophelia appears in speech, twenty times in total over the entire play, there were in the immediate vicinity of the name (when one pronounces it the English way, of course) some of the consonant or vowel, but above all the consonant, elements, of the name. The effect is like that of communicating vessels, like a diffusion of the consonants of her name in the neighbouring words or, leaving aside the prejudicial metaphor, certain words carried the same consonants, the same vowels as those in her name, and these words, lined up from the beginning to the end of the play, do not comprise a random list, but an accompaniment full of sense: the sense of the name within this play. These words sound out what characterises Ophelia and what constitutes her destiny .

And yet it is not a question, it cannot be a question of relationships of sense. First of all because a proper name has no sense. It is a designation. Anything etymological or descriptive, as in the Bible or in comedy, is obviously excluded from this. And further, because it is not only as units of sense, as words that have sense, that words are active.

At issue is *the continuous between designation and signification*. At issue is the text as system of its own discourse: it does what no other does. The work of the same author included. As a result of which the units in question are no longer entirely units of language. They are the units of a singular discourse. A semantics without semiotics. A poetics.

As such, it is no longer entirely a question of the paronomasia that Roman Jakobson analysed so idiosyncratically and astutely. As soon as paronomasia extends to an entire text, its nature changes. It is no longer of the order of rhetoric. The phonology of language, with the material of which it is constituted, gives no discursive value to its elements. A phoneme has no sense. Only an internal differential value within that language. Of which nothing transfers to pure semantics. But, however, a semiotics for a semantics.

The nature of this issue appears to exclude it from the usual problems of translating. But for the same reason that it appears to be untranslatable – since the phonology of a language is notoriously untranslatable, even Ezra Pound said so – it is essentially excluded from reading, and from sense, from the perception of sense. If we restrict language to sense.

But if we proceed from what exceeds sense, that which transpires ceaselessly, while speaking, without forgetting the body, while reading, while writing, then we have to admit that, in the unknown of language, there are para-semantics, or infra-semantics. Which necessarily evade meaning. Just as *force*, what Cicero called *vis verborum*, exceeds the notion of sense. Bringing to light the epistemological obstacle, paradoxically, that is the notion of sense. And if there is something that language does, even on the periphery of the readable, on the periphery of translating, it is a challenge for translating.

Before seeing if this is a problem of translation, and to what extent, we have to look at how a unit that traverses words functions, a unit that is not of the order of the discontinuous, but a unit of the continuous in the play. Always the relationship between the characters, but a relationship of significance. And I did not go looking, I simply found Ophelia.

This is not the first time that an encounter of this kind has taken place. Without any preconceptions in this regard. I noticed that in Hugo's *Les Travailleurs de la mer* [The Toilers of the Sea],[2] the immediate environment of the name Gilliatt, in its numerous occurrences, included words with the same consonants and which, as a whole, described his character and his fate. Which, in such a novelistic mass, can be neither a random sequence nor the effect of an intention. One would have to postulate, peculiarly, that the writing was one large slip of the tongue. It appears to me, faced with the ungraspable, more judicious to postulate a subject of the poem. That doesn't need to know what it is doing in order to do it, and does it; and you do not need to

---

2. I demonstrated this in *Écrire Hugo*. Henri Meschonnic, *Écrire Hugo, Pour la poétique IV*, (Paris: Gallimard, 1977).

know what it is doing either, nor how, for it to do it to you. Here begins the recitative within the literary, irrespective of what it is, novel, theatre, poem.

This is the poem of the prosody of Ophelia in *Hamlet*. The name of Ophelia has no sense. Or at least it has no identifiable etymology. If it did, this would be of no relevance. In any case, there is no allusion in that sense in the play. It is simply the name of the character who bears it. It is attached to her actions, her passions. But it develops something beyond this – its own signifiance.

This is a semantics of prosody. It makes the prosodic relationships (consonants, vowels) between the name *Ophelia* and the words in its immediate or very close environment, relationships of reciprocal motivation. Here – in *Hamlet* – language itself is a theatre within the theatre. The staging of the name *Ophelia* develops successive motifs of fear, farewell, beauty, the confrontation with Hamlet, as a relationship with her father (and then her brother), suffering, sweetness, sorrow, division from herself, tears, farewell, and love unto death.

Ophelia is named twenty times. Four times by Laertes. By Polonius, five times. Hamlet, five times, two of which are in the letter that Polonius reads; he is also the last one to utter her name. The king, three times – of which one is in the *affront* (the staged confrontation). The queen, three times, plus one where she speaks to her but does not utter her name (V, i, 232) – erasure of her name follows that of her life. Her name also appears four times in the stage directions: *Enter Ophelia* (after II, i, 74), *Lying down at Ophelia's feet* (after III, ii, 105), *Enter Ophelia, distracted, her hair down, singing* (IV, v), and finally *the corpse of Ophelia in an open coffin* (V, i, in the graveyard). I have not taken these into account for the interaction of the name with the signifiers in the dialogue, because these instances are not part of this.

But what merits some attention right away is that *fear*, which marks the entrance of Ophelia's name onto the stage, is uttered twice by the brother guardian of his sister, and once by Ophelia herself, to which she adds *affrighted*. And *dear*, twice by Laertes, once by Hamlet; *tears*, twice by Laertes. *Farewell*, three times – Laertes, Polonius and the queen. But *beautified*, twice, is Hamlet's, and *fair*, twice, Hamlet's alone. With *Nymph*. The king speaks only of her *fair judgment*, and her brother of her *fair and unpolluted flesh*. *Grief* is Polonius. And *sweet*, five times – the queen, Laertes, and the queen on a further three occasions.

I would only add, as a reminder of the signified, that Ophelia is twice qualified with *poor*, by the king and by Laertes.

Ophelia enters the stage in Act I, Scene ii, but remains a mute figure and leaves again. In Scene iii, she is with her brother, and the first word that accompanies, that precedes her name, in her brother's discourse, is that of fear, fear of Hamlet's desire, when her brother entreats her to reject the advances of the prince: '*Fear* it, *Ophelia, fear* it, my *dear* sister / And *keep* you in the *rear* of your *affection*. / Out of the shot and danger of desire' (I, iii, 33–5). A pairing, not insignificant, of *d*anger and *d*esire. Her name starts out framed by fear, and *fear* shares its initial consonant with Ophelia, and pairs in turn with *dear* and *rear*. For sense, Gide put, 'Crains cela, crains cela, ma sœur. Chère Ophélie . . .' and Lepoutre, 'Crains-le, Ophélie, crains-le, ma chère sœur'. If we think back to *horrible Harry*, this would need something like: 'C'est *affreux, Ophélie, affreux*, ma chère sœur'. Or: '*Fuis-le, Ophélie, fuis-le . . .*'.

Then Laertes bids her farewell. In fact, he will see her again only in her madness and she will no longer recognise him – *dramatic irony* (a concept lacking in French literary criticism – that unknowing prophecy of which only the spectator is aware) in[3] '*Farewell, Ophelia*, and remember well / What I have said to you' (I, iii, 84). *Farewell* is a word that Hamlet addresses to Ophelia three times in the course of the staged entrapment (III, i, 134, 139, 141). Laertes's final word to Ophelia is another *Farewell* (I, iii, 87). To which Polonius, in the following line, 'What is't, *Ophelia*, he hath said to you?', adds a further *farewell* to *Ophelia*. The summary of his recommendations, '*In few, Ophelia*, / do not *believe* his vows, for they are brokers . . .' (I, iii, 126), merely repeats the brother's injunctions in the father's suspicion.

Act II, Scene i. Polonius sends Reynaldo away, and the word that he utters, addressed to Reynaldo, the farewell, in the same line where he goes on to address Ophelia, is in direct contact with her name, where it does seem that it is not the destination – in other words, the sense – of the words that counts, in the sphere of signifiers, but their position, and their effect; *farewell*, like *fear*, has the initial syllable of *Ophelia*: '*Pol. Farewell!* [Enter Ophelia] / How now, *Ophelia*, what's the matter?' (II, i, 74). She replies, 'O my lord, my lord, I have been so *affrighted*' (75). A little further on she repeats (86), 'But truly I do *fear* it.'

The name of Ophelia starts her out in fear, and with an advance farewell to life, with a farewell to sensuality. The victim of her brother, her father, the king, and of Hamlet himself, victim in the process of becoming victim.

Then Polonius explains to the queen the cause, in his view, of Hamlet's madness, and reads her Hamlet's letter to Ophelia: 'To the *celestial*, and my *soul's idol*, the most / *beautified Ophelia*' (II, ii, 110). Her father's comment: 'That's an ill phrase, a vile phrase, "beautified" is a vile phrase.' It is in Hamlet's words that Ophelia's beauty is named, through his love, and

---

3. For the text and line references, I follow André Lorant's edition. William Shakespeare, *Hamlet*, trans., with an intro. and notes, by André Lorant (Paris: Aubier, 1988).

beautified, in direct contact with her name, participates in this, through the *f*, just as the name enters into an echo with *idol* and *celestial* through the *l*. Hamlet's letter continues with '*O dear Ophelia*, I am ill at these numbers' (II, ii, 120), which takes up Laertes's *dear*, but on this occasion directly attached to the name, not to the kinship term (*dear sister*). Another love, mixed with the name. This time through vowels.

Act III, the players have arrived, the two spies Rosencrantz and Guildenstern have made their report, the king is going to execute Polonius's plan for observing the encounter arranged between Hamlet and Ophelia. The king says: 'For we have closely sent for Hamlet hither / That he, as 'twere by accident, may here / *Affront Ophelia*. / Her *father* and *myself, lawful espials* . . .' (III, i, 30–3). The entire entrapment is in this *affront*, which distorts the encounter between Hamlet and Ophelia, since she is aware of the plan and since Hamlet has guessed but pretends not to know. This time, the system of signifiers that will kill off love and those who love each other is what makes with the name *Ophelia* the same system of significance.

This is what the queen addresses to Ophelia: 'And *for* your part, *Ophelia*, I do wish / That your good beauties be the happy cause / Of Hamlet's wildness' (III, i, 39–41). Thus, contrary to her desire, she makes Ophelia's participation in Hamlet's 'madness' enter into the name. Which her father succeeds in exacerbating, by insisting, '*Ophelia*, walk you *here*' (III, i, 44). This is what, in the same verse, he addresses to the king: 'Gracious, so please you, / We will bestow ourselves' ['gagnant notre retraite', Lorant says]. Ophelia is, *here*, the bait for Hamlet.

The old advisor, who can only hide himself (twice: this time with the king to spy on Ophelia and Hamlet; then with the queen to observe Hamlet, and the second time will prove fatal), hide himself and advise others to hide, has no idea of the extent to which he speaks the truth when he utters that this feigned devotion conceals an evil principle: ''Tis too much proved, that with devotion's visage / And pious action we do sugar o'er / The devil himself' (III, i, 48–50). This will effectively be the result of his ruse.

This is the moment at which Hamlet enters with his bitter tirade on death and life, but which changes theme and tone when he sees Ophelia – who softens his torments: '*Soft* you now, / The *fair Ophelia! Nymph*, in thy orisons / Be all my sins remembered' (III, i, 89–91). A prosodic superlative – three signifiers in direct succession to communicate her beauty (*fair*), the divinity of youth and femininity (*nymph*) and softness, three words away from the name of Ophelia, which through this becomes the signifier in its own right. But straight away Hamlet rigs the game, since the game is rigged in advance anyway, with his sarcasm, which turns love into offence and obscenity. This is the first of two passages containing three terms; the second will take place in the graveyard. The conclusion that of the opposite of love, Ophelia, who has remained alone, finishes on: 'O, woe is me, [a series whose main vowel is almost that of her own name] / T'have seen what I have seen, see what I see!' (III, i, 161–2).

The king has not been fooled by the excesses of Hamlet's language and does not attribute them in the slightest to the madness of love. Polonius is less clear, with his repetitive rhetoric, and completely contradicts his earlier advice: 'But yet do I believe / The origin and commencement of his *grief* / Sprung *from neglected love.* – How now, *Ophelia*?' (III, i, 176–8). *Grief* is an inverted echo of *Ophelia*, Hamlet's sadness is a counter-rhyme to Ophelia's name. And through this becomes in part, with *from neglected love*, Ophelia's very sorrow.

Scene ii, the performance of the players, Hamlet 'lying down at *Ophelia's feet*'. Then, the psychodrama having all too well succeeded, with Hamlet summoned by his mother, hidden Polonius killed by Hamlet, the queen is told of Ophelia's madness, who reappears (IV, v): 'Enter Ophelia, distracted, her hair down, singing', doubly mad, mad with sorrow (for her dead father, for her lost love), and insane.

The queen addresses her. Ophelia replies: 'Where is the *beauteous* majesty of Denmark?' (IV, v, 21). The queen: 'How now, *Ophelia*?' (22). A double reversal of beauty: she is no longer it and it is that of the queen, not of Ophelia. The commentaries say that Ophelia does not recognise the queen.

Then four verses of song, higgledy-piggledy, in other words with all the sense of a reversal of sense – this is precisely the role played by *fatrasie* – here the recognition that 'true love' has turned into false love, and that all appearances are turned upside down: 'How should I your true love know / From another one?' To which the queen replies, remaining within the sphere of common sense, which understands only sense: 'Alas, *sweet* lady, what imports this song?' (27). The second song speaks of the death of her father: 'He is dead and gone, lady, / He is dead and gone, / At his head a grass-green turf, / At his *heels a stone.* / O, Ho!' (32–3). The queen: 'Nay, but *Ophelia*' (34). This time, it is the signifiers of death that are closely related to and echo the name *Ophelia*.

The other songs mix the death of her father and the loss of her love; licentious words, out of place in Ophelia's mouth, also mark the loss of love. An inversion of Hamlet's sarcasm. The king, who enters after the second song, intervenes with a brief: 'Pretty *Ophelia*!' (54) – 'gentille', translates André Lorant. Ophelia continues, though she only replies: '*Indeed*, la? Without an oath, I'll make an end on't' (57). Where the *indeed*, connected via the echo of the vowel with *Ophelia*, signals, confirms, through the derision of the indecency, an end to love, and turns Hamlet's indecency towards her against him: '[*Sings*] By Gis and by Saint-Charity, Alack, and *fie for* shame! / Young men will do't, if they come to't, / By Cock, they are to blame' (58–61).

Ophelia leaves. Her words are half-rational, 'My brother shall know of it', a clear threat of revenge – half-insane: 'Come, my coach! Good night, ladies, good night. Sweet ladies, good night, good night.' André Lorant thinks that she is imagining 'being the wife of the heir apparent'. What is said without being said is that she is going out into the night. In all senses of the word *night*.

When the king considers the situation, in speaking to the queen, he reproaches himself for having buried Polonius in secret, he experiences Ophelia's madness as a misfortune that heralds further misfortunes: 'and we have done but greenly / In hugger-mugger to inter him; poor *Ophelia* / Divided *from herself* and her *fair* judgment, / Without the which we are pictures, or *mere beasts*' (IV, v, 83–6). Lorant translates *fair*, for the judgement, as 'clair'. One can see clearly here how a grasp of signifiers is a completely different thing to a grasp of the sense of words and their grammatical classification into empty words or full words. There is no word more full of significance here than this *from*, 'divided *from herself*', with the two consonants of the name *Ophelia*. The very definition of madness, this division from herself, entering into the composition of the name *Ophelia* through its consonants, just as the name spreads through the expression that designates it, this reciprocal expansion of the one into the other transforms the name into a second signifier, which ceaselessly transforms itself in this way from the beginning to the end of the name's presence in the piece.

Laertes returns, demands an account of the death of his father, sees Ophelia enter, mad: 'O *hear*, dry up my brains! *Tears* seven times salt / Burn out the sense and virtue of mine eye! / By heaven, the madness *shall* be paid with weight, / *Till* our *scale* turn the *beam*. O rose of *May*, / Dear *maid*, kind sister, *sweet Ophelia*! / O heavens, is't *possible* a young *maid's* wits / Should be as *mortal* as an *old* man's *life*?' (IV, v, 157–63). The *Ophelia*-system is far from being the only one here: other pairings create alliances between signifiers. Those of *maid* and *May*, even though they are not part of the composition of the name *Ophelia*, qualify Ophelia in an important fashion, since they associate her with the virginity of youth and everything that is culturally evoked by the month of May. Otherwise, what dominates is a semantic sequence that connects tears, affection (*dear*), sweetness and death. The death of her spirit prepares her physical death, whereas Laertes is thinking only of the death of his father.

The preparations of the king and Laertes to kill Hamlet. The queen enters, bearing the news of Ophelia's death by drowning. The queen's entire speech mixes Ophelia with the watery element, water already mixed with water through the element of tears – the river too is 'in tears' ('Fell into the weeping brook') and Ophelia is 'mermaid-like' ('like a nymph', Lorant translates) and in effect *mermaid* is the mythological equivalent, the divinity of the waters, of the *nymph* (Greek), a word with which Hamlet qualifies Ophelia. Who becomes 'like a creature native and indued / Unto that element' (IV, vii, 180–1), as if death was the return to her element. Laertes's reaction, a rhetoric as bombastic and in bad taste as his father's, but on the same theme, feigns (but in vain, he is crying) not to add to her the water of his tears, so as not to drown her even more, no doubt, which is what the text says in the first quarto: 'Too much of water hast thou, Ofelia; / Therefore I will not drown thee in my tears'. The folio by contrast: 'Too much of water hast thou, poor *Ophelia*, / And *therefore* I *forbid* my *tears*' (IV, vii, 186–7). Here again the grammar logic, which destroys tears, comes into conflict with the signifiers which the negation (*forbid*) has only presented, made present, all the more and which mix tears and the name of Ophelia.

But everything, in *Hamlet*, is under the sign, not even veiled, of signifiers: the Norman who praises Laertes's fencing is called *Lamord* (IV, vii, 92).

Act V, in the graveyard, Scene i. The king, the queen, Laertes accompany Ophelia's corpse, 'the corpse of *Ophelia* in an open coffin'. Laertes says, at three verses' remove from the name *Ophelia* uttered by Hamlet: 'And *from* her *fair* and *unpolluted flesh* / *May violets* spring' (V, i, 227). For the guardian of his sister, the beauty and freshness of flesh are disassociated from love. A different spring is called forth. Laertes has already manipulated the violet, 'A violet in the youth of primy nature' (I, iii, 7), to distance Ophelia from a spring love. As for the violets of which Ophelia spoke, 'they withered all when my father died' (IV, v, 184–5).

It is only at that moment that hidden Hamlet understands that it is Ophelia who is being buried: 'What, the *fair Ophelia*!' (V, i, 231). And the queen says: '[Scattering flowers] *Sweets* to the *sweet*. *Farewell.* / I hoped thou shouldst have been my Hamlet's *wife*. / I thought thy bride-bed to have decked, *sweet maid*, / And not t'have strewed thy grave' (232–5). This is the longest chain of *Ophelia* signifiers in direct proximity (they are more dispersed in Laertes's words a few lines above, 157–63). What is remarkable is that *sweet*, repeated, is caught between *fair* and *farewell*, and in this prosodic figure Ophelia's portrait and destiny coalesce. She is the character, I believe, who is most regularly bade adieu in *Hamlet*. And she begins and finishes more or less – but this more or less seems to me to be crucial – on *Farewell*: Laertes's *Farewell* (I, iii, 84) naming Ophelia for the second time, and that of the queen, next to the grave.

But there is Hamlet's final rejoinder. Laertes has thrown himself into the open grave, uttering words of such a rhetorical turn that they make

Hamlet emerge from his hiding place. According to the stage directions of the first quarto, he also throws himself into Ophelia's grave and, rivalling Laertes for bombast, he declares his love for Ophelia: 'I *loved Ophelia. Forty* thousand brothers / Could not, with all their quantity of *love* / Make up my sum' (V, i, 257). Here too one can distinguish between the rhetorical figure (hyperbole, or exaggeration), the sense of the words (the lack of relationship between 'Ophelia' and 'forty') and the reciprocal implication of a continued paronomasia, threading through the entire play such that it exceeds rhetoric to become poetics: a system of the text, a serial semantics. Here, hyper-conspicuously, Hamlet's love enters into Ophelia's name, and surrounds it, but both in death and beyond death.

The end of the name *Ophelia* in *Hamlet*. When, at the end of the duel rigged by the duke, Hamlet dies of poisoning, he evokes for Horatio the 'wounded name' that he will leave behind him if Horatio does not tell, 'O God, Horatio, what a wounded name, / Things standing thus unknown, shall I leave behind me!' (V, ii, 335–6). The name of Ophelia is therefore also a *wounded name*.

Discovering new readings is something that happens all the time. All one needs is a new perspective. This is the task of a poetics of rhythm, and of the continuous within language. Not only of hermeneutics. Not the same thing. Nor in the same way. And the creation of a new problem.

Among other things, a problem of translation. Insurmountable to the extent that *Belle Ophélie* no longer does anything like *Fair Ophelia*. What remains are approximations, towards other signifiers, barely translations in the current sense of the word: *frêle Ophélie, folle Ophélie*. That one can legitimately judge unacceptable. But then one doesn't want to see the problem either.

The mismatch contributes to making it mute. For example, when such a simple word – but everything that is *simple* is mistakenly simple – as *sweet*, used five times in the play with regard to Ophelia, is sometimes translated by André Lorant as *douce*: 'sweet lady' (IV, v, 27), says the queen, 'douce dame'; but *aimable Ophélie*, when it is Laertes (IV, v, 161), for 'sweet Ophelia'; and *douce* again, 'À la douce, ces fleurs douces' (V, i, 232) and 'douce fille' (234) for 'Sweets to the sweet' and 'sweet maid'.

It is about opening up problems of translating. Not closing them down. The conceptuality of the discontinuous of language closes them down. It is more fruitful for translating to put to work the significance, the semantic plurality of prosody. Which also raises the question of *why* we translate – of what we understand a translation to do.

PART 5

MODERNITY

The text of this section is taken from Henri Meschonnic's *Modernité modernité* (Modernity Modernity) from 1988 (Lagrasse: Verdier; new edition Paris: Gallimard, 1993, pp. 9–20). It constitutes the introduction to Meschonnic's dealings with the debate on modernity and, by extension, on post-modernity, on which he published a further monograph (*Pour sortir du postmoderne*, Paris: Klincksieck, 2009) and an edited volume (Meschonnic/Shiguehiko Hasumi, *La Modernité après le post-moderne*, Paris: Maisonneuve & Larose, 2002). He thus attacks the strong post-modern movement of the time as a misconception of the modern, against which he accentuates the on-going validity of a certain understanding of modernity, an understanding which operates beyond the categories of chronology and newness.

From the outset Meschonnic presents modernity as a battle and links it to the question of the subject, very much the central issue of the time and, of course, of Meschonnic's theory of rhythm. The notion of modernity, as Meschonnic understands it after a rereading of Baudelaire and Rimbaud, overflows the binarism and couplings of the sign and shows its limitations. Modernity becomes one of the central terms that demonstrates how his theory of language is key to every aspect of society, even though it mostly goes unnoticed. By changing all concepts – for instance, the one of rhythm – into the organisation of a discourse by a subject, Meschonnic arrives at a redefinition of poetics: not as the study of the functioning of literature, but as a poetics of society. This is related to the notion of modernity, understood not as historicism but as historicity, when modernity results from the past and at the same time being the infinity of sense. In his definition, a critique of modernity implies an understanding of what a subject is. Since modernity then becomes the present which remains present, it is another concept that allows us to think poetics as he developed it.

12

Modernity is a Battle

(in *Modernité modernité* (Modernity Modernity) from 1988 (Lagrasse: Verdier; new edition Paris: Gallimard, 1993, pp. 9–20).

Translated by Chantal Wright

Modernity is a battle. Endlessly beginning over again. Because it is a nascent state, indefinitely nascent, of the subject, its history, its sense. It endlessly leaves established thought[1] in its wake, those whose ideas are arrested, have arrested themselves, and who conflate their former youth with the ageing of the world. Modernity borders this cemetery of fossilised concepts with which we are encumbered. And which make us deaf. Deaf to what is coming.

Wanting to know what modernity is, I realised that it was the subject within us. Which is to say, the weakest point in the chain that holds art, literature, society together. In their practices, their concepts. The weakest because it is not included in the sign. Because it escapes it. Escapes its power. But this power extends everywhere and the only possible place for a critique of the sign is simultaneously closed off by the parade of the sign. The doubles of the individual and the social. In columns of two. From language to society, the same old game of the concepts of dualism. Which passes off the individual for the subject, to conflate them better, and, from its sacralisations to its fragmentations, to uphold the traditional theory of reason better. Its divisions, its accommodations.

Which makes art and literature the weak point of society and the sign in fact the strong point of a critique. The attempt to recognise the strategies and the stakes in the role-plays constituted by modes of thinking, of seeing, of feeling and the conservation of thought, of seeing, of feeling which direct

---

1. [Translator's note: Meschonnic writes 'les Assis de la pensée' here, most probably referring to the poem 'Les Assis' by Arthur Rimbaud, which describes the well-established bourgeoisie unwilling to change or move.]

ostentatious or hidden struggles. In the indiscernible reign of the sign and its values, which arrange themselves, in our world, according to the dual and tested schema of transcendence, indefinitely pure, the very operation of purity, and empirical forms, in turn exhaustible exhausted, of history.

Through which all the pairings (linguistic, philosophical, theological, anthropological, social, political) of the sign constitute a theologics of society. Much more than a scientific model of language. Part of that is the traditional opposition between the new and the old, farce and miracle of rupture.

One does not get out of it by rushing from one term to the other, by pitting the individual against the social, the ancient against the modern, any more than by pitting convention against nature, where language is concerned. Because it is the relation that holds the terms, not the terms that hold the relation. And this relation is the chain, the schema of the sign.

And yet this supposedly universal schema (cultural, historical) is constantly overflowed by the smallest word that one utters. Its fragility is figured in every poem, every work of art. Its weakness is its explicatory capacity. Its strength is pragmatic, political. Schema, in the sense of the organisation of something that is fixed, and frozen.

What overflows this schema is rhythm. Modernity. An atheologics of the subject. Irreducible to teleologies. Which nevertheless endlessly exert themselves to reconvert it into older modes. But this century will have notoriously made identity undergo alterity. Practices of translating those of ethnology, intercultural relations the pluralisation of the subject.

Art and literature, the poem in particular, will have exposed the fact that the poetics of the subject is a politics of rhythm. What takes place in the ostensible functioning and imperceptible ensemble of practices and concepts reveals what a society makes of sense, of history, and of the subject, through the concept-masks of the individual and the social.

This is why the theory of language has such a large role. It is the major site of foundation and battle for the radical historicity of sense and of society. Which is elaborated, following Humboldt and Saussure, and passes via Benveniste. Benveniste wrote that language serves for living. I will say that the theory of language, through the history and the status of the concepts a society lives with, and more than other social sciences, even economics and technology, which are generally judged much more vital, serves for living. Poetically and politically.

It is only seemingly a matter for specialists. There is not a phrase of a sociologist, of a psychologist, of a historian, or of a politician where it fails to exert its effects. All the more visible for going unnoticed by those who are speaking. Its role is crucial for understanding what we mean by modernity. For recognising it. Recognising ourselves in it. And through this even, perhaps only through this, becoming a subject of language. Of history. Of sense.

Which I also wanted to show. Working on an ethics of language muddled by have-you-seen-mes and fashionable imposters. This work, for pleasure.

Theory is not the serious place that we believe it to be. It is Guignol. Bluster solemnly disputes this. Personae. Masks. Roll up roll up, and you will see. Grasping how they move, and even animating them oneself, that is pleasure. The play has only just started. However one approaches it, one always arrives at the beginning. The play has no end, of course. No moral either. Maybe not having an end is the moral. We are all simultaneously spectators and actors in it.

To understand modernity, I had to retranslate certain words for myself. Because they spoke the language of the past, the language of the sign. From the start they returned the unknown to the known: the poem to *la langue*, the subject to the individual, modernity to the conflict between the old and the new. Which is to say, a return to the old ways.

Rhythm, understood as the formal schema of metric alternation, inscribed in the sign, has become the organisation of a discourse by a subject, so that all discourse manifests this subject, and so that this subject is organised by its discourse. Which overflows the sign. Culturally, rhetorically, poetically. Through which it can appear that the sign elicits a social metrics.

Poetics, initially the study of the functioning of literature, passing through recognition of the statuses of language, the strategies and stakes to which it gives occasion, becomes through this a poetics of society. A poetics of modernity. In which it remains itself. It is always a question of the poem. In the poem, it is a question of the subject, of its sense, its history, allegorically.

Of historicity. I wanted to show that this is one of the aspects of modernity. Both the always present and the contradiction held with everything that makes a moment, and that this moment passes. Not the dating. But together resulting from the past and the infinity of sense.

The classic trap of the sign is to take historicity for historicism – either that the only explanation is found through history, which reduces sense to the conditions of the production of sense, and infinity to a totalisation; or a variant, mere filiation, a progressive linearity. Where nothing takes account of the new. Thus transcendence dismisses historicity with historicism.

Working to recognise the effects and the how of discourses (and the concepts of discourse, masked by those of the sign and of *langue*), I learned to distinguish between polemic and critique by comparing them: polemic, a strategy of domination and conservation of strength; critique, a strategy of the recognition of strategies, and of sense.

And just as for historicism conflated with historicity, the strategy of the sign is to pass off critique as a polemic. Like this, it is on its own ground, that of strength. Where it doesn't have to reply. Nor even to listen. This too is Guignol.

Critique is this strategy, because it postulates not only the reciprocal involvement of language and history, of language and literature, but also of art and society. A mode of relation that rejects and consigns to the past regionalisations, habitual separations. What Horkheimer called traditional theory: it upholds society just as it is. I will add: it upholds theory just as it is. Critical theory is a traverser. Here, in the sense to which I am adhering, I am undertaking a critique of modernity.

I am not adding a voice to the chorus of those who proclaim its end. Because through that they settle it in its place. You know which fate Guignol reserves for them.

But the subject, what do you understand by the subject? I am looking for it, in looking for what modernity is.

To do this I had to dissociate what the enemies as much as the partisans of modernity conflate: avant-garde, and modernity. I reread Baudelaire, Rimbaud. They are invoked for the wrong reasons. As we had done with our Mallarmé. Once more modernity overflows the moderns.

The contemporary constantly runs after modernity. It does not always reach it. It is not the contemporary. Appears sometimes to fall short, then to go beyond. Uncatchable.

The old is a contemporary of the modern: sorcery in France, today. Magic, in advertising. Once again one takes what is new, the latest thing, for the modern.

Modernity is life. The faculty of the present. Which makes the inventions of thinking, feeling, seeing, of hearing it, the invention of forms of life. This is why there can be an after-modernism, not an after-modernity. Modernity is what reappears beneath all the stuffiness. Even in the 'petite vie' Baudelaire spoke of.

In a society that is moving backwards towards its future, by contemplating itself in its past, for the same reason which makes it privilege technoscientific adventure and the short term of plans of profitability rather than the long term of societal projects, the modernity of the subject is perhaps what prevents collectivity from becoming the programming of the individual.

Modernity is the projection of what it is to be in the present. The present, for the majority, is bound by the network of interests and powers, the network of conservation of the past.

Modernity is its utopia: this for which there is no space. Today, for example, the invention of a relation between culture and technology which emerges from the antagonistic coupling of adherence and rejection. And that relegates to the museum the syncretic sacred where Heidegger blends technocracy and dehumanisation, by placing under the same category of 'technology' the industrialisation of agriculture, the Nazi industry of death and the atomic bomb, in the past or to come.

The link between modernity and utopia creates, for example, a sort of active absence, like that of the educational project of the Ideologues, centred on letters and the humanities, sealed off by the Napoleonic techno-scientific model to the present day. A politics and a poetics of the subject. Against the rhetoric of the short term, a poetics of the long term.

Modernity, future of the present. I oppose it to another modernity. That which is made up of the history of modern art. Rather, of a certain manner of writing it. Which conflates art with the history of art.

End of the avant-gardes, the disappearance of resistances, the disappearance of challenge, the disappearance of faith in progress (among certain people, at the beginning of the century) or in art as religion, access to the sacred – and here we have the modern in the past.

Once again, the most recent arrivals more modern than the preceding ones, the have-been-moderns. Today, one is post-.

One seems to have more nostalgias than certitudes. To know less than before where one stands. One is furiously eclectic, and cynical. One does what one knows. Because one knows (too much) what one does. I am speaking of the post-moderns. The story of art-demystification-of-art, of art-rejection-of-art, devours everything. Cynicism for some, retreat for others.

There is also some anti- in the post-. Those who turn the past into a thesaurus. Who have no other future than the past. One can moreover reconcile the hyper-moderns and the anti-moderns: just as the post- are the neo-, and that they therefore constituted the ex-moderns as classical, they are all neo-classical. The patron of the neo-classical, Marcel Duchamp. See further on.[2]

Thus the post- is a we-have-seen-it-all-already. This is the farce that Nietzsche played to the century: he pulled the old Eternal Return trick on us. And how many fell for it. The salutary aspect: a rejection of theologies, religious or romantic. Because one no longer believes in them. The rejection of the history of art as 'sacred history' – 'our local tribal myth'.[3]

---

2. [Translator's note: Meschonnic will go on to deal with Duchamp in more detail at a later stage in *Modernité, modernité*.]
3. Thomas McEvilley, 'Art History or Sacred History?', in *Art and Discontent* (Kingston, NY: McPherson, 1991), pp. 133–67, p. 164. The cyclical analogy makes him evoke 'Alexandrian post-Modernism and late Roman Republican Modernism' (ibid., p. 141), but it is also a vigorous and erudite demonstration of the ignorance surrounding Antiquity, where perspective was concerned, which was rediscovered, rather than invented, in the Renaissance.

But the rejection of a sense-of-history, the atheological dissociation of *sense* and of *history*, dissociates history or rather the two senses of sense, that of *direction* and that of *intelligibility*, or rather only the first sense.

It is precisely the presupposition that these two senses of sense are indissociable, if not one and the same, which creates both sacred history and the crisis of sense in society. By upholding the two, or rejecting the two.

The typically post-modern position consists in driving the two meanings of sense together. With the alternative: sacred history or the 'pagan view', defined as 'there is nowhere to go but here' (ibid., p. 163). The 'realisation' is only a realisation of 'the present as the only living moment, affirming the loss of meaningful purpose and continuity as a liberation' (ibid.). I will return elsewhere to all these neo-paganisms with which we are being repaganised.[4]

But, postulating and endlessly verifying the necessary, reciprocal implication of language and history, I will say: it is only from sense as teleology that history can and must separate itself, so as not to recreate sacred history. To undo its eternal double game, transcendence of values and dereliction of history. To understand it, to cease to be its plaything, does not at all eliminate sense as intelligibility.

To eliminate it, or to aspire to do so (which could only be partial, and would return to localise, to flocculate sense) leads to a pseudo-liberation, an amnesia dedicated not to liberty but to a repetition of the same. The Eternal Return creates the substitute myth of sacred history: 'a return of an oscillation that has returned many times'.[5] The poetics of the feint, and of the ruse.

No more history. There is nothing more but time: 'History no longer seems to have any shape, nor does it seem any longer to be going any place in particular. [*It*] has dissolved into mere time, into Averroes's endless succession of moments without overall shape or direction' (ibid., p. 162).

Only there is one thing that post-modern detheologisation has not eliminated. This thing cancels the effect of its operation, unwittingly, in the same instant. It is the dualism of the sign. Its entire paradigm is there, this parade returns, this dance of the vampires to which all the replicas of form and of sense go in couples.

Thus the post-modernist proposes rewriting the history of art 'in terms of content', after those of 'form' (ibid., p. 165), without seeing that they have upheld traditional theory. Because it is traditional theory that was holding them. Differentiating between time and history presupposes the couple individual/social. The psychological and the sociological. Remaining in the individual, instead of going towards the subject. And the individual all the

---

4. In *L'Utopie du juif* [The Utopia of the Jew] (Paris: Desclée de Brouwer, 2001)
5. McEvilley, 'Art History or Sacred History?', p. 135.

more cut off from the social, and from the political, than time is cut off from history.

Through the subject, and in it, there is inseparably time and history, a present that is not 'the loss of continuity', but a permanent rewriting of the relations between continuity and discontinuity, which doesn't find its place in any of the categories of the discontinuous alone, which reigns in the sign. As Walter Benjamin wrote in 1940: 'History is the subject of a construction whose site is not homogenous, empty time, but time filled full by now-time.'[6] Which also holds to the proposition according to which: 'The concept of life is given its due only if everything that has a history of its own, and is not merely the setting for history, is credited with life.'[7]

Present, sense, subject – three different terms to approach a historicity that leaves in the past the dualism where partners oppose each other only to uphold the relation that makes them deaf to one another better, signifier against signified, individual against society.

The post-modern continues to play this comedy. We will also assist the anti-moderns. There are no two modernities the same. When I repeat: modernity modernity, the second word is not yet finished and modernity has already changed. This is why there is nothing there except for the clever Dicks of the day.

The laughter whose echo resounds into the future is that of the present which remains present. Modernity, that is this presence.

Modernity of Modernity

Who has been more modern than us? Who has pushed further the illusion that the past is *passé*, that the past's only role is to lead to us? But which epoch has also cultivated, to this extent, the idea that modernity, through being us, was behind us.

In writing about modernity, it is ourselves that we reflect upon, narcissistic, these recent times but regrets or blows that disturb our reflection. Modern post-modern immodern. Modernity is the sickness of the century. The new is not enough for it. The feeling of a new beginning. Of a change of the sense of words such that one no longer has bearings. No longer has partitions.

---

6. Walter Benjamin, 'On the Concept of History', trans. by Harry Zohn, in Howard Eiland and Michael W. Jennings (eds), *Walter Benjamin: Selected Writings*, vol. 4 (Cambridge, MA: The Belknap Press, 2006), pp. 389–411, p. 395.
7. Walter Benjamin, 'The Task of the Translator', trans. by Harry Zohn, in Marcus Bullock and Michael W. Jennings (eds), *Walter Benjamin: Selected Writings*, vol. 1 (Cambridge, MA: The Belknap Press, 2004), pp. 253–63, p. 255.

Modernity is not a movement. Cannot be conflated with any of those that one enumerates. Modernity is critique, and inverts itself into critique of modernity. It is provocation. But provocation, in itself, is not modern. One can never exhaust counting its faults and its true beginnings. From the new to the déjà vu.

In the constant we-do-not-yet-know-what-is-going-to-happen, we cry out at the crisis. The crisis of sense, of course. As if the world had always known where it is going. And for art, or writing, it is better not to know too much.

From the rejection of values to the marketplace of values, this is where art is situated. The challenge, the revolt, the creation of fables – a party with nibbles. An investment. The discourse on modernity no longer seems made up of anything but clichés that emerge one after the other, like frogs and snakes from the mouth of the young girl in Perrault's fairy-tale.

Yet the question that Aragon poses in his 'Introduction to 1930' cannot but return – 'What is modern today?'

The idea of the modern is so conflictual, promoted by that of creativity, or repudiated for contradictory motifs, that it is impossible for it to be objective. Avant-garde or museum, ancient artefact or terminus of history, it is continuous with itself even for those who disavow it.

Composed of forgotten or on-going scandals, of belated effects that work in the imperceptible, modernity reveals what we cannot understand, and try to hide through every form of knowledge. It is the collision of the modern and the contemporary. But we do not have the same present nor the same future according to whether we have had, or did not have, the same history. We do not have the same language.

Literature, and particularly poetry, has been the material of transformations in what language has been made to say, in a way that the relationship of the visual to the oral has been transformed in it, modifying each of the terms themselves. The sign has exploded, and has become rhythm. The thought of language too has been radically changed. The practices of the visible have invented a new historicity.

It is because all of society passes in and through language that the theory of language is the sense of its sense, the history of its history. Its dramas, its bluffs, its betrayals. From the radically historical to dehistoricisation. Its relationship to the cosmic, its relationship to the social.

Because literature – poetry – is within language that which is most sensitive to the pressures of the epoch, to the tensions of the known and the unknown, the subjective and the collective, it is what is most revelatory of language and of the social. Of their practices, their theories. And from this the games that lead into the current mode of modernity can be best perceived. Speaking of modernity, I am speaking of poetics. The poetics of the subject, the poetics of society.

Structuralism has been, and is still, the scientific ideology of serialisation, of formalism. Legitimising the bricolage of the skilful in literature. A scholastics of a Limousin schoolboy.[8] Education is infested by this substitution. Generalised semiotics has aggravated its dualism. Modernity likes to play Peirce against Saussure. Believing that it is following Saussure, it has chosen Peirce. The universal of the ahistorical and misleading sign, against the historicity of language.

Modernity likes to recognise itself in the figure of a hero. It triumphs everywhere, eponymous demi-gods, founding fathers. Reducing poetry emblematically to a single poet, philosophy to a single philosopher. The institution of the Nobel is the annual ephemeral illustration of this socialisation. Jakobson crowns Khlebnikov *the* poet of the twentieth century. For some, Heidegger is *the* philosopher of the century. A consensus is spreading today, in a significant manner, around the philosopher of consensus, Habermas, who reduces language to communication. Like fashion, modernity is eclectic. Eclecticism is a mask of dogmatism. There too we see what we make of language.

One of the dangers of anti-art, of the anti-work – not their initial appearance, but the tradition that issues from them – is to prepare the return of Sainte-Beuve. Of the pair of ancient beauties made up of psychologism and sociologism. This effect-of-theory of the sign. Well, one of the beginnings of modernity is Proust's *Contre Sainte-Beuve*. Linked to a practice and to a recognition of the work. And the passage from the notion of the work to that of practice, one of the traits of modernity, tends to present this research into specificity as outmoded. Which is apparent in this statement by Michel Butor: 'For a certain period it was considered "modern" to draw a complete separation between the work and the life of a writer; today nothing is more outmoded since the very notion of the work disappears to the benefit of the practice, the adventure etc. And it is not even that of *a* writer any more, one's own expression, rather it is always collective.'[9]

The modernity of the twentieth century represents itself, or is represented, in opposition to everything that precedes it. An anti-nineteenth

---

8. [Translator's note: In Rabelais, Pantagruel encounters a student, originally from the rural region of Limousin, who pretentiously 'enriches' his French with diverse Latin elements. Rabelais ridicules this counterfeit French, and the episode ends with a victory for the common usage of language.]
9. Michel Butor and Georges Raillard, 'Entretien sur la notion de modernité', *Cahiers du 20ᵉ siècle*, 5 (1975), p. 111.

century. More intelligent than the nineteenth, which passes for a stupid century. This impertinence is not deflated everywhere. It needs some help. Not so much to rectify a few misconceptions, which is what specialists do, as to untangle the mass of confusions that ended up seeming the veritable truth by virtue of being repeated. The mass of clichés about modernity and clichés of modernity. Which believe, for example, that they define the art of today without seeing that they talk about it like the art of always.

Modernity is a symptom. In which power is at stake. At the same time, unknown to itself. Indivisible, and irreducible to unity. It is its own myth: that of rupture. And its perverse deformation: the new. Conflated with the avant-garde, by many, even though disillusionment gives the allure of lucidity, belatedly. Therefore still illusory. Always that nineteenth-century dualism.

Whence the re-examination here of the sense of modernity, such as it is assumed to be today, continuous with Baudelaire, with Rimbaud. Cares that mask a deviation from sense, precisely where the conflict leads, a concealed conflict, from the modern and from the contemporary.

These elements put in their place may allow for a blow-by-blow analysis of the arguments of the partisans and adversaries of a modernity that has as many senses as it has partisans and adversaries. Those who put it in a museum. Those who put it in Vienna. Those who endlessly proclaim the end of something which changes name from time to time, but which in any case is at its end. Historicism, universalism, those two beautiful things of the nineteenth century, barely changed, are still there. Hegel is still there.

The comedy of the post-modern plays out in verbal one-upmanship and a love of blurriness that delight its worldly roles. Fairground thinkers lecture us. Even ethics is fashionable. Decidedly, one has to take care of everything.

This is why I hold on to the poem, like Dante holding Virgil by the hand – don't laugh, I know, the comparison is outmoded, worthy of Hugo, who was as stupid as his century –, traversing the hell of the modern. It is however at the same time the only opportunity we have to have language and its subject hold on to one another, and perhaps this crossing itself is a name, the only one that resists, of modernity.

PART 6
HISTORICITY AND SOCIETY

The following texts are taken from the posthumous volume *Langage, histoire, une même théorie* (Lagrasse: Verdier, 2012) (Language, History, One and the Same Theory), a book already mentioned as work in progress in *Critique du rythme* in 1982. This volume assembles texts from over three decades but all three of those chosen for this Reader seem to have been written for the 2012 publication and had not been published before. They are *For a Poetics of Historicity* (in *Langage, histoire*, pp. 55–8), *Rhythm, Theory of Language, Poetics of Society* (pp. 59–76) and *Realism, Nominalism: The Theory of Language is a Theory of Society* (pp. 717–26). They represent the ambition of Meschonnic's work from its very beginning: that is, to develop a theory of language that establishes a new basis for all the humanities and social sciences by overthrowing the reign of the sign in our episteme.

He focuses here on the connection between language and history through his notion of historicity, which is a situatedness that constantly leaves this situation and remains active in the presence. Only poetics, an awareness of what language is and does, he argues, enables to think beyond the sign and to develop a critical theory: that is, a theory aware of its situatedness. Meschonnic connects language to historicity, the political and the ethical. In the 'Meschonnic's Poetics of Society' introductory chapter, I refer widely to these texts.

13

For a Poetics of Historicity

(in *Langage, histoire, une même théorie,* Lagrasse: Verdier, 2012, pp. 55–8)

Translated by Marko Pajević

> *Die Geschichte ist Gegenstand einer Konstruktion, deren Ort nicht die homogene und leere Zeit sondern die von Jetztzeit erfüllte bildet.*[1]
> (History is the subject of a structure whose site is not homogeneous, empty time, but time filled by the presence of the now [Jetztzeit].)
>
> Walter Benjamin

The initial question of this book is twofold: is there a necessary, reciprocal relation between the theory of language and the theory of history? And what theory of history is needed for a radically historical theory of language? Victor Klemperer, in *LTI*,[2] had shown the strong connection that exists between language and history.

What is in question is the intelligibility of the connections between history and meaning that we need to think. The notions of Sense. It is this link that I have striven to think since the beginning of *Critique du rythme: anthropologie historique du langage*.[3]

I define critique as the work of recognising strategies, stakes, historicities. No connection, as I never stop saying, with polemics. Critique is *philological*, in the sense of Socrates: it loves discussion. Polemics keeps silent about the adversary, in order to be right. What follows is the equivalence that thinking

---

1. Walter Benjamin, 'Über den Begriff der Geschichte', *Gesammelte Schriften*, vol. I (Frankfurt am Main: Suhrkamp, 1980), p. 701. ('Theses on the Philosophy of History', in *Illuminations*, pp. 255–66, p. 263.)
2. Victor Klemperer, *LTI: Notizbuch eines Philologen* (Berlin: Aufbau, 1947). In English, *Language of the Third Reich: LTI: Lingua Tertii Imperii* (New York and London: Continuum, 2006).
3. Henri Meschonnic, *Critique du rythme: anthropologie historique du langage* (Lagrasse: Verdier, 1982).

equals critique equals liberty. Calling thinking that which renews thought. Against the maintenance of order. From which it must be recognised that any knowledge produces its ignorance, does not know that it produces it, and hence prevents its being recognised.

An example? The logico-grammatical punctuation of the nineteenth century impressed upon the texts of the sixteenth, seventeenth, eighteenth centuries, and which dehistoricises, depoeticises, whereas the article *ponctuation* of the *Encyclopédie* said explicitly that punctuation notes the breath. It is enough to compare the original of Montesquieu's *De l'esprit des lois*, in 1749, with the critical edition of the publisher Les Belles Lettres. There is no connection.

That is why thinking has to hurt, hurt them who think in the first place, outside of and against, and hurt academicism. From which follows a chain reaction. A critique of what is called meaning. And the connections between history and meaning. Since of language one has nothing but representations. And it is always the authorities, the experts, who are mistaken. With language, it is the sign that rules, with its series of the discontinuous. The binary. What is to be thought is the continuous of a serial semantics, language–body, and language–poem–ethics–politics.

This is something I do not stop saying. And that is why I posit that there are two historicities: one which is nothing but the inscription into the conditions of meaning-making, the other one which, albeit situated, constantly leaves this situation and remains active in the present. That is Humboldt's opposition between *energeia* (activity) and *ergon* (product) – product of its time. The entire question of the intelligibility of the present. In order not to be the imbecile of the present. Who are always recruited from the elite. My favourite example: Max Nordau who wrote in *Dégénerescence*, in 1893: 'Mallarmé is mentally disturbed; and by the way, Zola shares my opinion.' And Max Nordau was anything but stupid.

There is thus – I won't spend time on this here – a historicity of the translatable. When Latinist scholars translate *vis verbi, vis verborum* in Cicero ('the force of the word, the force of words') by 'the meaning of the word, the meaning of words'. Come on: everything has to be retranslated. That is why I call the current translations effacing translations.

Looking at the Bible, alongside the theologico-political there is the theologico-philological and the theologico-poetical. All enmeshed. Just one example: the famous translation 'God of the armies', where I translate, supported by the best of philological knowledge, 'God of the multitudes of stars'. It is well known what this has determined, ideologically. And, in the psalms, nowhere else but in my translation you can read that the humans are 'the sons of death' (Psalms 79: 11; 112: 21), elsewhere they are the 'condemned to death'.

If historicity implies that a text is a system of discourse, what a body does to language, then it is an activity which is an ethics-in-action of language, which presupposes that one cannot think history without thinking language, without having the sense of language, which is something else than the sense of words, this unit of the sign.

The sense of language, means to think a theory of the ensemble.

Langage, histoire, une même théorie[4] has limits which are at the same time visible and invisible. I believe that the true books are those whose invisible limits are stronger than those one can see. Intelligibility, in history and in thinking language – I posit that it is an interaction, of the order of the inseparable.

Which means that thinking is of the order of utopia: at the same time that to which the commonplaces do not grant any space, and that which has an internal force to impose thinking. This is why rhythm, as the organisation of the movement of speech in language, is the poetics of historicity. Instead of the poetics of the cosmic being metrics.

Ethics, stakes of the subject. Inseparable from the language–body, from the poem and from the political. When it is alone, according to the heterogeneity of the categories of reason which rules in our university disciplines, ethics – that is, the invisible comical of thinking – returns, without knowing it, to its origins: *to êthos*, 'the pig stable' in the *Odyssey* and in Herodotus. It is true that there were two words, *êthos* and *éthos*, 'the custom, the usage'.

By the connection between poetics and ethics, it is all of traditional philosophy which stands in question. This is why we have to de-Platonicise the notion of rhythm of which all dictionaries pretend to give the definition while speaking exclusively of metrics.

But with the art of language one deals with what Mallarmé called a 'rhythmical knot' – 'Every soul is a rhythmical knot.'[5] Where one has to hear as well what Apollinaire called 'personal prosodies'.[6]

Merleau-Ponty felt these things:

> We would undoubtedly recover the true sense of the concept of history if we acquired the habit of modelling it on the example of the arts and language. The close connection between each expression and every other within a single order instituted by the first act of expression effects the junction of the individual and the universal. Expression – language, for

---

4. [Translator's note: That is the title of the book this text is taken from (Lagrasse: Verdier, 2012).]
5. In Stéphane Mallarmé, *La Musique et les lettres* (Paris: Perrin, 1895).
6. Guillaume Apollinaire, 'Jean Royère', in *La Phalange, Œuvres en prose* (Paris: La Pléiade, 1992).

example – is what most belongs to us as individuals, for while addressing itself to others, it simultaneously acquires a universal value.⁷

A more intuitive than elaborated approach.

And Merleau-Ponty said already, in *Signes*:

> It is asked, '*Where* is history made? Who makes it? What is this movement which traces out and leaves behind the figures of the wake?' It is of the same order as the movement of Thought and Speech, and, in short, of the perceptible world's explosion within us. Everywhere there are meanings [. . .] . We are in the field of history as we are in the field of language or existence.⁸

But where are you speaking from? You will remember that once, this question was asked.

History is not constructed as language is. It is not about making the analogy, about making analogies. It is about reciprocal implication. History presupposes language, and language is the activity of subjects, which is made in history. The utopia of ethics and politics is poetics. That is bizarre, if not most improbable, only for the sign, its beneficiaries and its accomplices.

The place I speak from is the connection between my life and my poems, it is a practice, and it is from there that I am thinking about language, about the poem, about ethics, about the political. The sign is the treason of the intellectuals. Of those whom Alain called the 'philosophers of the institute'.

This is why nothing is more comical than thinking, and the comical needs to be shared.

---

7. Maurice Merleau-Ponty, *The Prose of the World*, ed. by Claude Lefort, trans. by John O'Neill (Evanston, IL: Northwestern University Press, 1974), p. 85. French version: *La Prose du monde* (Paris: Gallimard, 1969), p. 120.
8. Maurice Merleau-Ponty, *Signs*, trans., with an intro. by Richard C. McCleary (Evanston, IL: Northwestern University Press, 1964), p. 20. French version: *Signes* (Paris: Gallimard, 1960), p. 28.

14

Rhythm, Theory of Language, Poetics of Society

(in *Langage, histoire, une même théorie*, Lagrasse: Verdier, 2012, pp. 59–76)

Translated by Marko Pajević

There is some imprudence in speaking of a poetics of society. Because the question is immense, that is, it is difficult to measure. Because one can consequently approach it only from a long distance. Because it still is a utopia. The blank on our conceptual maps. And there is too much to say in order to say enough. One can hope only not to prove to be presumptuous or frivolous.

The paradox, with the apparent incongruity of the rapprochement of the terms poetics and society, is the imperial necessity of their rapprochement, the necessity of a poetics of society. By which I understand the study of the relation between the subject and the social, in such a way that it is no longer founded on a dualist theory of the sign, but on a historical anthropology of language, a theory of the historicity of discourse, which separates neither literature and language, nor language and life. Literature is here a major reactor for the theories of language, since it is founded in discourse, in rhythm, in the language–subject.

In the current state of the theoretical relations between the theory of language or language studies and the other social sciences, only poetics, as far as I know, can approach a political question that political philosophy does not seem to be either asking or being able to ask, so much it is installed in the sign.

This question, for me, starts out from the conflict between the sign and the poem. I have researched what certain philosophies, certain linguistics, and psychoanalysts, make of poetry, and how the subject is at stake in the relations of language with the sacred. Working in search of modes of relation between language, literature, history and the theories, theory of language, theory of literature, theory of history.

The critique of rhythm, itself inchoative and theoretical poem, aims at demonstrating, through the technicity which imposes itself, that the entire politics of language traverse, exactly, these technicities. There is not, on the one hand, a technical level, homologue to the signifier, and on the other hand, a social or political level, homologous to the signified of the sign.

The model of the sign is not a scientific model. The ambiguity of the relation between the cultural and the linguistic means that, as linguistic model, the sign is given–taken for the nature itself of language, of which its description, transparent, would be nothing but the copy, which precisely establishes its characteristics as cultural model. But this model is also, and maybe first of all, an anthropological paradigm: body and soul, the dead and the living, which overlap the scheme of signifier and signified, as the wordplay with the Greek words *soma–sêma* show, between the body, the sign and the tomb. This binary scheme is the patron of a chain binarisation: the letter and the spirit, dead scripture and living voice, abstract generic of words and concrete particularity of things and beings, the opposition of language to life. To this linguistic and anthropological model, Hegel added a theological scheme. A rationalist model of the rational and the irrational, as of prose and poetry – it is the pragmatic model of instrumentalism, which excludes literature, and first of all poetry, from ordinary language. It is this model which establishes the primacy of the notion of language, political primacy (unity of language, or dominated language/dominating language). Thus the force of the sign is considerable. But it is without any connection to scientific truth. It is first and foremost pragmatic and political. If its extension can have the reputation of being universal, its understanding has strong and weak points. Sufficient as it is for ordinary language, or what is taken to be, it turns out to be of no poetical value. Coming from there, one can demonstrate that the sign is overflown by the empirical. By the body. By the rhythm of the living.

From which follows the destabilisation of the sign by rhythm as the historicity of subjects in their discourse. From which follows the theoretical effect of rhythm on language. And the attitude change of rhythm, passing from traditional theory to critical theory. Traditional rhythm was a form of the signifier, which hardly modified the meaning, other than in the restricted category of expressivity, and the alternation of strong and weak, of symmetry and dissymmetry inscribed it in the ahistorical order of the cosmic. There, it joined the sign, which does not cease turning back towards the paradise lost of the union between the words and the things. But for the critique of rhythm, rhythm is an element of the radical historicity of language, in the historicity of discourse.

From this point of view, where the historicity of societies is prolonged in the historicity of language, the classical notion of rhythm is a collective phantasm, as is the classical theory of the sign, and both are linked the one to the other in the instrumentalist conformism which makes of it the theory needed by the pragmatics of power.

The subject can wake up from this dream of reason – and this awakening is already the start of what constitutes it as subject – only if it grounds the analysis of language on this major effect of rhythm. But this dream comes not out of a sleep of reason. It is not the sleep of reason that produces monsters. It is reason itself. Which means that, through the theory of language, what is at stake is not what language studies deal with, but rationality as well as sociality. And only, in the adventure of discourses, the analyses of this organisation of subjectivity, which historicises the modes of signifying, can, through this take on the empirical, assure us not to replace one collective phantasm by an egocentric phantasm.[1] There is more correspondence to the empirical functioning of language in the critique of rhythm than in the dualism of the sign. If only by the notion of orality as primacy of the prosodic and the rhythmical which replaces the duality–totality of the written opposed to the oral, by the triple distinction of the written, the spoken and the oral.

Rhythm, which works on and traverses the subject and the social, imposes a traversal procedure. Being a strategy of historicity in meaning, and a strategy of meaning in historicity, it imposes – but not in the structural mode – literature on language studies and the theory of language on literature, as the necessity of a theory of discourse on history, and of a theory of rhythm on psychoanalysis, a sociology on poetics and a poetics on sociology. From which follows, probably, that rhythm appears at the same time, according to the points of view, either as too technical or as too general, philosophical for the non-philosophers and outside of serious academia, cramped in their disciplines. This is why I take pleasure in quoting at this point Karl Popper, who said that 'a thing on its own such as an academic discipline simply does not exist' and 'What is called an academic discipline is nothing else but a conglomerate of problems and attempts to solve them, which has been artificially delimited and constructed.'[2] Through this, amongst other things, the critique of rhythm is not only the critique of the theories of language, but a critique of the humanities through rhythm.

Because rhythm and historicity are two aspects of one and the same

---

1. I take the terms of collective phantasm and of egocentric phantasm from Norbert Elias, *What is Sociology: European Perspectives* (New York: Columbia University Press, 1978) [German version: 1970].
2. Karl Popper, in Theodor W. Adorno, Karl Popper, Ralf Dahrendorf, Jürgen Habermas, Harald Pilot, *De Vienne à Francfort, la querelle allemande des sciences sociales* (Brussels: Complexe, 1979), p. 79 (trans. from the French by MP).

strategy for one and the same thing at stake: the historicity of language, of discourses, of subjects. This is in the first place the problem of a specific epistemology with an empirical status of meaning which encompasses language, history, the social – against the cladding of an epistemology of the hard or natural sciences on the so-called humanities. The perverted effect of this scientific cladding is that, behind its scientific posture, it produces an ideologisation. Thus the rapprochement of linguistics and biology, not to mention the abstract formalism that has separated theory from concrete language and discourse, that has produced a dehistoricisation of language and of linguistics – a regression of the field of historicity where Saussure had placed them (and which is different from the status of historical sciences, in the sense of the nineteenth century), towards the field of natural sciences, towards animal psychology and ethology. This state of affairs characterises a certain aspect of American linguistics, in Chomsky. But also an argumentation of the anti-arbitrary in some of Jakobson's last texts. And a part of the theses and of the success of René Girard: Michel Serres received *Things Hidden Since the Foundation of the World* by writing: 'Rats, rats, we are rats.' The shift itself from scientism towards ideology shows the link between epistemology, particularly for the humanities, and the political. But there is also a link between epistemology and ethics. What dehistoricisation, in the first instance, makes evident. Thus the connection between the abstract definition of the subject, in Chomsky, and the abstract notion of democracy, illustrated by his defence of Faurisson. Or the critique of the anti-Semite by the abstract democrat, in Sartre. Dehistoricisation is a demoralisation. A loss of the relations between the ethical, the political and the poetical, as theory of the subject in language. Another characteristic example of the loss of the connection between ethics and the political, in the link to a certain status of language and of literature, has been the work of Julien Benda. Since he pushed the dehistoricisation of values to the extent of considering their historicisation the 'treason of the intellectuals'. But did so, it is true, under circumstances and maybe misunderstandings which require closer scrutiny. It is the transcendence of values that takes place in the binary anthropology of the profane and the sacred. It has constantly stripped the profane of the values it outlined. Which left pure values, such as dogmata, and blemishes to history. A form that could be said to be particular to Gnosticism, and dualism, in the way the transcendence of values is, paradoxically, an origin of the crisis of values in the empirical.

A more recent example shows the topicality of the epistemological problem. This is Maurice Godelier's introduction to the official report on the state of the humanities in France. Organisation and funding of research took precedence, by some distance, over epistemology. But it is the state of this epistemology that is much worse than the one of its funding. A strange reflection on the humanities, as well, that takes for granted what makes its strategy itself, and what is at stake in them, and that is consequently in a state of slackness, a 'laxity' that, I believe, only René Rémond underlined in a discussion of the journal *Le Débat* (issue 22, November 1982). The vagueness appears straight away in the title of the report, *Les Sciences de l'homme et de la société en France* (*The Human and the Social Sciences in France*), which juxtaposes the traditional French designation *sciences de l'homme* (la Maison des sciences de l'homme) or *sciences humaines* (human sciences) with the English designation *Social Sciences*. It is unclear whether this represents an amplifying rhetoric, saying the same thing twice, or whether it represents two complementary fields. The distinction, however, is posited: 'We fear first of all that the human sciences might be sacrificed to the social sciences, and that the latter might definitely establish their hegemony over the former.'[3] But nowhere, neither before, nor after, is the distinction explained. In most cases, the two terms are juxtaposed, as in the title: 'The Uneven Development of the Human and the Social Sciences in France' (ibid., p. 31). Sometimes, in opposition to the natural sciences, 'human sciences' is used alone (ibid., p. 22). Finally, the distinction, which is posed, but remains vague – despite the entire starting section dealing precisely with epistemology – is put forward for abolition, though it is unclear what this abolition is meant to abolish and where only the notion of abolition is certain:

> For the mission, it is by now absolutely evident that the distinction and the border between the human sciences and the social sciences must be abolished, and that within the CNRS [National Centre for Academic Research], a vast sector must be created which incorporates them all and which gives them a general impetus. It is necessary that the human sciences cease to appear as the last remainders of what used to be called the 'humanities'. The distinction between 'human' sciences and 'social' sciences has no safe epistemological foundation. It permanently refreshes an ancient separation that the recent progress of these disciplines tends to reduce. In the midst of this vast sector, called 'human and social sciences', the mission proposes a new breakup of the sections. (ibid., p. 79)

Impossible to know whether the 'human' is on the side of the individual opposed to the social, or on the side of letters against sciences. And this vagueness is no coincidence. It results from a desire of generalised scientificity.

---

3. Maurice Godelier, *Les Sciences de l'homme et de la société en France: analyse et propositions pour une politique nouvelle, Rapport au Ministre de la Recherche et de l'Industrie* (Paris: La Documentation Française, 1982), p. 27 (trans. by MP).

This desire is formulated first of all as a *cooperation* between the human and the natural sciences:

> the human and the social sciences cannot develop outside of or against the movement of the 'hard' sciences which tend towards the knowledge of the physical universe, of nature and of life. Every society has developed and will develop within a determined ecosystem on which it acts, coming from material technics and determined intellectual knowledge. This is a first reason which imposes, at the end of this twentieth century and more than ever, the permanent exchange of knowledge and research cooperation between the human and the natural sciences. (ibid., p. 23)

But this quite banal request for complementarity, for 'interdependency' and 'reciprocal exchange' is made against the backdrop of an idea of science opposed to ideology, and whose model is the one of the hard sciences. Exactly in order to flee the imputation that the human sciences are 'immediately ideological and political'. We switch consequently from a cooperation to an epistemological *parity*, if not an *identity*. Must one, from the presence of the observer in the observed reality,

> conclude that the human and social sciences are no sciences? Or concede, if they are sciences, that they are based on an epistemological rationality which is completely distinct from the one of the hard sciences, on strange methods, imperfect, and in any case alien to those that ensure the efficiency of physics or molecular biology? I do not believe so. (ibid., p. 24)

This makes it clear that the hard and the natural sciences provide the only model of science. To veer away from it means to be inferior to them. This is the traditional state of the scientism of the nineteenth century. In complete contradiction to Passeron's conclusion, in his summarising balance of sociology: 'at times, the worst would be to copy what seems to be the best of hard sciences' (ibid., p. 219). The entire argumentation and vocabulary of Godelier show the alliance from twenty years ago, in spite of their apparent quarrel, between structuralism and Marxism: the confusion between structure and system, and the primacy of structure (ibid., p. 25), the confusion between scientificity and logico-mathematical formalisation: success lies in the translation of 'realities' into 'formal language'. This is the old myth of *progress*, with the metaphor of marching forward: 'anthropology has started to emancipate itself from the shackles of its origins and to set free a theoretical potential which will transport it even further in the future' (ibid., p. 33). And the magical term of *articulation*, so characteristic of the illusion of interdisciplinarity: 'the necessity to articulate the ones to the others and to develop together the sciences of the past and those of the present' (ibid., p. 38).

Behind the good intentions, nothing is more damaging to the human sciences than this false epistemological status, doubly situated, and dated, by its structuralism and by its Marxism (the opposition, as in Althusser, of science and ideology). The result is a conformism. That is what Popper, already in 1961, had called a 'misled naturalism'.[4] For linguistics, the subdivision between ordinary language (pragmatic and socio-linguistic), historical consciousness and informatisation, leaves space for poetics exclusively as 'ludic language', the part of *celebration* and of '*otherness*'. That is to say, the same divisions that obstruct the critique of rhythm. I find it hard to see how we can expect from this the 'long-term renewal of linguistic models'.[5] Because this is exactly the maintenance of traditional theory. Anthropology, on the other hand, is explicitly presented as a 'totalising discipline' (ibid., pp. 121, 135, 136): here again, the object precisely of a critique of anthropology. It is characteristic that the lexicalist linguistics of anthropologists as 'collectors of vocabulary' (ibid., p. 123) is not put in question. For history, according to Vovelle's report, it is always the quantitative, the serial, which are the 'major novelties' (ibid., p. 257). If that was the case, for a long time already there would have been nothing new in history. And learning discourse analysis (ibid., p. 258), which, indeed, is newer, makes of historians users of linguistic theories, of which they have no critical grasp. It seems that the 'methodological retardation' (ibid., p. 260) is on the side of the history of mentalities. The historian, just like the author of the report on philosophy, does not see himself connected to the history of thinking language, even if the latter writes exactly: 'At the articulations of knowledge, cultural forms and social practices, unheard of and productive problems come up. The future is born in the interfaces' (ibid., p. 496).

The relation of reciprocal implication between the epistemology of the human sciences, the ethical and the political, up to policy (research policy, cultural policy, politics in general), appears as the theoretical deferral of the relation between language, subject and history. This relation itself implies that the appellation of human sciences – linked to a totalising, unifying and mythologising anthropology – should rather be sciences of individuation. Because the status of the subject is what is at stake in language and in language theory, and, at the same time, because the subject is not the individual but the individuation. And that is precisely why literature, and poetry in particular, is revelatory of society, and of theory, because in it a subject is at stake, and through it any subject is, and because where a subject is at stake, the social is at stake.

4. In Adorno et al., *De Vienne à Francfort*, p. 78.
5. Godelier, *Les Sciences de l'homme et de la société en France*, p. 430.

From which follows the status of a theory of language, of the subject, of the social, as critical theory: by this postulation, proper to the Critical Theory of the Frankfurt School, that everything that concerns one sector of the social, here language, implies the social as a whole. Implies consequently the construction of a logic of relations, in such a way that the regionalisation of disciplines will be demonstrated as a denial of the theoretical and practical effects of the regionalisation – particularly the effects of the unthought, by which a non-theorisation of language manipulates ideologically the discourses on the social. This non-theorisation of language confirms the notion of traditional theory such as described by Horkheimer in 1937, as concurrent to the maintenance of society as it is. I should add: to the maintenance of theory as it is.

The critical status of theory is necessarily also critical of critical theory. The postulated link between practice and theory, between theory and critique remains efficient, productive. A critique of positivist science remains pertinent, and the notion, taken itself in a politisation of its era, remains of interest:

> There is no theory of society that does not imply political interests – including the one by 'generalising' sociologists –, and whose truth value could be judged in a supposedly neuter attitude and not in an effort of thought and action in return, integrated precisely in a concrete historical activity.[6]

But the critical theory of the thirties, a critique of abstract rationalism, worked itself within a rationalism, a truth of reason, an 'organisation founded on reason' (ibid., p. 49), a confidence in reason that considered itself to be the criterion for false rationalisations (Nazism, capitalism). Revolution was a rationalisation. It should lead to a rational organisation of society, 'satisfy the largest number of people'. At the expense of some individual problems which counted little in the eyes of liberation. What the critique did not do, in its distinction of diverse rationalisms, was the critique of its own rationalism. It was all about understanding how reason could have become an unreason, in the service of technics or of oppression. But conserving the 'Hegelian method'.[7] It has already been demonstrated how much the referral of the critical theory to its own interest could lead back a dogmatism of totality.[8] It is here that the question of rhythm and of language can bring about a shift of the critique, and of theory.

---

6. Max Horkheimer, *Théorie traditionnelle et théorie critique* (Paris: Gallimard, 1974), p. 56.
7. Max Horkheimer, *Théorie critique*, intro. by Luc Ferry and Alain Renaut (Paris: Payot, 1978), p. 26; English edition *Critical Theory* (NY: Continuum, 1982).
8. By Rüdiger Bubner, in 'Qu'est-ce que la théorie critique?', *Archives de philosophie*, 35 (1972), pp. 381–421.

Because it is in the very site of traditional philosophy that the traditional critique of Critical Theory takes place: with regard to the opposition between materialism and idealism. Theory is torn between its materialist concern, where its interest turns it back into an ideology, and its ambition of universal scientificity, of truth beyond interests. But the opposition between ideology and scientificity, between materialism and idealism, relativism and dogmatism, or relativism and universality – this entire paradigm that has a sense and a history for the problem of truth, and particularly for the identification between truth, theory and science (identification which defines Marxism), all of this has no sense for the theory of language. But it belongs properly to the Marxism of the thirties, which adds some Stalinism even in Horkheimer – *to impose reason by authority*: 'From the point of view of world history, indeed, the effort exerted on the very backwards social stratums in the city and in the countryside to teach them to repress their own narrow interests, would be a cure, which would be inevitable even under other circumstances. To their expired production mode corresponds a mental attitude which does not allow any rational adaptation, if not by means of authority, at the current state of knowledge.'[9] This very impossibility for the concepts of specificity and historicity of discourse to enter into the categories of Marxism, which want to be at the same time pan-epistemological, places the critique of rhythm in the situation of being the critique of the critical theory.

When Horkheimer in 1968 returned to his essays from 1932 to 1941 for a critical review, he apparently turned upside down the tasks of theory. Because the circumstances had changed and because 'What Marx had represented for himself as Socialism is in fact the administered world';[10] the first task is no longer the revolution, but the conservation of what can still be preserved of 'the autonomy of the individual person, the importance of the individual, their differentiated psychology, certain aspects of culture' (ibid., p. 359). The theology of original sin and a negative theology of 'absolute goodness' (ibid., p. 361) organise a theoretical pessimism, coupled, however, with a practical optimism. But if the position has changed, from rationalist optimism to religious pessimism, nothing has changed in this coupling. From one pole to the other, it is the same polarity. Rationality has become the automaticisation of society, but it is still 'a tendency immanent to the development of humanity' (ibid., p. 359). Still the same confidence, but it is disappointed. The polarity maintains the terms. To go from one pole to the other does not change

---

9. Max Horkheimer, *Kritische Theorie, Eine Dokumentation* (Frankfurt am Main: Fischer, 1968), vol. I, p. 156 (text from 1934).
10. In Horkheimer, 'La Théorie critique hier et aujourd'hui', in *Théorie critique*, p. 365 (text from 1970).

anything. No more than the blaspheme changes religion. None the less, it is still all about a critique of reason. Of its myths and its illusions. And it is exactly the critique of the theory of language that the Critical Theory lacks. For the historicity of practices, and of values, against its own normativity.

It is significant here that the only one in whose work this critique of language has developed, is Walter Benjamin, in connection with the Critical Theory but not working within it, and in an ambiguity between Judaism and Marxism, at least as it is habitually said, which makes of each of the terms a utopia.

Language as history of individuation, and the history of individuation as history of language, situate the primacy of discourse, against the one of language. Discourse as specific activity and as constitutive of subjects of enunciation. While the linguistics of *la langue* makes of discourse a use of signs. A secondarity which is modulated, mostly, to a pre-Saussurian reduction of language to naming, to a linguistics of the word, precisely the one used by historians for the analysis of political discourse. Which appeared in 1973 in *Histoire et linguistique* by Régine Robin. And more recently in the journal *Mots* (acronym of Mots/ordinateurs/textes/societies [Words/computers/texts/societies]), of the laboratory of political lexicology in Saint-Cloud, edited by the Fondation Nationale des Sciences Politiques [National Foundation of Political Sciences] since 1980. But the primacy of syntax, or the one of etymology as true discourse of the origin confused with sense, are also other forms of the primacy of *la langue*, and of the secondarisation of discourse. Like the traditional theory of rhythm. Or stylistics.

The primacy of discourse begins, I believe, with Humboldt. In particular in his *The Task of the Historian* from 1821, by the link he establishes between the notion of *Zusammenhang* (equivalent practically, and also morphologically, to the notion of sys-*tem*, the 'system of the events of the world'), and the notions of *Individuum* and *Individualität*, and in *Introduction to the Work on the Kavi*, in Chapters IX and X, as is shown, amongst other things, by the formulation 'Wir haben es historisch nur immer mit dem wirklich sprechenden Menschen zu thun.' ['*Historically*, our concern is always with *actually speaking* men'].[11]

One of the major paradoxes of the theoretical conditions of the possibility

---

11. In Wilhelm von Humboldt, *Über die Verschiedenheit des menschlichen Sprachbaus (Einleitung zum Kawiwerk), Gesammelte Schriften*, vol. 7/1 (Berlin: Behr, 1903–12), p. 42. English version: Wilhelm von Humboldt, *On Language: On the Diversity of Human Language Construction and its Influence on the Mental Development of the Human Species*, ed. by Michael Losonsky, trans. by Peter Heath (Cambridge: Cambridge University Press, 1999), p. 46.

of discourse is to have been founded in the conceptual work of Saussure, who, apparently, lies elsewhere. It's that the study of discourse inevitably provides a different reading of Saussure from the structuralist one, which didacticises and scholasticises it into language/speech [*langue/parole*], synchrony/diachrony, with the presupposition of rigour of the continuity between Saussure and the structuralists. For discourse, it is the strategy of historicity which is foundational in Saussure, with and in spite of its incompletion: the four principles: that is, the 'radically arbitrary' of the sign, condition of the radical historicity of language, and of discourse; the thinking of the functioning, at the same time against the origin and against the 'traditional sub-divisions' (lexicon, morphology, syntax); value, against the notion of sense; and system, against historicism, naming, but also against structure, which structuralism had confused with the notion of system. These epistemological principles of language are indispensable for a theory of discourse, even if Saussure has not conceived of them as such. Subsequently come into play the historical, conflictual and provisional, in the theory of discourse. From Benveniste to ethno-linguistics, from the philosophy of ordinary language to socio-linguistics.

The importance of the theory of discourse is also related to the necessity, for the historians, to deal with discourse. Which forces the question, generally eluded, of the notions historians have of sense and of discourse. Which cannot not be interposed between the *document* and them. And even more so to the degree that they believe that nothing is interposed. Thus there is a reversibility between the 'spontaneous philosophy' of language in the discourse of historians or the discourse on history, and a spontaneous philosophy of history in the discourse on language. These are the diverse figures of the relation to the political through language, and of the relation to language through the political.

What is illustrated by the analogical relations between discourse and history: history traced back to the narration of history, in Barthes; analogy inclined towards identity, in the generalised analogy of Jean-Pierre Faye; the postulation of discourse, overlooked by a linguistics of the word and by historicism, in Régine Robin; language and literature amiss due to the Marxist reduction to ideology, in Michel Vovelle.

Discourse engages the subject, and through this, a theory of creativity. Which presupposes that there is no creativity without subject, nor subject without creativity. It is characteristic that the two weak spots of the theory of language in generative grammar are – from this point of view, without talking about the rest – the notion of 'truly artistic creativity', distinguished by Chomsky from linguistic creativity, and the abstract status of the political implicated by the 'ideal speaker–listener, in a completely homogeneous linguistic community'.

From which two problems connect: the one of historicity (discourses, practices, subjects), to be distinguished from historicism, and the one of individuation. Historicity is a relation. Historicism is a transport: under the conditions of production of meaning, that is, a reduction of meaning to its conditions of production. Historicism is the completed, the past of meaning. Historicity is the indefinitely renewed encounter of the historical and the a-historical, of past and present moments of meaning. And the individuation and the discontinuity of life forms, of language forms, of subject-forms.

The status of the subject raises the question, of course, of how we understand 'subject', but also the question of the status of philosophical anthropology. In totalising anthropologies, the subject is confided to psychoanalyses, for example, which is its provider for the humanities. This is a complementary scheme, perfectly represented by Sartre, in his *Questions de méthode* [Questions of Method] and *L'Idiot de la famille* [The Idiot of the Family]: his 'ideology', plus Marxism (for the social and the political), plus psychoanalysis. By the juxta-disciplinary, a totality is conceived. The linguistic modelisation in structuralism, from Lévi-Strauss to Lacan, has been another one of its forms. The same for semiotics. However, empirically, meaning, history – the two terms being only aspects of each other – are in the infinite, not in totality, which is necessarily finite. The subject is infinite. To come back to the empirical, a critique of the notion of unit has to be done, of unity and of units. It is enough to let literature intervene, and its theoretical problems, in order to put an end to the totality–unity–truth, to bring back the forgotten rhythm, and the mutual critique of the political and the poetical. Thus the poetical and the political of Marinetti's Italian Futurism in the invention of a mode of enunciation and intervention, to which Mussolini himself paid homage in his article *fascismo* in the *Enciclopedia italiana* of 1932. Or in the poetical reception of the Russian Revolution of 1917 by Alexander Blok.

The non-theorisation of language forms a non-thought that manœuvres ideologically in the discourses on the social or on the political. The proof by etymology therefore provides a purely verbal circularity, a particular mode of tautology that, in an enunciation of political philosophy, replaces the analysis of the social by wordplay. Amongst the most beautiful cases is the one of the Christian etymology of the word *religion*, derived from *religare*, and not any more from *religere*, to signify 'the bond of piety, this dependency of the faithful on God'.[12] Often people refer to this etymology to illustrate the effect of social harmony, of *union*, procured by religion. So does Claude Lefort, in his article 'Permanence du théologico-politique' [Permanence of the Theologico-

---

12. Cf. Émile Benveniste, 'Religion et superstition', in *Vocabulaire des institutions indo-européennes* (Paris: Éditions de Minuit, 1969), vol. II, p. 272.

political],[13] where he opposes the thinking that separates the theological and the political, as it emerged from the French Revolution, to the thinking that unites them, and, citing the 'precious commentary' of Hegel (p. 14) who condemned this separation, he constructs two paradigms: the one of the *rupture* (*fracture, to separate, split, retreat, dis-intrication, division, fragmentation, heterogeneity, conflict*), and this is marked by the terms *error, illusion* (four times, p. 31) and *appearance*; and the paradigm of *union* (*unity*), marked by *certitude* (twice, p. 31), *the ancient certitudes*, paradigm of religion. They are not symmetrical since in the first one 'society remains in the search of its foundation' (ibid.) and in the second one, it is said 'that religion elaborates a primordial representation of the One and that this representation turns out to be the condition of the union of human beings' (ibid.), and this motif of union, marked and over-marked (by italicising the word), is nothing other than the gloss and the expansion of etymology that continues to tell the truth (*etumos logos*) about the truth, thus reinforcing the search for the religious in unity, 'the union of the social body' (p. 36), showing that for Michelet the Revolution 'was a Church itself' (p. 43) and 'It is clearly this establishment in *certitude* and this new *relation* that is *constructed* between the certain and the revealed that witnesses of a re-inscription of Michelet's thinking in the matrix of Christian religion' (p. 44, my italics). Lefort's thesis itself, 'would it not be better to posit a theologico-political *formation* as a foundation, logically and historically' (p. 54), and his conclusion, 'everything that moves into the direction of an explicitation of the contours of the social relation moves into the direction of the interiorisation of unity' (p. 60), are contained in the Christian etymology of the word *religion*, the meaning of which is given as *depth*, opposed to the *surface* of appearances – 'the arrangement of depth in the form of events' (p. 34), it is said of Michelet and we could say it again here. If this depth is not otherwise a circularity. The intelligibility that makes the social, the historical, necessarily presupposes meaning, *consequently a notion of meaning*. Marx already, in *Poverty of Philosophy*, criticised Proudhon's dissertation on the etymology of *servus–servare* in lieu of an argumentation of political economy. It seems indeed here that a discourse of political philosophy has been manœuvred by a notion of meaning, interior and anterior to its notion of religion. That is a common thing. So many discourses about prose or verse, or poetry, that develop the etymology of the word. The effects are not the same. But political philosophy as well has to *take care* of its language.

There is therefore a necessity, for all the humanities, to think the sense

---

13. Claude Lefort, 'Permanence du théologico-politique', *Le Temps de la réflexion*, 2 (1981).

of sense. To think this unthought can be done only by a theory of language that is also a poetics of language. Poetics, and more precisely the critique of rhythm, consequently plays a strategic role here. But this role is not at all the relief of the structuralist role of linguistics in the humanities. Which has been a role model, with all the scientistic ideology of this metaphorical use of the term 'model'. This role is not either, neither in its strategy nor in its effects, a role of domination. As, ostensibly, sociology presents itself, according to Bourdieu – an example of a sociology without poetics, which in its turn calls for a poetics of its sociology, and more generally the analysis of possible reciprocities between sociology and the theory of language and of literature. The role of poetics is to modify – and that is its proper theoretical effect – the ethical and the political, through which it implicates itself in the ethical and the political. Being a strategy of the subject, it would be rather a strategy of anti-domination, and of anti-hierarchy. The role of poetics is to be the problem without which the ethical and the political can constitute themselves only by forgetting the subject. Karl Popper said: 'It is therefore always the problem which is the point of departure.'[14] To which Adorno responded: 'It is only for him who can think society as other than the one that exists, that society becomes a problem in the terminology of Popper.'[15]

A poetics of society is thus a negative poetics. Firstly a critique of the absence of poetics in the social practices and in the humanities – not amongst the humanities, but within every single one of them. A critique of the absence of a theory of language in the theories of the social. A historical anthropology of language.

A poetics of society is consequently doubly utopian. Because the current state of science, humanities or social sciences, does not provide the space for it. And because it can only have its place by shifting them, and by shifting the theory of language itself, through the critique of rhythm. But even if the critique concerns a plurality of fields, including within language studies, at least it is the same critique.

And it is this critique that makes a poetics of society necessary. As a relation of reciprocal implication, and without hierarchy, the poetical and poetics, the political and politics. It is through the poetics of discourse, and not through the linguistics of discourse alone, that a theory of the subject can contribute to a thinking of democracy. And a thinking of the creativity which no longer opposes, as in the Greek tradition, the philosopher and the poet to the ordinary man, that is, to ordinary language. Utopia is thus at home in the

---

14. Karl Popper, 'La Logique des sciences sociales', in Adorno et al., *De Vienne à Francfort*, p. 77.
15. Theodor W. Adorno, 'Sur la logique des sciences sociales', in ibid., p. 104.

empirical. It is at home in every exposition of the subject. In the plurality of modes to signify, and in the maximal uptake of all of ordinary language. The poetics of society consists simply in attaching itself to the understanding of the labour that is done, in all the totalisations and the instrumentalisations of Reason and of the State, by the infinite of historicity.

15

Realism, Nominalism: The Theory of Language is a Theory of Society

(in *Langage, histoire, une même théorie*, Lagrasse: Verdier, 2012, pp. 717–26)

Translated by Marko Pajević

Realism, nominalism: it comes down to a problem of the sense of language, *Sprachsinn*, which I take from Humboldt. Language, in a sense which includes the whole sense of life. Not in the sense of national languages. What is at stake, is the sense of the individual. This is what I mean by *theory of language*: I mean interaction, *Wechselwirkung* – Humboldt again – the interaction of language, poem, ethics and politics. Here I start from the poem to think the ethical and the political, because what is at stake in the poem is the relation of reciprocal transformation between language and life, and this can take place only through a subject. And only the theory of language thus conceived makes it possible to think a poetics of society, and through this a political ethics of society.

To do this requires thinking language against the sign as representation, and show that the sign is nothing but a representation of language. For taking the sign to be the nature and truth of language prevents us from recognising it as a representation. A point of view. And Saussure has taught us that when it comes to language, we have only points of view. The sign prevents us from thinking the continuous, the interaction language–poem–ethics–politics. The sign is the discontinuous. It is theologico-essentialist. It makes it impossible to think either the subject or the poem.

At the same time that it essentialises, the sign engenders a heterogeneity in categories of reason through a generalised compartmentalisation of sciences [*savoirs*]. What Horkheimer called traditional theories, which is to say regional theories.

Ethics is what is at stake in the subject, the subjects that we are. A matter of thinking the relation between language, poem, ethics and politics. Which changes our relation to ourselves and to others.

Ethics is what we make of ourselves and of others. It is a doing, and a value-making. And value can only be the subject, and this immediately can only have a double sense: to make of oneself a subject, to make it such that others are subjects, to recognise others as subjects. And there is no subject unless the subject is the value of life. Unleashing from the individual all the subjects they carry within themselves. A dozen, and more.[1] This is quite different from morality, theologised or not, as social codification of commandments and prohibitions, of good and evil.

If ethics is what makes subjecthood, then ethics is necessarily nominalist: which is to say that each individual is this collection of subjects. This is what Montaigne said: 'Each man bears the whole stamp of the human condition.'[2] And the subject–individual is intermittent, as Groethuysen shows in *Philosophische Anthropologie*. No progress here. The defence of a poor little captain in the infamous Dreyfus Affair was nominalist, just as the defence of the Army's honour (even if it meant forgery) was politico-logical realism. A logical realism which made of the masses the subject of history. Another tattooed numbers on arms. A linguistic realism makes of the language a subject; the human being does not speak, according to Heidegger, except when they respond to language.

Here we have the full ethical and political potentiality of this old pair of notions, generally left by philosophers to logic, to metalinguistics, to the problem of universals.

Thus ethics is inevitably a matter of language. It's not about subjective judgements, matters of taste or emotion. It's about knowing how to deal with language, and how to think language.

Thinking language is quite different from knowledge [*le savoir*], from the sciences [*les savoirs*]. It has to do with what we don't know we are saying when we speak of the art of living [*savoir vivre*]. And Benveniste has written that 'language helps us *to live*'.[3] From which a certain number of consequences can be drawn for language, and for what one might call *to live*. Which necessarily implies that to think is first of all to invent thought, and at the same time to think the relationship between language and living. And if what is called thinking is given this strong sense, one can see at once that it is unimaginable how much we live in a culture that accustoms us

---

1. For a detailed discussion of this, cf. 'Poétique et politique du sujet', in *Politique du rythme, politique du sujet* (Lagrasse: Verdier, 1995), pp. 187–364.
2. Michel de Montaigne, *Essais* (1595), Book III, Chapter 2: 'Chaque homme porte en lui la forme entière, de l'humaine condition.'
3. Émile Benveniste, 'La Forme et le sens dans le langage', *Problèmes de linguistique générale 2* (Paris: Gallimard, 1974), p. 217.

not to think. And we don't even know. We hurry about our day-to-day business.

We are not yet thinking language, nor the poem, nor the ethical, nor the political, as long as we do not think them in their interaction, in their reciprocal implication, and in such a way that each of the terms modifies all the others and is modified by them.

So this isn't about the directly political, nor the political treated in isolation, as is usually done, separated from philosophical thought, or from the literary, for which Céline and Heidegger are the exemplary types. Which makes possible that minor miracle of intellectual cowardice, and of literature's and philosophy's non-thought, which consists in separating grand thought from petty politics, or Céline's great novels from his essays. What philologists would call the *lectio facilior*, whereas the *lectio difficilior* is stronger, which does not distinguish between the two.[4] Philosophy, and Heidegger's human–inhuman involvement with National Socialism. As Hugo didn't quite say, philosophy wants its tranquil moments.[5]

We are not yet thinking as long as we think within the cultural heterogeneity of the categories of reason: language set apart, for linguists, with all its subdivisions, according to languages and specialisms – all legitimate; literature and poetry, for the literary critics; art for the critics and historians of art; philosophy for the philosophers – the only ones who are supposed to think – and again according to its autonomous specialisms, ethics for the specialists in ethics, politics for the specialists in political philosophy, and then the specialists of aesthetics, not to forget psychology and sociology. As our university disciplines demonstrate.

But these habits of thought make for small-thought. All of these are knock-on effects of what linguists call the sign, and its series of dualisms: sound and meaning, for words, or signifier and signified (only the terminology changes), form and content, body and mind, oral and written (the living voice and the letter that kills or that is dead), poetic language as opposed to ordinary language, the separation between affect and concept as between individual and society, between identity and alterity, and finally the opposi-

---

4. As André Gide demonstrated in the *Nouvelle Revue Française* of April 1938 [vol. 295], in qualifying *Bagatelles pour un massacre* [*Bagatelles for a Massacre*] as 'lyricism', in his article 'Les Juifs, Céline et Maritain'.
5. [Translator's note: Meschonnic refers to Victor Hugo's poem *Ô Dieu! si vous avez la France sous vos ailes* [Oh God! if you keep France under your protection], in which the poet deplores the divisions and quarrels in France and concludes: 'À l'heure où le sommeil veut des moments tranquilles, / Les lourds canons rouler sur le pavé des villes!' [At a moment when sleep wants quiet moments / heavy canons roll over the cities' cobblestones!]]

tion between language and life. This is the cultural regime of the discontinuous, its anthropology of totality.

Thinking the interaction language–poem–art–ethics–politics allows us to break away from the anthropology of totality produced by the sign, in the series of its discontinuities, in order to think the continuous, and the infinite.

If one does not think the theory of language, according to the interaction I have spoken of, one is not thinking, and one does not know that one is not thinking.

To think language, poetics, ethics and the political according to their interaction, the criterion that seems to me here to be the reactivation of what is considered at the same time to be relevant only for logics and to be an outdated relic of the Middle Ages, and so forgotten that I have caught proclaimed philosophers in the act of confusing them:[6] it is that old couple of logical realism and nominalism.[7] For it is about understanding, and giving to understand (which means that everything in education needs to be transformed), its ethical and political effects. Without forgetting, although that is less vital, poems, and works of art. But yes, that is vital in a different way.

And reading the official version of logical realism, it is striking that the sign – in the linguist's sense – such as it presents itself, is a realist notion, since it claims to 'know the nature of things',[8] instead of being a representation of language, a point of view on language.

6. For instance, Rorty, cf. Meschonnic, *Politique du rythme, politique du sujet*, p. 418.
7. As objective references, I quote here the gist of the articles in *L'Encyclopédie philosophique universelle, II, Les Notions philosophiques, dictionnaires*, editor-in-chief Sylvain Auroux (Paris: Presses Universitaires de France, 1990). As one might expect, there are several articles for *réalisme*. The one that concerns us here states that it is about 'the acquisition of a direct and reliable knowledge of the world', which is then opposed to idealism and to nominalism, in so far as realism posits 'the reality of universals *ante res* [prior to things]', considering 'that they participate in a superior existence to individual sensible beings'. With the evocation, in the Middle Ages, of 'the quarrel of universals'. Realism is theological. It is presented as 'the possibility to attain the core of phenomena and not only a judgment of existence on different levels of reality'. It is notable that this is only a question of logic.

    Another article on *realism* opposes it to essentialism and instrumentalism. It is concerned with scientific knowledge. A final article concerns plastic arts and literature.

    The article *nominalism*, which evokes discussions amongst theoreticians, posits: 'nominalism refuses all realism of essence and acknowledges only the existence of individuals', and, a bit further on: 'it does not, however, reject abstract entities in favour of mere concrete entities'. The article considers nominalism only in logic and in mathematics.

    This is, so to speak, the official state of the two notions. It has hardly changed since the Middle Ages. Nothing on ethics, with its effects on the theory of ethics. That is the academicism of thought.
8. In the article *realism* that I just quoted.

Realism, nominalism, these notions seem to come out of a museum display, the Museum of the Middle Ages and the Museum of the Arts and Traditions of Language (which does not exist but its foundation is long overdue). It does not mean much to anyone any more, outside the technical debates among specialists of logic and of philosophy of science.

I posit on the contrary that these two notions are vital and within everyone's reach, in order to think language, ethics and the political in their interaction. And, actually, everybody knows it but does not know that they know it. This is what needs to be demonstrated, in order to transform thinking and reading. Realism, nominalism, I make of them a criterion for finding one's way in this interaction, for situating the relations between thinking language, ethics and the political, instead of separating them for comfortable reading.

And to my knowledge, this extension to ethics and to the political has never been done before. Thinking language as an ethics, and thereby as a poetics of society, is the means of liberating oneself from essentialism and its political effects, such as they have been pushed to their limits by Heidegger.

Here another problem arises, seemingly unrelated to what I have just said, and which constitutes a common pattern of thought shared by numerous philosophers, and certainly real, according to which European philosophy would have constituted itself on the erasure or denial, or negation, of the biblical origin of a certain number of values. While at the same time the cultural admits as a historical truth that the religious and philosophical West was founded on two pillars: Athens and Jerusalem.

I posit that it needs to be recognised that the two problems are linked. And not only because the misknown needs to be acknowledged.

That is because the paradox – a holy mountain of paradoxes – is that biblical Hebrew, the discourse in the Bible, sacralised as 'holy language',[9] as the Bible is called a 'sacred text' rather than a religious text,[10] that is to say, a text caught up in an entire mythology of Hebrew language; this discourse in the Bible, on the contrary, behind or under this layer of theologisation, is a language that is guided by a rhythm and a way of signifying which are irreducible to the Greco-Christian sign, and in which can be observed a nominalist functioning, emblematically at the opposite extreme to essentialising, massifying logical realism.

---

9. Biblical Hebrew says only that it is 'the language of holiness', *lechon haqódech*.
10. I presuppose here the definition of idolatry according to Maimonides, a cult devoted to a human product. I therefore say that the Bible is a religious text, rather than a holy one. Which also supposes the distinction that I make between the sacred, the divine and the religious, for which I refer the reader to my book *Un Coup de Bible dans la philosophie* (Paris: Bayard, 2004), p. 191.

I see the biblical as the major opposite of the sign and its theologisation of language, in its generalised dualism, its anthropology of totality, which opposes form to content, affect to concept, language to life.

That is because the biblical, language and values, is not simply an origin, as it is habitually taken to be, and what is confirmed in the imputations of denial or of oblivion. *The biblical is a way of functioning*.

Saussure said that each time one searches for the origin, one finds the way of functioning. That is what needs to be shown for the Bible, something one is not used to doing, so natural does it seem, historically, to take it as an origin. Something one says without knowing that one says it when one says: Athens and Jerusalem.

For in order to think what realism does, one must think what nominalism does. It is a question of ethics. Each must be considered in contrast with the other. And it is very simple to show what they do.

Logical realism presupposes a continuous relation between the word and what it designates. Nominalism owes its name to the fact that it considers words as names placed upon things.

From Abelard's time, in the twelfth century, there is one example which was abundantly discussed, that is the word, the notion of *humanity*. And this example is superb, because all by itself it concentrates the entire problem – obscured and unthought by logic – of the ethical and political consequences.

From the realist point of view, humanity exists, and humans are fragments of humanity. From the nominalist point of view, individuals exist, and humanity is the ensemble of individuals.

The example shows that when it comes to language, as Saussure said, there are only points of view. Here, both point of views, from each point of view, are true. But the logical, ethical and political consequences are not at all the same. Realism, concerning humanity, presupposes a generalised essentialisation, as a prerequisite. The individual melts in this mass, indistinctly. And this is the place to extend the reflection of Groethuysen: there are cultures where the notion of the individual does not exist, it is merely an element of a group. As in the *ummah*, the nation in the fusional religious sense, in Islam.

And everybody knows it without knowing: it is enough to say *Black, Jew, woman* (where the plural does not change much) or (in a certain use of the word) poetry, the novel, in order to be engaged in logical realism, with its ethical and political effects. Essentialising is massifying. It is etymologically the fascism of thought.

One of the most significant cases of logical realism is the massacre of Cambodians by the Khmer Rouge, as, before killing them, they took from the individuals their identity card, and thus they were only fragments of the Enemy to be slaughtered, in the name of the Revolution.

Nominalism alone can permit an ethics of subjects, that is, a politics of subjects. And this brings about a new point of view on what is called Athens and Jerusalem, on what the Bible does and the thinking that continues it, and on what has been done with it.

That is why for nominalism, paradoxically, I take the Bible not as origin but as a way of functioning.

The paradox, that many religious people probably misunderstand, is that I approach the Bible atheologically. Which means several things: its de-Christianisation, first of all, for Christianity has overlaid it theologico-politically, theologico-poetically and theologico-linguistically. The inverse paradox of the religious person, whose knowledge and faith are indisputable, is that what for them is the truth of the text, produces, without them knowing it, apparently, a residue: the form. The religious person, because they ponder a, *the* truth, does not see that truth functions *semiotically*, as, in the sign, meaning produces form. The result, which aims for the linguistically correct, is generally scandalously casual with regard to the signifiers.

But atheologically, apart from the hunt for sanctimoniousness and academicism, also means poetically, and more precisely following a poetics of the divine. In the sense in which I read it in Genesis and which makes me distinguish (which, to my knowledge, I am the only one to do) between the sacred, the divine and the religious, whereas for the religious person all three are indistinguishable.

I define the sacred as the fusion of the human and the cosmic, including the animal: the snake speaks to Eve, the ass to Balaam. The divine (Genesis 1: 20-1) is the principle of life that realises itself in each living creature. According to a nominalism of 'living souls'. The religious really only constitutes itself in the third book of the Pentateuch, commonly called Leviticus. It is the ritualisation of social life: the calendar of religious holidays, the restrictions, the prescriptions. And in the way it constitutes itself, it incorporates into itself the sacred and the divine, which become indistinguishable from the religious. In this sense, the religious participates in logical realism. It becomes the transmitter of ethics. It becomes a generalised theologisation which contains, potentially, the theologico-political. The theological is semiotic just as the sign is theological.

It is by its way of functioning as language that the Bible is not only an origin.

Biblical Hebrew has been so thoroughly sacralised, theologised, that the particularly remarkable functioning of thinking in Hebrew has been, to my knowledge and from my point of view, completely misunderstood, and which, contrary to the logical realism of the religious, is a nominalism. Its importance is particularly symbolic for the presence of thought.

It is the formation of certain abstract nouns. The best example, symbolic in itself of the entire problem, is the formation of the word which signifies 'life'. Life, that is, *'hayim*, masculine plural of *'hay*, living. What this word demonstrates, is that life is first of all the living.

Another example: 'youth'. That is *ne'ourim*, masculine plural of *ná'ar*, a young man: youth, that is first of all the young. Another example, savoury that one for its fate in translation. It is what has been traditionally translated by 'mercy' or 'compassion'. It is the plural of *re'hem*, which designates the uterus, the womb. Plural: *ra'hamin*.

In this nominalism of abstract nouns there is, on an ethical level, the absolute opposite to the essentialising realism of Heidegger and others. It is of major importance and very topical for thinking the relation between language, ethics and a politics of subjects.

Thinking nominalism is to think what Spinoza calls 'a human life': 'a human life I understand as one which is not defined by the circulation of blood alone, and other things, which are common to all the animals, but above all by reason, the true virtue and the life of the mind'.[11]

With all the coded language this expression brings with it, through its allusion to Uriel Da Costa, who committed suicide after his excommunication, and who had written *Exemplar Humanae Vitae* ('Example of a Human Life'), published after his death. Which makes this expression – recurrent in Spinoza – secretly a combat of the nominalism of the living against the theologico-political.

These things of the Bible, sacralisation itself – *sacred* text, *holy* language (where the Hebrew says merely language or language of holiness, *lechon haqódech*) – religion, paradoxically, prevents us from thinking them, precisely by not distinguishing between the sacred, the divine and the religious. Moreover, not only Jewish theology, through its confessionalisation, but most of all the Christian theologico-political prevents us from thinking these things, with what has been called the Jewish question, created by the Christian theologico-political, in its quest to be the *Verus Israel*.

Against the abstract thinking – void of humanity and of the universal – of the theologico-linguistic that in reality does not give forth anything but the universalisation of its own abstract model, it is vital to argue for the only strong thinking of the universal: that only the singular, in each case, is the

---

11. This can be found in the *Tractatus Politicus* (V, 5). In the text: '*Cum ergo dicimus, illud imperium optimum esse, ubi homines concorditer vitam transigunt, vitam humanam intelligo, quae non solâ sanguinis circulatione, & aliis, quae omnibus animalibus sunt communia, sed quae maximè ratione, verâ Mentis virtute, & vitâ definitur.*' See my book, *Spinoza: poème de la pensée* (Paris: Maisonneuve & Larose, 2002), p. 173.

universal. In other words, the universal is the infinite diversity of specificities, to be realised each time for itself, by itself, to be recognised as such by all the other specificities.

The living first of all. It is nominalism or death. For essentialism is the death of individuals.

Glossary

This glossary is limited to terms which are specific to Meschonnic's work.

Biblical Hebrew/*ta'am* (sg.)/*te'amim* (pl.)/taste/flavour: The accent system of biblical Hebrew consists of many conjunctive and disjunctive accents, thus contributing, by creating connections and disruptions, to the way of signifying. These accents are called *te'amim* (*ta'am* in the singular), which signifies the taste of what one has in the mouth, the flavour, this flavour being the reason for saying. This taste of language is hence not opposed to sense but carries it within it as the very movement of sense, in its continuous, in a serial semantics. This is the very meaning, and the first meaning, of orality, a parable of the body-in-language, of the physicality of language. Meschonnic therefore pleads for a ta'amisation of language and our ideas of language: that is, to take into consideration the rhythm of language. He claims to be the only translator and language thinker who pays attention to this particular accent system of the Hebrew Bible.

Body-in-language (*corps-langage*): This notion stresses the materiality of language, which is at once and inseparably speech sound and visual pattern, in their interaction within a discourse, which can be an entire text. Language is always embodied and this body is part of semantics and of signifiance.

Continuous and **Discontinuous**: The continuous (*le continu*) implies an interdependency of things, an epistemological interconnectedness, while in the discontinuous things are compartmentalised. The continuous is the key term in Meschonnic's theory of rhythm. It refers to the fact that sense in language is a matter not simply of the denotation of words, but of various elements of significance and their interaction in their historicity. In order to understand what language is and does, we need to consider language in its ensemble, its continuous, instead of in the discontinuous of its signs. The discontinuous considers language in terms of words or signs, in a linguistics of the word, or rhythm in terms of the discrete units of metre (metrical units, feet). The continuous includes the discontinuous but goes beyond this level and shows that there is more to language than its elements.

Discourse: This term is taken from Émile Benveniste and designates language in the form in which it is actually spoken: that is, its 'appropriation' by a speaker, in an individual realisation and as an entire utterance. This means that discourse considers language in its continuous instead of in split-up discontinuous units. Discourse implies a semantics of enunciation which allows for the full range of significance.

Effacers [*effaçantes*]: These are standard practices of translating inscribed in the sign and thus focused on rendering the meaning of words. Often, they also prioritise linguistic fluency over rhythmic features in the original. Consequently, they produce translations which do not take into consideration the rhythm of a text and thus efface large portions of significance.

Historicity: This key term means the situatedness and subjectivity of any discourse, implying also that the critique itself is situated and part of the discourse. In Meschonnic's theory of language, this term captures the contradiction that an activity is situated and circumstantial, but can constantly leave this situation and remain active in the present, in new presences. It is opposed to **historicism**, which is the completed, the past of meaning and a reduction of meaning to its conditions of production. Historicity designates a relation, the indefinitely renewed encounter between past and present moments of meaning. As such, it is unpredictable. This is a central term for poetics, since it creates the specificity of a literary work and shows that the sense of literature is not limited to the sense of the words at the time of their production. This implies the necessity of a theory of discourse for all disciplines of meaning because it shows the interaction between the theory of language and the theories of literature, art, the subject, ethics and politics. This is why Meschonnic's theory of rhythm is a **historical anthropology of language**.

Langue and ***Langage***: This famous distinction in French, for which there is no real equivalent in English, differentiates between a language system, a vernacular – that is, *langue* – and language generally, as the capacity of expression. In Meschonnic, however, *langage* is often used as the individual use of *langue*. In English translation, we are often obliged to use 'language' for both *langue* and *langage*, which in many cases poses no problem; where the opposition of *langue* to *language* is marked, *langue* is either translated as *language system* or kept in French as *langue*.

Orality: Meschonnic sees the duality of oral and written as part of the logic of the sign. In opposition to this, he rather constructs a tripartite constellation of the written, the spoken and the oral. He defines the **oral** as the mode of signifying, characterised by a primacy of rhythm and prosody in the movement of sense. Since the poetic subject of enunciation transforms discourse and is subject through this discourse, this primacy of rhythm and prosody implies an interdependency of subject and orality. This is the historicity of language and the mutual transformation of subject and discourse. The oral can be speech or writing, but literature would be the maximal orality since it is most attentive to rhythm. Orality is hence a key notion of Meschonnic's theory, impossible to separate from rhythm and the continuous.

Poetics: Poetics here is not equivalent to stylistics, as the term is often used in the Anglophone world. For Meschonnic, poetics refers rather to the theory of the specificity of literature, as the search for concepts that allow us to fathom the functioning of literature. However, this goes far beyond the realm of literature, since understanding this dimension of the functioning of language also impacts on our understanding of the functioning of the subject, and consequently, of ethics, politics and society as a whole. Poetics concerns the interaction of the form of language and the form of life.

Poetry and **Poem**: **Poetry**, for Meschonnic, is not necessarily the literary form nor the descriptive term to designate a corpus of written poems. He defines it rather as the activity of the poem: that is, the transformation of a form of life into a form of language, and reciprocally a form of language into a form of life. At times, he uses the term **poetry** in opposition to the **poem**, to refer to a fixed idea about what poetry should be like, as **poetisation**: that is to say, what precisely lacks the transformative, unique activity of a poem. On other occasions, however, the term poetry can also be understood as the activity of a poem.

Rhythm: Meschonnic's key term, based on Émile Benveniste's discovery of the pre-Platonic meaning of rhythm as form in movement. It is not the usual definition of a regular, alternating pattern, but rhythm as the individual organisation of language in speech, organising the elements of significance. It is an activity of discourse.

Semiotics and **Semantics**: With this distinction, Meschonnic refers to two modalities of sense, defined by Émile Benveniste in his article 'Sémiologie de la langue' ('The Semiology of Language', in Robert E. Innis (ed.), *Semiotics: An Introductory Anthology*, Bloomington: Indiana University Press, 1985, pp. 228–46). The semiotic mode belongs to *la langue* as system of signs: that is, a theory based on the model of the sign, words representing a signified. The semantic mode, however, results from discourse, or from an activity of a speaker putting language into action. It is concerned with the use and activity of language and thus with the organisation of life. Benveniste says that in semiotics a word is recognised, whereas in semantics it is understood.

Sense and **meaning**: These are constituted not only by the lexical but by all elements of significance. The French word *sens* is employed by Meschonnic in its semantic fullness, to encompass 'direction', an individual 'meaning' and a more generalised 'meaningfulness', and also the 'senses' themselves. Particularly noteworthy here is the fact that **sense of language** (*sens du langage*) can mean a sense *for* language and a sense *of* language, but also 'sense' such as it takes place *in* language and languages. Since both 'sense' and 'meaning' are ambiguous terms, with 'sense' being more often contextualised than 'meaning', we could not be fully consistent in our translation of *sens*; we tended rather towards 'sense' to underline the physical dimension of the term, but at times 'meaning' seemed more appropriate.

Serial semantics: With this expression Meschonnic suggests that the repetition of speech sounds/phonemes or linguistic patterns creates semantic associations between signifiers (as in rhyme) which function as networks or chains running throughout a discourse or (even long) text, working as an essential part of the meaning or significance of this discourse.

Sign: The sign consists of the signifier and the signified; in this conception, the signifier is traditionally considered to be secondary, as a means to designate the signified. In the theory of rhythm, the implied focus on the word unit is considered to be discontinuous and ignorant of large elements of significance. Meschonnic seeks to combat the sign's exclusive claim on sense.

Signifiance: This term, taken from Benveniste, designates a generalised semantics, a function of the ensemble of signifiers, which is linguistic and non-linguistic (particularly in spoken language). It is the way or the process of signifying, of meaning-making. This is opposed to **signification**, which means rather the result of the meaning-making process. It also needs to be distinguished from **sense**, which often refers to the sense of a word and its interpretation. The signification of a word depends, however, on its intonation and situation. For significance, the historicity of an enunciation, as well as its rhythmic organisation in prosodic chains, is vital.

Subjectivation: This takes place when a subject invents discourse and at the same time invents itself through its discourse. This is a specific subject, the **subject of the poem** (even though not in the sense of a literary genre but as activity). In order to understand this specificity, one needs to consider the semantics of the continuous of language. Meschonnic defines the **subject** as someone 'by whom someone else becomes a subject' [*est sujet celui par qui un autre devient sujet*], thus stressing the dialogical aspect. This also implies that the subjectivation of a text makes possible the reader's subjectivation.

Theory (critical and **traditional)**: Meschonnic follows Max Horkheimer in the differentiation of critical theory, which is a theory aware of its own conditions, and traditional theory, which remains within its proper boundaries and is therefore compartmentalised, and which leaves theory and society in place: that is, having no effect on them. A critical theory for Meschonnic implies a theory of language in his sense of poetics.

Thinking language: This is our translation of both the noun and the verb *pensée du langage/penser le langage*, or *Sprachdenken/Sprache denken* in German. Even though this transitive use of 'to think' is against English norms, it insists – more than 'thinking about' could – on the fact that our thinking is done not only with but in language. It is language reflection based on the fundamental force of language in its continuous.

Chronological Bibliography of Meschonnic's Books[1]

1967: *Dictionnaire du français contemporain*, in collaboration (Paris: Larousse).
1970: *Pour la poétique I* (Paris: Gallimard), 180 pp.
1970: *Les Cinq Rouleaux: Le Chant des chants, Ruth, Comme ou les Lamentations, Parole du sage, Esther*, translated from Hebrew (Paris: Gallimard), 240 pp.
1972: *Dédicaces proverbes*, poems (Paris: Gallimard), 124 pp. [Prix Max Jacob].
1973: *Pour la poétique II: Épistémologie de l'écriture, poétique de la traduction* (Paris: Gallimard), 458 pp.
1973: *Pour la poétique III: Une Parole écriture* (Paris: Gallimard), 342 pp.
1975: *Le Signe et le poème*, essay (Paris: Gallimard), 548 pp.
1976: *Dans nos recommencements*, poems (Paris: Gallimard), 86 pp.
1977: *Pour la poétique IV: Écrire Hugo* (vol. 1) (Paris: Gallimard), 306 pp.
1977: *Pour la poétique IV: Écrire Hugo* (vol. 2) (Paris: Gallimard), 218 pp.
1978: *Pour la poétique V: Poésie sans réponse* (Paris: Gallimard), 442 pp.
1979: *Légendaire chaque jour*, poems (Paris: Gallimard), 86 pp.
1981: *Jona et le signifiant errant* (Paris: Gallimard), 136 pp.
1982: *Critique du rythme: anthropologie historique du langage* (Lagrasse: Verdier), 730 pp. [new edition 1990; paperback edition Lagrasse: Verdier/poche, 2009].
1984: 'La Nature dans la voix', introduction to Charles Nodier, *Dictionnaire des onomatopées* (Mauvezin: Trans-Europ-Repress).
1985: *Voyageurs de la voix*, poems (Lagrasse: Verdier), 88 pp. [Prix Mallarmé, 1986].
1985: 'Présentation', 'Critique de la théorie critique' and 'Le Langage chez Habermas, ou Critique, encore un effort', in *Critique de la théorie critique: langage et histoire* (Paris: Presses Universitaires de Vincennes), 204 pp.
1985: 'Mallarmé au-delà du silence', in Stéphane Mallarmé, *Écrits sur le livre (choix de textes)* (Paris: Éditions de l'Éclat) (pp. 11–62).
1985: *Les États de la poétique* (Paris: Presses Universitaires de France), 284 pp.

---

1. This bibliography is taken from Serge Martin's blog, available at <https://mescho.hypotheses.org/bibliographie-des-oeuvres-dhenri-meschonnic> (last accessed 21 July 2018).

1986: *Jamais et un jour*, poems (Paris: Dominique Bedou), 48 pp.
1988: *Modernité modernité* (Lagrasse: Verdier) [paperback edition Paris: Gallimard, 'folio-essais', 1993], 316 pp.
1989: *La Rime et la vie* (Lagrasse: Verdier), 366 pp. [paperback edition Paris: Gallimard, 'folio-essais', 2006], 496 pp.
1990: *Nous le passage*, poems (Lagrasse: Verdier), 96 pp. [Artalect, audiobook (audiocassette)].
1990: *Le Langage Heidegger* (Paris: Presses Universitaires de France), 398 pp. (out of print).
1991: *Des Mots et des mondes: dictionnaires, encyclopédies, grammaires, nomenclatures* (Paris: Hatier), 312 pp.
1995: *Politique du rythme, politique du sujet* (Lagrasse: Verdier), 620 pp.
1995: 'Introduction' and 'Penser Humboldt aujourd'hui', in Henri Meschonnic (ed.), *La Pensée dans la langue: Humboldt et après* (Paris: Presses Universitaires de Vincennes), pp. 5–50.
1996: 'Avant-propos' (co-edited with Sylvain Auroux and Simone Delesalle) and 'Prosodie, poème du poème', in Henri Meschonnic, Sylvain Auroux and Simone Delesalle (eds), *Histoire et grammaire du sens: hommage à Jean-Claude Chevalier* (Paris: Armand Colin), pp. 7–10 and 222–52.
1997: *De la langue française: essai sur une clarté obscure* (Paris: Hachette), 356 pp. [lightly revised reprint in paperback: 'Pluriel', Paris: Hachette, 2001, 478 pp.].
1998: *Traité du rythme: des vers et des proses* (Paris: Dunod) (in collaboration with Gérard Dessons), 242 pp.
1999: *Poétique du traduire* (Lagrasse: Verdier), 474 pp.
1999: *Combien de noms*, poems (Paris: L'Improviste), 96 pp.
2000: *Maintenant*, poems (Aubervilliers: Les Petits Classiques du Grand Pirate).
2000: *Crisis del signo, política del ritmo y teoría del lenguaje, Crise du signe, politique du rythme et théorie du langage* (bilingual edition, Spanish trans. by Guillermo Piña-Contreras) (Santo Domingo: Ferilibro), 104 pp.
2000: *Je n'ai pas tout entendu*, poems (Creil: Dumerchez), 128 pp.
2000: 'Et le génie des langues?' and 'Poétique de la pensée: le latin de Spinoza', in Henri Meschonnic (ed.), *Et le génie des langues?* (Paris: Presses Universitaires de Vincennes), pp. 5–15 and 103–48.
2000: *Le Rythme et la lumière – avec Pierre Soulages* (Paris: Odile Jacob), 230 pp.
2001: *L'Utopie du juif* (Paris: Desclée de Brouwer), 428 pp.
2001: *Gloires*, translation of the Psalms (Paris: Desclée de Brouwer), 556 pp.
2001: *Puisque je suis ce buisson*, poems (Paris: Arfuye), 98 pp.
2001: *Célébration de la poésie* (Lagrasse: Verdier), 320 pp. [paperback Verdier/poche, 2006].
2001: 'Hugo continuant la Bible', in Henri Meschonnic and Manoko Ôno (eds), *Victor Hugo et la Bible*, in *Victor Hugo et l'Orient*, 7 (ed. Franck Laurent) (Paris: Maisonneuve & Larose), pp. 7–25.
2002: *Hugo, la poésie contre le maintien de l'ordre* (Paris: Maisonneuve & Larose), 256 pp.
2002: *Spinoza, poème de la pensée* (Paris: Maisonneuve & Larose), 312 pp.
2002: *Au commencement*, translation of Genesis (Paris: Desclée de Brouwer), 376 pp.
2002: 'La Modernité après le post-moderne' and 'Le Rôle de la théorie du langage pour une poétique et une politique de la relation entre la France et le Japon', in

Henri Meschonnic and Shiguehiko Hasumi, *La Modernité après le post-moderne* (Paris: Maisonneuve & Larose), pp. 11–12 and 165–88.

2003: *Les Noms*, translation of Exodus (Paris: Desclée de Brouwer), 360 pp.
2004: *Infiniment à venir*, poems (Paris: Dumerchez), 54 pp.
2004: *Un Coup de Bible dans la philosophie* (Paris: Bayard), 304 pp.
2005: *Et il a appelé*, translation of Leviticus (Paris: Desclée de Brouwer), 224 pp.
2005: *Tout entier visage*, poems (Paris: Arfuyen), 108 pp.
2006: *Vivre poème* (Paris: Dumerchez), 40 pp.
2006: *Le Nom de notre ignorance, la dame d'Auxerre* (Paris: Laurence Teper), 96 pp.
2006: *Et la terre coule*, poems (Paris: Arfuyen), 108 pp. [Prix de la littérature francophone Jean Arp].
2006: *Il Ritmo come poetica: Conversazioni con Giuditta Isotti Rosowsky* (Rome: Bulzoni), 160 pp.
2007: *Heidegger ou le national-essentialisme* (Paris: Laurence Teper), 200 pp.
2007: *Éthique et politique du traduire* (Lagrasse: Verdier, 2007), 185 pp.
2008: *Dans le désert*, translation of Numbers (Paris: Desclée de Brouwer), 292 pp.
2008: *La Vie je cours*, poems (Cannes: Tipaza), 16 pp.
2008: *Dans le bois de la langue* (Paris: Laurence Teper), 550 pp.
2008: *Parole rencontre*, poems (Mont-de-Laval: L'Atelier du Grand Tetras), 80 pp.
2009: *Pour sortir du postmoderne* (Paris: Klincksieck), 184 pp.
2010: *Demain dessus demain dessous*, poems (Paris: Arfuyen), 102 pp.
2012: *L'Obscur travaille*, poems (Paris: Arfuyen), 98 pp.
2012: *Langage, histoire, une même théorie* (Lagrasse: Verdier), 750 pp.

Name index

Abelard, 317
Adorno, Theodor, W., 44, 57, 77, 91, 99, 115, 157, 299, 310
Aeschylus, 142–4, 150
Alain, 97–8, 162, 296
Althusser, Louis, 78, 112, 303
Annensky, Innokenty, 190
Apollinaire, Guillaume, 62, 85, 109, 158, 187, 197, 295
Aragon, Louis, 65, 84, 150, 251, 288
Augustine, 134, 236, 240

Baïf, Jean-Antoine de, 116
Balzac, Honoré de, 188
Banon, David, 266
Barthes, Roland, 200–1, 307
Baudelaire, Charles, 25–7, 57, 78, 102–3, 151, 153, 158, 184, 190, 221, 279, 284, 290
Beckett, Samuel, 156
Bely, Andrei, 134, 139
Benda, Julien, 300
Benjamin, Walter, 213, 287, 293, 306
Benveniste, Émile, 3–4, 12, 16–23, 26, 31–2, 38, 41, 54–5, 67–8, 70, 74–5, 91, 109–10, 113, 199–200, 202, 221–2, 239, 244, 282, 307–8, 313, 322–4
Berman, Antoine, 225
Blok, Alexandr, 94–5, 119, 161, 189, 191, 196–7, 308
Bloomfield, Leonard, 68, 76
Blum, Léon, 207

Bonnefoy, Yves, 60, 125, 150
Bourdieu, Pierre, 310
Brassens, George, 215
Brecht, Bertolt, 63, 148–50
Brel, Jacques, 215
Brik, Osip Maksimovich, 127
Bryusov, Valery, 128
Buber, Martin, 30, 242, 253
Bubner, Rüdiger, 304

Céline, Louis-Ferdinand, 38, 314
Chagall, Marc, 190
Chomsky, Noam, 3, 24, 110, 112, 300, 307
Chouraqui, André, 242, 262–3
Cicero, 199, 258, 271, 294
Claudel, Paul, 138, 184, 264
Corneille, Pierre, 136, 153
Cornulier, Benoît de, 137, 145, 150–3
Cummings, E. E., 63

Dante Alighieri, 63, 79, 159, 259, 290
De Gaulle, Charles, 207
Deleuze, Gilles, 1, 116
Derrida, Jacques, 1, 9, 19, 21–2, 24, 48, 109, 200
Desbordes-Valmore, Marceline, 193
Deschamps, Eustache, 64, 184
Diaghilev, Sergei, 190
Diderot, Dénis, 79–80
Dostoyevsky, Fyodor, 190
Du Bellay, Joachim du, 63
Durkheim, Émile, 240

Ehrenburg, Ilya Grigoryevich, 190
Elias, Norbert, 299
Eliot, T. S., 58, 84, 96, 123–4, 158
Éluard, Paul, 63, 85, 110, 125, 183, 191, 194

Fet, Afanasy, 190
Flaubert, Gustave, 63, 94, 111, 123
Flavius Josephus, 238, 257
Fontaine, Jean de la, 136–7
Foucault, Michel, 29, 204
Freud, Sigmund, 69, 80, 99, 105–6, 168, 218, 220, 234, 261

Gala (Éluard Dalí), 191
Ghil, René, 58, 190
Gide, André, 190, 273, 314
Girard, René, 12, 300
Godelier, Maurice, 300–3
Goethe, Johann Wolfgang, 63
Gogol, Nikolai Vasilievich, 156
Góngora, Luis de, 162
Gontcharova, Natalia Sergeevna, 190
Gorki, Maxim, 190
Greimas, Algirdas Julien, 73, 75
Groethuysen, Bernhard, 313, 317
Guattari, Félix, 116

HaLevi, Yehuda, 266–7
Hegel, Georg Wilhelm Friedrich, 57, 82, 92, 122, 158, 204, 250–1, 290, 298, 304, 309
Heidegger, Martin, 2, 19, 21, 33–4, 38, 92, 105, 199, 203, 221, 240, 250, 284, 289, 313–14, 316, 319, 327–8
Heine, Heinrich, 190
Herodotus, 295
Hippocrates, 72, 74–5
Hitler, Adolf, 207, 267
Hjelmslev, Louis, 5, 62, 72, 75–6, 105, 112, 113, 117, 232
Hölderlin, Friedrich, 65, 170, 171, 215
Holz, Arno, 148
Homer, 156, 231, 238
Hopkins, Gerard Manley, 81, 184
Horkheimer, Max, 44, 73, 284, 304–5, 312, 325
Hugo, Victor, 58, 63, 78, 85–6, 94, 98, 125, 136, 156, 187, 236, 271, 290, 314
Humboldt, Wilhelm von, 3, 23–4, 26, 41–2, 49, 54, 84, 105, 108, 113, 205, 222, 232, 237, 249, 282, 294, 306, 312

Jacob, Max, 2, 159
Jakobson, Roman, 3, 63–4, 96, 110–11, 161, 216, 269, 271, 289, 300
Jankélévitch, Vladimir, 200
Jauss, Hans Robert, 217
Joyce, James, 63, 156, 191

Kafka, Franz, 156
Kaldhûn, Ibn, 159
Keats, John, 269
Khlebnikov, Viktor Vladimirovich, 63, 101, 191, 289
Klemperer, Viktor, 42–5, 293

Larionov, Mikhail Fyodorovich, 190
Lautréamont, 64
Lemaistre de Sacy, Louis-Isaac, 258
Lenin, Vladimir Ilyich, 190
Leopardi, Giocomo, 236
Lermontov, Mikhail Yuryevich, 190
Leroi-Gourhan, André, 98, 119, 134
Levinas, Emmanuel, 30
Lévy-Bruhl, Lucien, 64
Lomonossov, Mikhail Vasilyevich, 189
Lope de Vega, 162
Luther, Martin, 242, 258, 263

MacLuhan, Marshall, 61, 215
Maimonides, 214, 241, 261, 267, 316
Malherbe, François de, 126, 136
Mallarmé, Stéphane, 2, 63–4, 79, 89, 102, 145, 150–2, 169–73, 190, 233, 264, 284, 294–5, 326
Malleret, Ève, 177, 179, 191–2, 194–5
Mandelstam, Nadezhda, 193
Mandelstam, Osip Emilyevich, 79, 92, 159, 161
Marx, Karl, 4, 68–9, 78–9, 92–3, 104–5, 108, 117, 157–9, 163, 204, 221, 302–3, 305–9
Mauss, Marcel, 82, 203
Mayakovsky, Vladimir Vladimirovich, 83, 119, 183, 189–90, 192–3, 197, 200, 236
Merleau-Ponty, Maurice, 2, 295–6
Michaux, Henri, 191
Michelet, Jules, 309
Milosz, Czesław, 210
Milton, John, 156
Molière, 161, 210
Molina, Tirso de, 162
Molinet, Jean, 64

Montaigne, Michel de, 161, 251, 254, 255, 313
Morris, Charles, 72–3, 76
Mussorgsky, Modest Petrovich, 190

Nekrasov, Nikolay Alexeyevich, 189
Nietzsche, Friedrich, 88, 208, 285
Nordau, Max, 171, 294

Pasternak, Boris Leonidovich, 101, 189–90, 193–4, 196
Pêcheux, Michel, 210
Péguy, Charles, 60, 234
Peirce, Charles Sanders, 72–5, 289
Pétain, Philippe, 207
Plato, 16–17, 26, 34, 88, 99–100, 200, 207, 231, 237, 295, 323
Ponge, Francis, 64
Popper, Karl, 299, 303, 310
Pound, Ezra, 57, 58, 83–4, 119, 158, 239, 271
Proudhon, Pierre-Joseph, 309
Proust, Marcel, 63, 104, 110–11, 221, 289
Pushkin, Alexander Sergeyevich, 95, 128, 153, 189–90

Rabelais, François, 156, 289
Racine, Jean, 125, 153
Réda, Jacques, 63
Rémond, René, 301
Reverdy, Pierre, 91, 187
Ricoeur, Paul, 266
Rilke, Rainer Maria, 63, 148, 188–90, 194
Rimbaud, Arthur, 63, 84, 150–2, 170, 173, 279, 281, 284, 290
Ritsos, Yannis, 58
Robin, Régine, 306–7
Ronsard, Pierre de, 135–6, 236
Rorty, Richard, 315
Roubaud, Jacques, 107, 125, 136–7, 150–1

Saint-John Perse, 103, 169, 233
Sainte-Beuve, Charles-Augustin, 59–60, 104, 221, 289
Sartre, Jean-Paul, 69, 79, 94, 300, 308
Saussure, Ferdinand de, 5, 17–18, 23, 35, 62, 64, 68, 72–6, 89–91, 98, 105, 108, 112–13, 202, 204, 219, 222, 230–3, 269, 282, 289, 300, 307, 312, 317

Scève, Maurice, 236
Schelling, Friedrich Wilhelm Joseph, 190
Schlegel, August Wilhelm, 118–19, 127
Schopenhauer, Arthur, 190
Segond, Louis, 242, 258, 163
Serres, Michel, 300
Shakespeare, William, 227, 273
Shelley, Percy Bysshe, 99, 153, 182
Shklovsky, Viktor, 123
Sophocles, 118, 142–4, 150
Spinoza, Baruch, 25, 40, 240, 242–4, 249, 319, 327
Staël, Madame de, 189
Stanislavski, Konstantin Sergeievich, 18
Steiner, George, 225, 260–1
Sternberger, Dolf, 42–5
Stirner, Max, 102, 221
Stockhausen, Karlheinz, 197
Stravinsky, Igor Fyodorovich, 190

Tolstoy, Alexis, 190
Tolstoy, Leon, 190
Tomashevsky, Boris Viktorovich, 123, 128
Trabant, Jürgen, 43
Triolet, Elsa, 191
Trotsky, Leon, 190
Tsvetaeva, Marina, 177, 179, 188–97, 206
Tynianov, Iouri, 80–1
Tyutchev, Fyodor Ivanovich, 189–90

Ungaretti, Guiseppe, 236

Valéry, Paul, 63, 79, 82, 96–7, 101–5, 123, 205
Venuti, Lawrence, 225, 226
Verlaine, Paul, 136, 150–2, 190, 196
Villon, François, 189
Vovelle, Michel, 303, 307

Wagner, Richard, 208
Wittgenstein, Ludwig, 6, 30, 44, 175

Yesenin, Sergei Alexandrovich, 142

Zola, Émile, 188, 294
Zhirmunsky, Viktor Maksimovic, 123–4, 130–1, 135
Zumthor, Paul, 200–1, 203, 209, 214–17

Subject index

academicism, 167, 174, 182, 185, 187, 294, 315
activity, 17, 23–4, 27, 50, 53–4, 57, 59, 61–5, 71, 83, 165–6, 169–70, 177, 187, 201, 219, 234, 237, 252, 259, 263, 294, 296, 322
 of art and literature, 27–8
 ethical, 27–8, 295
 of giving form, 16–17
 of language/speech/discourse, 24, 28, 48, 54, 62, 64, 85, 116, 124, 155, 225, 248, 295, 306, 324
 of the mind, 41
 of the poem/poetic, 27, 53, 57, 62–3, 65, 79, 86, 167–8, 236, 239, 323, 325
 political, 27–8
 of the subject, 4, 27, 41, 54, 68, 100, 239, 296
anthropology, 15, 17, 25, 30, 32, 36, 53–5, 64, 69–70, 76–7, 82, 87, 90, 98, 101, 109, 111, 113, 133, 138, 155, 156, 180, 205, 208–9, 214, 230, 256, 270, 282, 293, 297, 298, 300, 302–3, 308, 310, 313, 315, 317, 322
Arabic, 82, 124, 127, 138, 146, 155, 159–60, 238, 267
automatisation, 121, 123

Bantu, 155
Bible, 6, 8–9, 11–13, 23–4, 36–7, 48–9, 81–2, 225–7, 229–31, 235, 237–67, 270, 294, 316–19, 321, 327
biblical, 9, 36–8, 48, 159, 216, 225–6, 238, 241, 244–8, 252–3, 255, 257, 259, 262, 266–7, 316–18, 321
binary, 21–2, 24, 35, 65, 127, 131–2, 151, 210, 226, 230, 232, 248, 294, 298, 300
biologism, 30, 204
biologisation, 204
body, 11, 17, 55, 63, 65, 78, 82, 112, 119, 155, 158–9, 180–2, 184, 199, 203–6, 208, 218–19, 226, 252, 271, 295, 298, 309, 314
body-in-language, 37, 199, 226, 233–4, 238, 245, 248, 321

Chinese, 92, 155, 160
Christian/Christianity/Christianism, 230, 237, 239, 248, 251, 253, 256–7, 258, 261–2, 265–8, 308–9, 316, 318–19
Christianisation/de-Christianise, 238, 241, 257, 318
cognitive science, 11, 163
consensus, 58, 231, 257, 289
 sign-consensus, 172
continuous, 6, 11, 18, 19–20, 22–3, 27–33, 35–6, 45, 50, 59, 74, 87, 105, 132, 169–70, 178, 180, 188, 192, 202, 227, 233–5, 237–40, 245–250, 258, 263–4, 270–1, 278, 288, 290, 294, 312, 315, 317, 321–3, 325
Critical Theory/critical theory, 44, 92, 110, 157, 221, 284, 291, 298, 304–6, 325
critique of rhythm, 4, 10, 12, 17, 32, 50,

SUBJECT INDEX | 333

53, 55, 57–8, 66, 70, 76–7, 81, 83–4, 91, 98, 110, 112, 115–16, 122, 155, 157–8, 160–1, 163, 198, 257, 291, 298–9, 303, 305, 310

democracy, 34, 105, 230, 300, 310
diachrony, 35, 232, 307
discontinuous, 18, 20–1, 28, 35–6, 170, 174, 188, 192, 202, 232, 234, 237, 245–6, 249, 258, 263–4, 271, 278, 287, 294, 312, 321, 324
discourse, 4, 12, 16–20, 22–4, 28–30, 32, 36, 45, 53–5, 57, 59, 61–2, 64–71, 73–81, 83–5, 88–92, 96–100, 103–27, 129–33, 135–7, 139–45, 147–51, 153–60, 162, 165, 170, 173, 178, 182, 187, 194, 197–8, 200–5 208, 210–11, 217–22, 231– 5, 239, 252, 261–3, 265–6, 270–2, 279, 283, 288, 295, 297–300, 303–10, 316, 322–5
discourse analysis, 45, 203, 210, 220, 303
Dreyfus Affair, 313
dualism, 28, 36, 57–8, 60, 62, 67, 75, 78, 86, 89, 97, 102, 104, 107, 117, 157–8, 163, 180–1, 207–8, 230, 245, 247–8, 253, 281, 286–7, 289–90, 299–300, 314, 317
duality, 111, 177, 198, 201, 217, 248, 299, 323

effacers (effacing translations [*effaçantes*]), 227, 237, 253, 260, 322
empirical, 4, 34, 55, 58–9, 68, 70–1, 73–4, 77, 82, 88–9, 108, 113, 118, 121–2, 153, 158, 163, 181, 196, 200, 203, 208–9, 220–1, 231, 237, 282, 298–300, 308, 311
empiricism, 72, 163, 198, 200
English, 5, 8, 15–18, 47–51, 96, 117, 127–9, 131–2, 138–40, 144, 147, 153, 156, 242, 251, 254, 260, 268, 270, 301, 322, 325
epic, 86, 100, 103, 122, 128, 138, 146–7, 162–3, 172, 189, 198, 216, 235
epistemology, 21, 34, 45, 61, 71–3, 75, 79, 104, 106, 112, 239, 271, 291, 300–3, 305, 307, 321
ethics, 21, 25, 27–30, 33–4, 38–9, 41–2, 44–6, 48, 62, 64, 71, 87, 89, 160, 170–1, 177, 197, 222, 225–6, 233–5, 239–40, 245, 249, 251–2, 263, 283, 290–1, 294–5, 300, 303, 310, 312–19, 322, 325

Europe, 12, 37–8, 40, 49, 92, 127, 159, 205, 210, 242, 262, 299, 308, 316
expressionism, 158, 184

flavour, 37, 238, 263–4, 321
formalisation, 64, 72, 76, 92, 117, 122, 179, 180, 215, 302
formalism, 12, 47, 55, 103, 110, 123–4, 158–9, 161, 180, 182, 202, 235, 289, 300
Frankfurt School, 44, 304
French, 2–3, 5, 7–8, 15–16, 18, 47–50, 57, 86, 109, 121–2, 125–8, 132–3, 135–9, 143–7, 150, 152–3, 165, 167, 172, 174, 184, 186, 188–94, 197, 209, 211–12, 215, 227, 229, 236, 241–2, 247, 250–2, 258, 261–2, 273, 289, 301, 309, 322, 324
futurism, 184, 308

Gaelic, 155
generative grammar/linguistics, 1, 73, 75, 78, 104, 108, 111, 113, 163, 210, 307
German, 7, 15, 22, 42–5, 47, 81, 91, 93, 105–6, 109, 120–1, 127, 130–2, 147, 188–91, 194, 203, 242, 250, 299, 325
Gnosticism, 300
Greek/Greco-, 7, 11, 37–8, 89, 91, 98, 109, 118, 122, 127, 135–6, 138–9, 142, 144, 146, 180, 237–8, 241, 247–8, 254, 257, 260, 268, 277, 298, 310, 316

Hebrew, 7–8, 11–12, 36–8, 41, 48, 81–2, 124, 155, 225–6, 237–8, 241, 247–8, 250–8, 260–4, 267–8, 316, 318–19, 321
Hellenisation, 226, 238–9, 251, 257
historicisation/dehistoricisation/historicise/dehistoricise, 59, 73, 87, 89, 98, 104, 155, 168, 170, 208, 242, 245, 248, 258, 279, 283, 288, 290, 294, 299–300, 307–8, 322
historicity, 21, 23, 28–30, 41–2, 45, 50, 53, 59–60, 63, 70, 72–4, 77, 85, 87, 88–9, 93, 95–6, 98, 104, 106, 108, 110, 113, 116, 119, 121–3, 129, 139, 141, 150–1, 155, 158, 160–1, 163, 170, 174, 182–3, 187, 198, 208, 212, 216–17, 221–2, 232–3, 235, 245–7, 249, 279, 262, 283, 287–9, 291, 293–5, 297–300, 305–8, 311, 321–3, 325

humanities, 11, 21, 25, 41, 47, 72, 166, 285, 291, 299–301, 308–10
human sciences, 31, 112, 301–3

ideologism, 239
ideology/ideological, 29, 41, 43, 58, 73, 78–9, 85, 92–3, 189, 191, 239, 251–2, 260, 285, 289, 294, 300, 302–5, 307–8, 310
Indo-European, 12, 160
infinity/infinite 24, 28, 30, 40, 42, 104, 113, 121, 163, 233, 236, 244, 249, 252, 255, 263, 279, 283, 308, 311, 315, 320
instrumentalisation, 204–5, 311
instrumentalism, 70, 104, 119, 201, 204, 298, 315
intellectuals/intellectuals, 1–2, 8–9, 21, 61, 94, 165, 296, 300, 302, 314
interaction, 25, 28, 33, 38, 45, 54, 57–8, 61–2, 80, 104, 143, 198, 233, 239, 272, 295, 312, 314–16, 321–3
intelligibility, 21, 29, 33, 286, 293–5, 309
isotopy, 75
Italian, 128–9, 236, 242, 267, 308

Japanese, 153, 160
Judaism, 262, 266–7, 306

knowledge, 21, 27, 29, 31, 43, 37, 50, 61–2, 66, 77–8, 90, 94, 100, 105–7, 134, 142, 161, 204, 221, 231, 234, 241, 149, 251, 255, 260, 263, 266, 288, 294, 302, 305, 313, 315–16, 318

Latin, 7, 12, 38, 121, 134–5, 138, 145–6, 184, 251, 254–5, 267, 294
lettrism, 207
life, 3, 6, 10, 14–15, 20–2, 25–30, 33, 35–6, 38, 40, 48, 54–5, 62, 65–6, 75, 82, 85–7, 95–6, 100, 103, 119, 134, 163, 165, 167, 170, 172–5, 177, 179–89, 191–2, 194–7, 207, 210, 232–3, 236, 239–40, 242–4, 251, 284, 287, 296–8, 308, 312–13, 315, 317–19, 323–4
linguistics, 1–9, 11–12, 17–19, 34–5, 42, 45, 54–5, 64, 67–8, 72, 74–6, 90, 104, 111–13, 117, 121–2, 129, 160, 199, 209–11, 214, 219, 222, 231–2, 249, 269, 297, 300, 303, 306–7, 310, 313, 321
literary criticism/critique, 2, 58

living, 3, 23, 29, 36, 38, 40, 65, 80, 93, 104, 173, 175, 180, 200, 203, 214, 230, 240, 244, 282, 286, 298, 313–14, 318–20

Malaysian, 158
Marxism/Marxist, 4, 68–9, 78–9, 92, 104, 108, 117, 157–8, 163, 204, 221, 302–3, 305–8
metaphor, 23, 43, 73, 78–80, 82, 94–5, 100, 105, 112, 116, 137, 173, 189, 191, 199, 205–6, 218–19, 222, 239, 252, 262, 265, 270, 302, 310
metaphorisation/demetaphorisation, 95, 204, 219, 265
metrics/metrical/meter, 4, 16–17, 22–3, 50, 55, 69, 71, 83, 102–4, 107–8, 113, 115–54, 158–62, 169, 172, 180–3, 185–6, 188, 199, 217, 221, 233, 238, 257, 260–1, 266, 283, 295, 309, 321

natural sciences, 73, 300–2
nominalism, 33–4, 36, 41–2, 291, 312–13, 315–20

oralisation, 194, 253
orality/oral, 12–13, 50, 55, 131, 155–6, 162, 171, 175, 178, 184, 193, 198–219, 234–5, 238, 264, 267, 288, 299, 314, 321, 323
orature, 201

paradigma/paradigmatic, 4, 68–9, 110–11, 202, 232, 245
parenthesis, 48, 201
pedagogy, 31, 61, 150, 212–14
phenomenology, 2, 63, 73, 82, 88, 101, 105, 169, 250
philology, 2, 5, 12, 43, 65, 67, 91, 106, 109, 113, 122, 212, 220, 237–9, 246, 249, 255–8, 262, 293–4, 314
poem, 3–4, 8–9, 12–3, 20, 24–5, 27–30, 47, 50, 54–5, 58, 60, 63–5, 67, 70–1, 73, 79–80, 82–3, 85–8, 91–2, 96, 98–101, 103–5, 119–21, 123–4, 127, 146, 159–62, 165, 167–75, 177, 186–97, 202, 205–7, 216, 218–21, 230–1, 233–7, 239, 241–8, 251–3, 259, 262–5, 271–2, 281–3, 290, 294–8, 312, 314–15, 323, 325
poeticise, 82, 263, 294
point of view (Saussure), 231, 233–5, 237, 312, 315, 317, 318

political, 3–4, 11–14, 27, 29, 34–9, 41–5, 55, 61, 69–70, 73, 78–9, 92, 94–5, 102, 104, 117, 158, 160, 163, 167, 191, 214, 230, 234–5, 237, 239–40, 242–3, 245–7, 249, 251–2, 257, 266, 282, 291, 294–8, 300, 302–4, 306–10, 312–19
politics, 4, 11, 21, 27–9, 33, 38, 42, 45–6, 68, 70–1, 157, 170–1, 180–1, 192, 197, 225–6, 233, 248, 263, 282, 285, 294, 296, 298, 303, 310, 312, 314–15, 318–19, 322–3
Port-Royal, 113, 136
Portuguese, 124
pragmatics/pragmatic, 45, 70, 82, 92, 104, 116, 144, 163, 199, 213, 282, 298–9, 303
presence, 21–2, 25–30, 33, 38, 94, 136, 161, 187, 192, 206, 214, 264, 276, 287, 291, 293, 302, 318, 322
psychoanalysis, 1, 69, 78, 84, 90–1, 99–100, 105–6, 163, 178, 184, 211, 218, 220–2, 234, 297, 299, 308
psychologism, 148, 221–2, 289
psychology, 65, 77, 109, 153, 174, 214, 300, 305, 314
punctuation, 81, 183, 200–1, 211–12, 248, 262–3, 294

realism, 33–4, 36, 39–41, 100, 103, 132, 158, 190, 201, 203, 222, 291, 312–13, 315–19
reason, 21, 27, 37, 40, 44, 60, 62, 70, 82, 97, 180–1, 183–5, 187, 193, 207, 231–2, 235, 243–5, 281, 295, 299, 304–6, 311–12, 314, 319
reasoning, 20, 99
recitative, 170, 217, 263, 272
religion, 1, 156, 199, 240, 250–1, 266, 285, 306, 308–9, 319
religious, 8–9, 13, 36, 63, 112, 230, 239–42, 245, 247, 249–50, 252–3, 255, 258, 265, 267, 285, 309, 316–19
rhetoric, 59, 62, 71–2, 79, 82, 92, 99, 116, 122–3, 144, 159, 184, 194, 199, 207, 213, 219, 222, 238, 250, 257, 260, 270–1, 275, 277–8, 283, 285, 301
rhyme, 83, 85, 107, 120, 124, 128, 132, 136, 138, 140–2, 144–5, 149, 159–60, 171, 177, 179, 180–9, 191–7, 206–7, 210, 233, 243, 257, 270, 275, 324
rhythmics, 55, 124, 127–9, 132, 138–42, 148–51, 153, 201, 237, 245, 248, 256, 265
Russian, 94, 95, 123, 127–8, 132, 134, 139, 141, 153, 188–93, 197, 236, 308
Russian formalism, 47, 103, 124, 161

Sanskrit, 138
scientism, 75, 231–2, 300, 302
semantics, 12, 19–20, 70, 74–5, 80, 83, 92, 101, 113, 132, 161, 184, 207, 271–2, 322–5
  serial semantics, 11, 225–6, 234, 239, 247, 263, 278, 294, 321, 324
semiotics, 1–2, 12–13, 15, 18, 20–1, 29–30, 54, 70–6, 207, 213, 222, 271, 289, 308, 324
shifter, 65, 158
signified, 15, 17–18, 24, 35, 48, 54, 60, 63, 65, 68, 74–5, 88, 180, 207, 210, 219, 230, 245, 272, 287, 298, 314, 324
signifier, 15, 17–18, 24, 35, 54, 60, 63, 65, 68, 70, 86, 90, 100, 106, 155, 157–8, 180, 193–4, 197, 207, 210, 219, 230, 241, 245, 270, 273–8, 287, 298, 314, 318, 324
social sciences, 59, 62, 163, 282, 291, 297, 299, 301–2, 310
sound, 5, 6, 28, 35, 89–90, 95, 97, 102, 117, 120, 161, 193–4, 196–7, 199, 203, 205, 214, 218, 225, 230, 235, 264, 268, 270 (sound out), 287 (resound)
sound patterns, 48, 50
sound poetry, 207, 214
Spanish, 128–9, 132–3, 135, 138, 141, 144, 146–7, 153, 171, 218, 242, 251
structuralism/structuralist, 1, 6, 12, 17, 53, 59–60, 64, 67, 70–1, 73, 78, 88–9, 104, 112–13, 202, 210, 213–14, 216–17, 220, 231–2, 269, 302–3, 307–8, 310
subject-form(er), 27, 81, 165–6, 168–9, 174, 201, 219, 263
subjectivism, 85, 221
subjectivity, 19, 25, 32, 38, 41, 45, 53, 77, 83–5, 87, 157–8, 174, 221, 299, 322
surrealism, 100, 158, 190
symbolism, 171
synchrony, 232, 307
syntagmatic, 4, 68–9, 108, 110–11, 124, 133, 137, 202, 232

ta'am/te'amim/ta'amisation, 37, 82, 123, 226, 238–9, 247, 252, 262, 321
teaching, 58, 61, 173, 213, 231, 255
technique, 57–8, 87, 181, 206, 213
theology/theological, 60, 90, 182, 230, 241, 243, 261, 267, 305, 319
totalitarianism, 39, 72
totality, 36, 55, 66, 70, 72, 74, 82, 104, 109, 188, 230, 233, 236, 299, 304, 308, 315, 317
transformation, 24–5, 27, 29, 43, 60, 69, 71, 84, 96, 110, 119, 122, 154, 160, 165–6, 173, 177–8, 183, 200, 202, 210, 222, 233, 236–7, 262, 312, 323
translation, 8–13, 17, 31, 33, 37, 45–51, 60, 64, 70–1, 81, 83, 90, 98, 113, 165, 186–8, 191–2, 200, 209, 225–7, 229–30, 235, 238, 240–2, 245–7, 249–56, 259–60, 262–3, 265, 267–8, 271, 278, 294, 319, 322, 324, 325

unity, 21, 23, 30, 34, 55, 66, 70–2, 74, 79–80, 82–3, 99, 104, 107, 159–60, 186, 204, 231, 253, 263, 265, 290, 298, 307–9
university, 1–3, 8, 17, 34, 43, 46, 49, 60–1, 67, 70, 72–3, 81–2, 88, 96, 98–9, 101, 132, 155, 159, 161–2, 199–200, 209, 213–14, 231–2, 251, 260, 295–6, 299, 306, 314
utopia, 27, 158, 201, 221–2, 232, 245, 247–8, 284–6, 295–7, 306, 310

versification, 87, 116, 125, 127, 131–2, 134, 139, 144–5, 147, 150, 153, 172, 188, 257
voice, 2, 5, 55, 82, 84, 107–8, 135, 150, 155, 167, 170–3, 177, 180, 191, 193, 198–209, 211, 213–19, 221, 230, 235, 254, 264, 266, 284, 298, 314

Western, 15, 37, 39, 48, 86, 95, 155, 191, 201

Yoruba, 155

EU representative:
Easy Access System Europe
Mustamäe tee 50, 10621 Tallinn, Estonia
Gpsr.requests@easproject.com

www.ingramcontent.com/pod-product-compliance
Lightning Source LLC
Chambersburg PA
CBHW082144230426
43672CB00015B/2842